WOODROW WILSON: THE LAST ROMANTIC

(A VOLUME IN FIRST MEN, AMERICA'S PRESIDENTS SERIES)

OTHER BOOKS IN THE FIRST MEN, AMERICA'S PRESIDENTS SERIES

Barbara Bennett Peterson, Editor

Theodore Roosevelt: A Political Life
Tom Lansford
2004. ISBN 1-59033-990-8

Citizen Lincoln
Ward M. McAfee
2004. ISBN 1-59454-112-4

George Washington, America's Moral Exemplar
Barbara Bennet Peterson
2005. ISBN 1-59454-230-9

President James K. Polk: The Dark Horse President
Louise Mayo
2006. ISBN 1-59454-718-1

Franklin Delano Roosevelt, Preserver of Spirit and Hope
Barbara Bennett Peterson
2006. ISBN 1-60021-117-8

John Quincy Adams: Yankee Nationalist
Paul E. Teed
2006. ISBN 1-59454-797-1

President Herbert Hoover
Don W. Whisenhunt
2006. ISBN 1-60021-476-2

Chester Alan Arthur: The Life of a Gilded Age Politician and President
Gregory J. Dehler
2007. ISBN : 978-1-60021-079-2

William Henry Harrison: General and President
Mary Jane Child Queen
2007. ISBN 978-1-60021-407-3

Thomas Jefferson: A Public Life, A Private Life
David Kiracofe
2008. ISBN 978-1-60456-061-9

John Tyler: A Rare Career
Lyle Nelson
2008. ISBN-13: 978-1-60021-961-0

WOODROW WILSON: THE LAST ROMANTIC

(A VOLUME IN FIRST MEN, AMERICA'S PRESIDENTS SERIES)

MARY STOCKWELL

Nova Science Publishers, Inc.
New York

For permission to use material from this book please contact us:
Telephone 631-231-7269; Fax 631-231-8175
Web Site: http://www.novapublishers.com

Library of Congress Cataloging-in-Publication Data

Woodrow Wilson : the last romantic / Mary Stockwell, author.
p. cm.
Includes bibliographical references and index.
ISBN-13: 978-1-60021-815-6 (hardcover)
ISBN-10: 1-60021-815-6 (hardcover)
1. Wilson, Woodrow, 1856-1924. 2. Wilson, Woodrow, 1856-1924--Political and social views. 3. Presidents--United States--Biography. I. Stockwell, Mary. II. Title.
E767.W95 2006
973.91'3092--dc22
[B] 2007029234

Published by Nova Science Publishers, Inc. ✦ New York

To my sister Roberta who read and proofed every page of this book and so helped me see Woodrow Wilson as "The Last Romantic."

CONTENTS

FOREWORD

President of the United States of America is an official title sought by many and won by only a few individuals. Most American presidents are of high merit and political acumen and reflected wisdom, leadership, and integrity. This series titled *First Men, America's Presidents* published by NOVA Science Publishers contains a book length biography of each president of the United States of America. Every book contains information on the president's early education, professional career, military service or political service prior to the presidency, interpretative discussion of both domestic and foreign policies during each presidency, and the conclusion of their political lives in public service. Every presidential biography in the Nova series has been written by a professional historian or political scientist well versed in the field of presidential scholarship. The two major themes of this series are the character traits marking success in the presidency, and the changes in the office of the presidency through America's history. Character matters in all walks of life, but perhaps matters most within the character of the president of the United States.

The duties of the president of the United States are delegated through Article II of the Constitution of the United States of America, and from the successive laws passed by Congress over time. Each president takes the Oath of Affirmation. "I do solemnly swear (or affirm) that I will faithfully execute the Office of the President of the United States, and will to the best of my Ability, preserve, protect and defend the Constitution of the United States." The president's duties and responsibilities under the Constitution are to serve as "Commander in Chief of the Army and Navy of the United States, and the Militia of the several States, when called into actual Service of the United States." The president may invite the counsel and opinions of his various department heads upon any subject related to the execution of the duties of their offices, either in writing or orally as has become the custom within the president's Cabinet. The president "shall have the power to grant Reprieves and Pardons for Offenses against the United States, except in Cases of Impeachment." Every president has realized that each must administer through constitutional principles, as each was elected by the voting majority of the people to be their chief executive through the Electoral College. Each president of the United States "shall have Power, by and with the Advice and Consent of the Senate, to make Treaties, provided two thirds of the Senators present concur." As the president directs both the domestic and foreign activities of the government, he has the power to "nominate and by and with the Advice and Consent of the Senate....appoint Ambassadors, other public Ministers and Consuls, Judges of the Supreme Court, and all other Officers of the United States, whose Appointments are not herein otherwise provided for, and which shall be established by law." The president also receives foreign ambassadors and officials on behalf of the American people. The president "shall have the Power to fill up all Vacancies that may happen during the Recess of the Senate, by granting Commissions which shall expire at the End of their next Session." The president under the Constitution shall give Congress a State of the Union address every year to acquaint them with his policy agenda and plans for the future. Usually in this address to Congress he recommends "to their Consideration such Measures as he shall judge necessary and expedient." Above all, the president of the United States "shall take Care that the Laws be faithfully executed, and shall Commission all the Officers of the United States." A strong role for the president had been envisioned by the Founding Fathers who rejected the obsolete Articles of Confederation and replaced the framework of government with the Constitution of the United States. Article II of the Constitution outlining the powers of the presidency provided that the office of the president would be held by one individual. It provided the president with enumerated powers including the power of the veto, and stipulated that the president's election would be above the control of the Congress to ensure the separation of powers and the system of checks and balances. It stipulated that the president, vice president, and all civil officers of the United States *must govern in the name of the American people* lest they "be removed from Office on Impeachment for, and Conviction of Treason, Bribery, or other high Crimes and Misdemeanors."

From presidents George Washington through John Quincy Adams candidates for the presidency were selected in caucuses of senators and congressmen and then the state legislatures indirectly chose the president through the selection of Electors to the Electoral College. This system had worked for Washington, Adams, Jefferson, Madison and Monroe—they were statesmen who held wide appeal within Congress and the state legislatures and claimed to represent the people. But as demands for greater democracy in the election process were heard, the process was changed. In the outcome of the election of 1824, John Quincy Adams was chosen president by the Congressional House of Representatives under constitutional law after no candidate had received a majority of the electoral ballots in the Electoral College. Jackson, the candidate who had received the most popular votes was not chosen president and his supporters called for more direct popular participation and worked to introduce changes. Hence, the voting process was altered in the name of democracy. In the election of 1828 President Andrew Jackson triumphed after voting had been given directly to the people and removed from the state legislatures. Democracy further triumphed by the elimination of the congressional caucuses in naming presidential candidates and the holding of national political party conventions to name them instead, allowing greater voice and participation of the people. The institution of the party convention to nominate presidential candidates remains, although winners in various state primaries command party delegates to vote the choice of the people. The presidency, molded by the character and designs of each president, oversees command, administration, diplomacy, ceremony, legislation, and public opinion. The modern strength of the presidency is a reflection of the mighty power of the United States within a global world.

The majority of America's presidents have served for one four-year term or less as some died in office. Four presidents served out part of their predecessor's term and won subsequent re-election in their own right: Theodore Roosevelt, Calvin Coolidge, Harry S Truman, and Lyndon Baines Johnson. Only one president, Grover Cleveland, was elected to two discontinuous terms of office and thus was both the twenty-second and the twenty-fourth president of the United States. Several outstanding presidents have been elected to two four-year terms or more. They were: George Washington, Thomas Jefferson, James Madison, James Monroe, Andrew Jackson, Abraham Lincoln, Ulysses S. Grant, Grover Cleveland, William McKinley, Woodrow Wilson, Franklin D. Roosevelt, Dwight D. Eisenhower, Richard Nixon, Ronald Reagan, William Jefferson ("Bill") Clinton, and George W. Bush. Only one president, Franklin D. Roosevelt, was elected for a third and fourth term. Eight presidents have achieved their office as a result of being the vice-president of a preceding president who died in office or resigned: John Tyler, Millard Fillmore, Andrew Johnson, Chester Arthur, Theodore Roosevelt, Calvin Coolidge, Harry S. Truman, Lyndon Baines Johnson, and Gerald R. Ford. Additionally, John Adams, Thomas Jefferson, Martin Van Buren, Richard M. Nixon and George H.W. Bush also rose from the office of vice-president to president. Besides the vice-presidency as a stepping stone to the presidency, two thirds of the presidents elected had held congressional office earlier in their political careers. Twenty presidents had served as Governors of states or territories before being elected. They were: Thomas Jefferson (Virginia), James Monroe (Virginia), Andrew Jackson (Florida), Martin Van Buren (New York), William Henry Harrison (Indiana), John Tyler (Virginia), James K. Polk (Tennessee), Andrew Johnson (Tennessee), Rutherford B. Hayes (Ohio), Grover Cleveland (New York), William McKinley (Ohio), Theodore Roosevelt (New York), William Howard Taft (The Philippines), Woodrow Wilson (New Jersey), Calvin Coolidge (Massachusetts), Franklin D. Roosevelt (New York), Jimmy Carter (Georgia), Ronald Reagan (California), William Jefferson Clinton (Arkansas), and George W. Bush (Texas). Some states with larger voting populations and hence more electoral votes have seen their native sons rise to the presidency of the United States. The American presidents have come from both coasts, east and west, and from both the upper tier and the lower tier of states geographically, north and south. When elected, the president becomes the president of 'all the people', not just those of his political party. Since the president acts as America's commander in chief, the majority of the presidents of the United States have served in the U.S. military. George Washington, Andrew Jackson, William Henry Harrison, Zachary Taylor, Franklin Pierce, Ulysses S. Grant, Rutherford B. Hayes, James Garfield, Chester Arthur, Benjamin Harrison, and Dwight David Eisenhower served in the capacity of generals. James Monroe, John Tyler, Abraham Lincoln, William McKinley, Theodore Roosevelt, Harry Truman, John F. Kennedy, Lyndon Baines Johnson, Richard Nixon, Gerald R. Ford, Jimmy Carter, Ronald Reagan, George Herbert Walker Bush, and George W. Bush also served their country in military service at various ranks, and always with dedication. The youngest elected president was John F. Kennedy (1960) at forty-three. The youngest man to ever serve as president was Theodore Roosevelt who at forty-two assumed the office following William McKinley's assassination. The average age for an elected president was fifty-four. The oldest elected president was Ronald Reagan at sixty-nine (1980) and seventy-three (1984).[1]

One of the major features of American constitutional development has been the growth of the presidency both in power and prestige as well as in new Cabinet positions, departments and agencies under the control of the president. The Federal government has grown mightily in comparison with the states' governments since the inception of the Constitution. Increases in presidential powers have been occasioned by wars, depressions, foreign relations, and the agenda of the presidents themselves. Henry F. Graff, Emeritus Professor at

---

[1] David C. Whitney and Robin Vaughn Whitney, *The American President (*Garden City, New York: Doubleday, 1993), v-ix.

Columbia University, described the office of the president as "the most powerful office in the world" in *The Presidents*. The Executive Office of the President (EOP) was created during the administration of President Franklin D. Roosevelt upon passage by Congress of the Reorganization Act of 1939. The EOP originally included the White House Office (WHO), the Bureau of the Budget, the Office of Government Reports, the National Resources Planning Board, and the Liaison Office for Personnel Management. In addition, wrote Henry F. Graff, the 1939 Act provided that an "office for emergency management" may be formed "in the event of a national emergency, or threat of a national emergency."[2] Today the White House Office has become "the political as well as policy arm of the chief executive." The larger, all encompassing Executive Office of the President has expanded through time to include a myriad number of departments in addition to the first five listed above and the president is advised by nearly 60 active boards, committees and commissions. During and immediately after World War II the following additional departments within the purview of the EOP were organized: Committee for Congested Production Areas, 1943-1944; War Refugee Board, 1944-1945; Council of Economic Advisers, 1946-; National Security Council, 1947-, and National Security Resources Board, 1947-1953; During the Cold War, additions to the EOP were made adding the following departments: Telecommunications Adviser to the President, 1951-1953; Office of the Director for Mutual Security, 1951-1954; Office of Defense Mobilization, 1952-1958; President's Advisory Committee on Government Organization, 1953-1961; Operations Coordinating Board, 1953-1961; President's Board of Consultants on Foreign Intelligence Activities, 1956-1961; Office of Civil and Defense Mobilization, 1958-1962; and National Aeronautics and Space Council, 1958-1993. By the Sixties, some of the earlier departments organized in the 1939 to 1960 decades were allowed to close, with newer agencies with a new focus and expanded technology taking their place. These newer agencies included: President's Foreign Intelligence Advisory Board, 1961-1977; Office of Emergency Planning, 1962-1969; Office of Science and Technology, 1962-1973; Office of Economic Opportunity, 1964-1975; Office of Emergency Preparedness, 1965-1973, National Council on Marine Resources and Engineering Development, 1966-1971; Council on Environmental Quality, 1969-; Council for Urban Affairs, 1969-1970; and Office of Intergovernmental Relations, 1969-1973. By the mid-Seventies, once again there was a general reorganization with some of the earlier departments and offices being swept away and replaced by newer

[2] Henry F. Graff, Editor, *The Presidents* (New York: Charles Scribner's Sons, Simon & Schuster Macmillan, 2nd edition, 1996, Appendix C), 743-745.

agencies reflecting new presidential agendas. Many of the new agencies reflected the urgencies in domestic policies and included: the Domestic Council, 1970-1978; Office of Management and Budget, 1970-; Office of Telecommunications Policy, 1970-1977; Council on International Economic Policy, 1971-1977; Office of Consumer Affairs, 1971-1973; Special Action Office for Drug Abuse Prevention, 1971-1975; Federal Property Council, 1973-1977; Council on Economic Policy, 1973-1974; Energy Policy Office, 1973-1974; Council on Wage and Price Stability, 1974-1981; Energy Resource Council, 1974-1977; Office of Special Representative for Trade Negotiations, 1974-; Presidential Clemency Board, 1974-1975; Office of Science and Technology Policy, 1976-; Office of Administration, 1977-; and Domestic Policy Staff, 1978-1981. Many of the departments, councils and agencies organized as part of the Executive Office of the President by the late Seventies and early Eighties included: Office of Policy Development, 1981-; Office of the U.S. Trade Representative, 1981-; National Critical Materials Council, 1984-; Office of National Drug Control Policy, 1988-; National Economic Council, 1993-. By the 21st century the EOP continued several effective agencies started earlier: Council of Economic Advisers, 1946-; National Security Council, 1947-; Council on Environmental Quality 1964-; Office of Management and Budget 1970-; Office of Science and Technology Policy, 1976-; Office of Administration, 1977-; Office of the U.S. Trade Representative, 1981-; Office of Policy Development, 1981-; and the Office of National Drug Control Policy, 1988-. In addition to the White House Office of the President, the Office of the Vice President functions and is administered as part of the EOP.[3] At the turn of the millennium the department of Homeland Security, 2001-, was established by presidential executive order and administered by the Executive Office of the President that continues to be evolutionary in response to new issues, demands, and events.

Capable presidents have responded to America's changing needs and responsibilities by retooling their administrations to meet new crises, opportunities, and challenges. This series, *First Men, America's Presidents,* published by Nova, explains the personal and public life of each president of the United States. Their qualities of character and leadership are aptly interpreted and offer strong role models for all citizens. Presidential successes are recorded for posterity, as are the pitfalls that should be guarded against in the future. This series also explains the domestic reasons and world backdrop for the expansion of the Executive Office of the President. The president of the United States is

---

[3] Henry F. Graff, Editor, *The Presidents* (New York: Charles Scribner's Sons, Simon & Schuster Macmillan, 3rd edition, 2002, Appendix), 743-747.

perhaps the most coveted position in the world and this series reveals the lives of all those successfully elected, how each performed as president, and how each is to be measured in history. The collective life stories of the presidents reveal the greatness that America represents in the world.

Dr. Barbara Bennett Peterson
First Men, America's Presidents Nova Series Editor
Professor of History, Oregon State University (retired)
Emeritus Professor University of Hawaii
Former Adjunct Fellow East-West Center
Professor of History, California State University San Bernardino, Palm Desert

Preface: The Image of a Man

There are images that linger in the minds of Americans when remembering their presidents. Some of these images are so vivid that no historian can ever truly overcome them. Washington will be forever remembered rowing with his men in the frozen night toward Trenton or riding alongside them in the bloody snow all the way to Valley Forge. Jackson with his shock of white hair stands high atop a barricade shouting through the smoke and down the ages at the British and the Creeks and the Bank of the United States. Lincoln remains a lonesome prairie boy with a poet's heart who recalls the ties that bind our nation together and reminds us that somehow these cords must keep our fragile republic from disappearing off the face of the earth.

When Wilson comes to mind, he too brings images that are hard to overcome. His large bespeckled eyes and his sturdy chin seem to tell us that he is unflinching in his determination to do things his own way. Harsh and uncompromising is the face of Woodrow Wilson. We remember this as we watch him striding down the streets of Paris with confetti falling all about him and crowds cheering him on to the mirrored halls of Versailles. He has made the world safe for democracy and now he has come to teach the old order how good government works in the modern world. But as we watch him passing before our eyes, as if in a silent movie that is going much too fast, we know the wheel of fortune will turn and the arrogant savior will be toppled. His dream of peace everlasting and a League of Nations that would secure it will be trampled in the old world and the new. Neither Europe nor America will bend to his will or heed his warning of a more terrible war on the horizon if his way is not followed. In breaking with his league, Wilson's own countrymen will break him in two. A stroke will level him, and he will die forgotten and alone in a decade racing happily toward the destruction he has warned about so eloquently.

There is only one word for the Wilson of our dreams and that is failure. Perhaps if he could have bent his will a bit more, we say, he might have won his vision of a world transformed. Instead his refusal to compromise sent us deeper into chaos, and so our final view of Wilson is that of an old man waiting to die while the whole world plunges once again toward war. The image is so powerful that we never look away from it long enough to see that we are living in the fulfillment of many of Wilson's dreams rather than in their failure. We expect the president to work at home and abroad on our behalf to achieve a better life for us and maintain our prosperity. We assume he will explain all of this to us in regular messages both to Congress and the people themselves. We often demand that he face reporters in regular press conferences. We expect him somehow to be in touch with our deepest dreams as if attuned to the very beat of our collective hearts, and if he cannot express these dreams in stirring words, we are disappointed. If a president is not in tune with us, we make sure that he is miserable until he leaves office. On a grander scale, we assume that war is not inevitable and that the peoples of the world can live in peace if they would but work together to achieve it. We believe that all nations can exist side by side without war if they but honor the rights of their own citizens and those of other countries. We make and then abide by treaties that allow us to trade peacefully with other nations. We as a country have spent much of the last century making the world safe for democracy and forging alliances to keep it that way. The Europe that we once rescued is no longer at war with itself but is instead a democratic union linked together with agreements that we in part helped to forge. People on every continent, not just Europe, are struggling to achieve the vision that was first so clearly seen by Woodrow Wilson.

If we can admit that we are living in Wilson's world, at least in part, should we not also give him some credit for dreaming it, instead of calling him a failure through and through? When remembering Woodrow Wilson, we must look past our own vision of a failed leader and instead see how he came to dream these things for the world. Order, peace, respect for nations, freedom for individuals, written constitutions with rights protected – everywhere we see the mark of an American president who believed wholeheartedly in these principles and who risked all to make the world safe for them. It is this man that we must find behind the failure that still stands so powerfully before us. To understand our world, we must understand the vision that made it. To understand this vision, we must seek out the man who first dreamt it, and so this book is dedicated to the mind and spirit of Woodrow Wilson, the last romantic to dream that such a world was possible simply by imagining it.

Part of the trouble in trying to understand Wilson comes from the fact that historians begin and end with his failure to win his nation's approval for the League of Nations. His greatest detractors have set the parameters of the debate by searching for some fatal flaw in Wilson's character that made this failure inevitable. William Allen White, a Progressive supporter of Wilson's arch enemy Theodore Roosevelt, led the way in *Woodrow Wilson: The Man, His Times and His Task*, one of the first biographies of our 28th president. White characterized Wilson as a man with a second rate mind who was not up to the tasks set before him. Sigmund Freud weighed in against Wilson in a work he co-wrote with William C. Bullitt entitled *Thomas Woodrow Wilson: Twenty-eighth President of the United States—A Psychological Study*. Freud diagnosed Wilson as a man bound for failure since he suffered from a deep Oedipal complex that originated in his relationship with his domineering father. British economist John Maynard Keynes argued that Wilson's naiveté when dealing with other world leaders led to his failure to achieve a just peace following the Great War in his work *The Economic Consequences of the Peace*. Defenders of Wilson, most notably Ray Stannard Baker and Arthur Link, have prepared multi-volume studies to prove that the man they revere so much truly was admirable. But there is always a sense in their works that they are defending a case to which no one is listening. It is as if we are mesmerized by the images we carry with us of Wilson adored in the streets of Paris and Wilson lying in his bed in the White House felled by a stroke. Could such a figure, at once arrogant and pitiful, have achieved anything of lasting value?

If we can turn our attention away from the final battle in Wilson's long life and remember the more than 60 years that preceded it, we can gain a better picture of who he truly was. No president comes to a great crisis in his tenure of office as an empty slate. Instead the president is a person shaped from the moment of his birth to the great events in which we are so interested. It is a look into the whole life of a president that gives the best insights into what our national leader does at a critical moment in history. Historians have understood this most clearly in their studies of Abraham Lincoln. No one ever concentrates simply on the success or failure of Lincoln's presidency without taking a long look back to the frontier cabin in Kentucky where he was born. Jefferson is often forgiven major mistakes, like the Embargo of 1808, because we always remember the quiet young red head struggling in the summer of 1776 to write our Declaration of Independence. The same is true of Franklin D. Roosevelt whom no scandal can ever truly tarnish when we see this vital man reduced to spending his life in a wheelchair.

Historians need to take a long view of the life of Woodrow Wilson if they are to see the deep romantic spirit that buoyed up his every public action. From his childhood in the ruined South to his presidency during the Great War, he remained a person moved first and foremost by his emotions and his imagination. If Wilson could not see and feel the truth in his own mind, then he could not act. Once he had a clear vision to which he could deeply commit his heart and soul, all life became an adventure for him. For Wilson, his mind was not a place where he could hide from reality like so many other educated men, but was instead a gateway into his heart and then back out to the world. "I cannot understand the lives of those men who seem to feed on their minds," he told his first wife Ellen Wilson in one of the last letters he ever wrote to her, "They seem to me something less than human."[1]

Perhaps if there was a tragedy in Wilson's life, it was in his failure to recognize that sometimes a great vision for the future only comes about after much suffering. A vision alone rarely moves people in its direction, especially if it requires them to give up the worst in themselves. Only in days when the best becomes a necessity, and not a dream, do such visions come true. As the world plunged into the horrors of the Second World War, the vision of Wilson seemed both realistic and necessary in the face of the madness of fascism. Today as political commentators openly speculate if we are in the first stages of World War III, it is a good time to take a look again at the man who first believed that all war must come to an end and that all nations must live together as democracies and brother nations. From the time he first played that he was a great hero chasing pirates on the imaginary seas of his childhood until he fell from grace along with his failed league, Thomas Woodrow Wilson was first and foremost a romantic who believed that if we could imagine the best possible future for all mankind, then we need only sail forth toward it and surely we would arrive there. The words that William Wordsworth wrote in honor of Lord Nelson, another great hero who fought for a better future on the high seas of the world, best capture the spirit that lay at the heart of Woodrow Wilson and his presidency:

> "It is the generous Spirit, who, when brought
> Among the tasks of real life, hath wrought

---

[1] Woodrow Wilson, "Letter to Ellen Wilson, September 21, 1913," *The Priceless Gift: The Love Letters of Woodrow Wilson and Ellen Axson Wilson*, edited by Eleanor Axson Wilson (New York, Toronto and London: McGraw-Hill Book Company, Inc., 1962), 305.

Upon the plan that pleased his childish thought:
Whose high endeavours are an inward light
That make the path before him always bright."[2]

[2] William Wordsworth, "Character of the Happy Warrior," accessed at http://www.readbookonline.net.

Chapter 1

A CHILD OF WAR AND DREAMS

A boy never gets over his boyhood ...

Woodrow Wilson[3]

Throughout his life, Woodrow Wilson would always be able to recall his very first memory. It happened on a day in November in the year 1860. Not quite four years old, he was standing at the gate in front of his family's house in Augusta, Georgia. As he looked out onto the street, he heard someone passing by and saying in an excited voice that Lincoln had been elected and that there would be a war. Not knowing who Lincoln was or what war was, he ran back up the path into his house to ask his father what it meant.[4]

The war predicted by the excited voice did come to pass and Wilson carried memories of it with him for the rest of his life. His family's church was turned into a hospital for sick and wounded Confederates brought there from the bloody battle at Chickamauga, while its yard became a prison for Union soldiers marched across town from the railroad depot. Wilson often remembered how many brave young men his minister father buried during the long and terrible war, and how still the soldiers kept coming to the church and through the town, more ragged in appearance each year. He recalled another time when he sat on a post at the same gateway where he had first heard the news of Lincoln's election. "Go, get your

---

[3] Donald Day, editor, *Woodrow Wilson's Own Story* (Boston: Little, Brown and Company, 1952), 7.

[4] Woodrow Wilson, "Abraham Lincoln: A Man of the People, February 12, 1909," *The Public Papers of Woodrow Wilson: Educational, Literary and Political (1875-1913)*, Volume II, edited by Ray Stannard Baker and William E. Dodd (New York and London: Harper & Brothers Publishers, 1925), 83.

mule!" he shouted in the slang of the day at the tattered men as they disappeared down the dusty street. He remembered a Sunday too when his father told the congregation that there was a terrible battle raging in Virginia and that the ladies were to head over to the local ammunition factory after the services were done. It was their duty, he said, to roll cartridges for the Confederacy.[5]

There were still more terrible days ahead like the time when news arrived that General Sherman was close at hand. Wilson remembered how the men worked hard to pile bales of cotton in the town square in the hope that if Sherman came through Augusta, he would burn the cotton and leave the city standing. General Sherman headed straight from Savannah to Columbia, South Carolina, and never marched on Augusta. Still danger continued for the town, most especially in the last days of the war when food was scarce and vagrants descended on the city. Wilson often spoke of the delicious soup his mother made from the peas usually left in the fields for the cows to eat. He remembered keeping vigils late into the night in the parsonage as homeless men, black and white, wandered through Augusta. Thieves broke into his father's church and stole chairs and carpets and even the communion table. Robbers came back a year later, taking the newly replaced furniture and even part of the fence from around the church.[6]

There were still two more days after the war had finally ended that stayed in Wilson's memory forever. On one of them, he peered through the blinds of an upstairs room in his family's home to watch as Jefferson Davis was taken in a carriage through the streets of Augusta on his way to prison in Florida. On the other day, a bright May morning in the year 1870, he anxiously stood with all the other people in town, waiting for a chance to get a glimpse of Robert E. Lee who had come to visit Augusta. A friend of young Wilson broke from the crowd and raced up to Lee. He handed him the most beautiful rose he had been able to find just hours before in his mother's garden. Lee stood up from his chair and took the rose, thanking the boy for the gift and asking if he could present it to his daughter. Before the stunned child could answer, Lee turned and handed the flower to a young woman sitting behind him. Never had the people of Augusta seen a more glorious man. Wilson was able to get close to the general too. He remembered the

---

[5] William Allen White, *Woodrow Wilson: The Man, His Times and His Task* (Boston and New York: Houghton Mifflin Company, 1924), 27-33; Josephus Daniels, *The Life of Woodrow Wilson 1856-1924* (Chicago, Philadelphia and Toronto: The John C. Winston Company, 1924), 36.

[6] Arthur Walworth, *The Life of Woodrow Wilson*, Volume I (Second Revised Edition) (Boston: Houghton Mifflin Company, 1965), 8; Daniels, *The Life of Woodrow Wilson*, 37.

wonder of standing right next to Lee and looking up for a long time into his sad and noble face.[7]

But as much as these images of war would stay with him for the rest of his life, they would be but a small part of the deeper and more memorable story of his childhood. This story was played out among the people who lived in the house he ran to on that fall day in 1860. He probably headed to his father's study at the left of the main door. It was lined all the way to the ceiling with books and smelled of the tobacco that his father smoked almost constantly in his clay pipe. Wilson often said that the smell of books was forever wonderful to him, but that he never smoked because his father had done enough for both of them in his lifetime. His father loved tobacco so much that he hoarded it in the attic of the manse throughout the Civil War along with a little gold.

How many other times Wilson had already run to his father when troubled he was never able to recall. But for the rest of his life, and as long as his father lived, he would seek out this "incomparable" man for advice, especially when he needed to make an important decision. Even after his father had died, Wilson would stop and ask himself what his father would have done in the same situation he was now facing.[8] Joseph Ruggles Wilson was a tall and handsome man with a shock of dark brown hair that his family said turned the color of Sea Island cotton as he grew older. He had a deep voice that he made good use of in his careers as a Presbyterian minister and a college professor. He was the kind of larger than life man who filled up every room he entered and who made all heads turn as he passed. There was nothing dour or sadly pious about this clergyman. Instead, he was a lively fellow with a great sense of humor that came out in an endless stream of puns and stories.[9]

Reverend Wilson must have towered over the little boy everyone called Tommy on that troubling day in November telling him that all would be well. In his own heart, he hoped that the North would simply let the southern states go if they chose to secede. He had come to Georgia just three years before and fully sympathized with the cause of the South. Wilson kept slaves himself and housed them in quarters behind the manse near the barn. He believed that slavery could be considered part of God's wise and providential plan for the human family, but

---

[7] Walworth, Life of Woodrow Wilson, I, 8; Daniels, Life of Woodrow Wilson, 37; White, Woodrow Wilson, 32, 42-43.

[8] Walworth, *Life of Woodrow Wilson*, I, 8; Woodrow Wilson, "Letter to Joseph Ruggles Wilson, December 16, 1888," *Papers of Woodrow Wilson (PWW)*, edited by Arthur S. Link (Princeton: Princeton University Press, 1966), VI, 30; Ray Stannard Baker, *Woodrow Wilson: Life and Letters, Youth, 1856-1890*, Volume I (Garden City, New York: Doubleday, Page & Co., 1927) 30.

[9] Ibid., 8.

only if slaveholders helped their charges become more civilized and slaves worked hard to become better people. Joseph Wilson hoped that northern Presbyterians would somehow come to understand this and so the fight over slavery would not split the church in two.

But after the attack on Fort Sumter just five months later, Reverend Wilson could only stand by and watch helplessly as all hope for continued unity in his church slipped away forever. Like so many other Southern delegates to the Presbyterian General Assembly in Philadelphia in June of 1861, he was stunned and saddened when a resolution expelling all slaveholders from the church was passed. He headed back home with other southern ministers to Atlanta where the Presbyterian Church of the Confederate States of America was founded and then invited everyone to come to his own church in Augusta where the first General Assembly of the new denomination, better known as the Southern Presbyterian Church, was held. For the next forty years, he served as the clerk of the General Assembly and even had his son Tommy help him when he was older. Once he even won the high honor of being elected its Moderator for a year.[10]

While he wholeheartedly embraced the cause of the South, even serving for a short time as a chaplain in the Confederate army, Joseph Wilson was not a native born Southerner. He was the son of Scotch-Irish immigrants James Wilson and Anne Adams, and had been born in Steubenville, Ohio in 1822. His parents had both come from somewhere in Northern Ireland, probably on the same boat, in the year 1807. His father was just twenty years old when he came to America and might have been born near Strabane in Londonderry. His mother was only seventeen and could have come from County Down or County Antrim since she loved telling the tale of how she could see the "wind-whipped linen" hanging out to dry on clotheslines across the Irish Channel in Scotland on bright and cloudless days.[11]

When James Wilson landed in Philadelphia, he headed straight for 15 Franklin Court, the home of Benjamin Franklin. He might have been inspired to do so by reading the *Autobiography* of another ambitious young man who had run away from his brother's printing shop in Boston to start a new life for himself in Philadelphia. Franklin had been dead for nearly twenty years and his home now served as the headquarters of the *Aurora*, a Democratic-Republican newspaper devoted to the ideals of Thomas Jefferson and edited by the arch anti-Federalist William Duane. Young James Wilson was hired on the spot and quickly mastered

---

[10] Walworth, *Life of Woodrow Wilson*, I, 7, 12; White, *Woodrow Wilson*, 29-30.

[11] Josephus Daniels, *The Life of Woodrow Wilson 1856-1924* (Chicago, Philadelphia and Toronto: The John C. Winston Company, 1924), 29; Baker, *Life and Letters*, I, 13-14.

the printing trade. He married Anne Adams a year later and soon had a growing family of his own. By the opening months of the War of 1812, he had become the editor of the *Aurora* himself.[12]

Ambitious and restless like so many of their fellow Scotch-Irish immigrants, James and Anne Wilson started to dream of a better life in the west. When the War of 1812 finally came to an end, they made the long trek overland to Pittsburgh, and then settled first in Lisbon, Ohio before heading on to Steubenville. Here James Wilson became the editor of a frontier newspaper that he renamed the *Western Herald and Steubenville Gazette*. He turned on the party of Thomas Jefferson when it embraced Andrew Jackson, and soon became a dedicated Whig. He served in the Ohio Legislature and also as an associate judge of the Court of Common Pleas. A pro-tariff and anti-slavery man, he opened a bank and sponsored a railroad that built the first bridge across the Ohio River. He taught his children how to set type as soon as they were able, and left his wife and sons in charge of the *Western Herald* when he went off to Pittsburgh to start another newspaper under the masthead "Principles, Not Men." More serious than the lively "Paddy Wilson," Anne spent her days on the Ohio frontier raising a family of seven boys and three girls with an iron will. She made sure each one of them attended the local Presbyterian church every Sunday, and never forgave one of her daughters for eloping with a young man whom she considered unsuitable.[13]

While most of their sons seemed bound for a life in business or politics on the western frontier, the Wilsons' youngest boy Joseph Ruggles appeared more suited for a life as a minister or teacher back east. Like his brothers and sisters, he learned to set type when young and even had his own newspaper when still just a boy, but he had a searching mind and a love of words that convinced his parents to send him to school. He graduated from Jefferson College in western Pennsylvania as the valedictorian of his class and taught for a time in the little town of Mercer. He soon felt called to the ministry and studied for a few months at a local seminary before heading to Princeton. He received a Bachelor of Divinity degree from the college, and then returned home to Steubenville where he taught in the town's male academy.

On a fall day in 1846, Joseph Wilson was raking leaves in the front yard of his parents' house. When he looked up from his work for just a moment, he saw a young woman walking by and staring at him through the fence. She said later she was taken by the beautiful kid gloves that the handsome boy was wearing as he

---

[12] Henry Jones Ford, *Woodrow Wilson: The Man and His Work; A Biographical Study* (New York and London: D. Appleton and Company, 1916), 2; Wilson Family Bible, *PWW*, I, 3-4.

[13] Baker, *Life and Letters*, I, 6-14.

raked. The young teacher fell instantly in love with the girl with the large blue grey eyes and a mass of curls about her face. She was Janet Woodrow, the daughter of Reverend Thomas Woodrow, a Presbyterian minister from Chillicothe. Most everyone who knew her called her Jeanie or Jessie. She was totally unlike the dashing young man who had fallen so completely in love with her. She was quiet and shy, and some people even called her somber, but it may have been because her young life had not been an easy one.

The fifth child of the Reverend Thomas Woodrow and his wife Marion Williamson, Jeanie was born in Carlisle, England in 1826. Her father had come south from his native Scotland to minister at a Presbyterian church there and also to run a school for young children. He had purchased land from the Duke of Devonshire on Warwick Road where he built a small house under the shadow of a castle. Jeanie recalled how she would stand in the garden behind the house and toss a ball against the castle wall. Jeanie sailed for America along with her parents and seven brothers and sisters when she was just eight years old. The voyage was so terrible that high winds sent them all the way back to Ireland even after their ship had nearly reached the shores of Newfoundland. Jeanie Woodrow would always remember watching the waves of the dark sea rise high above the ship and then crash down on deck. One swell was so powerful that it swept her overboard. The crew threw her a rope and watched in amazement as the little girl grabbed it, holding on for dear life until she was pulled from the violent sea that she would hate for the rest of her life.

There was little comfort in the new world for the Woodrows. Jeanie's father left the family in New York City and headed north to hold prayer meetings in Poughkeepsie and then to seek a position as a minister in Canada. By the time he returned, his wife was dead, broken by the long sea voyage past any hope of recovering. The shattered family moved first to Ontario and then came to Ohio where Reverend Woodrow secured a church and a new wife in Chillicothe. Soon there were other children in a second family, sons and daughters whom Reverend Woodrow would remember in his will even as he failed to mention Jeanie and the other children from his first marriage. As sad and withdrawn as these many shocks must have made this young woman, she was bold enough to say "Yes" when Joseph Ruggles Wilson asked her to be his wife. They were married on June 7, 1847 by her father at the manse of his church in Chillicothe, and so began the life of the parents of Tommy Wilson.[14]

Jeanie Wilson soon discovered that her husband was as restless and ambitious as his own father had been before him. For a little while, he preached at a small

[14] Ibid., 14-23.

church in Chartier's Manse, Pennsylvania. A daughter named Marion was born there to the couple in 1851. Joseph Wilson next took a job teaching rhetoric at his alma mater Jefferson College before moving on to Hampden-Sydney in Virginia where he taught chemistry and the natural sciences. Another daughter named Annie was born there in 1853. Finally in the early summer of 1855, Joseph Wilson was called to minister at the First Presbyterian Church in Staunton, Virginia, an old trading town in the Shenandoah where many a Scotch-Irishman had passed through on his way to a better future down the Great Valley. The family settled into a spacious white brick parsonage where they were waited on by a staff of free blacks who cooked for them in an open fireplace in the basement and carried water from a well in the yard. The manse sat high on a ridge across the way from the church which stood on a small hill. Reverend Wilson could often be seen sitting on the porch at the back of the house, looking past his wife's garden toward his church and writing his sermons on Saturday afternoons.[15]

Sometime close to midnight on December 28, 1856, Jeanie Wilson gave birth to her first son in a large room just off the main hall of the parsonage. She named him Thomas Woodrow after her father and older brother. The little boy was placed in a wooden crib and watched over by his mother and sisters and the family's black servants. Just a few days after Tommy was born, Staunton was hit by a terrible snowstorm that cut the town off from the world for nearly two weeks. The family did not seem to mind for they were overjoyed at the birth of their little Tommy. Joseph Wilson was especially happy to have a son with large blue-grey eyes just like his mother. She was happy too, believing her son to be the best baby that a young mother could possibly have. She said so in a letter written to her father in April 1857:

> "The boy is a fine healthy fellow. He is much larger than either of the others were—and just as fat as he can be. Every one tells us, he is a beautiful boy. What is best of all, he is just as good as he can be—as little trouble as it is possible for a baby to be. You may be sure Joseph is very proud of his fine little son—though he used to say daughters were so much sweeter than sons ... our little boy is named 'Thomas Woodrow.'—Your affectionate daughter Jeanie Wilson."[16]

When Tommy was not quite a year old, his family was on the move again, heading farther south to Augusta, Georgia where Reverend Wilson had accepted a position as the minister of the First Presbyterian Church. Augusta was a trading

---

[15] White, *Woodrow Wilson*, 28.

[16] Janet Woodrow Wilson, "Letter to Thomas Wilson, April 27, 1857," *PWW*, I, 7.

town and manufacturing center of some 16,000 people on the Savannah River. Here cotton planters from the surrounding countryside brought their crop for sale and shipment out to the Atlantic and the world. Slaves made up nearly half of the city's population. Reverend Wilson had visited Augusta some months before at the invitation of his wife's sister Marion who was married to a local doctor named James Bones. She had asked her sister's husband to come to town to preside at the marriage of their brother James Woodrow. The young preacher with the crystal clear mind and resonant voice made such an impression on the local congregation that they asked him to return and become their permanent minister. His church, one of the oldest in Augusta, stood with its high tower and white spire in a grove of trees right in the center of town. The congregation promised to build a parsonage across the street from the church with a fenced yard out front along with a small garden in back for Jeanie Wilson and a stable behind the house for Reverend Wilson's black horse.[17]

When Tommy Wilson was a grown man, he would look back to the red brick parsonage of the First Presbyterian Church in Augusta, Georgia as his first real home. Above all else, it was a place filled to the brim and overflowing with the love of his father and mother. He was fond of saying that it was in this house that he learned to be a Christian. He even came to believe that the best way to become a Christian was to live in the presence of people who truly loved Christ and tried to be like him. Joseph and Jeanie Wilson were two such people and their quiet faith shaped young Tommy right down to his very depths. He would long remember how good and kind these two souls truly were. Even with so many burdens to carry during the war, his father would often take time in his busy day to play chase with him in the yard. His mother was always waiting to comfort him when he ran to her, a "mischievous bundle of nerves" as she often called him, and buried his face in her skirts. His parents taught him that the best way for children to learn their faith was by breathing it in as the very atmosphere of their home.

This did not mean that the Wilsons ignored the outward practices of their Presbyterian faith. They knelt down together as a family each day and listened as Reverend Wilson led them in their prayers. On Sunday mornings, Jeanie Wilson along with her two daughters and little son sat in the fourth row of the church marked out for the minister's family, listening intently to Joseph Ruggles Wilson's sermons. Tommy would sometimes look up when his father stopped and searched for the right phrase to make a point in his sermon. He would try to think of the word himself, and when his father finally found it, a thrill would run up and down Tommy's spine. He would also listen intently to the sad melodies of the

---

[17] Baker, *Life and Letters*, I, 28-32.

organ, sometimes being so overcome with emotion that tears would stream down his cheeks. He especially loved the tune "Twas on That Dark and Doleful Day," a song about the crucifixion of Christ that was often played during the Presbyterian communion service. Later at home on Sunday evenings, Tommy and his family would gather again around the piano and sing even more hymns.[18]

While he would struggle like many other young Presbyterians to learn his catechism, Tommy Wilson would never question the essential truths of his faith that he learned in childhood. All the great Christian beliefs – the just and loving God made known to the world in Christ, the purposeful motion of the universe and mankind, both on their way back to God, the inevitable sense of God's plan for every person and his imprint down to the last fiber of life itself – were planted forever in little Tommy's soul. Of all the truths of the faith, none was more beautiful to him than the idea that God had made a promise to his people to save them. Somehow and somewhere men and women had fallen from the heights that God had intended for them into the depths of sin and suffering and death. But God could not forget his people and so came among them with promises that he would help them. After the great flood, he told Noah that he would never again send such watery destruction to the earth. Then he spoke in the very depths of his friend Abraham, telling him to come with his wife Sarah out of Ur so that he might become the father of a people as numerous as the fish in the sea or the stars in the sky. He spoke again to Moses from the depths of a burning bush, revealing his own name and promising to deliver his people from their captivity in Pharaoh's land. He gave them the law as the way back to the happiness he had originally planned for them from the beginning of time. He asked that his people promise to abide by it, and then he whispered more truths to his prophets, promising to send a redeemer. Finally he sent his own son as the savior who made the last and greatest promise, the everlasting covenant between God and his people, sealed with his own passion, death, and resurrection.

Tommy's love of the promises of God surely came in part from his father, most especially from his preaching and teaching about the Old and New Testaments. But as he grew older, he became convinced that his love of God's promises had more probably come to him from his mother's side of the family. From little on, he came to know his mother's relatives much better than those of his father. Reverend Wilson's support for the Confederacy broke the bonds between himself and his own family who remained loyal to the Union. Two of his brothers had even become generals in the northern army. In contrast, Jeanie Wilson made sure Tommy and the rest of her children were close to her own

---

[18] Woodrow Wilson, "Letter to Eleanor Wilson, April 19, 1888, *PWW*, V, 719.

family. They already knew her sister Anne and her brother James who both lived in Georgia. As soon as the Civil War ended, she took her children back to Ohio for a visit with their grandfather, aunts and uncles, and many cousins. Reverend Woodrow often came south from then on to visit his daughter and grandchildren. Tommy remembered him as a man of deep prayer who carried his Bible with him every morning to breakfast. He loved to sing old Scottish folk songs and relax in the evenings by doing mathematical puzzles. Tommy best remembered the day that his grandfather came to preach in his father's church. Reverend Woodrow had left his glasses at home and had to use ones borrowed from a member of the congregation. Tommy anxiously looked up at the pulpit, listening to his grandfather read his sermon with his thick Scottish accent and watching the borrowed spectacles slip down his nose. Right at the moment when the glasses were about to slip off, he pushed them back up and calmly continued on with his sermon.

Tommy was proud to be one of the Woodrows. Originally spelling their name "Wodrow," this ancient Scottish family could trace its ancestry back for hundreds of years. Each generation was full of ministers and scholars, Presbyterians to the last, who were part of a line known as the Covenanters. In 1557, they had promised their allegiance to one another in resisting the Catholic Church and the English crown. These people bound themselves to each other not just to resist an old and troubled world, but rather to build a new and more righteous one. While he would one day choose the professions of his father's side of the family, writing and politics, Tommy Wilson would remain convinced that the flame that burned most deeply within him was the fiery spirit of the Scottish Covenanters, and back through them even farther to the proudest Highland clans and to Robert the Bruce himself.[19]

While building a living faith in their family was important to the Wilsons, so was allowing them to remain in their childhood dreams for as long as possible. Above all else, they were certain that letting their family – Marion, Annie, Tommy, and little Joseph who was born in 1866 – remain in their imaginations was important in helping them become responsible adults. Tommy would always remember his childhood as a time of dreams. He considered himself much luckier than so many other children who were forced into becoming adults too quickly. He especially loved the many fairy tales his mother told him, taken from a book called *The Talisman*. She made him costumes and watched with delight as he played out scenes before her from the stories she had taught him. When Tommy showed no inclination to go past dreaming and learn how to read himself, neither

[19] Baker, *Life and Letters*, I, 47.

his mother nor his father seemed too worried. Mrs. Wilson remembered how she had been forced to learn Latin when she was just six years old and she did not want Tommy suffering in the same way. His parents did get him a pair of glasses, thinking the problem might be his vision. But when this made no difference, they continued to read to him, convinced that someday, when he was ready, he would take it up for himself.[20]

Listening to Reverend Wilson read aloud from the greatest works of the day became one of the favorite pastimes of the Wilson family while they lived in Augusta. Almost every night, after dinner and before prayers, all the Wilsons would gather in the parlor. Tommy would stretch out on the floor flat on his back, while his sisters would sit in chairs side by side with their mother. Jeanie Wilson would usually be knitting. Everyone waited for Reverend Wilson to enter the room and sit down on the floor next to Tommy with his back leaning against an overturned chair. Then he would open up a whole world for his family by reading novels, poems, and travel books to them. There in the parlor of the Wilson parsonage came David Copperfield lost and bewildered in the crowded streets of London. There stood William Wallace and all the other brave Scottish chieftains, defying England and all the Plantagenets to the last. There too came Natty Bumppo and faithful Chingachgook running deep in the dark forests along the Hudson in pursuit of the hated Magua. Night after night, all the adventurers and heroes of the past would light up before Tommy's eyes through the beautiful voice and ringing laughter of his father.[21]

Reverend Wilson found another way to teach his son how to master words even while he was unwilling or unable to read. He was convinced that Tommy must win a command of words for one day he would leave the world of childhood dreams behind and take his place among the world of men. In order to be a part of this world, and so serve both his fellow man and God who had placed him there, he must be able to express himself clearly. His father took it upon himself to show little Tommy how to describe what he saw in the world in his own words. Every Monday morning, he could usually be seen wandering through the cotton warehouses and the ammunition factories of Augusta with his little blonde son in tow. The boy would listen intently as his father explained, like one adult to another, how a cotton gin worked or how a piece of machinery operated.

Later in the day when Reverend Wilson returned home with Tommy, he would ask his son to explain back to him exactly what he had seen. He told him to

---

[20] Stockton Axson, *Brother Woodrow: A Memoir of Woodrow Wilson* (Princeton, New Jersey: Princeton University Press, 1993), 9-29.

[21] White, *Woodrow Wilson*, 38.

find the simplest and clearest way to capture his thoughts and convey them to his listeners. "When you frame a sentence, don't do it as if you were loading a shotgun," he would say, "but as if you were loading a rifle … shoot with a single bullet and hit the thing alone!" He could give such advice to his son because he was convinced that a boy was not a blank slate, but a thinking person with a profound awareness of the world even if he could not clearly voice it. Words allowed a child to speak the truths that he already carried within him. They were the way to let out the great splendor within the human heart. Mastering words was like breaking open a hard shell around a seedling, or coming up above the surface of the water after swimming from the bottom for a long time. A boy is not a "gut to be stuffed," Joseph Wilson was fond of saying, but a real person who must be given the means to express what he already knew within him. If a boy could learn to master words, he would be able to find not only his own self but his purpose in the world.[22]

After teaching their son as much as they could in their own home, Reverend Wilson and his wife finally sent Tommy to school when he was nine years old. The war had come to an end, and a Confederate veteran named John Derry had returned to Augusta and opened a classical academy for boys. Every morning Tommy and the other students would listen as a psalm was read before reciting the Lord's Prayer together. They then spent the rest of the morning studying Latin and history with Mr. Derry, and in the afternoon, they took up writing and bookkeeping with another teacher named Mr. Pelot. Under their watchful eyes, Tommy Wilson finally learned to read on his own, although he would always say that it took him two more years to master his letters.

But this time in young Wilson's life was important for more than just learning how to read. He at last made friends outside the circle of his own family. They were boys like himself who had survived the Civil War and who now grew to manhood in its wake. Joe and Phil Lamar were the sons of a minister and lived next door to the manse. They went to John Derry's academy along with other boys like Pleasant Stovall, Tom Gibson, and William Keene. Stovall was the boy who rushed up to Robert E. Lee with the beautiful rose in his hand. One of the best friends of young Wilson was Will Fleming. He attended a different academy in town but usually saw Tommy on Sundays when his family worshipped at the First Presbyterian Church. Wilson remembered the many afternoons when he would ride out to the Fleming plantation on his father's black horse and spend the day playing with his friend Will.[23]

---

[22] Day, editor, *Woodrow Wilson's Own Story*, 8.

[23] Axson, *Brother Woodrow*, 48-77.

Back in Augusta, Tommy and his schoolmates started their own baseball team called the Lightfoot Club. They obeyed the rules written for them by Tommy in the club's constitution. They climbed up the ladder to the loft in his father's barn and held secret club meetings under the watchful eye of their mascot Lucifer. They had found a picture of him advertising ham in a magazine and tore him out to be their guardian. He watched over them as they played hooky together on the day the circus paraded down the main street of Augusta, and then headed to the warehouses to pack their behinds with cotton to cushion them from the whipping they were sure to receive once they had finally arrived back in school. Tommy and his friends did receive a whipping from Mr. Derry and he would remember for his whole life what little good the cotton did to soften the blows.

While the other children in his class seemed driven to succeed later in life, Tommy Wilson appeared to be a nice, if not very bright boy, who would accomplish little once he was older. His friend Joe Lamar would go on to become a justice of the nation's highest court, and Will Fleming would serve in the Georgia legislature. Tom Gibson would become the Minister to Switzerland, while William Keene would become the Dean of the Law School at Columbia University. Sadly in the eyes of most who knew him, especially his teacher John Derry, Tommy Wilson seemed bound for less spectacular heights. But what Mr. Derry and just about everyone else outside of his own family could not see was the great change going on in the mind of young Wilson. It was a change that could hardly be measured by his school assignments or the enthusiasm he showed in class. Reading on his own had become a wonder to him that opened up whole new worlds and even his own future to him. After years of listening to his father read aloud to the family, he could at last be moved by books on his own.[24]

If the first memory of his life was hearing news about the election of Lincoln, then his first memory of himself as a reader came through a book known to many other young people of his day. It was *The Life of George Washington* by Parson Weems. He could barely read on his own when this book somehow fell into his hands. The story of the heroic Washington who could never tell a lie and who rose to such heights in service to his country deeply touched the young Wilson. As he lived and breathed with Washington on every page of the book, Tommy came to discover something on his own for the first time, not something his father or a teacher had shown him. He would long remember that this book gave him his first glimpse of the amazing ideals upon which his nation was founded. "I recall having thought even then," he later wrote, "that something doubtless more than common must have possessed that cause for which our fathers fought." Like the

[24] Baker, *Life and Letters*, I, 47.

Founding Fathers he was learning about in his reading, Tommy was inspired to write a constitution himself, not for his nation but for his Lightfoot Club. He made certain that the boys who climbed the loft to play with him in his father's barn understood parliamentary procedure and practiced it in their many debates.[25]

There were other books too that lit his imagination and they were usually ones filled with brave heroes and their daring adventures. He especially loved reading the Leatherstocking Tales of James Fenimore Cooper. Even as he grew older and his friends left make believe behind, he would read Cooper's books and then pretend that he was one of the characters. His playmate in these adventures was not a fellow schoolboy but his cousin Jessie Bones. She was five years younger than Tommy, a tomboy ready and willing to play with her cousin who could not leave dreams behind as quickly as his other friends. Tommy and Jessie would hunt choke cherries and rub them into their arms and faces to turn them as red as any Indian in the tales of Cooper. Then they would hide behind bushes and jump out to scare the "settlers," unsuspecting black children who were hurrying on their way back to their settlement in the piney woods on the edge of town. Once when playing at hunting deep in some imaginary woods, Jessie climbed high in a tree and Tommy took dead aim at her with a makeshift bow and arrow. His shot at the make believe squirrel was right on target, and Jessie fell to the ground unconscious. "I am a murderer; it wasn't an accident; I killed her!" Tommy cried as he carried her back home. The little girl revived and was soon ready to play with him once again.[26]

There were other times when Tommy Wilson preferred to play his imaginary games on his own. This was especially true when he went off into his favorite world of ships and pirates and long sea battles. Often neighbors would see him sending his toy sail boats out along the drainage ditches that carried storm waters in front of the manse. What his neighbors could not see was the great story of adventure he told himself as he sent his ships upon the waves. In his own mind, he was not the blonde freckled son of the local minister, but dashing Admiral Wilson who sailed the seas in search of pirates. As he ran through the grove of trees about the parsonage, he captained an enchanted ship that he called the *Avenger*. When the battles were over, the brave admiral would head up the stairs of his family's home to his bedroom with the high ceilings and windows that looked out toward the white spire of his father's church across the street. Here he kept a ship's log

---

[25] Ibid., 38-39.

[26] Ibid., 38-39.

and recorded all the victories he had won, the prisoners he had set free, and the treasure he had recovered.[27]

Tommy's secret life as an admiral in the grove of trees about the manse in Augusta came to an end in 1870. Just a few months before he turned fourteen, his father decided to move the family across the Savannah River to South Carolina. He had accepted a position as a professor of Pastoral and Evangelical Theology and Sacred Rhetoric at the Columbia Theological Seminary. Still scarred from the fire and ruin of Sherman's march through their city, the people of Columbia were eager to rebuild their town and educate young Presbyterian preachers once again. The seminary itself was a mere building near an open field on the outskirts of town, but here Reverend Wilson was happy to teach once again. He would also serve as the minister of the First Presbyterian Church in Columbia. Together the two salaries would allow him to provide a comfortable life for his family, even in the midst of a city whose business district, one mile long and three blocks wide, was still in ruins.

Jeanie Wilson was also happy with the move to Columbia. Her brother James Woodrow, an accomplished scientist who had studied with Louis Agassiz at Harvard and received a doctorate from Europe's renowned Heidelberg University, also taught at the seminary, and he would now be able to help guide her dreamy young son toward adulthood. Jeanie Wilson was delighted that she could finally build a home for her family. She had received an inheritance from her brother William Woodrow who had died in Nebraska, unmarried and with no children. She took great care in the construction of her family's first home of their own, choosing the lot it would be built on, planting the magnolia trees herself, and working with the carpenters until everything was just right. Here in this white clapboard house with its wide porch and picket fence, Jeanie Wilson hoped that she and her husband would live for the rest of their lives.[28]

For Tommy, it was not an easy move. He would come to love Columbia, and remember this place more fondly than any other one in which he would live as a boy. But he would regret the move, remembering how much more terrible uprooting a family can be for a child than for an adult. He found it difficult to learn and even more difficult to make friends. He attended a school called the Barnwell Academy, and did well in English and composition, but struggled to master ancient languages and mathematics. His uncle James Woodrow often said to him, "Tommy, you can learn if you will." He reminded him too that even if he did not aspire to be a scholar, then surely he must study hard in order to become a

[27] White, *Woodrow Wilson*, 36-37.
[28] Ibid., 45, 55.

gentleman. Tommy did his best to do better in his studies, and was most inspired by sitting in on his father's lectures. He still loved to read with Reverend Wilson, especially the works of Charles Lamb and Daniel Webster. They would often try their best to see if they could say things better than either writer, but they always found, with Webster especially, that there was simply no better way to say what he had said.[29]

In beautiful and lonely Columbia, Tommy turned more and more inward, spending long hours alone. He found himself torn between wanting to become an adult and take his part on the world stage, and retreating into the world of his childhood imagination in order to stay there forever. He came to see the life of adults as a great drama where men and women played their parts, and where children stood in the wings waiting for cues to enter and become part of the drama themselves. He found one such cue to move out into the wider world in the pages of a boy's magazine. In the November 1872 issue of *Frank Leslie's Boys' and Girls' Weekly,* he read an article on the Graham shorthand method written by Joseph Snipes, a court reporter in New York City. Tommy cut out and pasted nearly fifty articles on shorthand in scrapbooks he kept his whole life. He had chosen a difficult system of shorthand to master, one so complex that it would be overtaken in the business world by the more flexible Gregg system. But the complexity did not matter to him, and he saved his money to buy one book after another, moving from the simplest to the most advanced manual. He became so fascinated with the intricacies of the system that he even took to writing to Joseph Snipes himself. Snipes wrote back, asking him if Columbia had recovered from the war. Wilson answered there was no finer main street in all the world except maybe Broadway in New York City.[30]

In all these changes, the move to Columbia, the growing solitude amidst the loss of the first home he could remember, and the attempts at mastering shorthand, young Tommy Wilson was learning about himself more deeply each day. There were times when it seemed he was ready to come out of his childhood, and then there were other times when he hoped to stay in his dreams for as long as he possibly could. Another move toward adulthood came in his own personal quest for a religious experience of his own. Some of the best memories of his days in Columbia came from the long afternoons he spent in the room of an older fellow student at the Barnwell Academy. His name was Francis Brooke and he often called Tommy and other young men to his quarters to talk about God and to pray together. Brooke had a deep and burning faith in Christ, and his ability to

---

[29] Ibid., 47.

[30] Joseph F. Snipes, "Letter to Thomas Woodrow Wilson, September 10, 1873," *PWW*, I, 29.

express his belief inflamed Tommy's own soul. After learning about Christ from his parents for his entire life, Tommy at last felt the movement of grace within himself, and formally entered the Presbyterian Church along with two other young men in July 1873. Tommy would never speak of the experience that brought him into the Presbyterian Church, but he always said that the Barnwell Academy would forever be holy ground in his memory.[31]

As much as religion had touched him, and led him into the world of adults, the dreams of his childhood still pulled him back within himself. In these dreams, he was sometimes the Commander in Chief of the Royal Lance Guards or the Royal Rifle Brigade, but more usually he was Admiral Thomas Wilson, sometimes also called Lord Eagleton, the greatest commander in Her Majesty's Royal Navy. He kept lists of the names of his officers, his ships, and even his horses, and often wrote detailed instructions to the men who served under him. Most of his officers were young men he actually knew, like Francis Brooke who served as a Captain Major of the Royal Guards, and Douglas McKay, one of the young men who entered the church with him in the summer of 1873, who was a Lieutenant Commander of the Royal Navy. He kept the lists and orders in notebooks, and pasted articles on warships, yachts, and horse races that he had cut out of British magazines side by side in scrapbooks. He loved ships so much that he even started his own imaginary merchant fleet. He called it the Atlantic and Great Western Steamship Line, and listed himself, Lord Thomas Woodrow Wilson, the Marquis of Huntington, as its founder and owner.[32]

While Tommy was usually a British commander in his dreams, he became an American ship captain in the most intricate story he imagined during the summer of his sixteenth year. The story became so real to him that he seemed for a time to live in two separate worlds. As he walked the streets of Columbia, read books with his father, and prayed with his friends, he also sailed the Pacific in search of a "nest of pirates" that had long been ravaging the South Seas. Young Captain Wilson wrote daily reports to the Navy Department describing his hot pursuit of the pirates who always escaped him. On one dark night, he finally caught up with their hideous ship covered in black rigging. It led Wilson and his men on an exciting chase to an unchartered island that they could not find on their maps. They followed the ship into a narrow inlet only to be met by a wall of solid rock. For a moment, brave Captain Wilson hesitated, wondering if this could be a trap. Then he ordered some of his men into a small boat to explore the inlet. They rowed past the wall of rock and discovered that the island was actually an atoll.

---

[31] Baker, *Life and Letters*, I, 66-67.

[32] Ibid., 66-70.

Captain Wilson and the rest of the crew followed them into a wide and beautiful bay where they discovered more enemy ships and the dismantled hulls of the American navy. He and his men defeated the pirates, rescued all the captives and ended once and for all this threat to freedom on the high seas.[33]

But even while he sailed the seas in search of bloodthirsty pirates, Tommy Wilson was beginning to dream of a life for himself that would let him be a hero in this world. He gave no inkling of this dream to his immediate family. It was still just a whisper in his mind but he was slowly coming to believe that maybe a heroic life waited for him some day in politics. He finally confessed this dream not to his father or mother, but to his cousin Jessie who had come to visit him in Columbia. She noticed the picture of a man that she had never seen before hanging above the desk in Tommy's bedroom. When Jessie asked who this man was, her cousin answered, "That's William Gladstone, the world's greatest living statesman, and I aim to be one too someday!"[34]

But how he would ever find his way into that world remained a mystery to Tommy. He knew that the dream his parents held for him was that one day he would become a minister. In September 1873, when he was not quite seventeen years old, they sent him to Davidson College in Mecklenburg County just across the border in North Carolina. Here they expected him to begin the formal studies that would lead to his life's work in the Presbyterian Church. Finding himself on a path not of his own making, Tommy Wilson experienced the first real unhappiness that he had ever known in his young life. The dreamy boy quickly found out that he would not be pampered at Davidson College as he was at home. Instead he was expected to rise early every morning and chop his own firewood. He soon was known on campus as the boy who could sleep longer than anybody else and still make it to morning services and breakfast. His lack of drive and determination was equally apparent when he played second base on the freshman baseball team. His coach was fond of saying that young Wilson would make a great player someday if only he was not so lazy.

Many of the struggles Wilson faced in his freshman year came from the fact that he was far behind his fellow students academically. It was painfully obvious that he knew much less than most of the other boys who had come to Davidson. He had the most difficult time in mathematics and ancient languages. In his first term, he studied the Old Testament along with Latin, English, Greek, and algebra. In the second one, he continued his studies of the Old Testament and algebra, and

---

[33] William Bayard Hale, *Woodrow Wilson: The Story of His Life* (Garden City, New York: Doubleday, Page & Company, 1912), 44-46.

[34] Axson, *Brother Woodrow*, 200-248.

took classes in English composition, vocabulary, rhetoric, and geometry. He was also required to read Cicero and Horace in Latin, and Xenophon and Herodotus in Greek. He took some comfort in the fact that he proved himself to be a ready debater in the college's freshman literary society and he even wrote a new constitution for the group. But by the end of the first semester, he began to miss meetings along with classes and baseball practice, complaining of an upset stomach and exhaustion.[35]

There were many things that seemed to break young Thomas Wilson in two in his first year at Davidson. Most importantly, he was terribly homesick. To be away from his entire family for the first time was hard, but he especially missed his father and his mother. He wrote home to Reverend Wilson more than anyone else, pouring out his love for him. He kept an anxious count of how many letters he had written to his family and friends and then how many times they had answered him. In his loneliness, he began to regret the time he had wasted and the wrong he had done when just a child in Augusta. His anxiety was increased by the embarrassment he felt at being so far behind his fellow classmates. He wondered if he might be better suited for business school, and he was soon determined to work up the courage to ask his father if he could attend one. In the meantime, his classmates teased him about his backwardness, and their ridicule made him feel unloved for the first time in his life. In a class in English grammar, the teacher asked, "What is that kind of meat that comes from a well-fed young cow?" Tommy answered, "Mouton!" From that day on, he had to bear the humiliation of being called "Monsieur Mouton!"[36] He was so hurt that he wrote home to his mother complaining that no one loved him and that he was truly worthless. She answered that this was simply untrue for many people in Columbia thought highly of him, considering him a fine and handsome young man. These were hollow words for a troubled, self-conscious young man, indeed, to be thought highly of only by his mother.[37]

Even more troubles came into the life of young Thomas Woodrow Wilson in the winter of his seventeenth year. These troubles were not of his own making but instead concerned his father. Reverend Wilson was stunned when members of the local Presbyterian congregation decided to replace him as their minister. For a man who up until this time had been so successful, this was an insult and a failure that he could not tolerate. He retaliated by requiring the students at his seminary to attend Sunday services with him at the school and not at the First Presbyterian

---

35 Baker, *Life and Letters*, I, 71.

36 Ibid., 72.

37 Janet Woodrow Wilson, "Letter to Thomas Woodrow Wilson, May 20, 1874," *PWW*, I, 50.

Church. He won the support of many of them but some complained that they preferred to go to church in town. The issue made it all the way to the General Assembly which sided with the students who wished to attend the church off campus. Reverend Wilson could not bear this humiliation and soon found another position for himself as the minister of the First Presbyterian Church in Wilmington, North Carolina. He and his wife Jeanie along with their youngest son Joseph left the house that had been built for them forever, and headed to Wilmington in the summer of 1874. They stayed first in the home of a local merchant before moving into the newly remodeled manse at Fourth and Orange Streets. Anne Wilson stayed behind for she was the wife of Dr. George Howe, the son of the family's next door neighbors in Columbia. Marion had married the Reverend Anderson Ross Kennedy two years before and was now living in South Carolina.[38]

The troubles of his father hurt him deeply and seemed even to mirror his own heartbreak. For the first time that he could remember, not only was he unhappy, but so was his father. The sadness had been so overwhelming for him that he could not find words within himself to express it. Halfway through his first term at Davidson, he had come upon a poem in a magazine called the *Southern Presbyterian*. The work captured his own terrible fears for it was the prayer of a child lost and alone in a troubled world. "The way is dark, my Father! Cloud on cloud is gathering thickly o'er my head, and loud the thunder roars above me," cried the opening lines of the poem. Tommy carefully copied all sixteen stanzas into a notebook. He must have taken comfort in the fact that God at last answered the lost child in the poem, reminding him that his own well beloved Son had once borne an even heavier cross. "For him bear thine, and stand with him at last, and from Thy Father's hand, thy cross laid down, receive a crown."[39]

After one year at Davidson, and in the midst of his family's troubling move to Wilmington, Tommy Wilson's prayer to return home was answered. His family would give him time to rest and regain his health. But they would expect him to continue to prepare for a return to college and most probably to the ministry. His father, his uncle James Woodrow, and even his grandfather Reverend Thomas Woodrow, would help him with his studies. His father would also hire tutors to drill him in Latin and Greek. He would take up the practice of reading with Tommy once again, but now it would be side by side as they poured over and discussed every edition of the *Nation* and the *Edinburgh Review*. Tommy would

---

[38] Baker, *Life and Letters*, I, 72.

[39] Copied by Thomas Woodrow Wilson from the *Southern Presbyterian* (November 6, 1873) (see *PWW*, I, 33-35).

also be able to spend more time with his mother. He could now take long walks with her down the tree-lined streets of Wilmington. People in her husband's new congregation would say that she was cold and withdrawn, too proud for a minister's wife, taking no help from anyone but instead doing everything for her family on her own. Tommy never saw her this way. For him, she was forever the beautiful woman with the blue-gray eyes that seemed to change colors with her moods who filled her family's home with flowers and music. He gallantly seated her in the family's pew every Sunday morning, remembering always that he was the mama's boy who had clung to her skirts as a little boy and that from her very apron strings he learned to love and care deeply for all women.[40]

During his one year in Wilmington, Tommy retreated into the arms of his mother and father and even deeper into the waiting arms of his imagination. It was not an easy thing for this eighteen year old boy to leave the pirate ships and great sea battles of his childhood behind. A hero's life as a daring naval commander still called to him, especially as he explored the docks of Wilmington. On any given day, sailing ships and merchant vessels from fleets all over the world arrived in the city's great harbor where the Cape Fear River met the Atlantic. Tommy Wilson spent his days wandering along the docks, mastering every type of ship and all the semaphores, and talking to anyone he could about the sea. Sometimes he would ride far out into the Atlantic on a great ship and then return to shore on the pilot vessel. Once he hurt himself when he fell into the hold of a boat, but he soon recovered and went back to the docks to learn even more from the sailors. If only he could go to sea, or maybe even to the Naval Academy in Annapolis, he could become the hero he so longed to be.[41]

When he returned home from a day along the wharves in Wilmington, he filled up notebooks with his own drawings of the ships he had seen and all their flags. He poured over the sea-going adventures of Sir Walter Scott and Captain Frederic Marrayat. David Bryant, the family's butler, remembered that if he could not find young Mr. Wilson, he need only go up to the boy's room and there he would be, curled up on his bed with his head in a book. Sometimes Reverend Wilson would even have to wait supper until his son finished his reading and came downstairs to be with the family. Back up in his room, Tommy took time from his reading to master shorthand, and even wrote to Andrew Jackson Graham, the founder of the system, asking him for private lessons. Graham answered politely, showing him how to copy out complex words like purity, period, variety, Albany, melody and enigma. But when Wilson asked for private lessons, Graham

---

[40] Woodrow Wilson, "Letter to Eleanor Axson Wilson, April 19, 1888," *PWW*, V, 719.

[41] White, *Woodrow Wilson*, 60-61.

wrote that he was ill and could not take on any more students. He encouraged young Wilson to continue in his study of phonography for it would help him when he returned to college someday. Tommy also wrote to his two sisters Marion and Anne as well as to John Leckie, his former roommate at Davidson College, and Douglas McKay, the young man who had joined the church with him the year before. Leckie playfully warned him to be careful as he made his first moves out into the society of young women so as not to get his "wings scorched," while McKay buoyed up his spirits by telling him that one day they would both be Senators.[42]

Even as he prepared for college, he still loved best to sit down at his desk and fill notebooks with instructions to the ships that continued to sail only in his imagination. One of the most important tasks he set for himself in Wilmington was the writing of a constitution for the Royal United Kingdom Yacht Club of Great Britain and Ireland. Once again styling himself as Lord Thomas Wilson, the Duke of Carlton, he served as the Commodore of the club which had thirty English, Scottish, and Irish schooners. He owned two of the largest ships – the *Eclipse* and the *Sea Bird*. His roommate at Davidson College was now an Irish nobleman named Sir John William Leckie, the proud owner of the *Independent*. His grandfather Thomas Woodrow captained a 220-ton Scottish ship called the *Lorne*. As Commodore, Lord Wilson had much greater control over the club than any of the other officers including the Vice Commodore, Rear Commodore, Secretary, and Treasurer, all of whom were elected to four year terms. His position was comparable to that of an admiral in her majesty's fleet. He ran all the club's meetings and had an absolute veto power over the club's laws, even if the vote among the members was unanimous. The Commodore also sponsored the most important of the ten regattas held each year by the club, and handed out three prizes of his own design in gold, silver, and wood.[43]

While he sailed in his imagination along the high seas of the world, Tommy made one good friend in Wilmington. His name was John Bellamy and he lived with his family next door to the Wilsons. The two boys loved to head to a place on the edge of town called the Delgado Mills, formerly an ammunition magazine for the Confederacy, but now a park with rolling hills and shade trees. The boys

---

[42] Ibid., 57-59; Andrew Jackson Graham, "Letters to Thomas Woodrow Wilson, August 8, 15, and 28, September 7, 14, 16, and 25, 1874, *PWW*, I, 57-59; Marion Wilson Kennedy, "Letter to Thomas Woodrow Wilson, June 14, 1875," *PWW*, I, 65-66; Annie Wilson Howe, "Letter to Thomas Woodrow Wilson, July 1, 1875," *PWW*, I, 67-68; John William Leckie, "Letter to Thomas Woodrow Wilson, May 7, 1875," *PWW*, I, 63-64; Douglas McKay, "Letter to Thomas Woodrow Wilson, June 25, 1875," *PWW*, I, 66-67.

would lie under the trees for hours reading aloud from their favorite books and discussing every character. Years later when he had become a lawyer and member of Congress, Bellamy remembered that his friend was never content just to read a book, but instead had to talk about every part of the work right down to the last detail. Wilson's favorite book at the time was *The Pirate* by Sir Walter Scott. He was fascinated by a character in it named Yellowley, a strange fellow who rode a donkey and quoted Latin. He could identify with the strange character for he had made something of a name for himself around town as the first person in Wilmington to ride a bicycle. He also found the two main women characters in the book, Minna and Brenda, more fascinating than most of the girls he had met in Wilmington. "There's not a girl in Wilmington who can carry on a conversation requiring much reading," he often complained to his friend John Bellamy.[44]

When they were not reading on the hills at the Delgado Mills, the two friends spent some of the last days of the summer of 1875 swimming in the Cape Fear River. They would head to Dock Street and dive into the tides flowing in and out from the Atlantic. They played baseball on a neighborhood team, and went to picnics with the other young people in their set. Wilson found one girl fascinating enough to correspond with her but he later never spoke her name or said why the courtship ended. Yet no matter what they were doing, the conversation would almost always turn back to books and sometimes to politics. Bellamy later remembered that Wilson was especially puzzled by the concept of political greatness. "What makes a man great?" was a question ever before his mind. He would list the great men of the past and present – Oliver Cromwell, William Gladstone, Robert E. Lee, and Stonewall Jackson were always at the top of it – and then try to determine why each one was great. Quietly to his friend, Thomas Woodrow Wilson was speaking the growing dream he held within himself of someday leading a heroic life on the sea or in politics.[45]

But his dreams of a daring life on the stage of grownup men and women would have to wait. Any plans for a career at sea came to an end when Wilson's mother, still frightened by the ocean crossing of her childhood, said "No" to both the merchant fleet and the Naval Academy. She and her husband agreed that their bookish and dreamy son still seemed suited for the ministry. Perhaps he would understand that better once he had enrolled at his father's alma mater. Their son would be sent north to Princeton, and there be taught at last the best way to take

---

[43] Thomas Woodrow Wilson, "The Royal United Kingdom Yacht Club: Vessels, Officers, Rules and Regulations," *PWW*, I, 54-58.

[44] George Osborn, *Woodrow Wilson: The Early Years* (Baton Rouge: Louisiana State University Press, 1968), 32-33.

his place in the world of men. In September 1875, Thomas Woodrow Wilson packed his most valuable possessions in his father's old black valise and headed by boat to Baltimore and then by train to New Jersey. His parents must have wondered if he would ever become the minister they knew he could be, and he must have wondered if there was any possibility left for him to become the dashing hero of his imagination.[46]

[45] Ibid., 34; Baker, *Life and Letters*, I, 78-79.
[46] Osborn, *Woodrow Wilson: The Early Years*, 35.

Chapter 2

A STUDENT AT PRINCETON

Father, I have made a discovery; I have found that I have a mind.
Woodrow Wilson[47]

When Thomas Woodrow Wilson arrived in Princeton, New Jersey in the late summer of 1875, the few people who later remembered meeting him saw nothing special in the young man. They described him as tall and awkward with a face that seemed somewhat angular and even homely. He was serious and shy, and appeared to have not a single friend in town.[48] None of them suspected the depths of the imagination that lived in the college freshman who had come up from North Carolina to begin his studies in the first week of September. They were unaware of the mighty battles he had fought against pirates on the high seas, the splendid constitutions he had written for his baseball team and his imaginary yacht club, or the fact that he had bravely trailed Natty Bumppo and Chingachgook deep into the forests along the Hudson River. They could never have guessed that the bashful Southerner carrying his father's old black suitcase as he searched for a place to stay was about to set forth on a greater adventure than he had ever known in childhood. It would take him from solitary dreams about heroic deeds to a deep understanding of the nature of good government and the best way he could play a part in it.

Wilson himself seemed unaware of the great changes that were about to come upon him. At the moment, his more immediate concern was finding a room. After he learned that there were no spaces left for freshmen in the dormitories on campus, he called on the Duffields, friends of his family in Princeton, who let him

---

[47] Quoted in Axson, *Brother Woodrow*, 15.

[48] Mulder, *Woodrow Wilson: The Years of Preparation*, 34.

stay with them for a few days. He finally rented a room from Mrs. Josiah Wright in her boarding house on Nassau Street just across from the college. His lodgings were on the second floor and looked directly out toward the Princeton campus.[49] Once settled, Wilson finally had time to think about the great changes that lay before him, and he did what he had always done when such moments had come upon him since childhood. He opened a notebook at his desk, took up his pen, and wrote down his thoughts. He listed the important events and turning points in his life starting with his birth in Staunton, Virginia on December 28, 1856, heading next to the places where he had lived while growing up, Augusta, Columbia, and Wilmington, and then adding his time at Davidson College. He ended with the simple words that he had entered the freshman class of Princeton in September 1875 as a member of the Class of 1879.[50]

He also made a list of everything he had brought with him in his father's valise. There were ten new shirts and one old one, a half a dozen new cuffs and collars each along with a half a dozen old ones, and six pairs of socks. He had handkerchiefs, night shirts, and drawers for summer and winter. Finally he started a running log of his expenses that included his weekly room and board of $10, school supplies like paper, pencils, and ink, fees for cleaning his winter coat and mending his pants, a few more pennies for apples, pears, and candy, and a bit more for the New York *Times* and a phonographic magazine. There was also the price of the books he would need for his classes like Demosthenes, Thucydides, Herodotus, Latin grammar, and the dreaded algebra.[51]

The shy boy could not stay in his room forever making lists. He knew that his father expected him to call on James McCosh, the President of Princeton. The Reverend Wilson had even written a letter to McCosh which Wilson had been carrying with him all the way from Wilmington. In his first days at the college, he was simply too bashful to take it to him. McCosh, a Presbyterian minister like Tommy's father, had paid a visit to the family in Columbia, where he met young Wilson and said he would be expecting him at Princeton someday. Tommy finally overcame his natural reticence and went to the President's office where McCosh received him kindly and made him feel more at home. Wilson felt even better when a boy from Alabama named Frank Glass took him under his wing, inviting him to join several other Southern students at an upper class eating club for his first two weeks on campus.

---

[49] Bragdon, *Woodrow Wilson: The Academic Years* (Cambridge, Massachusetts: Belknap Press, Harvard University Press, 1967), 21; Baker, *Life and Letters*, I, 81-82.

[50] Wilson, "Shorthand Vita, September 7, 1875," *PWW*, I, 72.

[51] Wilson, "Two Items from a Notebook, September 7 to December 18, 1875," *PWW*, I, 73-74.

But it was when he struck up a friendship with Robert McCarter, a freshman who lived next door to him on the second floor of Mrs. Wright's boarding house, that Wilson finally felt at home at Princeton. Wilson had not made a good first impression on McCarter who remembered his fellow freshman as "pimply-faced" and "hungry looking" with not one friend in the entire class. But McCarter soon discovered that the quiet and retiring young Wilson had a marvelous mind and an amazing ability to converse on any subject. He was warm and friendly under his painfully shy exterior. It was not long before the two were inseparable, spending hours together in McCarter's room talking late into the night.

Two things became obvious to McCarter about Tommy Wilson very quickly. One was that the young man loved his family dearly especially his father. He was truly devoted to the Reverend Wilson and often referred to his father's opinions when debating many topics. The second one was that Wilson had a deep love for the people of the South who had suffered so much during the Reconstruction. McCarter later remembered that young Tommy was "full of the South" and that one evening they argued late into the night with Wilson "taking the Southern side and getting quite bitter." On another night when other boys in the boarding house joined in the debate on the Reconstruction, Tommy's face went white, he shouted, "You know nothing whatever about it," and stormed out of the room.[52]

But while he was a ready debater and an excellent conversationalist, Wilson soon found himself far behind his fellow freshmen once classes began. As always, he did well in writing, speaking, and reading, loving history and literature especially, but he trailed behind the others in mathematics and ancient languages, especially Greek. He was soon known to his instructors as a very serious student who quietly tried his best to master Demosthenes and Herodotus. Wilson was not as impressed with his efforts as his teachers were, and continued to be troubled by his own laziness. He knew he could do better if he only tried harder, but he just could not get excited about his coursework or other formal activities on campus. Even debating which had been so important to him at Davidson College did not seem to interest him at Princeton. He joined the American Whig Society, a debating club that once had James Madison as a member, but only participated in one debate in October when he defended the principle that "Rome was not built in a day."[53]

When he truly cared about something, like baseball, he threw his heart and soul into it. He and his fellow classmates at the Wright Bower, the freshmen's

---

[52] Daniels, *The Life of Woodrow Wilson*, 46; "An Interview with Robert H. McCarter, June 15, 1940," cited in Bragdon, *Woodrow Wilson: The Academic Years*, 21-22.

[53] Baker, *Life and Letters*, I, 85-86.

name for their boarding house on Nassau Street, started a team called the "Bowery Boys." They played against other groups of Princeton students who had formed teams of their own. Wilson loved baseball so much that he sometimes played two games a day, and once went six straight days playing a game on every one. On days when no games were scheduled, he loved playing catch. He also rooted for the Princeton baseball team and loved cheering on the college rowers. Like other students, he ran along the Raritan Canal shouting for the Princeton rowing team during competitions on campus. He joined in the celebrations after every victory, helping to set off firecrackers and cannons, and light bonfires in the night along with the other boys.[54]

By Easter break of his first year at Princeton, Tommy Wilson worried that, while he had become a fine baseball player, he had made little progress in his own intellectual development. He brooded that he was a lazy student who was always sick, unable to shake a cough that he had suffered from for some time. He loved his family and the friends he had left behind in Wilmington and Columbia, but he regretted that he never seemed to have enough energy to write the many letters he planned to send them.[55] Just as he had not realized his potential at Davidson, so again he was not reaching his potential at Princeton.

Wilson might have been surprised to learn that his classmates saw him in a wholly different light. They had noticed some remarkable transformations in their serious but always pleasant companion during his freshman year at Princeton. They considered him "one of the most original and superior men in the college" because he was not afraid to think for himself.[56] While other students worked diligently on the projects assigned to them, Wilson could often be seen in his favorite spot in the stairwell on the Chancellor Green Library on campus reading books he had chosen for himself. While they were content to accept whatever their professors told them, Tommy Wilson had a deep ache for the truth and a conviction that he could somehow find it on his own.

While Tommy Wilson had not yet seen the effect of his personal quest for the truth on himself, he did confess to his sister Annie that he was spending much more time reading widely in the great writers of the past, most notably the historical works of the early 19th century English writer Thomas Macaulay. In a letter to her at Easter in 1876, he said that he "would give anything to become as great a writer as Macaulay."[57] There was something amazing in the way Macaulay

---

[54] Bragdon, *Woodrow Wilson: The Academic Years*, 23.

[55] Wilson, "Letter to Annie Wilson Howe, April 19, 1876, *PWW*, I, 127-128.

[56] Baker, *Life and Letters*, I, 85.

[57] Wilson, "Letter to Annie Wilson Howe, April 19, 1876," *PWW*, I, 128.

could describe the history of England that made all the dead facts, the long lost names and the forgotten places, come to life before his eyes. Even if he had no interest in a topic, if Macaulay wrote about it, then he got excited about it too. Wilson admired Macaulay's ability to write as if he remembered the past through his own personal experience rather than through his own research in the present. It was as if Macaulay actually stood in ancient Greece and Rome, or really wandered through London's troubled Whitehall during the reign of Charles II or the angry streets of Paris during the French Revolution as he wrote his stories of the past.

Wilson became so enamored of the writings of Macaulay that he could not shake one line he had read from his mind. He knew that Macaulay had relied on the diary of Samuel Pepys to reconstruct the world of Restoration England. So he read Pepys' diary and decided to start one himself. He had been keeping an "Index Rerum" since February where he listed all the interesting facts he had come across in alphabetical order.[58] He carried pocket notebooks with him where he quickly wrote down items that he later copied into larger volumes, either in shorthand or longhand. But on Saturday, June 3, at 19 years of age, he decided to follow in the footsteps of Samuel Pepys and keep a record in shorthand of the daily events in the life of Thomas W. Wilson.

At the top of the first entry, he drew four columns with books about shorthand tucked below two connecting archways. In the center, he traced a large medallion with a symbol for "My Journal" in shorthand. He then wrote that while he thought Pepys was a "strange man," he had contemplated keeping a diary like his for sometime. But today he had little else to say beyond the fact that the Harvard baseball team beat Yale 3 to 2. He was overjoyed along with the rest of the Princeton student body because Yale had humiliated Princeton in a crushing 12 to 9 defeat just one month before. Another freshman named Alanson Enos treated him to a dish of ice cream to celebrate, but Wilson was soon unhappy when he remembered that his friend McCarter had gone home for a few days. He knew it would be a long and lonesome weekend, but at least he could be grateful to God for the blessing of excellent health.[59]

In the last weeks of his freshman year at Princeton, he filled his diary with a countdown to the baccalaureate. Four more weeks, three more weeks, and finally just two more weeks until he would go with his friend McCarter to the chapel on campus and listen to President McCosh say farewell to the students and faculty alike. In between, there was more baseball, sometimes two games a day for the

---

58 Wilson, "Memory, Macaulay's," cited in "Index Rerum," *PWW*, I, 108.

59 Wilson, "Journal Entry for June 3, 1876," cited in "Wilson's Shorthand Diary," *PWW*, I, 132.

Bowery Boys, but sadly one defeat after another for the Princeton team. While he was always excited about baseball, Wilson wrote of his boredom with his studies, especially Greek. Although he found nothing wrong with the works of Xenophon, he questioned why reading had to be so prescribed for college students. The *Memorabilia* was not a stupid book, he wrote, but it was "stupid to read any book when you know you are obliged to read it." Most everything else also seemed to bore Wilson, including going to religious services on the weekends. The sermons he heard were usually dry, unemotional, and poor in their logic. For a change of pace, he went to an Episcopalian service with one of his friends, but dismissed the entire experience as "a ridiculous way of worshiping God."[60]

Besides baseball, the only thing that excited Tommy Wilson's mind in late May and early June was his continuing study of the works of Thomas Macaulay, especially his *History of England*. "If all history was written thus I would read little else," he confessed in his journal.[61] He was mesmerized by Macaulay's descriptions of the reigns of Charles II, James II, and William and Mary. They were so vivid that young Wilson felt he had been transported back to the world of kings and nobleman more than two centuries before. The very principles of good government were laid out before him as he learned of Parliament's struggles to end the long and troubled reign of the powerful Stuart monarchs. Surely the story of the Glorious Revolution was the most important tale of liberty ever played out in the history of the world. Wilson was convinced that the form of government England developed at this time was the best system the world had ever known. Only a limited constitutional monarchy could truly guarantee liberty for the people.[62]

Wilson spent so much time reading about England's troubles in the late 17th century, and what these struggles meant for the development of political principles in the modern world, that he began to worry that it might affect his health and his academic career. Except for more baseball games with the Bowery Boys, he had forgotten to take any other exercise, preferring instead to read Macaulay hour after hour. He finally stopped himself long enough to study for his exams in geometry, Latin, French, and the much hated Greek. While he knew that he must do well in his exams and so succeed as a student at Princeton, he could not stay away from Macaulay for too long. Once his exams were finished, he was

---

60 Wilson, "Journal Entries for June 4, 1876," cited in "Wilson's Shorthand Diary," *PWW*, I, 132.

61 Wilson, "Journal Entry for June 5, 1876," cited in "Wilson's Shorthand Diary," *PWW*, I, 133.

62 Wilson, "Journal Entries for June 4, 5, and 6, 1876," cited in "Wilson's Shorthand Diary," *PWW*, I, 133-135.

back in the library to check out the next volume of his *History of England*. "Oh that I could learn to write thus," he confessed in his journal.[63]

When the day of Princeton's baccalaureate finally arrived on June 25, 1876, Wilson and his friend McCarter headed to the chapel to listen to President McCosh. But they were quickly bored and skipped out to lay under the shade of the nearby trees until the baccalaureate was over, discussing their disappointment that there had not been nearly as many pretty girls at the ceremony as there usually were in church on the weekends. Wilson returned to his room to pack and was soon upset with himself for collecting so many things in the past year. After he finally finished packing, he said good-bye to all of his friends in the Wright Bower and won a promise from McCarter that he would write to him. Early on the next morning, he boarded the train that came through the campus and headed for Baltimore. It was a hot and dusty trip, and Wilson was happy to get on the boat that would take him to North Carolina. He sat up on the deck in the bright sun and cool breeze all the way to Portsmouth, and was only disappointed that there were no pretty girls on board. He headed on to Wilmington, arriving there in the early evening of Tuesday June 27.[64]

He found his mother and little brother Josie alone at the family home. They were overjoyed to see him and told him that the Reverend Wilson had gone to the commencement ceremonies at Davidson College. Wilson was just as happy to see his family, but he was very concerned that his mother's health appeared to be failing. Only fifty years old, she was always tired and often in pain, and needed to rest frequently throughout the day. Wilson took it upon himself to help around the house. He played with Josie, sometimes drawing pictures of ships for him and often taking him to the market in the mornings to buy groceries and other supplies for the family. When two new rooms were finished at the back of the manse, Tommy brought pieces of furniture down from the upstairs for his mother and even varnished them. He helped her lay carpets in the new rooms. He found he liked staying at home, doing chores and running errands. When his mother urged him to go out and meet some of the young ladies in town, he complained that he found most of them dull and uninteresting, and preferred to stay in his room, reading Macaulay of course.

He took his reading of Macaulay so much to heart that if the historian praised a writer as important, then Wilson had to read him. In the summer of 1876, he

---

[63] Wilson, "Journal Entries for June, 12, 13, and 14, 1876," cited in "Wilson's Shorthand Diary," *PWW*, I, 138-140.

[64] Wilson, "Journal Entries for June 25, 26, and 27, 1876," cited in "Wilson's Shorthand Diary," *PWW*, I, 145-146.

took Macaulay's advice, and moved past Samuel Pepys and on to William Shakespeare. Wilson had already read *Romeo and Juliet*, and was not impressed with the tale. But he now plunged into tragedies like *King Lear* and was overwhelmed at how Shakespeare brought the misery of this troubled old man to life. He also loved Shakespeare's comedies like *Much Ado about Nothing* and, most especially, *The Merry Wives of Windsor*. Othello, Iago, Macbeth and his wife, John Falstaff, and young Prince Harry – each one lit up before his eyes through the magical words of Shakespeare just as the charming King Charles and his arrogant brother James appeared before him through the vivid descriptions of Macaulay.[65]

When his father returned from Davidson College, Wilson had long talks with him, at first mainly about the many friends he had made up north. There were games, too, since his father had kept up with one of the latest trends from Europe and built a billiard table for his family in the basement. The father and son would play as many as three games a day together throughout the summer. They also enjoyed more discussions on a variety of topics, the most important one being the relationship between poetry and philosophy. Both agreed that poetry belonged to the world of children more than to the world of grown men. It came naturally to a people in the early stages of their civilization, but was less important to them as they advanced and became more philosophical. Wilson even got his friend McCarter caught up in the family debate on the relationship of poetry and philosophy through frequent letters over the summer.[66]

When he was not spending time with his family, Tommy retreated to his room where he went ever deeper into his study of the past. Having lived through the revolution that the Civil War brought upon the South, and still seeing its effects during the Reconstruction, Tommy found some comfort in studying a time when England had also faced a revolution and come out of it, according to Macaulay, a much better nation. Perhaps in these books there was some hope of finding a solution to the troubles he knew in his own country. If he had seen one world come undone and then be reborn in his lifetime, and now watched it happening once again in the pages of Macaulay's history of England, then perhaps he could find the principles upon which the best government should be built. If he could understand where England had gone wrong in its civil war, could he not one day see where his own nation had also gone wrong? It was as if he looked into a

---

[65] Wilson, "Journal Entries for June 28, July 3, and August 1, 3, and 5, 1876," cited in "Wilson's Shorthand Diary," *PWW*, I, 146-148, 162-163, 166.

[66] Wilson, "Journal Entry for June 29, 1876," cited in "Wilson's Shorthand Diary," *PWW*, I, 147; Robert Harris Carter, "Letter to Thomas Woodrow Wilson, July 10, 1876," *PWW*, I, 152.

mirror that reflected his own nation when he went up to his room, threw himself on his bed, and read volume after volume of Macaulay's *History of England.* Every chapter seemed to hold secrets about the past and present that Wilson was determined to unlock.

Still he was not ready to admit that his fascination with English history at its most troubled might reflect a concern for his own country as it passed through the dark days of the Reconstruction. In his diary, he made no connection between the tales of political ruin and rebirth that he loved to read and the struggles of his own nation. In fact, he found himself in the midst of his country's Centennial celebration in the summer of 1876 thoroughly disgusted with the American political system. He had made a name for himself in the Wright Bower all year as the defender of the English system of government as the best one the world had ever seen. Now he sat in Wilmington, glancing at newspaper accounts of celebrations all over the country, and becoming angrier as he read. On Tuesday July 4, as so much of the rest of the nation, at least the north and west, celebrated one hundred years of American freedom, he spent the day fixing a toy boat for his brother Josie, writing a letter to his sister Annie, and playing billiards with his father. He finished the 21st chapter of Macaulay's history and made it through most of the 22nd one as well. He also had time to make this bitter entry in his diary to mark the day:

> "The one hundredth anniversary of American independence. One hundred years ago America conquered England in an unequal struggle and this year she glories over it. How much happier (?) she would be now if she had England's form of government instead of the miserable delusion of a republic. A republic too founded on the notion of abstract liberty! I venture to say that this country will never celebrate another centennial as a republic. The English form of government is the only true one."[67]

Just a few days later when he read about the massacre of General George Armstrong Custer and the 7th Cavalry at the Little Big Horn, Wilson felt no patriotic stirrings, but instead chalked up the disaster to Custer wanting "to make something of himself."[68]

Much of the disgust for his country came from his dislike of the ruling Republican Party, whom he always referred to in his journal as the "Radical Party," and the misery he believed it had brought on the South during the Reconstruction. Wilson attended a rally in town just a few days after the Fourth of

---

[67] Wilson, "Journal Entry for July 4, 1876," cited in "Wilson's Shorthand Diary," *PWW*, I, 148-149.

July where he heard speakers call for a Democratic victory at the polls in November. He listened to one man who spoke for two hours, never getting tired or losing interest in what the man was saying. He hoped the rumors were true that Governor Samuel Tilden of New York would get the Democratic nomination, win the Presidency, and end the rule of the Radical Republicans in the South and the rest of the nation forever. But his disgust with his own nation was not simply directed at northern politicians. He looked around him and saw much that dissatisfied him in the South as well. Wilmington was a disgrace, a dirty place where people did not have the decency to take care of their property. He helped his father gather and stack the lumber that was strewn about their own backyard, and then wrote an editorial to the local newspaper calling for the town government to cleanup Wilmington.[69]

Shortly after he swept out the backyard with his son, Reverend Wilson prepared to leave for a vacation on his own in the north, a habit he had developed when his children were still small. Tommy helped his mother pack, handing one item after another to her which she carefully placed in Reverend Wilson's trunk. While away, Reverend Wilson relied on his son to act in his place as the clerk of the Southern Presbyterian Church. Tommy did his best to keep up with the correspondence but confessed in his diary that at times the task was daunting. He was sad to see his father go, but happy when he learned that Annie Howe would soon be coming to Wilmington with her son for a vacation. Tommy was delighted to see his older sister again, and thought she looked much better than she did when he saw her during Christmas vacation. He spent many hours playing in the manse with his brother Josie and his toddler nephew Wilson.[70]

With his father in the north, Tommy Wilson took his mother and brother to several local churches for Sunday services, and was often quite dissatisfied with the uninspired sermons he heard. He was also upset at the way his fellow Christians quietly rejoiced in their own salvation and then never did anything to make the world a better place. In August, he decided to do something about it himself. He wrote a series of four articles under the pen name of Twiwood for the Wilmington North Carolina Presbyterian in which he presented his own growing vision of life and the role that faith should play in it. Certain that not a soul would read them, and after letting his mother suggest corrections, he began with a piece

---

[68] Wilson, "Journal Entry for July 7, 1876," cited in "Wilson's Shorthand Diary," *PWW*, I, 150.

[69] Wilson, "Journal Entries for July 7 and August 10, 1876," cited in "Wilson's Shorthand Diary," *PWW*, I, 150, 174-175; A Citizen, "Letter to the Editor," *Wilmington Journal*, July 14, 1876," *PWW*, I, 150-151.

[70] Wilson, "Journal Entries for June 29 and 30, August 12, 1876," cited in "Wilson's Shorthand Diary," *PWW*, I, 147, 178.

called “Work-Day Religion.” He argued that most Christians confined their faith to Sunday mornings. They were filled with the love of God from the time they entered the church right up until the moment they left it. Then all thought of following Christ in their average “work-day” lives was forgotten. They made no attempt to help out at the local church and never brought Christ into the workplace. “Life is a work-day,” Wilson boldly proclaimed. Christians will be called to account on the last day by Jesus himself who will ask them to show how they used the talents he gave them for the good of the others in their daily lives.[71]

In “Christ’s Army,” the second piece published a week later, Wilson picked up the same theme, but now in more heroic terms. He described two great armies, one led by Christ and the other led by the Prince of Darkness, arrayed like medieval warriors as they faced each other on the battlefield of the world.

> “Immediately behind the great Captain of Salvation come the veteran regiments of the soldiers of the cross with steady tread, their feet shod with the preparation of the Gospel of Peace, girt about with truth, their breastplates of righteousness glittering beneath their Master’s love, each one grasping the sword of the Spirit ... From the opposite side of the field, advancing from the tents of wickedness, come the hosts of sin led by the Prince of Lies himself, riding upon death’s horse. Behind him a mighty army marshaled by fiends under the dark banners of iniquity.”

There was no turning back from this contest for all must decide which army they would join. The great battle between good and evil was then played out in daily life, and on the last day, the world would learn on which side every man, woman, and child had been fighting. Wilson urged his readers to remember that by faithfully doing their duty, even in some quiet corner of the world, they stood shoulder to shoulder with their God and Savior Jesus Christ in a battle for the very soul of the world.[72]

In the next week, Wilson followed up with instructions on the best place to go for guidance on how to live one’s daily life in a truly Christian way. The guidance was in the Bible. Wilson complained that modern Christians seemed to look for guidance everywhere but in the Bible. He reminded them that all the civilized nations of the world looked to the Old Testament as the foundation of their laws, and that by following the example of Christ in the New Testament, a person could

---

[71] Wilson, “Journal Entry for August 9, 1876,” cited in “Wilson’s Shorthand Diary,” *PWW*, I, 174; Twiwood, “Work-Day Religion” (Wilmington *North Carolina Presbyterian*, August 16, 1876), *PWW*, I, 176-178.

learn of the love of God and the best way to live a perfect life in this world and so gain an everlasting one in the next. He assured his readers that if they spent their whole lives studying this work, they could not "exhaust one half of its treasures."[73]

Wilson submitted his final editorial on September 1, just four days before he left Wilmington for his sophomore year at Princeton. He called it "A Christian Statesman," and in it he gave voice to his own growing love of politics and the possible place that he, the son of a Presbyterian minister and a devout Christian himself, might play in it. Again he stressed the theme that had preoccupied him all summer – that today Christianity is confined to certain walks of life. It is fine for a minister and even a soldier to be a Christian. But most would think it quite comical to say a businessman, a lawyer or a statesman was a Christian. "Religion is thought out of place in the business office," wrote Wilson, and sadly, "a lawyer is too often justified in a lie; and we should be tempted to smile at hearing of a praying statesman." But surely this is wrong, argued the passionate young editorialist, for would not faith help the businessman, and the love of truth and justice aid the lawyer? Even more importantly, would it not be the Christian statesman, motivated by duty to both God and man, who could do the most to promote good in the world? Wilson reasoned that the love of truth must motivate all men in their daily lives, no matter what profession they chose, and that a statesman must be above party or popularity when he struggled to do what was right for the world. Once he found the truth, a statesman must fight for it with humility, never attacking his opponents and always being aware of his own weaknesses. A statesman, Wilson concluded, must "let his whole conversation and life be such as becomes a Christian, and, therefore, a gentleman."[74]

In the logic of this small piece, just four paragraphs long, Wilson seemed to have written an outline for a future that he was still not willing to admit he longed for wholeheartedly. His ambition, first mentioned to his cousin Jessie in childhood, and now the obsession of his reading, was just below the surface, not yet ready for him to view fully or acknowledge completely. For now, he must pack his trunk, buy his last supplies for his trip back to college, and head by boat and train to Princeton. His good-bye to his mother, his brother Josie, his sister Annie, and "dear little Wilson" was heart-wrenching, more difficult than any

---

72 Thomas Woodrow Wilson ("Twiwood"), "Christ's Army" (Wilmington *North Carolina Presbyterian*, August 23, 1876), *PWW*, I, 180-181.

73 Thomas Woodrow Wilson ("Twiwood"), "The Bible" (Wilmington *North Carolina Presbyterian*, August 30, 1876), *PWW*, I, 184-185.

74 Thomas Woodrow Wilson ("Twiwood"), "A Christian Statesman" (Wilmington *North Carolina Presbyterian*, September 6, 1876), *PWW*, I, 188-189.

other parting of his young life. He thanked God for the blessing of his wonderful home, his health and his strength. Then he made his way to Baltimore on a boat that was crowded to overflowing, and headed by train to Philadelphia, where he joined his father who was waiting for him to tour the Centennial Exhibition. Wilson was amazed at the technology on display, especially a machine that automatically addressed envelopes, but was most impressed with a display of arts from England, the nation he most admired.

After touring the exhibition for two days, Wilson went with his father to Wannamaker's Department Store where he bought clothes for the winter. On the next day, they rode together by train to Princeton. Wilson was proud when his father preached a sermon at the college. Students and faculty alike gathered around Tommy Wilson and congratulated him for having such a wonderful father. He said good-bye to the Reverend Wilson whom he loved so dearly on September 11, and then settled down for his second year at Princeton and the Wright Bower.[75]

He tried his best to keep up with the diary he had begun nearly a year before but soon found that he had little enthusiasm for it. Still it was a good place to record the deep anxiety that he and so many of his fellow countrymen felt for their nation as the presidential election grew closer. Wilson hoped that Samuel Tilden, the Democratic Governor from New York, would defeat the Republican from Ohio Rutherford B. Hayes. Perhaps the humiliation of the South would then come to an end at last. He duly recorded every state election held in the fall of 1876 that seemed to predict a Democratic win in the presidential race. If Indiana, Ohio and West Virginia went for the Democrats in October, he wrote, then surely Tilden would win in November.[76] On the night after the election, Wilson joined other Democrats on campus for a bonfire. But even as they cheered the many speakers who hailed Tilden's victory, students who supported the Republicans brought news that the papers now said Hayes had won by 4 electoral votes. Wilson finally collapsed in his bed in the Wright Bower at 11 that night, exhausted from the "shouting and excitement."[77]

When he awoke the next day, he discovered that the confusion over who had won the election continued. Conflicting reports came in from all over the state and the nation about who the next president would be. Some said it was Hayes, but others said it was Tilden. While he did not know which side to believe, Wilson

---

[75] Wilson, "Journal Entries for September 5 to 11, 1876," cited in "Wilson's Shorthand Diary," *PWW*, I, 189-192.

[76] Wilson, "Journal Entry for October 11, 1876," cited in "Wilson's Shorthand Diary," *PWW*, I, 208.

[77] Wilson, "Journal Entry for November 8, 1876," cited in "Wilson's Shorthand Diary," *PWW*, I, 222.

confessed in his diary that he was "of course inclined to believe the Democratic reports before the Republican." So was Janet Wilson who wrote to her son Tommy that it seemed "too good to be true" but it looked as if there would soon be a Democratic Governor in North Carolina and a Democratic President in the White House. She encouraged her "darling boy" to ignore any nasty taunts from Republican students on campus if Tilden had won, and to be equally patient if the unthinkable happened and Hayes was elected.[78]

In the agony of waiting to hear once and for all who would become the next President of the United States, Wilson did his best to keep up with his classes in French, mathematics, English, and psychology. But the disputed election was never far from his mind, and he tried his best to find words to capture the hope that his country would put aside the bitterness of the contest between Hayes and Tilden. He sat down at his desk in the Wright Bower and drafted a speech called "The Union." He would never give the speech that surely would have shocked his many roommates who still remembered how white his face had turned whenever the South was criticized. But now for the first time in his life he felt a flicker of patriotism for his bold young country that had thrown off the shackles of the old world and set up a Constitution based on its best models. Yet try as he might, the words failed him so he wrote down long passages from Daniel Webster and Andrew Jackson. "Without union our liberty and independence would never have been achieved," he copied from President Jackson's Second Inaugural Address, "without union they can never be maintained." In the end, Wilson could only hope that one day the North and the South "would soon be seen marching hand in hand with their great progress with the world," and that maybe someday he would be able to find words to move a nation like Andrew Jackson once did.[79]

Finding the right words was imperative for the Princeton sophomore not just because he was upset about the election but because he had come to believe that the most important thing a man could do was to become a great orator. Sometime in the spring of his freshman year, he had come upon an essay called "The Orator" written by an anonymous author. He would always remember the day he sat in the stairwell of the Chancellor Green Library on the Princeton campus and read that great speakers like William Pitt and Edmund Burke could move whole nations through the courage and conviction of their words.[80] If only he could be a leader like Pitt, calling his nation to war and greatness, or one like Burke, daring to stand

---

[78] Wilson, "Journal Entry for November 9, 1876," cited in "Wilson's Shorthand Diary," *PWW*, I, 223; Janet Woodrow Wilson to Thomas Woodrow Wilson (November 8, 1876), *PWW*, I, 223.

[79] Thomas Woodrow Wilson, "The Union," *PWW*, I, 226-228.

[80] Baker, *Life and Letters*, I, 88.

up for what was right in the face of evil, then surely he would have found his purpose in life. The thought of these two men fighting for what they believed in lit up in his mind, and their words rung in his ears as if he had heard them himself in Parliament. But he could not yet find such words in himself, and instead could only hope that one day he would learn to speak with a passion so deep that it could stir an entire nation.

As he came to realize the important role an orator could play in a nation, Thomas Woodrow Wilson seemed to step off the deck of the imaginary pirate ships of his childhood and onto the floor of the Congress where he saw himself leading men one day through the sheer brilliance of his words. Even as the picture of his future began to form in his mind, he was already convinced that the words he would speak someday must not come from a desire for self-glorification, but instead must arise from a profound understanding of the best path his nation should take. Ideas were beginning to form deep within him about the future direction of his country, but his struggle with the speech on the Union showed just how far he was from being able to speak on this important matter. He found it was much easier to write about ideas that came from his childhood rather than from his own uncertain future or that of his nation. In an article he penned for the North Carolina Presbyterian called "One Duty of a Son to His Parents," he urged his young readers to be the best gentlemen that they could possibly be in these turbulent times. By so doing, they would be the best sons they could possibly be. Surely if a young man was a gentleman in the world, behaving properly to everyone he met, then he must be a gentleman at home and treat his parents with respect.[81]

Shortly before leaving for home in December 1876, Wilson wrote another essay on "Christian Progress" for the same paper. He reminded his readers that the life of a Christian was one of struggle on a long journey. "In order to advance," he explained, "the Christian must needs strain every muscle." But still it was a pleasant journey since the road led to eternal life and Christ himself walked side by side with us on the way to true happiness.[82] When he arrived back in Wilmington for Christmas vacation, he found his father lost in a private struggle of his own. In the words of Janet Wilson, he was "blue," still depressed from the troubles in Columbia when the students at the seminary did not want to listen to his sermons. He had never been able to find real happiness in his new church in

---

[81] A Son, "One Duty of Son to His Parents" (Wilmington *North Carolina Presbyterian*, October 8, 1876), *PWW*, I, 205-207.

[82] Thomas Woodrow Wilson ("Twiwood"), "Christian Progress" (Wilmington *North Carolina Presbyterian*, December 20, 1876), *PWW*, I, 234-235.

Wilmington. Wilson's mother tried her best to cheer up the family, and would soon come up with a plan to take her sons Tommy and Josie to Georgia in the upcoming summer to visit her sister Marion Bones who had been quite ill. She wanted Tommy to have fun with his cousin Jessie again, and get some good exercise riding on horseback in the countryside around Rome. If Wilson spoke with his mother or father about his growing plans to become a great speaker and so a great leader, he did not confess this in his diary. In early September, he was sad to leave his family's home in Wilmington on the first leg of the long journey back to Princeton, but happy when he turned to see his little brother Josie running after him with a handkerchief he had had left behind. A few days later, Mrs. Wilson wrote to Tommy that the little boy had fought back tears when he handed the hankie to his older brother, not wanting him to know how much his family missed him, and then ran back home to her where he burst into tears.[83]

Back in Princeton, Wilson was relieved to move out of the Wright Bower and into Witherspoon Hall, a new dormitory on the campus. He considered Mrs. Wright a difficult woman who was given to whims, and he was happy to be away from the many arguments that broke out in her boarding house.[84] The move also seemed to match something happening deep within himself. Some of his companions noticed how much their friend was developing as a person. Hiram Woods, a boy from Maine, said that while other students seemed to drift at Princeton, young Thomas Wilson had a keen sense of purpose and direction.[85] Wilson attended classes and did the same assignments as the other students, but he had also developed an uncanny knack for picking other books to read that would help him grow as a future leader. Every new book he borrowed from the Chancellor Green Library or the collection of the American Whig Society held a clue to the world he would one day enter as a grown man.

As he combed through stories about the great leaders of the past, Wilson became concerned again with the question of political greatness, a problem that he and his friend John Bellamy had debated while lying on the hills at the Delgado Mills in the summer before his freshman year at Princeton. He worked hard on a speech called "The Ideal Statesman" where he tried to summarize all he had learned so far about what a man must do to become the best political leader he could possibly be. For Wilson, there was simply no higher calling for a man than to be a statesman. But how could a man become the perfect statesman? First, he must be a great lawyer, knowing the laws of his own nation and those of other

---

[83] Janet Woodrow Wilson, "Letter to Thomas Woodrow Wilson, January 17, 1877," *PWW*, I, 237.
[84] Janet Woodrow Wilson, "Letter to Thomas Woodrow Wilson, March 7, 1877," *PWW*, I, 251-252.
[85] Baker, *Life and Letters*, I, 93.

nations as well. He must also be an excellent historian who made the story of all mankind the main topic of his studies. Beyond that, the ideal statesman must be above partisan politics, and must also have a kind of genius that set him apart from the average man. Could anyone ever live up to such perfection? Only, Wilson concluded, if this ideal statesman "worked with an energy" that was "almost superhuman" and "looked to uninterested spectators like insanity."[86]

Although he did not mention it in his speech on "The Ideal Statesman," Wilson remained convinced that the mastery of words was the single most powerful talent that a political leader must develop. He was so determined to master the art of speaking himself that he often went alone into the woods near Princeton to recite famous speeches. A friend found him there one day reciting the words of Edmund Burke. He was determined to do the same thing in the summer when he was back home in North Carolina. He would go to his father's church, climb up in the pulpit, and read aloud the speeches of Gladstone, Webster, and even Demosthenes to the empty pews.[87] He was equally convinced that he could hone his skills in real debates about things that mattered in the modern world. While he continued to participate in the debates of the American Whig Society, even winning a second prize for his speech "The Ideal Statesman," he grew tired of talking about outdated and abstract topics. He wanted to discuss the real issues of the day with his friends and decided to found his own debating society.

Wilson called it the Liberal Debating Club and founded it in the late winter of 1877 with nine of his closest companions. They included his first friend at Princeton, Robert McCarter, and one of his newest friends, a boy from New York named Charles Andrew Talcott who shared his dream of becoming a politician one day. Tommy got a chance to write a constitution for the club, his fourth so far since writing one for the Lightfoot Club, another one for the freshman literary society at Davidson, and the last one for his imaginary yacht club. The purpose of the debating club was twofold. It was to form a brotherhood of young men who would "encourage each other in every possible way" while at the same time upholding the ideals of "justice, morality, and friendship." The President, who was elected by all the members, would oversee the debates, while the Secretary of State, who was appointed by the President, would maintain all the records of the society. The most important issues of the day would be considered "bills" that would be passed on to all members for discussion and debate. Every member of

---

[86] Thomas Woodrow Wilson ("Atticus"), "The Ideal Statesman," *PWW*, I, 241-245.

[87] Baker, *Life and Letters*, I, 92.

the club must give an opinion on each issue, and also promise to keep the proceedings of this special club a secret.[88]

It was soon obvious to many students besides his closest friends in the Liberal Debating Club that Tommy Wilson was becoming a leader on campus. In the early spring of 1877, when he was depressed from struggling with a lingering cold that just would not go away, he was elected to the board of editors of The Princetonian, a position he would assume at the start of his junior year. He wrote home excitedly to tell his parents. His mother, who had also been sick throughout the winter, was overjoyed that her darling boy had at last been recognized by his fellow students, but his father warned him not to be "puffed up." Wilson took his father's warning to heart, and wrote the first of many editorials for The Princetonian on "True Scholarship." The message of the short piece was clear. A student must not seek knowledge for self-glorification, but for the good that it would allow him to do for the world one day.[89]

When Wilson headed home for his summer vacation in June, he could be proud that he had done well in his schoolwork, better than in his freshman year. He ranked 30th in his class, and did his best in Latin and English but also did well in French, Greek, Natural Science and even Mathematics. But this success seemed unimportant to him. He had a growing awareness that he had come unto himself, as he would later describe it when he was much older, and was now determined to learn how to write and speak in a way that moved men's souls and even changed history. He was overjoyed to see his family, and soon headed with his mother and younger brother Josie out to the home of his aunt Marion Bones in Rome, Georgia. He loved riding in the countryside on horseback, playing with his two nephews, Wilson and little George who had been born in the previous October, and helping his mother take care of Josie. But he was also determined to improve his oratory and wrote letters to his father in Wilmington asking for advice on speech writing.[90]

Back at Princeton for his junior year, Tommy Wilson found both his mind and his friendships deepening. He looked for new political heroes to study and searched for new books that would move him as much as Macaulay's histories had once done. He was not content to discover things on his own but instead gathered a group of fellow students around him in a room two doors down from

---

[88] Thomas Woodrow Wilson, "Constitution of the Liberal Debating Club" (February 1 to March 15, 1877), *PWW*, I, 245-249.

[89] Joseph Ruggles Wilson, "Letter to Thomas Woodrow Wilson, March 27, 1877," *PWW*, I, 254-255; Thomas Woodrow Wilson, "True Scholarship," Editorial in *The Princetonian*, Printed May 24, 1877, PWW, I, 268-269.

[90] Joseph Ruggles Wilson, "Letter to Thomas Woodrow Wilson, July 26, 1877," *PWW*, I, 287-288.

his own in Witherspoon Hall. Known as the "Witherspoon Gang," they debated every topic "under the sun" in the early evening after they had attended a college prayer meeting. They spent their days together, too, as members of an eating club called the "Alligators." They mixed their love of ideas and debates with an equal fondness for storytelling. Tommy was considered the best storyteller because he peppered his tales with a whole series of characters and dialects. He could even entertain his friends with songs and a hornpipe dance. Wilson would always remember these days with the "dear boys" of "No. 9 East Witherspoon" as some of the happiest times of his life.[91]

Even as he talked and laughed with his friends, Wilson continued to search for political leaders to study and someday emulate. He found an unlikely hero in the person of Otto von Bismarck, a man who seemed to break every rule that Wilson considered necessary for political greatness. As a child and young adult, Bismarck had exhibited none of the signs of genius that Wilson had identified in the ideal statesman. He took no interest in politics, and preferred instead to spend his time fox hunting. But when the rising tide of revolution swept through Europe in 1848, ambition came alive within him and overnight he found the will to reshape the continent in his own image. Bismarck united Germany, stripped the Catholic Church of its former power, and humiliated France. At last he showed clear signs of the superhuman energy that Tommy Wilson considered necessary in a great leader.

In October, Wilson started work on a piece about Bismarck that he hoped to use both as an essay and a speech. The essay was accepted for publication in *The Nassau Literary Magazine* in November, but it did not win a prize for the best article as Wilson had hoped. He sent a copy of the piece home to his parents for their comments. His mother wrote back that she loved the work, but his father gently reminded him that there was a great difference between a written piece of work and a spoken one. He urged his son to rewrite the essay with shorter sentences and more vivid language. "Sentences ought to resemble bullets," he explained, "compact and rapid, & prepared to make clean holes." Wilson did exactly as his father had said, cutting the speech in half and ending with the dramatic phrase that "This was a man." He gave the improved speech on Bismarck at an American Whig Society competition in December. When his father wrote another letter on how to write speeches a few weeks later, Wilson copied the instructions down in shorthand in a notebook in the form of simple

[91] Baker, *Life and Letters*, I, 98-99; Thomas Woodrow Wilson, "Letter to Charles Talcott, December 31, 1879," as quoted in Baker, *Life and Letters*, I, 99.

rules that he could always follow to make sure his written words were equally powerful once spoken.[92]

Just as he seemed to be finding his way in the world, Wilson received disturbing news from home. William Leckie, the boy he had roomed with at Davidson College, had been killed. Tommy tried to understand the circumstances of Leckie's death, but the letters from his mother and his sister Annie gave conflicting accounts of what had happened. Slowly the story emerged. Leckie was working as a school teacher, saving money to attend the local seminary where he would become a Presbyterian minister, the deepest dream of his widowed mother's heart. But he disappointed his family when he fell in love with the daughter of the woman who owned the boarding house where he was staying. Greatly distressed over his mother's refusal to allow him to marry the girl, Leckie seemed to take his anger out on his students. He beat one boy so viciously that the child's father or someone close to him shot William dead. It was an unbelievable tragedy for Mrs. Leckie and a strangely chilling good-bye to the path toward the ministry that Wilson had once traveled himself.[93]

The news of Leckie's death deeply troubled Tommy Wilson and even seemed for a time to shatter his growing self-confidence. He wrote home to his mother that he feared for his own future and did not know what would ever become of him. Janet Wilson answered him quickly, reminding her darling boy to concentrate on the present moment and the future would take care of itself. "Don't be too ambitious, dear," she wrote, "for that kind of ambition brings only worry."[94] She even came up with a plan to take her family out to Fremont, Nebraska where she had inherited a beautiful piece of property. She told her son that the family could head west in three or four years time, but just to "think about it" for now.[95]

Tommy Wilson cheered up greatly when he was named the managing editor of *The Princetonian* in February. Throughout the spring of 1878, he wrote even more editorials for the paper, choosing topics that ranged from the college glee club, the need for a voice coach on campus, and a scolding to his fellow students

---

[92] Thomas Woodrow Wilson ("Atticus"), "Prince Bismarck," *PWW*, I, 307-313; Janet Woodrow Wilson, "Letter to Thomas Woodrow Wilson, November 5, 1877," *PWW*, I, 314-315; Joseph Ruggles Wilson, "Letter to Thomas Woodrow Wilson, November 5, 1877," *PWW*, I, 315; Thomas Woodrow Wilson, "Bismarck," *PWW*, I, 325-328; Joseph Ruggles Wilson, "Guide in Writing," *PWW*, I, 340-341.

[93] Janet Woodrow Wilson, "Letter to Thomas Woodrow Wilson, November 10, 1877," *PWW*, I, 316-317; Annie Wilson Howe, "Letter to Thomas Woodrow Wilson, December 20, 1877," *PWW*, I, 331.

[94] Janet Woodrow Wilson, "Letter to Thomas Woodrow Wilson, January 22, 1878," *PWW*, I, 342.

[95] Janet Woodrow Wilson, "Letter to Thomas Woodrow Wilson, February 23, 1878," *PWW*, I, 361.

for their often immature behavior. Wilson's spirits rose even more when he discovered a new book on English history. It was the recently published work of John Richard Green called *A Short History of the English People*. Wilson thrilled at the story of England from the days of the Anglo-Saxons to the reign of Victoria. He wrote an enthusiastic review of Green's history for *The Princetonian* in May, telling his readers that a multi-volume addition of the work was already being printed. Even in this shorter history, Green has clearly shown that the history of the English people was the history of the American people. But Wilson could not help but worry that Americans in their noble experiment had stretched the sacred principles of liberty they had inherited from the English to their utmost. As a "lusty branch of a noble race," they must be sure to add luster rather than stain to this great heritage, warned the young editorialist who seemed to grow more enamored of England each day.[96]

Wilson spent the first half of his summer vacation back in Columbia at the home of his sister Annie Howe. He found it hotter than he had ever remembered, but was glad to see that the charm of the Old South he had known as a boy was alive and well. The people seemed to have accepted the outcome of the recent presidential election and remained as fascinated with politics as ever before. Wilson stayed interested in politics himself by working his way through the multi-volume edition of the *History of the English People* and by outlining an essay on William Pitt, a hero he had grown to admire deeply while reading Green's work. Still he was happiest playing with his youngest nephew George who loved to make his uncle chase him through the house on all fours. Wilson also liked spending time with other young people in town especially several girls he had known in his childhood who still called him "Tommie." Back in Wilmington later in the summer, he brooded for a time that he had dropped to 37th place in his class, a fact he blamed on his lack of interest in physics and the unfairness of his natural science professor. Yet he was happy that the weather cooled in late July, and that he could sit at the open window of his family's house and feel the breezes from the sea.[97]

The pace of life picked up for Thomas Woodrow Wilson in his senior year at Princeton. He took a regular load of classes, but spent much of his free time managing The Princetonian. His favorite topics continued to be activities on

---

[96] Thomas Woodrow Wilson, "Review of Green's *A History of the English People*, May 2, 1878," *PWW*, I, 373-375.

[97] Thomas Woodrow Wilson, "Marginal Notes in John Richard Green's *History of the English People*, July 27, 1878," *PWW*, I, 387-393; Thomas Woodrow Wilson, "Letter to James Edwin Webster, July 23, 1878," *PWW*, I, 383-385; Thomas Woodrow Wilson, "Letter to Robert Bridges, July 27, 1878," *PWW*, I, 385-387.

campus like baseball, football, the glee club, speech contests and the rowdy behavior of his fellow students. He was also chosen as the President of the Baseball Association, a position that greatly alarmed his mother who urged him to give the job up for more serious pursuits. The increased responsibilities of his senior year had an effect on his grades. While they remained high in history, ethics, political science, and English, they tumbled to new lows in chemistry and astronomy.

Although his parents were upset with the poor grades, blaming the unfair professors rather than their own son, Wilson was not long discouraged. He truly believed that he had found himself at Princeton primarily through the reading he had done on his own rather than in his class assignments. As he headed into the last months of his college career, he began to reflect on the many books that he had chosen to read from the Chancellor Green Library and the collection of the American Whig Society. He then took time to do what he had done on the very first day he arrived in Princeton. He sat down and wrote out a list of what at the moment seemed to be the most important things in his life. But instead of a careful list of the clothes he had brought with him and the purchases he had made, he now wrote down every significant book he had read in each of his fours years at Princeton. Here was Shakespeare and Macaulay in his freshman year, and Burke and Locke in his sophomore year. By his senior year, he had read nearly 60 books, mainly in politics and literature.[98]

Wilson also continued to make great strides in his own writing. He gave up his diary, concluding that it was much more pleasant to read one than to keep one, and decided instead to concentrate on political essays. He became even more fascinated with his new hero, William Pitt, and wrote an article on him for *The Nassau Literary Magazine* that won an award for best essay. The piece read more like poetry rather than history since Wilson spent only one line on Pitt's actual career, specifically his triumphs in the Seven Years War, and the remainder on a description of his complex character. In the work, Pitt appears as a man who lives counter to his age. He is a commoner who storms through the halls of power, challenging the privileged classes to think more of their nation than themselves. He has a wild and passionate heart in an age filled with rational and cynical men. He pushes his country forward to greatness and empire through the sheer force of his own personality. In this man, Wilson found a flawed genius who was far more complex than any one he had previously studied. Pitt seemed to have stepped straight out of the plays of Shakespeare rather than the works of Macaulay or

[98] Joseph Ruggles Wilson, "Letter to Thomas Woodrow Wilson, January 10, 1879," *PWW*, I, 443-444; Thomas Woodrow Wilson, "My Reading – Principal Works," *PWW*, I, 442-443.

Green. Wilson was also haunted by the fact that a great politician like Pitt could be utterly alone at the end of his life. He was troubled that the great commoner, so long ignored after all he had done for his country, rose to accept the title of the Earl of Chatham, and then fell from grace, never to rise again.[99]

Early in his final semester at Princeton, Wilson began work on an even more serious piece. Moving far beyond the character studies he had done on heroes like Bismarck and Pitt, he now tackled the question of where the American political system had gone wrong. In an essay entitled "Cabinet Government in the United States," he began with the premise that most modern Americans had come to doubt their own government. The mood of fear and anxiety that blanketed the nation could not be blamed on the chaos of the presidential election in 1876 or even the Civil War and its aftermath. Instead the cause of the country's current woes could be found in the very construction of the Constitution.

Wilson argued that the men who gathered in Philadelphia in the summer of 1787 had made a near fatal mistake when they decided that members of the executive branch, specifically the officers of the President's cabinet, could not sit in either branch of the national legislature. Unlike England where the Prime Minister's Cabinet sits in Parliament, the United States had adopted a system that drew a sharp divide between the executive and legislative branches. This decision left the President powerless to draft and pass legislation necessary for the success of his administration. Instead, the many standing committees in both chambers of Congress wrote the legislation behind the scenes. In such a system, the great orators, and the play of their debates that Wilson so admired, were hidden from view and ultimately unnecessary. The President could not sway the decision-making process since his ministers were not a part of the legislature and so could not speak on his behalf. For a young man who could see Pitt and Burke in his mind's eye giving magnificent speeches in the House of Commons, the mere thought of the American system was stifling. That decisions were made behind closed doors rather than on the center stage of the floor of the House or the Senate was the essential flaw in the American system according to Thomas Wilson who had come to understand this in reading so many books on history and politics at Princeton. The argument he made was powerful enough for the young author to win publication of his essay in the International Review in the summer of 1879.[100]

Oratory as the sincere expression of a person's most deep seated beliefs had clearly become one of the highest ideals in the life of young Wilson. In his eyes, a

---

[99] Thomas Woodrow Wilson, "Journal Entry for May 1877," *PWW*, I, 270; Thomas Woodrow Wilson, "William Earl Chatham," *PWW*, I, 407-412.

[100] Thomas Woodrow Wilson, "Cabinet Government in the United States," *PWW*, I, 493-510.

nation's fortunes rose and fell on the ability of its greatest leaders to put forward the clearest vision of the country's future in the most beautiful and stirring terms. He was determined to master the art of writing speeches and then delivering them in a powerful way in order to prepare for a life in government. He was so committed to this ideal that he could not debate a topic that he did not believe in wholeheartedly. This became apparent in the spring of 1879 when he refused to participate in the Lynde Debate, the most important speech competition held between top seniors at the Princeton Commencement. Many of his friends hoped that he would represent the American Whig Society in the contest, but he lost interest very early when he learned that one of the preliminary debates would be on the issue of whether it would be "advantageous to the United States to abolish universal suffrage." He confessed to his father that the topic did not interest him in the least since he was completely against giving the vote to every man. After drawing lots to argue the question in the negative, meaning he would have to speak in favor of universal suffrage, Wilson withdrew from the contest, saying he could not debate in favor of giving every man the vote when he was so deeply against the practice. Preferring the English system that had property qualifications for voting, he was convinced that only people who somehow had a stake in society should be allowed to participate in elections.[101]

The seniors who decided to stay in the competition ended up debating "Ought Chinese Immigration to be Prohibited?" at the commencement exercises in June. While some of his companions may have been disappointed that he did not participate in the Lynde Debate, Wilson's family and closest friends understood why he had stepped down. The integrity of his convictions mattered more to him than the fleeting glory of a college prize that would soon be forgotten. In the final weeks of school, he preferred instead to put all of his energy into writing the speech he would give at the commencement on the ties between England and the United States. Everyone who heard him agreed it was a magnificent speech given by a young man who truly seemed to have a sense of purpose for his own life. Wilson confessed this purpose in letters written to his friend Charles Andrew Talcott throughout the spring and summer of 1879. They made a solemn covenant with each other promising to live up to their highest ideals and to achieve their dream of serving in politics. Someday they would greet each other as Senators in Washington. In the back of his mind, Wilson could even see himself as the Governor of Virginia or the Secretary of the Navy. In order to achieve at least one of these goals, he would continue to perfect his writing on political themes and

---

[101] Arthur S. Link, "Editorial Note: Wilson's Refusal to Enter the Lynde Competition," *PWW*, I, 480-481.

strengthen the power of his voice. He also made the decision to attend law school at the University of Virginia in the upcoming fall. The law would be the gateway into the political world he had dreamt of throughout his college career, and the road he would begin to go down in order to one day stand beside the likes of Edmund Burke and William Pitt.[102]

He graduated from Princeton in June 1879, knowing full well that he had been on an adventure that truly shaped him to his very depths. It had brought him out of the lonely dreams of his childhood into a world where his imagination remained alive and now showed the clear path he must take to achieve political greatness. He was determined to keep in touch with the friends he had made in college, and hoped he would meet many of them in the halls of Congress in some distant future. He returned home to his family in Wilmington, and his mother, who had been ill throughout much of the year, soon packed the family up for a vacation high in the Blue Ridge Mountains. She took Tommy, Josie, her daughter Annie, and her three grandchildren, Wilson, George, and a little girl also named Annie, westward into the cool mountains where they stayed first in Horse Cove, North Carolina and then in Walhalla, South Carolina. Wilson enjoyed the relaxing time with his family, but continued in his political studies, producing an essay on the government of France. Although still favoring the English system of politics over all others, he showed great respect for the French people as they struggled again to establish a democracy under the Third Republic when they had so few traditions of self-government upon which to build this brave experiment.[103]

As the summer of 1879 drew to a close, Thomas Woodrow Wilson, now 22 years old, seemed totally different from the dreamy child who had once struggled to learn how to read or the awkward shy boy who wandered about the Princeton campus carrying his father's old black valise and looking for a place to stay. But inwardly he was still somewhat uncertain about himself, and even began to brood that while he had achieved much at college, he had not found the love of a woman that so many of his fellow graduates were now pursuing. Would he find love not just of the law but of a woman who would support him as his mother had so faithfully supported his father? This small ache in his heart was the only cloud on

---

[102] Joseph Ruggles Wilson, "Letter to Thomas Woodrow Wilson, April 17, 1879," *PWW*, I, 477; Charles Andrew Talcott, "Letters to Thomas Woodrow Wilson, May 21 and June 1, 1879," *PWW*, I, 484-486; Thomas Woodrow Wilson, "Letters to Charles Andrew Talcott, May 21 and July 7, 1879," *PWW*, I, 484, 487-488; Baker, *Life and Letters*, I, 105.

[103] Thomas Woodrow Wilson, "Letter to Robert Bridges, September 4, 1879," *PWW*, I, 539; Thomas Woodrow Wilson, "Self-Government in France," *PWW*, I, 515-539.

the horizon of his future as he prepared to leave for Charlottesville and the start of classes at the University of Virginia in October.[104]

[104] Thomas Woodrow Wilson, "Letter to Charles Andrew Talcott, July 7, 1879," *PWW*, I, 487-488; Thomas Woodrow Wilson, "Letter to Robert Bridges, July 30, 1879," *PWW*, I, 489-491.

Chapter 3

LESSONS FROM LAW AND LIFE

The profession I chose was politics; the profession I entered was the law. I entered the one because I thought it would lead to the other.

Woodrow Wilson[105]

When Thomas Woodrow Wilson stepped off the train in Charlottesville, Virginia in the fall of 1879, he was in some respects a changed man. He had grown sideburns over the summer as was the fashion of the day and now looked every inch a grownup.[106] But in his heart, he was still the boy who had dreamt of glory as a ship captain chasing pirates in the South Seas and then dreamt of it again as a college student who hoped to shake the halls of power with his oratory. He was certain that the route to fulfilling these dreams lay through the law, and so he had come to Thomas Jefferson's university to study it. However, he would soon discover that dreaming of greatness and achieving it were two entirely different things. Like Icarus in the Greek stories he so disliked translating, Wilson would fly high on every course he had set for himself in college, before tumbling to earth, and finding his way at last.

The first hint that the road to greatness might not be as easy as he imagined came in the shock of being in a new place that was not at all like Princeton. Wilson complained in letters to his college friends that he missed them all terribly and that he did not find the same sense of camaraderie with his fellow students in law school as he had known as an undergraduate. The beautiful campus high in the mountains with its wide lawn and domed buildings lined with white porticoes, all laid out by Jefferson himself, belied a more brutal atmosphere than Princeton.

---

105 Woodrow Wilson, "Letter to Ellen Louise Axson, October 30, 1883," *PWW*, II, 500.

106 Woodrow Wilson, "Letter to Robert Bridges, September 4, 1879," *PWW*, I, 541.

Students were seldom rowdy or immature at this university, but were instead totally dedicated to their studies. They lived side by side with their professors who had full control over them and the institution. Wilson confessed to his friend Robert Bridges that only students who had some collegiate experience under their belts could survive on this highly competitive campus. The self discipline and raw determination needed to succeed at the University of Virginia was more than the average freshman could bear.[107]

The college itself was still trying to overcome the terrible blow that the Civil War had dealt to its enrollment. So many young men had gone off to fight for the Confederacy and most of them had never returned. Many of those who did come back could not raise the money for a college education or a law degree for themselves or their children. In the fall semester of 1879, there were just 328 young men enrolled at the university. Only two instructors taught in the college of law, Professor John Minor and Professor Stephen Southall. Wilson enrolled in courses taught by both men, and quickly learned that while conditions on the campus were Spartan, the minds of the two instructors who taught him were in no way diminished. He found Professor Minor to be an especially brilliant and challenging teacher. A kind man who led his students in Bible study in his lecture hall on Sunday mornings, Minor was a taskmaster who drilled his students in the intricacies of the law during the rest of the week. He had just completed a massive study which served as the main text in his classes. It was a 5,000 page work in four volumes entitled *Institutes of Common and Statute Law* which students were expected to master in their two year program in the law at the University of Virginia. Wilson also studied constitutional, mercantile, and international law with the equally gifted Professor Southall.[108]

At first, Wilson had a hard time adjusting to a world of intense study, demanding professors, and poor accommodations. He complained to his mother about the room he had taken far from the main campus in a place called Dawson's Row. There was nowhere to eat in the dormitory so Wilson had to pay an extra $18 a week for meals at Mrs. Massie's boarding house. He found the food was just as terrible there as it was everywhere else in Charlottesville. He was also concerned that he would have a hard time making new friends. His mother sympathized with her darling boy's plight and worried that the poor food might upset his delicate stomach. She tried to comfort him with the fact that it would just not be possible to make the same kind of friends in law school that he had

---

[107] Baker, *Life and Letters*, I, 111-112; Woodrow Wilson, "Letter to Robert Bridges, November 7, 1879," *PWW*, I, 580-583.

[108] Baker, *Life and Letters*, I, 112-115.

made in college. When it appeared that Wilson might be in danger of withdrawing into himself, like he had done after leaving Davidson College, his father wrote gently but firmly that he must not go down this path again. He urged his son not to think of himself as better than the other young men who were studying with him in Charlottesville. "Guard against the temptation of imagining yourself to be perfect," wrote Reverend Wilson to his lonely and ever bashful son.[109]

Taking the advice of his parents to heart, Wilson soon found it was easier to make friends than he had at first imagined. While he regretted that he did not have the natural charm of so many other young men born in the South, he was able to overcome his natural reserve and open up to others. A student named Richard Heath Dabney, who was preparing for a career as an English professor, became his closest friend. "Dab" considered Tommy Wilson to be one of the funniest and most intelligent young men he had ever met. They spent long hours together hiking around the campus, playing toss, and telling jokes to one another. Both Wilson and Dabney were chosen as members of the Phi Kappa Psi Fraternity. Wilson also joined the Glee Club, where he sang first tenor, and was made the secretary of the Jefferson Society, one of only two debating clubs on campus. He soon won a reputation for his ready speech and quick wit, and was even asked to present medals to student athletes at a special ceremony in the university's gymnasium. Wilson was asked for copies of the comments he made about each young man, so they could be published in the college's student newspaper, but he had spoken off the cuff and could not later remember his exact words.[110]

Despite his growing popularity, Wilson was becoming ever more uneasy about his work at the University of Virginia as the fall term neared its end. He complained in letters to his friends and family alike that the law was a "hard taskmaster." He had dreamt of a political career and the straight path he would take to it by becoming a lawyer, but he now found himself totally bored with the study of the law. The glowing path that would lead him to stand beside the likes of William Pitt and Edmund Burke was now a dry and dusty one. He poured his despair out most completely to his Princeton classmate Charles Talcott, the boy he had made the sacred covenant with just months before to achieve personal greatness. It now seemed long ago when he had come up with the simple dream that if he remained true to his most cherished beliefs, mastered the art of speaking, and studied the law diligently, then the world of politics would somehow open

---

[109] Janet Woodrow Wilson, "Letter to Thomas Woodrow Wilson, November 18, 1879," *PWW*, I, 584; Joseph Ruggles Wilson, "Letter to Thomas Woodrow Wilson, November 19, 1879," *PWW*, I, 585.

[110] Thomas Woodrow Wilson, "Letter to Robert Bridges, November 7, 1879," *PWW*, I, 580-583.

magically before him and beckon him into a bright future. He confessed that he wished he could find some way to love the law as much as he loved politics and history. While he found that the study of law fed his mind, he longed desperately for it to feed his heart as well.[111]

As he struggled to master the law, Wilson also tried to continue his political writing. Even with a much tougher schedule of courses ahead of him than he had known at Princeton, he kept up with the latest political scholarship and commented on it in essays he wrote in his spare time. In his first days in law school, he picked up a new book called *A True Republic* written by Albert Stickney. Like many other political writers of the day who were trying to find a way to end the corruption that marred national politics, Stickney argued that all elected officials, including the President, should be allowed to hold office as long as they proved to be of good character. Wilson responded to Stickney's ideas by reworking his essay on cabinet government into a new one that he called "Congressional Government." In it, he agreed that the President should be allowed to serve for life as long as he was virtuous and continued to do an excellent job. But he also argued that the President should be able to choose his Cabinet officers from members of Congress who would be allowed to keep their seats in the House or Senate. By so doing, the President would have the support of Congress in winning important legislation. In Wilson's eyes, it was the President, and not the Congress, who must set the legislative agenda for the country.[112]

Just before the end of his first semester at the University of Virginia, Wilson wrote to his father and asked him for advice on getting his political writings published. In the most tactful way possible, Reverend Wilson let his son know that he was not completely happy with his desire to follow a literary career rather than a legal one. He knew Tommy was trying hard to take one step after another to get into the great game of politics. But he also knew that his son was hoping for too much success too soon. "You expect your ideas at once to be heard," he wrote just days before the Christmas holiday in 1879, instead of realizing that a man must slowly build a career first in law before launching into one in politics. It takes time to win the respect of men, he cautioned. Reverend Wilson also worried that his son could not support himself by means of a literary career so instead

---

[111] Thomas Woodrow Wilson, "Letter to Charles Andrew Talcott, December 31, 1879," *PWW*, I, 591-593.

[112] Thomas Woodrow Wilson, "Marginal Notes," *PWW*, I, 546-548; Thomas Woodrow Wilson, "Congressional Government," *PWW*, I, 548-575.

advised him to stick with the law. If nothing else, his worried father explained, do not "let existing opportunity slip from your grasp."[113]

Knowing how troubled her son was in his struggle with the law, Jeanie Wilson suggested that he spend the Christmas holiday with his cousins in Staunton. It was just a 40 mile train ride across the crest of the Blue Ridge Mountains to the new home of his uncle James and his aunt Marion Bones. Tommy would surely be cheered up by spending time with his cousin Jessie who was now a lively 17 year old student at the local Presbyterian academy for girls. The daughters of Thomas Woodrow, the uncle after whom Tommy Wilson had been named, were also students at the academy. Wilson's father had spent time with Jeanie, Mary, and Harriet Woodrow during the previous spring when he visited Staunton, and was delighted to find that his nieces were all affectionate, sweet, and pretty young ladies.[114]

Wilson took his mother's advice and traveled in late December by train to Staunton where he was welcomed into the house of his uncle and aunt. He was happy to spend time with his childhood playmate Jessie, but he was soon completely captivated by his cousin Harriet Augusta Woodrow. She was a dark haired and blue-eyed beauty who was four years younger than the 23 year old Wilson. Called Hattie by her family and friends, she was most often described by them as vivacious. She was a keen lover of music and was able to play many instruments. Wilson admired this talent in her, but was most touched by her beautiful voice. Something in the way she sang "The Last Rose of Summer" pierced his lonely heart. At family gatherings where all the cousins would perform, Wilson clapped and cheered the loudest for Hattie, paying no attention to the raised eyebrows of his relatives who thought it unseemly for one cousin to be so fond of another. In the dreams of the romantic young Thomas Woodrow Wilson, Hattie had become his fair damsel and he had become her "chosen knight."[115]

When he returned to the University of Virginia in early 1880, he liked his studies no better, but now found that he had something to live for at the end of each week. He boarded the train on Friday and headed to Staunton where he stayed at his uncle's house through Sunday and even into the next week whenever he could not bear the thought of leaving Hattie. When he returned to Charlottesville, he wrote chatty letters to his dear "Rosalind" as often as he could,

---

[113] Joseph Ruggles Wilson, "Letter to Thomas Woodrow Wilson, December 22, 1883," *PWW*, I, 589-590.

[114] Janet Wilson, "Letters to Thomas Joseph Wilson, June 2, 1789 and January 5, 1880," *PWW*, I, 486-487, 593.

[115] Thomas Woodrow Wilson, "Letter to Harriet Woodrow, April 14, 1880," *PWW*, I, 647-650.

convinced that she was as unhappy as he was at each parting. He was so in love with Hattie that he began to miss his law classes, preferring to wile away his time in Staunton in the hope that he could spend just one more moment with his beloved cousin. Wilson's failure to attend class alarmed his law professors who marked him absent at least 19 times in the spring of 1880.[116]

For the first time in his life, Wilson had to face questions from his father about his bad behavior. Reverend Wilson wrote to Tommy that the family no longer seemed to receive as many letters from him as they once did. The ones that did arrive spoke not a word about his schoolwork, his plans to become a great orator, or his struggles with the law. Tommy even seemed to have lost interest in a literary career. In contrast, his father wrote, "Your capacity for spreeing seems to be enlarging." He was quite upset when he received a report from the University of Virginia on his son's frequent absences but happy that his professors still considered him a student worth saving. Whatever trouble his son was passing through in the spring of 1880, his father assured him that while he was disappointed in his son, he would never turn on him. "Be sure that you are not less dear to me, or less in my confidence as your father and friend," wrote Wilson's father, "than you have always been."[117]

Contrary to what his father said about him, Wilson had not completely given up his old ambitions. He was chosen by the members of Phi Kappa Psi to attend the fraternity's national convention in Washington, D.C. in February where he enjoyed debating law and politics with other young men from around the country. In the following weeks, he wrote a biographical essay on the contemporary British politician John Bright and a character study of his childhood hero William Gladstone. Both pieces were accepted for publication in the *Virginia University Magazine*.[118] In April, he threw himself into preparations for a debate against a law student from Maryland named James Cabell Bruce. Dismissing the younger man as a "puppy," he was certain that he would easily win the debate against Cabell on whether or not the Catholic Church was a threat to American institutions. Wilson was proud of his own natural debating style and thought everyone would consider Bruce's old-fashioned mannerisms quite comic. As Wilson expected, his opponent put on a dramatic performance when he

---

[116] Thomas Woodrow Wilson, "Letter to Charles Andrew Talcott, May 20, 1880," *PWW*, I, 656-657; Editorial Note on "Report of James F. Harrison," *PWW*, I, 659.

[117] Joseph Ruggles Wilson, "Letters to Thomas Woodrow Wilson, April 17, May 6 and 14, and June 7, 1880," *PWW*, I, 650-651, 654, 659-660.

[118] Thomas Woodrow Wilson, "Letter to Robert Bridges, February 25, 1880," *PWW*, I, 603-607; Thomas Woodrow Wilson, "John Bright, March 6, 1880," *PWW*, I, 608-621; Thomas Woodrow Wilson, "Mr. Gladstone: A Character Sketch, April 1880," *PWW*, I, 621-642.

condemned the Catholic Church as a longstanding enemy of human freedom and a particular threat to the United States. Wilson countered with a much calmer speech in which he argued that, while the Catholic Church was in many respects as evil as Cabell characterized it, the institution still held no real threat to the thriving American democracy which was rooted in both Anglo-Saxon and Protestant traditions. Certain he had won the debate, he was surprised when, after much deliberation, the university awarded Cabell the "Best Debater" prize and gave Wilson the less prestigious "Best Orator" prize.[119]

But even with these efforts, Wilson's main interest in the late spring of 1880 remained his growing love for Hattie. He wrote long letters to her, telling her how much he missed her and asking for news about her family, especially her younger brother James who had taken quite a liking to Tommy. James was planning to attend Princeton and enjoyed asking advice from his older cousin about the college. Wilson loved best to portray himself as a carefree romantic in his letters to Hattie. He told her how he had joined his fellow glee club members in serenading their sweethearts in the moonlight under the windows of their homes in Charlottesville. He told his parents that such outings with the glee club would only strengthen his voice for debating and the law someday.[120]

As late as June 1880, in the final weeks of his first year in law school, Wilson was still ignoring all pleas from his professors and his family to attend class more regularly. When he stayed too long in Staunton after attending graduation at Hattie's academy, he finally had some pangs of conscience knowing that he had done the wrong thing. Wilson returned to Charlottesville where Dr. James Harrison, the head of the faculty at the University of Virginia, scolded him and even threatened to dismiss him from the law school.[121] Tommy's continuing bad behavior also upset his father deeply. Reverend Wilson still struggled with the "blue" despair that had come over him ever since leaving Columbia. He felt a growing resentment toward the many members of his congregation in Wilmington who demanded that he spend more time ministering to their daily needs rather than preparing his carefully crafted sermons. His sadness now deepened as his son, who had always been the perfect child, seemed to be going down some mysterious road to ruin. Reverend Wilson was losing the little blonde boy who

[15] Janet Wilson, "Letter to Thomas Woodrow Wilson, October 28, 1879," *PWW*, I, 579; News Item in the Virginia University Magazine, April 1880," *PWW*, II, 643-646; Editorial Note, "Wilson's Debate with Cabell Bruce," *PWW*, I, 654.

[120] Woodrow Wilson, "Letter to Harriet Augusta Woodrow, April 14, 1880," *PWW*, II, 647-649; Joseph Ruggles Wilson, "Letter to Thomas Woodrow Wilson, April 17, 1880," *PWW*, I, 650-651.

[121] Editorial Note on "Report of James F. Harrison," *PWW*, I, 659.

had followed him through Augusta hanging on his every word and there appeared to be no way to win him back.

Wilson's mother tried her best to step into the fray as a peacemaker. Throughout the year, she had written the kindest letters to her son, often telling him that from early on he had been the greatest joy and comfort in her life. No matter what Tommy needed, she collected it for him and sent it north, sometimes with extra money. Once he decided that he wanted a scrapbook that he had kept in the summer after his first year at Princeton. It was filled with romantic scenes from history and literature that he had cut out of magazines purchased for him by his father. She promised to search high and low until she found it, never asking why he needed this memory of his boyhood in the midst of his legal studies. If he ever seemed troubled in his letters, she urged him to cheer up for surely things would get better. She also said that maybe he and his brother Josie could spend the summer in Staunton with their cousins while she and Reverend Wilson traveled to Europe. When there was not enough money or time for this, she made sure Tommy came home to Wilmington where he spent his vacation helping Reverend Wilson with his work as the secretary of the Southern Presbyterians.[122]

At the end of summer, Tommy headed back to Charlottesville along with his mother and brother Josie. Mrs. Wilson came north to make sure her son got a room closer to campus with better food that would not upset his delicate stomach. Later both she and her husband sent one letter after another from Wilmington encouraging Tommy in his study of the law. Reverend Wilson especially worried about the deep anxiety that seemed to be creeping into his son's personality. He urged Tommy not to imitate his own blue moods. Instead he told him to look forward to an exciting future that could be achieved through oratory and the law. He was overjoyed to hear that his son was planning to take elocution lessons in the fall semester. He promised to continue looking for the best place to set up a law practice and even wrote that Tommy could rest at home for a year or so after he had graduated.[123]

Wilson tried his best to master the law in the second year of formal study, but still found that he had no enthusiasm for it. His stomach became terribly upset as he tried to quiet his own growing doubts about pursuing a law career. He also could not escape the uneasy feeling that Hattie might not love him in the same way he loved her. Each line of every letter betrayed the uncertainty of a young

[122] Janet Wilson, "Letters to Thomas Woodrow Wilson, February 19 and May 5, 1880," *PWW*, I, 603 and 653.

[123] Joseph Ruggles Wilson, "Letters to Thomas Woodrow Wilson, October 5 and 19, and November 19, 1880," *PWW*, II, 682, 685-686, 687.

man who knew without a doubt that his cousin adored him, but then again did she? His doubt increased when he thought of the many handsome beaus who swirled about her in Staunton, and the many more who pursued her back home in Chillicothe.

Even with these worries, Wilson tried to lift his spirits by joining in campus activities similar to the ones he had known as an undergraduate at Princeton. He put much of his energy into writing a new constitution for the Jefferson Society.[124] But even with these renewed efforts to participate in college life, by early December 1880, Tommy decided he could not bear another day at the University of Virginia. Suffering from what his doctors diagnosed as acute dyspepsia, he withdrew from his courses before taking his final exams and packed his bags for home. He had already made plans with his parents to continue his law studies in Wilmington. He would rest and get his health back, and would also work hard to prepare himself for the bar exam. His father would help him set up an office in a big Southern city and he would write to his many friends to see if anyone knew a young man who would like to go into business with him. Perhaps most importantly, he would hurry across the Blue Ridge Mountains to spend Christmas with Hattie. He would tell her that his college days were over and that his real life, which he hoped she would share with him, was about to begin.

Tommy Wilson was deeply disappointed when he arrived at the home of his uncle James Bones in Staunton only to be learn that Hattie had gone north to the wedding of a girlfriend in Springfield, Ohio. Back in Wilmington, he wrote immediately to her, never telling her how sick he had been with dyspepsia or that he was soon on the mend once he returned home. Instead he told her how excited he was to learn from his cousin Jessie that Hattie had gotten the slice of cake with the bride's ring in it at the wedding reception of her friend. This meant that she would be the next bride in the family. If Hattie could read between the lines, she would see how much Wilson was hoping that he would be the groom. But rather than speak of such things directly, he told her of the beautiful little mare his parents had bought. She hated the cold and shivered in the early morning when Wilson took her out riding. How he wished Hattie could go riding with him on these winter days. Perhaps, he quietly suggested, Hattie might consider coming to Wilmington to spend the summer with Wilson and his family.[125] Surely then, he must have thought, their love would blossom in the loving glow of his parents' house and in the city with the warm breezes that came in from the sea.

---

[124] Thomas Woodrow Wilson, "A New Constitution for the Jefferson Society," *PWW*, I, 689-699.

[125] Thomas Woodrow Wilson, "Letter to Harriet Augusta Woodrow, May 10, 1881," *PWW*, II, 63-66.

As he dreamt of the summer he would spend with Hattie, he regained his health and soon seemed to be his old self again. When his law books arrived from Charlottesville, he organized a plan of study and kept to it faithfully. He was grateful that Professor Minor's drills in the law had prepared him to work on his own. Wilson was also happy to be back with his brother Josie. With no good schools in the neighborhood, the Wilsons were teaching Josie at home. His older brother now took over the task of tutoring him in Latin. They spent their spare time dreaming of sailing about the world, and Tommy showed Josie how to make lists of imaginary navies and staff them with friends and family alike. By the early spring, Wilson felt so much better that he even started writing again. He penned one editorial after another that he usually called "Stray Thoughts from the South." In these pieces, some of which were published in the *Wilmington Morning Star* and the *New York Evening Post*, he joined with other voices calling for the New South to rise up and wipe away all memories of the Old South. The reliance on slavery in the southern states had set the region far behind the North in economic development. Now the young men of the South must embrace industry, commerce, and especially education to bring their homeland into modern times. Wilson also hated the practice of decorating the graves of the Confederate dead every May and even convinced his father not to support or participate in such activities.[126]

Relieved that their son appeared to have recovered from the wrong path he was heading down just months before, Jeanie and Joseph Wilson went to work making sure Tommy stayed on track. His mother organized an evening of music and song in the family home. She invited all the young women in the neighborhood to come meet her brilliant son who had come home from law school. His father made him think about where he would like to establish his law practice once he was ready. Reverend Wilson had carefully studied the situation and decided that the boom town of Atlanta would probably be his best bet. Knowing their son would soon be burdened with the responsibilities of adult life, and never again be so free to come and go as he pleased, they decided to send him to Chillicothe, Ohio during the late summer of 1881. He could work in the law office of his uncle Henry Woodrow, and also spend one last carefree summer visiting all of his Woodrow cousins.[127]

Tommy Wilson agreed with his parents' plans for him, but went north in the late summer of 1881 with a plan of his own. He had decided to ask Hattie to

---

[126] Joseph R. Wilson, Jr., "Letter to Thomas Woodrow Wilson, August 20, 1881," *PWW*, II, 74-75.

[127] Thomas Woodrow Wilson, "Letter to Charles Andrew Talcott, September 22, 1881," *PWW*, I, 79-80.

marry him. He was convinced that he had his parents support in this, and was also certain that his uncle Thomas Woodrow would not object. He was overjoyed to see Hattie once again and was delighted to learn that she had prepared a round of parties and picnics for him with all of their cousins and other young people in town. It was at one of these dances in his uncle's house on the night of September 25 that he took hold of Hattie, led her outside, and asked for her hand in marriage. He was stunned when she turned him down on the spot with no hesitation. She simply said that it would not be proper for cousins to marry and then left to go back to her guests. Angry and embarrassed, Wilson decided to leave for home immediately. He packed his bags and headed for the local hotel where he spent a sleepless night, rocking between the despair over Hattie's refusal and the renewed hope that she might come to her senses. He found a torn piece of paper and used it to write a desperate note to Hattie, asking her to change her mind.

> "Now, Hattie, for my sake, *and for your own*, reconsider the dismissal you gave me to-night. I cannot sleep to-night—so give me the consolation of thinking, while waiting for the morning, that there is still one faint hope left to save me from the terror of despair."

If it was only her concern that her father might object to cousins marrying, he was certain that he could overcome this problem. Signing his name "Woodrow" rather than Tommy, he had the note delivered to Hattie's house, but no answer came back to him.[128]

On the following morning, he went to see his uncle James who told him there was no need for him to go, but the broken hearted young man headed for the train anyway. Hattie's brother James followed him all the way to the station trying to console him, but there was nothing anyone could say to relieve his misery. His despair deepened at the station when he met the handsome Edward Freeman Welles, who had just arrived with several friends to attend the many parties that Hattie had planned for her cousin Tommy. He happily greeted Wilson, but Tommy received him coldly, knowing the rumors that this was the boy Hattie truly loved and would soon marry. Surely Hattie could not prefer this empty dandy to a young man like himself with such depths and substance. He consoled himself with the thought that Eddie Welles must have had "a feeling of relief to get me out of the way."[129]

---

[128] Editorial Note, "Wilson's Proposal to Hattie Woodrow," *PWW*, II, 84-85; Woodrow Wilson, "Note to Harriet Augusta Woodrow, September 25, 1881," *PWW*, II, 83.

[129] Woodrow Wilson, "Letter to Harriet Augusta Woodrow, September 26, 1881," *PWW*, II, 86.

As his train took him across the Ohio River into Kentucky, his stomach became more and more upset. He had come north with dreams of love fulfilled and now he was heading home cast down in shame and despair. At Ashland, he found there would be a six hour delay until his connecting train arrived. He waited in the hot and crowded lobby of the town's main hotel. Since there had been no answer to his sad and pleading note, he decided to write again to his darling Hattie. The tone of the letter was desperate. He demanded that Hattie go to the local photographer in Chillicothe and have her picture taken. It must be done in the exact way that Wilson described in his letter. Hattie must wear her pink dress and must be photographed with her hair swept up like she wore it in the mornings. She must hold her head slightly toward the right. For some reason, he wanted to remember Hattie this way. There must be only one copy of the photograph. Hattie could keep the original but the copy must be sent to him. Tommy assured his cousin that he would pay for everything. Finally, as if to say his life had changed forever on the night of September 25, 1880, he again signed his name "Woodrow."[130]

When he arrived back home a week later, he immediately wrote to Hattie in the chatty tones of his earlier letters. He told her of the terrible heat he had endured on the long trip back to Virginia. He tried to make her jealous by saying how he had gotten off the train at Charlottesville where he met the two young daughters of John Minor. They were delighted to see him and made him come back to town with them to spend time with their father. Finally he made his way to Columbia, where he stayed for a time with his sister Annie. She had just given birth to a daughter named Jessie, the "prettiest little creature" that Wilson had ever seen. Annie was surprised to see him "*alone*," meaning she had expected him to arrive with his bride. He was now back in Wilmington, preparing for his new life as a lawyer in Atlanta. He spoke of the coming Christmas holiday when Marion would come home with her two boys and Annie would arrive with her four children in tow. Wilson wrote that he hoped his poor father's nerves would be able to take the noise of the "united households." Cousin Jessie Bones was coming, too, and he still hoped there was a chance that Hattie might come with her. Even under the breezy tone of his second letter to Hattie, the terrible effect of the crisis he had passed through remained clear. The boy everyone had known as Tommy was gone. Once again, he signed the letter with his new name – Woodrow.[131]

---

[130] Ibid., 85-87.

[131] Woodrow Wilson, "Letter to Harriet Augusta Woodrow, October 3, 1881," *PWW*, II, 87-89.

Though words could barely capture all he had suffered, he tried to express his grief in a long poem that he finished in the early winter of 1881. Called "A River's Course," the poem spoke of a river that tumbled out of the mountains on its way to the sea. Somewhere on its long course, the river passed by an island where an abandoned castle stood. The walls of the castle showed the marks of long forgotten battles. The windowless tower was covered with ivy, the great hall with its crumbling oak table and brittle tapestries stood silent, and the rusty bell high in the parapet rang no more. Only eagles, owls and sparrows now made their home in the castle along with the howling wind. At last, the river passed by the castle and headed to a bright new city. The people of the city paid little heed to the dark history that the river had seen and still carried with it. Finally the river flowed on toward a manor house where two brothers played on the lawn as their mother watched over them. Then it hurried past them and joined the deep wide currents of the sea.[132]

In just 25 stanzas, Wilson had captured the entire story of his life from the time he first played in the yard of his father's manse in Augusta until the present moment when he rested from his heartbreak in his family's home in North Carolina. For as long as he could remember, he had lived in an imaginary world where great deeds were done by heroic men. As a boy, he dreamt of hunting down pirates on the high seas, and as a young man, he dreamt of stirring a nation to even greater deeds by the power of his words. But somehow all of these dreams had come crashing to an end when his lady fair had refused his proposal of marriage. Now Wilson, like the river, must go on without his childhood dreams and his beloved. Off he would go to crowded Atlanta where no one would ever know the imaginary world he had grown up in. Still before this would happen, he would spend a last few peaceful months with his mother and his brother Josie in the town of Wilmington by the sea.

He wrote only one more poem called simply "A Song" that betrayed his quiet hope that maybe Hattie would change her mind and come back to him. He was still convinced that she loved him as much as he loved her and confessed all of this in a letter to his college friend Robert Bridges. It was just her fear that she would displease her father that now kept them apart. But the shortness of this second poem, when set against the great length of "A River's Course," betrayed his own suspicion that this would never happen. His despair filled pages, but his hope could only fill one stanza:

"Sing, ye feathered songsters,

[132] Woodrow Wilson, "A River's Course," *PWW*, II, 91-94.

Sing in full concert all your quaintest strains,
Each richest note that melody contains,
Each pleasant chord, each harmony sonorous
Join ye in one ringing chorus;
Your voices raise in sweetest praise:
My love is won and joy fills all my days."[133]

As gentle as this poem sounded, there remained a deep well of bitterness in Woodrow Wilson over the failure to win Hattie that had to come out of him. The target he chose to vent his wrath was the editor of the *Wilmington Morning Star*. Wilson had submitted a few editorials on education in the South to the *Morning Star*. They had been published with no author's name attached and had gone on to win some acclaim in the state. Wilson was angry that the editor took credit for the pieces and so he now referred to the man as "Sham." He decided to practice his talent for "satire and ridicule" by attacking favorable comments the editor made in his paper about the Catholic Church in the late winter of 1882. Calling himself "Anti Sham," Wilson launched his editorial attack in the pages of the *North Carolina Presbyterian*. He ridiculed "Sham" for saying that several Catholic bishops gave better sermons than most Protestant ministers. He also criticized him for praising the efforts of young Catholic men in the state to form a benevolent society. Still smarting not just from his loss of Harriet, but also from his failure to best the "puppy" James Cabell Bruce in the debate at the University of Virginia, Wilson launched into a systematic account of the evils perpetrated by the Catholic Church throughout the ages. He must have thought that if only he had spoken with the same fury just a few months before, then surely he would have come home from Charlottesville as "Best Debater" rather than merely "Best Orator."[134]

Wilson knew that he could not stay in his room brooding over lost love and jousting with the local newspaper editor forever. He must find a young man who was willing to be his partner in a law firm in Atlanta. He wrote to many of his friends from both Princeton and the University of Virginia asking for help in this matter. Finally, a letter arrived from a student he had barely known in law school. He was Edward Ireland Renick, a young man from Maryland who was four years older than Wilson. He had completed his law studies at the University of Virginia in 1881 and then headed to Atlanta where he opened his own practice with a friend. At first, he wrote giving advice to Wilson saying that the best place in town for an office was near the Supreme Court and State Capital and the best

---

[133] Woodrow Wilson, "Letter to Robert Bridges, March 15, 1882," *PWW*, II, 107; Woodrow Wilson, "A Song," *PWW*, II, 94.

[134] Woodrow Wilson, "Letter to Robert Bridges, March 15, 1882," *PWW*, II, 108; Anti-Sham, "To the Editor of the N.C. Presbyterian, March 15, 1882," *PWW*, II, 113-117.

place to board was at the home of Mrs. Boylston. She was a kind and cultured woman from Charleston. She treated her guests more like family than paying customers. But in late April 1882, Renick suggested that Wilson come and join him in his law practice. His former partner had just left to start a practice with someone else so Renick wrote to Wilson saying, "I would be pleased to have you as his successor." He said his office was "a much coveted one" just across the street from the State Capital that housed Georgia's main library and a post office. It was a large room with fresh paint and wallpaper. A chandelier and two windows that faced onto the street provided plenty of light. There was a desk, table and chairs, a bookcase, and more than enough room for two lawyers who were just starting out in their trade. They could split the cost of the $9.00 a month rent and even have their own servant for just an extra 50 or 75 cents a month. He would also get a room for Wilson at the home of the lively Mrs. Boylston.[135]

Within just two weeks of receiving the offer from Renick to join his law firm, Woodrow Wilson headed for Atlanta. He told his friend Robert Bridges that the move made him "more hopeful and confident than anxious." Now as he sat in his new office in the middle of May, he pulled out an old pocket notebook from his college days and filled it with a list of his expenses. At the many turning points in his life, Wilson was often comforted by taking stock of where he had been, what he owned, and what his expenses would be. His father had promised to send him $50 a month until he could get on his feet and make his way in the world. So now he carefully calculated how he could survive on just $40 a month. His greatest expense would be his room and board, followed by his office rent and all the supplies he would need in the law trade. He had to calculate for the professional shaves and haircuts he would need to keep his sideburns and his new moustache in perfect shape. He also set aside $100 for the traveling expenses he would need to attend the Triennial Reunion of the Class of 1879 at Princeton.[136]

Although he had told his college friend Robert Bridges that he was more excited than anxious about moving to Atlanta, it was soon obvious that this was not truly the case. Within just days of arriving in Georgia, he became ill just like he always did when he faced stressful situations. He complained of a terrible taste in his mouth along with a sour stomach and hemorrhoids. He turned to Dr. George Howe, the husband of his sister Annie, for help. Howe advised his brother-in-law, whom he and the rest of the family now addressed as "Woodrow," to take at least

---

[135] James Ireland Renick, "Letters to Woodrow Wilson, January 15 and April 29, 1882," *PWW*, II, 96-97, 127-128.

[136] Woodrow Wilson, "Letter to Robert Bridges, May 2, 1882," *PWW*, II, 128; Woodrow Wilson, "An Account of Personal Expenses, May 16 to June 15, 1882," *PWW*, II, 129-130.

two of the pills he prescribed for him each day. These pills were meant to improve the function of his liver. Dr. Howe was certain that Wilson would start feeling better in just a few days. But if he did not, he told him to write back for more advice and a better diagnosis.[137]

While Wilson's health did improve, his spirits did not, and he soon admitted to his family and friends alike that he hated the practice of law. Although Renick was a fine young fellow and Mrs. Boylston was an equally charming woman, there was no way around the fact that the day to day business of the law turned his stomach. If Wilson had any remaining illusions that the law was the direct path into the glories of politics, they disappeared in his first weeks in Atlanta. Instead, he found the profession to be a grubby and demeaning one. His dislike of the oppressive nature of the courts took on the quality of poetry:

> "I cannot breathe freely nor smile readily in an atmosphere of broken promises, of wrecked estates, of neglected trusts, of unperformed duties, of crimes and quarrels. I find myself hardened and made narrow and cynical by seeing only the worst side of human nature."[138]

It infuriated him that the older lawyers in town seemed to have a lock on all the important cases while the younger men had to fight among themselves over the scraps that were left to them. The world of the law was peopled with shady characters who had never heard of the likes of William Pitt or Edmund Burke. Wilson did his best to survive in his new profession as long as he could. He won some local notoriety by testifying on behalf of free trade before the Tariff Commission in September and passed the bar exam in October. Judge George Hillyer who presided over the questioning of Wilson in the Fulton County Courthouse later remembered him as nothing "short of brilliant" in his answers.[139] Still by December of 1882, Woodrow Wilson was determined to find a way out of the law and into a career that better suited him.

Needless to say, Reverend Wilson was worried that his son seemed incapable of finding his way in life. He was convinced that some of his son's despair came from his failed romance with his cousin Hattie. He wrote about this to his son while on a visit to the Woodrow clan back in Chillicothe. First, he tried to comfort him by telling him that everyone still thought highly of him, even Hattie, but then he went on to explain the bitter truth. "I honestly and firmly believe," he wrote,

---

[137] George Howe, Jr., "Letter to Woodrow Wilson, May 31, 1882," *PWW*, II, 131.

[138] Woodrow Wilson, "Letter to Robert Bridges, May 29, 1883," *PWW*, II, 343.

[139] Woodrow Wilson, "Testimony before the Tariff Commission, September 23, 1882," *PWW*, II, 140-144; Editorial Note, "Wilson's Practice of Law," *PWW*, II, 144.

"that the marriage you desired would have made you happy only for a very little while." He admired his son for still caring about Hattie's happiness "even though she may not care for yours in the way you desired."[140] Hoping his son would forget Hattie, he urged him not to give up on the law. He knew it was hard for a young man with such great dreams to get started and slowly move up the ladder of success. But there was no better way to get experience in the real world, not just in the imagination, than by practicing law. "My beloved boy you have only one thing to do," he explained, "to stick to the law and its prospects be they ever so depressing or disgusting."[141]

Joseph Wilson had been overjoyed when his son passed the bar, hoping that he would recognize it as an important turning point in his life. He wanted him to realize that since the law touched on so many things he loved, like history, philosophy, morality, composition and oratory, then surely it would bring him happiness one day. But still Wilson's father worried that his son was plagued with the same sadness and self doubt that haunted him. He could not bear the thought that his brilliant son would waste as much precious time being downcast as he had done in his life. Wilson's father had at last come to the conclusion that depression was useless and that only a strong hope in the future could keep a man going in the worst times. "*Think as highly of yourself as possible*," he wrote to Woodrow just days after he had passed the bar. He admitted to his son that he now regretted how often he had allowed himself to be depressed. To him, it would be an unbearable misery to think that he had transmitted this same illness to Woodrow. "A cheerful trust in God as the best & greatest of Helpers and an equally cheerful trust in yourself as your own helper," he wrote, "will carry you through to a triumphant issue."[142]

As Christmas of 1882 approached, Jeanie Wilson made one last effort to keep him in his law practice. She told him not to come home for the holiday since this time was a sad one for the family. They had never been happy living in Wilmington and she worried that their depressed mood would only bring him down. She admitted that they missed him terribly, especially his father who by now wanted him to move back home. But she wanted him there only when he knew what he planned to do with his life. If he came back any sooner, then he would consider himself a failure. His mother would not allow him to feel this

[140] Joseph Ruggles Wilson, "Letter to Woodrow Wilson, August 28, 1882," *PWW*, II, 138.

[141] Joseph Ruggles Wilson, "Letter to Woodrow Wilson, August 14, 1882," *PWW*, II, 135.

[142] Joseph Ruggles Wilson, "Letter to Woodrow Wilson, October 21, 1882," *PWW*, II, 145-147.

way, telling him instead that "You have been a comfort to me all your sweet life."[143]

Over the holiday, Jeanie Wilson suggested that Woodrow, a name she admitted she could not get used to saying, should work instead on the case she had given him to handle. Wilson's mother had inherited property in Nebraska from her older brother William Woodrow. She was given the property along with her sister Marion and her brother James who had subsequently sold his portion of the estate. Now that her sister Marion had died, she also wanted to sell her part of the inheritance. However, James Bones, Marion's husband, gave a series of excuses why this could not be done immediately. Bones had gone bankrupt some time before and needed every penny he could get his hands on. Jeanie Wilson was convinced that her share of the property was worth much more than the $6,800 quoted to her by Bones, and she had grown tired of the many excuses that he gave as to why he could not pay her even this small amount. She had given her power of attorney to her son Woodrow and now expected him to get her out of the tangled mess once and for all.[144]

Sometime in the winter of 1883, as he stayed in Atlanta working on his mother's case along with the few others that had come his way, Woodrow Wilson came to a profound understanding of himself. He realized that he often threw aside his notes on cases to read about politics and history. In fact, he had spent much of the past year studying biographies of John C. Calhoun, Alexander Hamilton, and John Randolph of Roanoke along with Alexis de Tocqueville's *Democracy in America*. Still enamored of Great Britain, he was deeply upset that the French aristocrat saw the American character and nation as wholly unique and rarely explained either in terms of the country's English heritage. He was still committed to finding a way to reshape American politics more along the lines of the British system. He sent his manuscript for *Government by Debate* off to several publishers in New York. While every publisher rejected the book, Wilson remained determined to be as famous a writer as De Tocqueville one day. He hoped to improve his powers of expression by forming a club with other young attorneys to debate contemporary issues. He called his new debating society the "Georgia House of Commons" and promptly drafted a constitution for it based on the best British models.[145]

---

143 Janet Wilson, "Letters to Woodrow Wilson, December 6 and 24, 1882," *PWW*, II, 276- 278.

144 Janet Wilson, "Letters to Woodrow Wilson, December 6, 1882," *PWW*, II, 276.

145 Woodrow Wilson, "Marginal Notes, October 28, 1882, *PWW*, II, 149-152;" Woodrow Wilson, "Critique of De Tocqueville's *Democracy in America*, January 19, 1883" *PWW*, II, 295-296; Woodrow Wilson, "Government by Debate: Being a Short View of Our National Government As

As he sat in his office that looked out toward the Georgia State capital, he found he must face the fact that if he was not cut out for the law, then maybe he was also not cut out for politics. Since he was a little boy, he had dreamt of one day becoming a great leader who would move his nation toward a glorious future with his stirring words. He had chosen the law as the surest pathway to that end. But now as he endured the day to day world of negotiating deeds and contracts, he wondered if he was not better suited to the life of a scholar of politics rather than to the life of a statesman. He could probably make a decent living for himself by studying and teaching government, rather than practicing law or running for office himself. By the spring of 1883, he had decided to give up his work at the firm of Renick & Wilson and apply for admission to the graduate school at Johns Hopkins University. There he would study politics and history under the noted American historian Herbert Baxter Adams. Perhaps he could even use the work he had already done on congressional government as the foundation for his doctoral dissertation.

Once he told his parents of his decision, he was relieved to learn that they supported him wholeheartedly. Both his father and mother went to work writing letters to friends and family about how to win funding for his graduate education. They urged him to apply for a fellowship and asked his uncle James Woodrow for advice on how he should go about completing such an application. While Jeanie Wilson was happy that her son seemed to have found himself at last, she urged him to settle the case of the family's property in Nebraska with his uncle James Bones before he headed to Johns Hopkins in the fall of 1883. For some reason, she had begun to worry about her husband's health. She had started to brood that the men in Reverend Wilson's family often died young. If something happened to her husband, then she would need the money from the land sale to support herself and Josie.[146]

Jeanie Wilson advised her son to contact Abraham Brower, the husband of his cousin and childhood playmate Jessie Bones. Brower and his new bride were living near Uncle James in East Rome in a home they called Oakdene. Wilson knew Brower well since he had agreed to represent him in a libel case and had even recently been certified to practice in the federal courts in order to handle the matter. His mother's hunch about Brower proved correct and correspondence with him helped to settle the longstanding case. Brower wrote to Wilson that, as far as he knew, his mother-in-law Marion Bones had left her portion of the Nebraska

---

It Is and As It Might Be. An Essay in Five Parts," *PWW*, II, 159-275; Woodrow Wilson, "Draft of a Constitution for a 'Georgia House of Commons,' January 11, 1883," *PWW*, II, 288-291.

[146] Janet Wilson, "Letters to Woodrow Wilson, March 17 and 26, 1883," *PWW*, II, 319-320, 323-324.

property to Jessie and her two other daughters with her husband James as the executor. But instead of simply overseeing the land on behalf of his three children, Bones had used money from his wife's estate to finance several business ventures. Wilson's mother was also convinced that her brother-in-law had used some of the profits to build a new house in Georgia. Brower assured Wilson that his wife and her two sisters were totally unaware of their father's actions. In fact, Jessie fully supported Aunt Jeanie's claim to her share of the property and would ask her father for an immediate division of the land. By the end of March, Wilson had won a promise from Uncle James to divide the property, and in the first week of April, he traveled to Rome to work out the details of the agreement.[147]

On Sunday morning, April 8, 1883, Woodrow Wilson headed with his uncle to services at Rome's First Presbyterian Church and had no idea that his life was about to change forever on that day. As he sat with his family waiting for the communion service, he noticed a girl in a nearby pew, probably because she looked something like Hattie Woodrow. Wilson saw her pretty face with large brown eyes and her brown hair covered by a heavy crepe veil. "What splendid, mischievous, laughing eyes!" he thought, "I'll lay a wager that this demure little lady has lots of life and fun in her!"[148] He got a better look at her when she came over after communion to speak with the elderly mother of James Bones. Wilson was told that she was Ellen Louise Axson, the daughter of the Reverend Samuel Edward Axson, the pastor of the First Presbyterian Church in Rome and a friend of the Reverend Joseph Wilson. He could not get her face out of his mind and was determined to call on her that very afternoon.

When Wilson arrived at Ellen's home just a few hours later, Reverend Axson assumed that the young man had come to see him. He invited Woodrow into the parlor and asked him why he thought congregations in Presbyterian churches had gotten so small in recent years? Not wanting to offend Reverend Axson, but also not wanting to miss a chance to see Ellen's "bright, pretty face" again, he blurted out, "How is your daughter's health?" Finally understanding the reason for Wilson's visit, Axson asked Ellen to come join them in the parlor. After he headed back to the home of his Uncle James, Wilson worried that Ellen might have thought his performance was quite comic as he struggled to answer her father's questions. However, not wanting to fall in love with the girl too quickly, he was able to hold his feelings in check for a few days until he ran into her again as she was walking home from a friend's house. Wilson followed her all the way

---

[147] Janet Wilson, "Letters to Woodrow Wilson, March 17, 1883," *PWW*, II, 319; Abraham T. Brower, "Letter to Woodrow Wilson, March 3, 1883," *PWW*, II, 312-319.

[148] Woodrow Wilson, "Letter to Ellen Louise Axson," *PWW*, II, October 11, 1883, 468.

to her father's manse and lingered at her door, delighted that he had found such a wonderful companion. By the time he came back in the next week to take her on two more walks through the town, he had fallen completely in love with Miss Ellen Louise Axson.[149]

Wilson returned to Atlanta, but he could not stop thinking of his "charming brown-eyed lassie." She was the ideal woman he had first dreamt of while reading the novels of Cooper and Scott when still a boy. Ellen Axson was beautiful but strangely unaware of it just as she was brilliant without any hint of arrogance. She was charming and ladylike with no coyness or cruelty anywhere in her character. Above all else, she was extremely well read with a keen sense of beauty. Wilson was overjoyed that she knew Shakespeare, Wordsworth, Emerson, Dickens, and Tennyson among others. She quoted these authors not to show off her knowledge but because their words meant so much to her that she had truly made them a part of her very being. Her love of beauty made her an excellent artist and she even made a little money for herself doing charcoal portraits.[150]

After all he had recently been through in his young life, especially the loss of Hattie and the failure of his law career, Woodrow Wilson suddenly had a sense that he had finally found his path in life. He was now more certain than ever that he should make a life for himself as a college professor and that he must win Ellen Axson as his bride. In early May, Wilson wrote to Johns Hopkins University asking to be admitted as a graduate student in history and political science. He listed his B.A. from Princeton, his recommendations from renowned professors like John Minor, and his published article on "Congressional Government" as the major reasons why he should be awarded a university fellowship. By the end of the month, he was back in Rome, Georgia to work on his mother's case, but more importantly to court Ellen. As soon as he arrived at his cousin Jessie's home at Oakdene, he wrote a note to "Miss Ellen Axson" asking her to go riding with him at precisely 5 p.m. that evening. Almost immediately, Ellen sent a note back to "Mr. Wilson" telling him that she would be waiting for him at that precise hour.[151]

During late May and June, Wilson spent much of his time traveling back and forth between his law office and his cousin Jessie's home at Oakdene. He packed up his books and all his belongings in Atlanta for shipment to Wilmington and bought a typewriter to help him complete the paperwork related to the settlement

---

[149] Ibid., 468-471; Editorial Note, "Wilson's Introduction to Ellen Axson," *PWW*, II, 333-335.

[150] Woodrow Wilson, "Letter to Robert Bridges, July 26, 1883," *PWW*, II, 393-394; Stockton Axson, *Brother Woodrow*, 80-111.

[151] Woodrow Wilson, "Draft of a Letter to the Faculty of The Johns Hopkins University, April 14, 1883," *PWW*, II, 337-339; Woodrow Wilson, "Note to Ellen Louise Axson, May 28, 1883," *PWW*, II, 363; Ellen Louise Axson, "Note to Woodrow Wilson, May 28, 1883, *PWW*, II, 363.

of Aunt Marion's estate. He wrote to his mother that not only had the problem of her inheritance been solved, but he had also just met the girl he was determined to marry. Back in Rome, Wilson worked out the final details of a deal with his Uncle James that gave a little over $18,000 to his mother. He spent the rest of his spare time taking long walks with Miss Ellen and escorting her to concerts and picnics in town. He won a promise from her in late June to write to him after he went home to Wilmington in July. Back with his own family, he prepared to enter Johns Hopkins by reading as much as he possibly could on the colonial period of American history, certain that if he ever hoped to understand the American political system, then he must start in these formative years. Here "the keys to all our legal systems, both state and federal, are to be found," he wrote to his friend Bridges. He discovered that his reading of English history was coming in handy for he could now see how the Constitution had developed over time and was "in no sense a manufactured article."[152]

Wilson was soon delighted to learn that Ellen Axson was as wonderful a letter writer as she was a conversationalist. She wrote in a guileless way about all the town gossip and told him how she spent much of the high days of summer playing chess with her brothers Edward and Stockton. She was quite upset when she learned that Wilson's mother was sick with typhoid fever and urged him to bring her to Rome where she could regain her strength by playing with Jessie's beautiful baby girl Marion. Wilson answered Ellen's letters by telling her about all the events in his day. Unlike his letters to Hattie which had been so guarded, he filled every note to "Miss Ellie Lou" with images of his time in Wilmington so vivid that the events seemed to leap right off every page. At one moment, he was playing with his shy and beautiful niece Jessie, letting the little girl ride on his back as her pony throughout his parents' house. She was the youngest daughter of Annie Howe who had come home with her four children to take care of Jeanie Wilson. In the next moment, he was at the local market trying to buy all the meat and vegetables he would need to cook the family's meal that night. Then again he was sailing down the Cape Fear River with Annie and her children and tumbling on shore with them for a picnic where he felt the breezes from the sea while wishing his dearest Ellie could be with him.[153]

In August, Wilson traveled with his mother, his brother Josie, and his sister Annie and her children first to Flat Rock and then to Arden in the mountains of

---

[152] Editorial Note, "Wilson and His Caligraph," *PWW*, II, 366-368; Woodrow Wilson, "Deed of Partition, June 27, 1883," *PWW*, II, 373-375; Woodrow Wilson, "Letter to Robert Bridges, July 26, 1883," *PWW*, II, 393-394.

[153] Ellen Louise Axson, "Letter to Woodrow Wilson, July 12, 1883," *PWW*, II, 383-386; Woodrow Wilson, "Letters to Ellen Louise Axson, July 16 and 30, 1883," *PWW*, II, 387-390, 395-399.

North Carolina. They hoped that Jeanie Wilson would get even better once she was away from the humid coast and up in the cooler climate of the western country. Wilson was planning to stay with his family until the middle of September when he would have to leave for Baltimore to begin his doctoral studies at Johns Hopkins. Ellen wrote to Wilson that she might be coming up first to Flat Rock and then to Morgantown where she would be visiting friends. He sent notes to every place he thought she might be as she traveled north, but the letters always missed her. Finally, after receiving a letter from Woodrow saying he could visit her in Morgantown, Ellen wrote back that she must leave immediately for Georgia since her father was quite ill and wanted her home immediately. She had not told Woodrow how troubled her father had become since the death of her mother in childbirth less than two years before. At just 23 years of age, she felt responsible for her father, her two brothers, and her baby sister Margaret who was living at the time with a relative in Gainesville, Georgia. She headed back to Rome, perhaps worrying that she had not only missed seeing Woodrow, but maybe had missed a chance for a life of her own one day.[154]

Disappointed that Ellie Lou had gone home, Wilson left for Johns Hopkins University on Friday September 14. Later on that same morning, he got off the train in Asheville. As he walked through the town, he looked up at a second floor window of the Eagle Hotel and saw a young woman he knew was Ellen just disappearing from view. He raced up to meet her and was overjoyed to learn that she had only just arrived. Her train was delayed so she must spend the day in Asheville. Wilson begged her to remain until Sunday when he would have to leave for Baltimore. Although worried about her father, she decided to stay with Woodrow in Asheville. She even went riding with him out in the country and then up to Arden to meet his mother. Back at the Eagle Hotel where he had taken a room, Wilson could not sleep because he had decided to ask Ellie to marry him and he agonized over how he should do it. He could not bear the thought of the beautiful Miss Ellen Louise Axson refusing him as Hattie Woodrow had done just two summers before. In her room, Ellen was also in agony since she knew the question that was coming her way. She was prepared to turn Wilson down saying that now was not the right time for an engagement since he must concentrate all his efforts on winning his Ph.D.[155]

---

[154] Woodrow Wilson, "Letter to Ellen Louise Axson, September 1, 1883," *PWW*, II, 148; Ellen Louise Axson, "Letters to Woodrow Wilson, September 1 and 7, 1883," *PWW*, II, 414-417, 419-420.

[155] Editorial Note, "The Engagement," *PWW*, II, 426-427; Woodrow Wilson, "Letter to Ellen Louise Axson, September 18, 1883," *PWW*, II, 433-435.

On Sunday, September 16, 1883, just about an hour before his train was to leave for Baltimore, Wilson proposed to Ellen in the hallway of the Eagle Hotel. She sat "dazed and tongue-tied" as he explained, with strangers looking on, that he loved her and that it would interfere with his work at Johns Hopkins if she turned him down. At first, embarrassed and confused, she said that she was not worthy of him and that she could never make him happy. She even said she was homely. But then remembering how her heart pounded when he drove up in the buggy in front of the hotel to take her riding, and suddenly feeling an overwhelming sense of loneliness at the thought of his leaving for school, she said, "Yes!" Wilson kissed her for the first time and ran out of the hotel for his train. Down the street, he remembered that he did not know Ellen's ring size. He raced back to the hotel, borrowed a ring from her, and ran again for the train to Baltimore.

Ellen Axson later admitted that at first she was too excited and lonely to be happy about saying "yes" to Woodrow Wilson's proposal. But on the next day, Monday September 15, 1883, as she took the train from Asheville to Knoxville, she experienced some of the happiest moments of her young life. She would always remember the day when she traveled home along the French Broad River into the Great Smoky Mountains of Tennessee. It was a "white day" filled with the brilliant light of late summer. Everything she looked at – the flowers, the fields, the trees, the blue sky – turned into "fairy vistas" in an "enchanted land." Wilson, in contrast, had felt only happiness from the moment he asked Ellen to marry him. As he rode the train out of Asheville to Baltimore, he watched and listened to everyone near him in the crowded car, remembering the details so he could later tell them all to Ellen in a letter. He felt his heart swelling with such joy that it "nearly burst its tenement." He seemed to hear soft music playing in the distance as he realized he loved Ellen with all his heart. While he might never go down in history as a great leader, he was at least on his way to becoming a professor of politics and he would surely always be a hero in the eyes of the young woman who would one day be his bride.[156]

[156] Ibid., 435-436; Woodrow Wilson, "Letter to Ellen Louise Axson, September 18, 1883," *PWW*, II, 428.

Chapter 4

THE SEASON OF PREPARATION

The season of preparation has been long, and will yet last a little while; but there's still time, God willing, to do some good, honest, hard work in which the accumulated momentum of the time past may be made to tell.

Woodrow Wilson[157]

When Woodrow Wilson arrived at the train station in Baltimore at midnight on September 18, 1883, he found his father waiting for him in the dark. This would be the last time that Reverend Wilson would wait anxiously for his son to arrive at yet another turning point in his life. Joseph Ruggles Wilson had patiently stood by his boy's side as he stumbled at Davidson College and found his footing once again at Princeton. When Tommy then decided to attend law school, he came up with the tuition and even sent him $50 a month. He nursed his son through the heartbreak of his failed romance with his cousin Hattie and then helped him set up his law practice in Atlanta. When his precious Tommy, now calling himself by the more grownup "Woodrow," decided to try for Johns Hopkins, he wrote to every one he knew trying to win him a fellowship. Although he failed at this, he was still determined to pay for his son's graduate education and also send him extra money to live on each month. He wanted more than anything else for his son to succeed at this latest venture and now stood ready in the dark of this September night to take Woodrow to the local hotel and then find him comfortable lodgings on the next day. But now as he heard the news of his boy's engagement, he felt just a small twinge of sadness. He knew that neither he nor his wife would be the center of the younger Wilson's world anymore. Ellen

[157] Woodrow Wilson, "Letter to Ellen Louise Axson, December 28, 1883," quoted in Baker, *Life and Letters*, I, 168.

Louise Axson would have most of his son's love "to the ousting of everything else." The sensitive little boy who had made so many wrong turns in his life seemed to be at last on a sure path to a happy future.[158]

Reverend Wilson congratulated his son on his engagement and promised to love Ellen as much as it was possible to love anyone. His mother was also happy once she heard the news. When Woodrow worried that his mother would think he did not love her anymore, she told him that she could never envy such a great blessing in his life. "I know you still love me," Jeanie Wilson wrote a few weeks after learning about her son's engagement. She was delighted that Woodrow had found a sweet girl like Ellen Axson who would love him as much as his parents did. She even told her son that he had actually fallen in love with Miss Ellie Lou when he was just a little boy. The Axsons brought their baby daughter with them on a visit to the Wilsons in Augusta many years before. Tommy Wilson was smitten with the beautiful child and demanded that he be allowed to hold her. His mother could still see her son so tiny himself cradling baby Ellen in his arms.[159] Woodrow's sisters were just as happy as their parents were that their brother had found such a lovely bride to be. They hoped that the old Tommy who was so light hearted would now return to them. But little brother Josie was the happiest of all. He had encouraged Woodrow to ask Ellie to marry him during the family's summer vacation in Arden since he was certain that Miss Axson would say "Yes!" "I told you so," he now wrote to Woodrow, adding with glee, "I wonder what cousin Hattie will say when she hears it!"[160]

Wilson himself was amazed at how suddenly everything in his life seemed to be falling into place. He looked back and saw how things had gone from bad to worse when he was heading down the wrong path. Law school was a mistake that had become even more complicated for him when he embarked on a one-sided romance with Hattie Woodrow. His life had become still more troubled and confused when he tried to practice law in Atlanta. But from the very moment he decided to pursue a career as a professor of history and politics, good things started to happen in his life. He met Ellen Axson at her father's church in Rome, Georgia and later proposed to her just days after looking up and seeing her in the window of the hotel in Asheville. He was now determined to complete his studies at Johns Hopkins, become a professor, and marry Miss Ellie Lou. He explained

---

[158] Woodrow Wilson, "Letter to Ellen Louise Axson, September 18, 1883," *PWW*, II, 428.

[159] Janet Wilson, "Letter to Woodrow Wilson, October 3, 1883," *PWW*, II, 453-454; McAdoo, *The Priceless Gift,* 147-149.

[160] Annie Wilson Howe, "Letter to Woodrow Wilson, September 18, 1883," *PWW*, II, 430-431; Joseph Wilson, Jr., "Letter to Woodrow Wilson, September 19, 1883," *PWW*, II, 432-433.

the tie between his graduate work and his marriage most clearly in a letter to Reverend Samuel Axson asking for his daughter's hand in marriage. He wrote to Ellen's father from the Mount Vernon Hotel on the morning after he arrived in Baltimore. "My course work will cover two years," he explained, "and our marriage at the end of it must depend on my securing a professorship."[161]

In Wilson's opinion, there was no better place to prepare for his new career than Johns Hopkins University. Here he would study under the renowned scholar Herbert Baxter Adams, a historian from Massachusetts with a Ph.D. from the University of Heidelberg, who had introduced new methods for researching and writing history from Germany. Adams trained his graduate students in the seminar method. Instead of listening to lectures and taking tests, students in a seminar setting met with their professor each week to discuss and present their own research. Adams held a seminar session with his students every Friday night from 8 to 10 P.M. at a long red table in the Bluntschli Library on campus. Wilson participated in these sessions and also enrolled in International Law and Sources of American Colonial History with Professor Adams. His other courses were Advanced Political Economy with Professor Richard Ely and English and Constitutional History with Professor J. Franklin Jameson.[162]

During his first weeks at Johns Hopkins, Wilson seemed to walk in "cloudless climes and starry skies."[163] He was overwhelmed by his love for Ellen Axson and thrilled at the prospect of his marriage to her. The companionship that this love made possible swept Wilson into an emotional state he had never known before. He often mused that he had not felt this way when he had fallen so hopelessly in love with Hattie. His engagement to Ellie allowed him to pour out every thought and feeling he experienced in long letters to his fiancée. Shortly after settling into a boarding house just three blocks from campus, he confessed to Ellen in a letter written in his large clear hand that "somehow I take very kindly to this new business of love-letter writing." He also recognized the deep need he had to be surrounded by people who loved him. "There never was a man," he wrote, "more dependent than I am upon love and sympathy."

Responding to her ardent fiancé, Ellen answered with page after page written in a more hurried script. Her letters were filled with exclamation points and the words sometimes carried into the margins filling up every space on the page. She

---

[161] Woodrow Wilson, "Letter to Reverend Samuel E. Axson, September 19, 1883," *PWW*, II, 430-431.

[162] Baker, *Life and Letters*, II, 177.

[163] George Gordon, Lord Byron, "She Walks in Beauty," *English Romantic Writers* (New York: Harcourt, Brace & World, Inc., 1967), 791; Woodrow Wilson loved the English Romantic poets and became especially fond of quoting them in his letters to Ellen Axson during their engagement.

had known a few suitors in Rome but had never been the object of such adoration. She was amazed at how nearly every letter from Woodrow told her that she filled his thoughts by day and his dreams by night. Once her betrothed even dreamt that he was chasing her through his parents' house in Wilmington as if they were children playing a game. "Love certainly leads a man into writing," Woodrow explained, "as he never dreamt of writing before!"[164]

Wilson also came to love poetry more than ever before and filled his letters to Ellen with quotes from the most popular poets of the day. Once he had considered poetry a sign of the childishness of a civilization that had not yet developed philosophy or science, but now he responded to Ellen's ability to weave quote after quote into her letters by including long passages from writers like William Wordsworth, Dante Gabriel Rosetti, and George Otto Trevelyan in his own. Sometimes he added quotes that captured his deep passion for Ellen in a better way than he could ever express himself:

> "We are apart: yet day by day,
> I bid my heart more constant be.
> I bid it keep the world away,
> And grow a home for only thee
> Nor fear but thy love likewise grows,
> Like mine, each day, more tried, more true."[165]

At other times, he quoted poems that invited Ellen into his boyhood world of brave heroes and romantic adventures on the high seas. He was especially moved by a passage from "Tristram of Lyoness" written by Algernon Swinburne, and hoped Ellen would be too:

> "About the middle music of the spring
> Came from the castled shore of Ireland's king
> A fair ship stoutly sailing, eastward bound
> And south by Wales and all its wonders round
> To the lourd rocks and ringing reaches home
> That take the wild wrath of the Cornish Foam …
>
> To the wind-hollowed heights and gusty bays
> Of sheer Tintagel, fair with famous days."[166]

---

[164] Woodrow Wilson, "Letters to Ellen Louise Axson, September 9 and October 2, 1883," *PWW*, II, 445-447, 449-450.

[165] Woodrow Wilson, "Letter to Ellen Louise Axson, March 8, 1884," *PWW*, III, 71.

Wilson even tried his own hand at poetry again when celebrating Ellie's 25th birthday, but he could not find the words that captured how wonderful he thought she truly was. Phrases like "bright eyes," "purity of heart," and "beauty's charm" seemed to pale in comparison to the reality of the young woman he loved so much. When words failed him, he could do little more than praise May as the month in which Ellen Louise Axson was born.[167]

Even with all the happiness that entered Wilson's life through his engagement to Ellen, it was not long before he was upset about another part of his life. He decided very early on that he did not like graduate school. Within just a month of his arrival at Johns Hopkins University, he concluded that he was not fond of the seminar method of teaching. He agreed with a classmate who compared it to a scene in Dante's *Inferno* where souls came up from a burning sea only to be pushed back into the boiling foam by demons. Wilson blamed part of the misery on Professor Adams' "ill-served" lectures. Adams often spoke of his fondness for Machiavelli, and Wilson claimed this fascination was apparent in the professor's delight in watching his students suffer by reading one primary source after another. By the winter semester, Wilson was even more brutal in his criticism of Herbert Baxter Adams. "You may know I speak soberly of this man," he wrote to Ellen, "because I came here to admire him, and I remain to scoff." He was equally unimpressed with Professors Ely and Thompson, and only enjoyed listening to the Harvard philosopher Josiah Royce who lectured to the students at Johns Hopkins in the winter of 1884. "I wish I could live with Dr. Royce for a few months. He is one of the rarest spirits I have ever met," he confessed in a letter to Ellen. Wilson admired Royce's ability to catch his listeners up with his own thoughts, taking them into a world where many disconnected ideas came together in one great truth.[168]

For his part, Professor Adams was sympathetic to the young lawyer turned scholar who disliked him so much. In fact, Wilson's strong face reminded him of a race horse with his head thrown back and his nostrils quivering in "revolt against academic bridles." Just three weeks into his first semester at Johns Hopkins, Wilson told Adams he preferred to study on his own. Adams agreed to let him concentrate on a topic that had intrigued him since his college days. While Wilson would continue to attend his classes and participate in the Friday night seminar sessions, he would be allowed to spend the rest of his time researching

---

166 Woodrow Wilson, "Letter to Ellen Louise Axson, April 4, 1884," *PWW*, III, 143-144.

167 Woodrow Wilson, "Letter to Ellen Louise Axson, May 13, 1885," *PWW*, III, 178-180.

168 Baker, *Life and Letters*, I, 229-230; Woodrow Wilson, "Letters to Ellen Louise Axson, February 2 and 17, 1884," *PWW*, III, 10 and 26.

and writing on his favorite theme of "Congressional Government." He was determined to concentrate his best efforts on comparing the inefficient American system of government to the superior methods of the British Parliament.[169]

While he was happy to win the right to study on his own, Wilson was clearly a man facing a dilemma. On the one hand, he hoped to complete his graduate studies quickly so he could marry Miss Axson. But on the other hand, he knew that if he became a professor, then he would probably never be a politician. Since the days when he had first stepped onto the deck of an imaginary ship, placed a picture of Gladstone above his desk, or preached to the empty pews of his father's church, he had dreamt of becoming a statesman like Edmund Burke or William Pitt. In fact, much of his obsession with the British system of government came from the vision he had formed in his youth of brave men standing up in the House of Commons and swaying the English nation with their words. While politics was the world he most truly wanted to be a part of as an adult, the path to it through the law had collapsed all around him. Wilson had found the study of the law deadly dull and the practice of the law corrupt and demeaning. But if he now headed away from the law and into the academy, then he must accept the fact that he would never be the statesman he had dreamt of becoming since he was a boy.

Wilson's failure to achieve his childhood dream led him to take a clear look at the realities of American life in his own time. In a letter to Ellen written in late October 1883, he explained that his childhood hopes of a political life had been based on an understanding of his nation's past rather than its present or future. When the country was young, only a handful of men had an education. These lawyers, doctors, and ministers were the natural leaders of their communities. They could easily step forward to serve in political offices and then return to their own careers. Wilson considered Daniel Webster the best example of this older tradition in American politics. Webster could serve in the Senate where he gave magnificent speeches on the indestructible nature of the Union, while at the same time supporting himself as a practicing attorney. But now Wilson looked around him and saw the world that made Daniel Webster possible was passing away. Life was brutally competitive for even the most talented and ambitious young men. A person needed to put all of his efforts into only one profession if he was ever to make a living for himself and the people he loved. "Nowadays," he explained to Ellen, "a man cannot do two things at once." If he was a lawyer, then that was the only job he could have. The same held true if he chose to be a professor. He must do everything he could to win his Ph.D. and secure a teaching position. Sadly, Wilson concluded that politics in the United States in the late 19th century

---

[169] Baker, *Life and Letters*, I, 180.

belonged only to the wealthy. "This is the time of leisured classes," he wrote dejectedly to Ellen, "and the time of crowded professions." A person like himself who had to make a living had no time for "intervals of office-holding and political activity." Even more pointedly, he explained that a man "without independent means" must give up all hopes of taking an active role in the political affairs of his country.

Still Wilson's decision to give up a life in politics in favor of becoming a professor did not mean that he would turn his back on his country. He would make every effort to lead a "literary life" in which he would analyze American political institutions in a way that no one had ever done before him. He described this new adventure that he was about to set out on to Ellen, certain that she would be at his side through it all.

> "I want to contribute to our literature what no American has ever contributed, studies in the philosophy of our institutions, not the abstract and occult, but the practical and suggestive ... what is the philosophy that makes our institutions useful?"[170]

Wilson's journey from failed politician to future professor would have been unbearable for him if Ellen Axson had not been in his life. "*I love you beyond all else in the world*" was a common sentiment in his letters to her during his first year at Johns Hopkins. His relationship with her allowed him to work out his own powerful emotions and conflicting thoughts with some lessening of the anxiety and depression he had recently experienced. For a little while at least, his headaches and upset stomachs subsided as he unburdened himself to a young woman who seemed to love him without question and to support him in all things. Still he worried that Ellen might reject him after he told her about his failed romance with Hattie Woodrow in the fall of 1883. Even though Ellen continued to write chatty letters to him filled with gossip about neighbors and friends in Georgia along with quotes from her favorite poems and Bible stories, Wilson detected a certain reserve in her correspondence and feared that his proposal of marriage to his first cousin had shocked her. Finally, he asked Ellen directly what was troubling her:

> "What are these things, my love which you would like to ask and hear, and say, but which you cannot gain the courage to write?"[171]

---

[170] Woodrow Wilson, "Letter to Ellen Louise Axson, October 30, 1883," *PWW*, II, 499-505.

[171] Woodrow Wilson, "Letter to Ellen Louise Axson, September 27, 1883," *PWW*, II, 442-445.

For Ellen Axson, Wilson's love for Hattie Woodrow was not a problem. In fact, she was touched by how innocent her husband-to-be was if this was the one great scandal in his life. She assured him that his failed romance with his first cousin did not shock her, and in the coming months she would even tease him about his tendency to fall in love with relatives. After Jessie Bones had paid her a visit, Ellen asked Woodrow a pointed but humorous question:

> "How is it that you did'nt fall in love with her? "seeing as how" you don't share my prejudice against pressing "first" cousins into that sort of service!"[172]

What troubled Ellen in the fall of 1883 was not something in Wilson's life but something in her own. Ever since her mother died in childbirth just two years before, her father had become increasingly depressed and had even given up the ministry. Reverend Axson sent his newborn daughter Margaret and five year old son Eddie to live with relatives. Stockton, a shy and sensitive boy of 14, was packed off to boarding school. But Samuel Axson demanded that his eldest child Ellie stay with him. He took her to Savannah where they lived in the manse of the Independent Presbyterian Church with her grandparents. There Ellen Axson tried everything she could possibly imagine to cheer her troubled father. She even offered to travel with him to new places that might lift his spirits only to watch him fall deeper and deeper in despair.[173]

Ellen sent hints in her letters to Woodrow about the desperate situation she was in. One of her recurring complaints was that she could only write to him late at night when her father was finally resting. Sadly, Wilson was too caught up in his graduate studies and too anxious about his own future to read between the lines. He did not realize the seriousness of the situation until January 1884 when Reverend Axson became violent and had to be committed to the Georgia State Mental Hospital in Milledgeville. Wilson hurried to Savannah to be at Ellen's side, and returned to Rome in May after learning that Reverend Axson had committed suicide. Wilson told Ellen – whom he insisted on calling by his own new special name of "Eileen" – that she must never keep any dark secrets or sadness from him:

---

[172] Edward Axson, "Letter to Woodrow Wilson, June 9, 1884," *PWW*, III, 211.
[173] Axson, *Brother Woodrow*, ix-x.

> "I want you to make me a promise. Don't show me only your smiles in your letters, but tell me ... tell me of everything that perplexes you or makes you sad."[174]

Wilson's "Eileen" responded to this demand with a graciousness that would later characterize their married life together. She loved Woodrow dearly, but she knew that in some ways he was as acutely sensitive as her father. If she was to be a good wife, then it would be her duty to keep all worry and sorrow away from him.

After her father's death, Ellen was determined to be the steadying influence in the lives of all the people she loved. She had done this for her father and now she would do the same for her young husband. She read every word of Wilson's first lecture on Adam Smith, cheered him on as he struggled to turn his ideas on congressional government into a full-length manuscript, and felt his headaches and sour stomachs as if they were her own. While she grieved the loss of her father, remembering him as "the best, the purest, truest man I ever knew," she would not allow Wilson to interrupt his studies to help her. She was adamant that he complete his course work at Johns Hopkins and not accept a possible position at the University of Arkansas, just so they could marry. In the meantime, she would wait to see if her father had left her any money in his will. If there was no money in her father's estate, then she would get a job teaching art in Rome. By doing this, she could help her grandparents raise her sister and two brothers. If she did inherit money, then she would enroll in the Art Students' League in New York City in the fall of 1884 and spend the year before her marriage learning to be a better sketch artist and portrait painter.[175]

Wilson headed back to Johns Hopkins in the fall of 1884 as a university fellow. Ellen, who had received a small inheritance from her father's estate, came by train with her fiancé as he traveled from North Carolina. They spent one day together in Washington, D.C. where they visited the Corcoran Art Gallery. The couple next headed to New York City where Ellen enrolled at the Art Students' League and rented rooms with other students at 60 Clinton Street. Back in Baltimore, Wilson kept up his letter writing to Ellen and threw himself into his work on "Congressional Government." He was anxious to complete the work and find a publisher for it. However, as he looked forward both to his marriage to Ellen and his life as a scholar, he became more and more frustrated with Johns Hopkins which he now derisively referred to as the "Greatest Educational Show

---

[174] Woodrow Wilson, "Letter to Ellen Louise Axson, February 2, 1884," *PWW*, III, 3-6.

[175] Ellen Axson, "Letters to Woodrow Wilson, June 2 and 29, 1884," *PWW*, III, 201, 221-223.

on Earth." He was still smarting over a variety of disappointments that he had a hard time accepting. Wilson had truly wanted to find a job in order to marry Ellen Axson earlier than originally planned, but the University of Arkansas had called off its search for a history professor.

Even now as he continued his quest for a teaching position, he still brooded that his dreams of leading a political life had come to an end. Before returning to his second year in graduate school, he had confessed to his friend Charles Talcott that he would most probably not be able to fulfill the pact they had made to achieve greatness as statesmen in their last halcyon days at Princeton. Much as he had explained the situation to Ellen Axson, he now told his college friend that he had come to realize that the law, his chosen path into politics, was not for him. After much soul searching, he had become convinced that the days when a working man could serve in politics were over. How anyone could be a politician who was not independently wealthy he simply did not know. What he did understand was that he was not now nor would he ever be a wealthy man. He must give up all dreams of political glory and settle on a profession before it was too late. "As I had no independent fortune to fall back upon for support," he had decided to become a professor of history and political science.[176]

Despite the quiet despair that lay along the edges of his happiness in the fall of 1885, his work on "Congressional Government" was proceeding well. In the previous January, he had published many of his main ideas on this topic in an article called "Committee or Cabinet Government?" in the *Overland Monthly*. He had continued to extend his manuscript and now read chapters of the book to the Friday night seminar sessions in the Bruntschli Library. While he worried that he usually bored his listeners, telling Ellen that "my audience looked as tired as I was when I got through," the report of his performance in the records of the seminar read differently:

> "The principal paper of the evening was by Mr. Wilson who read the introduction to his work on Representative Government … Mr. Wilson's work is better than anything in that line that has been heretofore in the Seminary."[177]

Wilson's argument was essentially the same one he had made when he first took on this topic as an undergraduate at Princeton. His beginning presupposition was always based on a general lack of respect for the American system of

[176] Woodrow Wilson, "Letter to Charles Andrew Talcott, July 5, 1884," *PWW*, III, 230-232.

[177] Woodrow Wilson, "Letter to Ellen Axson, November 11, 1884," quoted in Baker, *Life and Letters*, I, 218; Ibid., 219.

government, especially its legislative branch. “Other legislative bodies are noisy,” he explained, “but not with the noise of the House of Representatives.” He was fond of describing the lower chamber of Congress as a great hall filled with relentless chatter. Its more than 300 members sat in their easy chairs, talking with their neighbors and clapping their hands for pages to come pick up messages. For Wilson, this comic scene masked the essential flaw in the American political system. The members of the House of Representatives never actually engaged in an open debate on any significant piece of legislation. Instead, the real work of the House went on behind the scenes in a maze of standing committees. Wilson considered these committees “selfish” since they fought almost exclusively for the whims of their current members. Somehow through the confusion, bills did make it to the floor of the House for a vote, but the outcome was always a forgone conclusion since the members supported or opposed legislation based strictly on party lines. The whole system was far too tame for a young man like Woodrow Wilson who was still convinced that passionate oratory, and not standing committees, must move a nation’s chief assembly.

According to Wilson, the solution was not in dismantling the two party system. The creation of such groups was inevitable in a representative democracy. England had shown this with the rise of the Tory and Whig Parties after the nation’s civil war finally came to an end. Instead, the solution would come in amending the Constitution in several key places. First, the length of terms for the President and members of Congress must be extended. This would especially give the President a chance to shape legislation as he saw fit for the benefit of the country. Second, the President must be allowed to choose his cabinet members from the Congress. Finally, these men must retain their positions in the Congress and thereby help the President pass his legislative program.

In an age of weak Presidents and powerful Congresses, Wilson was calling for a closer link between the executive and legislative branches primarily to increase the power of the Presidency. He wanted the chief executive to have the same ability to craft legislation in the United States that the Prime Minister had in Great Britain. “Committee government is too clumsy and too clandestine a system to last,” he explained, “English precedent and the world’s fashion must be followed.” For all of his love of England, Wilson’s childhood obsession with the British Parliament had actually matured into a call for increased power for the American President at the expense of the Congress. He hoped to link the executive and legislative branches in order to strengthen the one and weaken the other. Pushing aside all discussion of the separation of powers, he argued:

> "So long as the two great branches are isolated, they must be ineffective ... Congress will always be the master, and will always enforce its commands on the administration ... The only hope of wrecking the present clumsy misrule of Congress lies in the establishment of responsible cabinet government."[178]

Wilson was overjoyed in late November 1885 when Houghton Mifflin agreed to publish *Congressional Government: A Study of American Government*. In the final version of his manuscript, Wilson attempted to tone down some of his more strident criticism of the American political system when contrasting it with the British one. He tried to be more subtle, showing how the American government had developed over the previous century and how it worked at the present time. "The object of these essays is not to exhaust criticism of the government of the United States," he wrote in the Introduction, "but only to point out the most characteristic practical features of the federal system." Still he did not go into a real analysis of the current political situation in the country that might have helped him make his argument better. He never mentioned how the power of the Presidency had been eclipsed by Congress since the death of Lincoln or how the Republican Party had taken control of the nation's legislative branch during the Reconstruction and had never let it go. Instead, he preferred to write about English history and British politics when making his main point that the greatest struggle in the modern world was the battle between congressional or committee government on the one hand and parliamentary or cabinet government on the other. He concluded by assuring his readers that while he criticized the way the American government worked, his call for reform was made in the same spirit that had led the Founding Fathers to write the Constitution. While Wilson's book would go through several printings, he would never change one word of the text from the original version.[179]

Wilson was excited that his book generally received good reviews. Many commentators were impressed that a work on the Constitution finally placed the document in its modern context rather than at its point of origin. Wilson clearly saw that the Constitution was not merely a piece of paper but was instead a living process that forged a government which had developed over time. It was not written in stone and could be changed if modern Americans identified and

---

[178] Woodrow Wilson, "Committee or Cabinet Government?" *The Public Papers of Woodrow Wilson (PPWW): College and State: Educational, Literary and Political Papers (1875-1913)*, Edited by Ray Stannard Baker and William E. Dodd (New York and London: Harper & Brothers Publishers, 1925), 95-129.

[179] "Editorial Note on *Congressional Government*," *PWW*, IV, 6-13; Woodrow Wilson, "Congressional Government: A Study in American Politics," *PWW*, IV, 13, 134-160, 172, 179.

implemented the correct reforms. Like any first time writer, Wilson loved going into bookstores and asking the clerks if they had a copy of *Congressional Government*. Only one thing worried him as he looked through the first edition of his book. He had dedicated it to his father, calling him "the patient guide of his youth, the gracious companion of his manhood, the best instructor and most lenient critic." He became concerned that Ellen might think she was not as important to him in the writing of the book as his father had been. He sent one of the first two copies of the book he received to Ellen with a letter explaining she was the true inspiration behind the work. Every line in the book, he explained, was written "in the light and under the inspiration of your love." Indeed, Wilson had been inspired to write each word as if he was speaking directly to Ellen. "As your love runs through my first book," he confessed, "so it must be the enabling power in all that I may write hereafter."[180]

At the very moment that Wilson's first book was published, he received an offer to become a professor at Bryn Mawr, a new college for women that had just been opened under the auspices of the Quakers outside of Philadelphia. In late November, Professor Adams asked Wilson to come to his office where Dr. Carey Thomas, the Dean of the Faculty at the college, and Dr. James Rhoads were waiting to meet him. Dean Thomas was the daughter of one of the trustees of Johns Hopkins and she also held a Ph.D. from the University of Zurich. She hoped to build undergraduate and graduate programs for women at Bryn Mawr that were as strong as the ones for men at Johns Hopkins. Wilson was quite uncomfortable speaking with a woman as accomplished as Carey Thomas, and later told Ellen that altogether "it was a queer experience, wasn't it?"[181] He was relieved to go off to lunch alone with Dr. Rhoads, the President of Bryn Mawr. At the impromptu interview that followed, Rhoads, a devout Quaker himself, asked the young man a series of simple yet direct questions. Did Mr. Wilson believe that Providence played a role in history? Is there progress in Christianity like there is in science and philosophy? Can war ever be justified? Wilson answered a resounding "yes" to the first two questions and a more qualified one to the last saying that war could only be justified by necessity. Rhoads asked him if he had a personal faith of his own and Wilson assured him that he was a Presbyterian of good standing. Rhoads liked every answer he heard and finally explained that he and Dean Thomas had been authorized by the board of the college to find the best

---

[180] Baker, *Life and Letters*, I, 221; Woodrow Wilson, "Letter to Ellen Axson, December 2, 1884," quoted in Ibid., 220-221.

[181] Woodrow Wilson, "Letter to Ellen Axson, November 27, 1884," *PWW*, III, 492.

candidate to organize Bryn Mawr's history department. They were both certain that they had found the right man for the job in Woodrow Wilson.[182]

While he was not convinced that an education based on German methods was appropriate for young ladies, Wilson was excited at the prospect of a job waiting for him at the end of the year. He might not be able to finish his Ph.D. by then, but he would be able to marry "his precious little queen." Although it would be strange to teach a class filled with women, it would at least be the start of his married life with Ellen. He had begun to worry about the suitors who were vying for Ellen's attention in New York and so he decided to take the job at Bryn Mawr since this would ensure their marriage in the coming summer. Wilson had become especially alarmed when Ellen wrote about the many young men who were escorting her around town. One suitor was so persistent that he refused to go home after he walked Ellen to her boarding house. An angry Wilson wrote back, "Oh! Why am I condemned to live thus separated from you!" If only he had been there, he declared, the bold young suitor would have been told never to speak to Miss Ellen Axson again or he would have received quite a thrashing![183]

It was all too clear to Woodrow Wilson that his sheltered fiancée from Georgia was having the time of her life in New York City. She wrote letter after letter back to her "dear Woodrow" describing her classes at the Art Students' League. "We are so fascinated with it, that we can scarcely tear ourselves away to go elsewhere!" was a typical comment. Back in her room, filled with dingy furniture but with large windows that let in much light, she and her new friends would sit around a large table covered with a red cloth in the evenings. There they would recount everything that had happened and everything they had learned at the league on that day. They would also diligently practice their art. Ellen's favorite subject was a fellow student named Florence, but sometimes she even tried sketching herself. She became especially fond of Katie, the maid who took care of all the students. "She is a bright, merry and exceedingly pretty Irish girl; just as pleasant cheery and kind hearted as she can be!"

Everything in New York fascinated Ellen Axson especially if it gave her the opportunity to see and do what she had never done before. One night she went with friends to see the famous actress Ellen Terry star in *The Merchant of Venice*. She raced back to her room where she wrote page after page in her excited script to Wilson. "Oh! It was glorious—the loveliest thing I ever saw or imagined is certainly Ellen Terry! … it was more beautiful than a picture,--it was as beautiful as a dream!" She had another memorable experience at a parade for James G.

[182] Ibid, 489-493.

[183] Ellen Axson, "Letter to Woodrow Wilson, October 10, 1884," *PWW*, III, 345-346.

Blaine, the Republican candidate for President, just a week before the election. She later told Wilson that she was still loyal to the Democratic Party and had not gone over into the "enemy camp." In fact, the young man who accompanied her to 5th Avenue to see the parade as it headed down to Madison Square made sure she was wearing a Democratic badge to show her support for Grover Cleveland. Ellen knew that Woodrow might be shocked that she went to a Republican rally, but she told him she had never seen such a parade before and would not miss it for the world.[184]

As he became more anxious about Ellen in New York, Wilson also started to worry about his ability to complete his Ph.D. by the end of the year. Soon his dyspepsia returned with a vengeance along with "ominous headaches." He complained to Ellen and his parents that his drive to win a doctorate by the spring of 1885 was wrecking his health. When he finally decided that he would leave Johns Hopkins after two years of study without the Ph.D., everyone supported him. Ellen wrote, "*No* degree can be so valuable a possession as health." She went on to encourage him by predicting, "I believe they will give you the degree under *any* circumstances and I wouldn't worry much about it!"[185] Wilson's parents also supported his decision, but could not worry too much about their son since they were preparing to leave Wilmington and move to Clarksville, Tennessee. Reverend Wilson had given notice to his congregation that he had accepted a teaching position in the Divinity School at Tennessee University and would be heading there within the year.

With the approval of his fiancée and his parents, Woodrow Wilson set his sights on leaving Johns Hopkins in May, marrying Miss Ellie in June, and starting his teaching career at Bryn Mawr in September. Throughout the spring of 1885, Wilson's excitement about his upcoming marriage reached a fever pitch. While Ellen remained calm, even serene, Woodrow became more and more agitated over every detail of their impending wedding. He dashed off one letter after another to Ellen asking her if they should honeymoon in the South or New England? Which place would be better – North Carolina or New Hampshire? No matter where they stayed, would the $500 he saved be enough? If they married in Savannah, should they leave right after the ceremony or stay one night in Georgia before heading

---

[184] Ellen Axson, "Letters to Woodrow Wilson, October 31 and November 22, 1884," *PWW*, III, 390-391, 470-471.

[185] Ellen Axson, "Letter to Woodrow Wilson, February 19, 1885," *PWW*, III, 269-271.

north? Wilson felt that the last question was especially important since it would determine if Ellen wore a wedding gown or traveling clothes at the ceremony.[186]

Even in the midst of his anxiety over every detail of the wedding, Wilson's happiness over the thought of his coming marriage knew no bounds. He filled his letters to Ellen with praise for her every virtue. Without a doubt, Miss Ellen Louise Axson was the most perfect woman any man had ever known. Just two months before the ceremony, he confessed, "Oh, darling, into what a new world your love has brought me!" She was the woman of his imagination whom he had been dreaming about for so many years. For her part, Ellen tried to steady her ardent fiancé by reminding him that his hope for a blissful marriage with a perfect woman might be an illusion. "Instead of life with poor little me, my dear," she wrote, "you are describing heaven." She asked Wilson not to think of her as "the most satisfying companion that ever man had" because then she would only disappoint him. She hoped he would see her as less than perfect so that he would not be disappointed no matter what happened in their married life together.[187]

Ellen Axson returned to Savannah in June 1885 to await her marriage to Woodrow Wilson on the 24th of the month. She spent her time making her own wedding dress and veil. She confessed to her betrothed that she was sad about only one thing as the day of their marriage approached. It was the fact that her letter writing with her dear Woodrow would come to an end. Ellen knew that for the rest of her life she would always look for the postman even though her husband would now be at her side. In the last letter she wrote to Wilson before their marriage, she explained, "How strange it seems to think that we will have no more need of letters!—how strangely sweet!" Still after all the sorrow in her life, she was overwhelmed as she realized God's providence had been carefully laying out her life for her. She knew that the loving Father in heaven had planned her marriage to Wilson and that he would richly bless them. With God's help, she would be the best wife she could possibly be and one that a man like Woodrow truly deserved. As she ended her last letter to him before her marriage, she wrote:

> "And now good-bye, my dear one, till Tuesday, I love you, darling as much as you would have me love you. Make out your check for *any* amount and I can fill it. Perhaps you have not yet sounded all the depths of my heart. Yet to the very bottom *it is all yours*,—and I am for life—and death."[188]

---

[186] A good example of the "fever pitch" of Wilson's letters to his fiancée is the last one he wrote before his marriage; see Woodrow Wilson, "Letter to Ellen Louise Axson, June 21, 1885," *PWW*, IV, 733-735.

[187] Ellen Axson, "Letter to Woodrow Wilson, May 13, 1885," *PWW*, IV, 588.

[188] Ellen Axson, "Letter to Woodrow Wilson, June 20, 1885," *PWW*, IV, 729-730.

On the evening of June 24, 1885, Ellen Axson married Woodrow Wilson in the parlor of her grandfather's manse. Dr. Axson and Reverend Wilson took turns reading parts of the ceremony. Ellen wore the white dress and veil that she had made herself, while Woodrow wore his best Sunday suit. The bride and groom were so obviously in love that all the women in the room wept for joy for them. The happy scene was only interrupted when Eddie Axson, Ellen's brother, and Wilson Howe, Woodrow's nephew, took an immediate dislike to each other and decided to fight it out on the parlor floor. Ellen was shocked, but Woodrow was delighted. Nothing could make him sad on this most wonderful day which he called "the happiest moment of all my life."[189] That evening the couple left for their honeymoon in North Carolina, and on the next day, the wedding was announced in the *Savannah Morning News*:

> "Miss Ellie Lou Axson, daughter of the late Rev. Edward Axson, of this city, and Mr. Wilson, son of Rev. J. R. Wilson, of Wilmington, N.C., were married last evening in the residence of Rev. Dr. I. S. K. Axson, pastor of the Independent Presbyterian church. The ceremony was performed by the groom's father and the bride's grandfather. The nuptials were celebrated quietly, only the immediate friends and relatives of the contracting parties being present."[190]

The Wilsons spent their honeymoon at Arden Park, a resort in the mountains of North Carolina. Ellen Wilson loved the name of the place because it reminded her of Shakespeare, while her husband loved it because he could afford it on their $500 budget. They stayed in a small cottage at the resort that was covered with vines and near footpaths that led into the piney woods. Ellen and Woodrow stayed at the resort for two weeks and spent the rest of the time traveling to visit relatives. The couple especially loved reading aloud to each other from their favorite works as they walked in the woods about their cottage. Ellen recited passages from romantic poems and novels, while Woodrow read from his favorite political writers like Walter Bagehot. Wilson was so in love that he often sang to his new bride as they walked in the woods, and so happy that he wrote letters to his parents throughout his honeymoon describing the joy he was experiencing as a husband. His parents were traveling in New York, and his mother wrote back to her son describing their own joy about his marriage:

---

[189] McAdoo, *The Priceless Gift*, 147; Baker, *Life and Letters*, I, 238; Woodrow Wilson, "Letter to Ellen Louise Axson, June 21, 1885," *PWW*, IV, 733-735.

[190] "A News Item in the *Savannah Morning News*, June 25, 1885," *PWW*, IV, 735.

> "I need not tell you that we have thought and talked about you a great deal. We are so glad to think of your happiness in each other. I love to think of you in that beautiful place—of your happy wanderings from day to day."[191]

His parents were not so impressed, however, with his choice of a college where he would begin his teaching career. Both Wilson's mother and father would have preferred that he take a position at a more established school where the students were men, not women. Reverend Wilson could not help teasing him about the college's strange sounding name, and even wondered if there was not some way to get out of his commitment to the Quaker school. "Are you in truth tied—tethered—where you are, at that unpronounceable college?" he asked.[192]

Despite his parents' concerns and even some of his own, Woodrow Wilson arrived in Bryn Mawr with his bride in September 1885. The new school was about ten miles outside of Philadelphia in the rolling and wooded countryside along the Lancaster Pike. The place chosen by the Quaker businessman who had endowed the school with $800,000 was a historic one. George Washington had led his men down the Gulph Road that ran through the campus on his way to Valley Forge. The battleground at Brandywine and site of the massacre at Paoli were nearby. Since this was the first year that the college was open, there were only five buildings on campus. One was for the administration, while another was the dormitory for 35 undergraduate and seven graduate students. The three other buildings on campus were the Deanery, where Dr. Carey Thomas lived, the Scenery which looked out onto some of the most beautiful countryside in Lancaster County, and the Betweenery where most of the faculty were assigned living quarters. The Wilsons took up residence in two rooms in the Betweenery, still so overjoyed by their marriage that they paid little attention to their primitive living conditions.

Wilson went to work preparing his lectures, often staying up late into the night as he wrote by the light of a kerosene lamp. In his first semester, he taught one class in Ancient History. He set up the course in such a way that Greek and Roman history alternated week by week. He even gave the students two grades, one in Greek history and one in Roman history. In the second semester, he carried on the study of Rome from the last conquests of its empire to the rise of Charlemagne.

---

[191] McAdoo, *The Priceless Gift*, 147; Janet Wilson, "Letter to Woodrow Wilson, July 27, 1885," *PWW*, V, 9.

[192] Joseph Ruggles Wilson, "Letter to Woodrow Wilson, February 18, 1886," *PWW*, V, 125.

Wilson began his course in Ancient History by telling the students something of his own philosophy of history. At this early stage in their study of history, Professor Wilson asked his students to work on gaining some "genuine living interest" in the past. He told them that while history was a grave study requiring much effort on their part to master, they should remember that it must always be pursued with charm and imagination. He told his class to look back into the ancient world as if it was their own time, and then to look into the present as if it was not their own. "Suppose that you had yourself wished to thrust Pericles from power," he challenged them, "or that Socrates was the grandfather of your college-mate." Wilson then tried his best to make the past come to life for his students through lectures that often left them spellbound. He also made them join in the process of studying the past through discussions and oral reports.[193]

While the young professor was well prepared and dedicated to his craft, he soon began to worry that he was not getting through to his students. The young ladies were so quiet and respectful that he could never be sure any of his points hit their mark. They especially missed his humor, never uttering a sound when he told a joke or made a pun. He finally decided to shave off his moustache in the hope that his students would laugh at his jokes once they could see his facial expressions.

But despite his doubts about the effectiveness of his teaching, Professor Wilson was making a powerful impression on his students. Many long remembered their young professor as "always smiling." He was "witty" and filled with an "infectious gaiety." Others thought of him as a "very courteous Southern gentleman" even though he spoke with a decidedly Northern accent. A student named Mary Tremain remembered how friendly, urbane, and pleasant her professor was in his first year of teaching. For Miss Tremain, Woodrow Wilson, with or without his moustache, was the "most interesting and inspiring lecturer I have ever heard." Another student noted how Professor Wilson always entered the classroom smiling, animated, and ever in a good humor. His lectures seemed to be perfect essays that were "well rounded and with a distinct literary style." Another student explained Wilson's approach to teaching history this way:

> "Never have I known another mind that could reason so profoundly and as clearly, with such breadth of reason … he did not recognize the importance of detail, but … the fundamental underlying laws and causes, whether economic, political, and social problems, fascinated him and absorbed his best energies."

---

[193] Baker, *Life and Letters*, I, 251-260; McAdoo, *The Priceless Gift*, 148; Editorial Note, "Wilson's Teaching at Bryn Mawr, 1885-1886," *PWW*, V, 16-17; Woodrow Wilson, "Notes for Four Lectures on the Study of History, September 1885," *PWW*, V, 20.

Wilson's only graduate student in his first year of teaching at Bryn Mawr was Jane Bancroft. She later recalled how she met with Professor Wilson in the winter semester for two or three hours a week in a seminar room in Taylor Hall. She enjoyed the often one-sided conversation with her young professor who spoke more as a friend or a colleague than as a teacher. He told her about the Constitutional Convention of 1787 and the writings of Alexander Hamilton and John Marshall. But most of all, he loved talking about his favorite subject of congressional government as opposed to cabinet government.[194]

While Wilson found teaching women a strange experience, liking it sometimes but remaining uncomfortable with it at others, he struggled even more when dealing with Dean Thomas. He had simply never met a woman so forthright and direct. She was only a few days younger than Wilson, but had already received a Ph.D. Now she pressed Wilson to finish his program at Johns Hopkins since everyone of her other new professors, both men and women, had their doctorates. Wilson promised to return to Johns Hopkins by the end of his first year at Bryn Mawr and take the exams that would give him his Ph.D. While the Dean won her point on the matter of Wilson's doctorate, she gave him free reign to develop a two-year plan of study in history and political science as he saw fit. In history, Wilson started his students off in Ancient History in their first year at Bryn Mawr and then scheduled them for Modern History in their second year. While the class in Ancient History would take them up through the reign of Charlemagne, the course in Modern History would cover the entire history of England and France along with the Italian Renaissance and the German Reformation. At the end of the second year, Wilson would lecture on special topics in American history. His talks on the history of his own country would include the founding of the colonies, the battle between England, France, and Spain for control of the New World, the American Revolution and the War of 1812, the rise of the Federalist Party, and the nation's westward expansion up to the Missouri Compromise. Wilson made sure that the Civil War would not be covered in his class on Modern History. The two year course in political science would include political economy and opinion, the English and American constitutions, and a history of political institutions.[195]

Despite the respect he had won from his students and his dean, Wilson was soon deeply dissatisfied with his work at Bryn Mawr. He complained in letters to his many friends from his own school days that he longed to teach young men

---

[194] Baker, *Life and Letters*, I, 261-262.

[195] Woodrow Wilson, "Revised Course of Study for Students in History and Political Science, February 1, 1886," *PWW*, V, 104-106.

whom he could challenge to reason and debate. While he had given up his dreams of leading a political life, he still hoped to win the respect of his peers through his brilliant analysis of political institutions. If he could not be a William Pitt, then surely he could become the next Alexis de Tocqueville. Wilson became convinced that he would have a chance to show his skills as a political analyst at a meeting of Princeton alumni in New York City in March 1886 where he had been asked to speak on "The College and the Government." The event was held at Delmonico's Restaurant where the balcony of the dining hall was trimmed with the college colors of orange and black along with a banner won at a football game on Thanksgiving Day. The more than 250 alumni who crowded into Delmonico's were ready for a good time. They sang old college songs, told jokes and stories, and puffed on the best cigars. Ignoring the raucous atmosphere around him, Wilson launched into a deadly serious speech on the need for every university to hire a Professor of Politics who would teach students the fundamentals of government. Even when the crowd turned against him, shouting jokes at him and even milling about the hall to talk to each other, Wilson recited every word of his carefully prepared speech. Later many alumni remembered that the 20 minute speech seemed to last more than an hour. They wondered how such a deadly dull and self important young man could ever be an effective teacher.[196]

The dejected Wilson went home to Bryn Mawr certain that he had ruined any chance of ever teaching at his alma mater one day. Only his father, still ever sympathetic to his intense young son, was able to console him while keeping the dream of teaching at Princeton alive. Just weeks after the debacle, a night Wilson would always remember as the only time that a crowd ever laughed at him, his father wrote:

> "As to your alumni speech I have no doubt you underrate the impression it made. I grant that such speeches are hard to make – but if you succeeded in interesting the *more* thoughtful men, they will remember what you said … *if* you could get a foothold at Princeton."[197]

Wilson took comfort in the fact that he had returned home to the most loving wife any man had ever known. Ellen did everything she could to make life pleasant for her sensitive young husband. While servants had taken care of her for much of her life, she gladly took on the many duties that came with being the wife of a poor professor. In the first months of her marriage, she rode the train twice a

---

[196] Editorial Note, "Wilson's 'First Failure' in Public Speaking," *PWW*, V, 134-137; Woodrow Wilson, "An Address to the Princeton Alumni, March 23, 1886," *PWW*, V, 131-141.

week into Philadelphia where she took lessons at Mrs. Rorer's cooking school. Wilson's sisters were especially amazed that the once pampered Ellen was soon an excellent cook. In the evening when her chores for the day were done, she sat by Wilson's side, often sewing but at other times helping him with his research and writing. She even taught herself German so she could translate texts that Wilson needed in his work.

Above all else, Ellen Wilson wanted to become a mother. Her deepest wish came true when she became pregnant just two months after her wedding. As the time drew closer for her to deliver her child, she became more determined than ever to have her baby in Georgia. There were many reasons for this but the biggest one was her fear of childbirth. Ellen's mother had died giving birth to her sister and she knew how many southern women were never the same after having babies. If she survived, she did not want to become an invalid. She would go to the home of her mother's sister, Louise Hoyt Wade or "Aunt Lou" as everyone called her. Ellen's aunt was a woman known for her courage in standing up to Sherman's army and much beloved by everyone in Gainesville for her wisdom. Aunt Lou had servants who would hover over Ellen and a trusted family physician who would deliver the baby for next to nothing. Her final reason for heading to Georgia was the necessity of sparing her husband the agony of watching her in childbirth. Still Ellen Wilson told none of her concerns to her young husband and instead insisted that she would not allow a child of hers to be born "north of the Mason Dixon Line."[198]

In the first week of April 1886, Woodrow Wilson took his pregnant wife to the station in Philadelphia and put her on a train bound for Georgia. He then headed to Washington for a visit with his former law partner Edward Renick who had a job working in the Department of the Treasury. Now that Grover Cleveland was president, Wilson hoped that he might win a position in the new administration, but he found no openings during his visit. He got a better reception in Boston where the editors at D. C. Heath & Company asked him to write a textbook called *The State* on the essentials of government. Wilson returned to Bryn Mawr, excited about his writing assignment, but still so worried about Ellen that he could not bear to stay in their rooms in the Betweenery. He moved into a local boarding house and waited for news of the birth of his first child.[199]

On May 16, 1886, Ellen Axson Wilson gave birth to a healthy daughter named Margaret or "Maggie" after her maternal grandmother. Aunt Lou remarked

---

[197] Joseph Ruggles Wilson, "Letter to Woodrow Wilson, April 5, 1886," *PWW*, V, 153.
[198] McAdoo, *The Priceless Gift*, 147-149.
[199] Ibid., 151.

on her niece's bravery in bringing forth her first child with not one cry or complaint. Wilson was overjoyed when he received the news of his daughter's birth by telegram. He immediately wrote ecstatically to Ellen saying, "Oh, my darling, my darling, what shall I say to you now! My little wife is a mother; the baby has come—little Maggie has come! Oh, my little queen, how full my heart is—how infinitely I love you and the baby!"

Still even in the midst of such happiness Wilson was anxious to know if the baby looked like his wife or himself. He wanted the baby to be beautiful like her mother and not ugly like her father. Just five days after the baby was born, Aunt Lou finally let Ellen write back to her husband and assure him that "It is a little beauty, darling." – the prettiest little baby you ever saw – pretty, plump, and healthy how good the Heavenly father is to us!"[200]

Ellen missed her husband terribly but obeyed Aunt Lou's instructions about resting for at least a month after the birth of her daughter before even thinking about returning to Bryn Mawr with him. Once Aunt Lou allowed her to write on a regular basis, she filled up page after page of letters to her husband in her excited hand. She so wanted Woodrow to meet his daughter that she drew a circle at the top of one letter, touched it to the baby's lips, and then wrote "A Kiss from Baby" underneath it, explaining that Maggie "sends her love to her Papa & a kiss planted just in the middle of the little circle." Ellen was amazed at the letters that came back from her husband. He poured out his love for her in the most emotional terms possible while at the same time responding to her every comment and concern. It was clear that he missed her terribly. When she wrote that her two brothers Eddie and Stockton were coming to spend some time with her, Wilson was happy that her "adopted children" would soon be in Gainesville, but worried that she might forget him in all the family happiness. He reminded "his wife, his life, his queen, his Eileen" that he would be there soon to settle the doctor's bill. She answered that her heart was so full words simply failed her. She was unable to capture the overwhelming love she felt for her husband and her daughter. She could only say that the letters Wilson had written to her after she became a mother were the most beautiful ones he had ever penned. Could it be, she wrote, that she had truly become the woman of his dreams? She told him that she would treasure these letters above all others for the rest of her life.[201]

---

[200] Woodrow Wilson, "Letter to Ellen Wilson, April 17, 1886," *PWW*, V, 159: Ellen Wilson, "Letter to Woodrow Wilson, April 21, 1886, *PWW*, V, 166.

[201] Ellen Wilson, "Letter to Woodrow Wilson, April 27, 1886, *PWW*, V, 177; Woodrow Wilson, "Letter to Ellen Wilson, May 5, 1886," *PWW*, V, 197-198; Ellen Wilson, "Letter to Woodrow Wilson, May 12, 1886," *PWW*, V, 217.

By the start of his second year of teaching, Woodrow Wilson had his wife and baby daughter Maggie back with him at Bryn Mawr. In the spring semester, he moved his family into a large rambling house farther out from the college on the Gulph Road. It was an old parsonage for a Baptist church, and would be the perfect place to raise their growing family and take care of their relatives who were coming up from the south. The Wilsons needed the larger house since Ellen was expecting the couple's second child in the summer of 1887. They had also asked Ellen's brother Eddie Axson and her cousin Mary Hoyt to come to live with them since the two young people could get a better education in the north than they could ever possibly get in the south.

Ellen especially loved the big old house because of the privacy it afforded the family. She stayed busy all day cooking, cleaning, and sewing as well as stoking the furnace, pumping water from the well, and sweeping the yard. Wilson returned home from his classes and worked hard on his new book, *The State*, with Ellen helping him outline and research his book long into the night. She even drew a portrait of Gladstone for her husband to put above his desk in the study and so inspire him. Mary Hoyt remembered this idyllic time in her own life and the life of the Wilsons, recalling years later that:

> "I have often thought how hard it was for them never to have had their home to themselves. He would have liked it very much, just with Ellen, I think; and yet I cannot express to you the loveliness of life in that home. It was filled with so much kindness and courtesy, with so much devotion between Ellen and Cousin Woodrow, that the air always seemed to have a kind of sparkle."[202]

Still even cousin Mary Hoyt could see that Woodrow Wilson was restless. Every afternoon he would take long walks by himself in the woods where he composed his lectures, writing them down in shorthand and then transcribing them on a typewriter when he got back home. He seemed happiest on Sundays and on Friday evenings when he read aloud to his family, just like his father had once done. "He had the tenderest heart in the world and could never read aloud anything sad, because his voice would always break" Cousin Mary Hoyt remembered, "He had, I think, the most beautiful speaking voice in the world." Wilson also loved to sing irreverent college songs and more solemn hymns like "Art Thou Weary, Art Thou Languid?" But all the happiness masked Wilson's growing frustration with his failure to write anything that was truly great. He worked diligently on his manuscript for *The State* but remained dissatisfied that

[202] Baker, *Life and Letters*, I, 287, 289.

he was writing only a textbook filled with deadly dull facts. He hoped to write a great book one day called *The Philosophy of Politics* that would examine all the governments in the civilized world.[203]

Wilson also longed to be free of Bryn Mawr and win an appointment as a professor at a men's college, preferably his alma mater Princeton. When Ellen went to Gainesville in the late summer of 1887 to await the birth of their second child, Wilson wrote to her of his frustration, saying, "When I think of my little wife, I love this 'College for Women,' because *you* are a woman: but when I think only of myself, I hate the place very cordially." He also began a confidential journal like the one he had kept in his undergraduate days as he tried to work out his conflicting thoughts about teaching women and the growing boredom he felt as he lectured on the same topics week after week.

> "October 20: Lecturing to young women of the present generation on history and principles of politics is about as appropriate and profitable as would be lecturing to stone-masons on the evolution of fashion in dress. There is a painful absenteeism of the mind on the part of the audience. Passing through a vacuum, your speech generated no heat. Perhaps it is some of it due to undergraduateism, not all to femininity."[204]

Ellen returned to Bryn Mawr in the fall of 1887 with baby daughter Jessie, who had been born in Aunt Lou's house in Gainesville on August 27, to find her husband happy to see them but troubled over his own future. He was still the thoroughbred waiting for his chance to run his course in life and win a great race. The path he had laid out for himself to achieve greatness was in writing about politics but in his own eyes he had done nothing exceptional on this road since the publication of *Congressional Government.* "Thirty-one years old and nothing done!," he complained. He seemed almost to be bursting from his very skin as he sought one project after another by which to express his own deep thoughts about life in general and his nation in particular. He looked out at a world that more and more prided itself on being scientific. Wilson found nothing wrong with science and even argued that Americans must learn to study their own politics and economics in a more systematic way. While he was a devout Presbyterian, he was also a staunch supporter of scholars like his uncle Professor James Woodrow who believed in the theory of evolution. Still he warned that too great a reliance on scientific explanations for every part of the human experience would ultimately

---

[203] Ibid., 288-289.

[204] Woodrow Wilson, "Letter to Ellen Wilson, October 4, 1887," *PWW*, V, 605; Woodrow Wilson, "Confidential Journal, October 20, 1887," *PWW*, V, 619.

destroy the individual. The American way of life was especially based on the individual who must not be eclipsed in the race to describe all things scientifically.[205]

Deep down inside, Wilson still longed to play an active role in government. His "old political longings" were "set throbbing again" when Edward Renick told him there might be a chance for him to become an Assistant Secretary of State. However, when he did not get the job, he realized that merely being known as the promising young author of *Congressional Government* would never get him a position in the State Department. He felt the certain end of his childhood hopes about politics when he received word in April 1888 that his mother had died suddenly on the 15th of the month. While his mother's health had been failing for sometime, especially since she contracted typhoid fever and malaria five years before, he knew nothing of her last illness until he received the letter telling him that she was dead. He was devastated when he arrived in Clarksville only to find the "house shut up with father and Josie gone to Columbia with dear mother's body." He returned home deeply worried about Reverend Wilson who with his daughters married and Josie in college would now be all alone. The pain was so intense that he could hardly bear it. In his grief, he turned to Richard Heath Dabney, his best friend while in law school at the University of Virginia, explaining to him how his mother's death marked a passage in his own life:

> "My mother was a mother to me in the fullest, sweetest sense of the word, and her loss has left me with a sad, oppressive sense of having somehow suddenly lost my youth. I feel old and responsibility-ridden. I suppose that feeling will in time wear off, however, and that I will ultimately get my balance back again. In the meantime, I crave your sympathy, old fellow—I need all you can give."[206]

Wilson's unbearable sorrow over his mother's death was somewhat eased when he was offered a professorship in history and political economy at Wesleyan University, a college for men in Middleton, Connecticut. He stayed at the college for two years, teaching a variety of courses including the history of England and France, the Constitution of the United States, the history of institutions, political economy and statistics, and Roman and Greek history. He also taught a course in the United States that started in colonial times, came up through the Civil War, and ended with the presidency of Grover Cleveland. Both the faculty and students

---

205 Baker, *Life and Letters*, I, 289.

206 Woodrow Wilson, "Letter to Ellen Wilson, April 17, 1888, *PWW*, V, 718; Woodrow Wilson, "Letter to Richard Heath Dabney, May 16,1888, *PWW*, V, 726.

loved their new professor, finding Wilson an inspiring lecturer, a pleasant colleague, and a wonderful friend. Professor Wilson was especially happy to be teaching young men again, and enjoyed coaching both the football squad and the debating team. He liked to joke that when the football team was winning, he bragged to everyone how he was their coach. But whenever the team was losing, he said he was a member of the faculty and had nothing whatsoever to do with sports. Wilson was also happy to write a new constitution for the college debating team which he renamed the Wesleyan House of Commons.[207]

During his second semester at Wesleyan, Wilson contracted with Johns Hopkins University to give a series of lectures in public administration. Wilson was winning a reputation as one of the first scholars in the nation to write about this subject. For six weeks in the winter of 1889, Wilson lived in Baltimore where he taught a new group of young historians like Frederick Jackson Turner who would soon win fame for his frontier thesis and Reuben Goldthwaites who would prepare some of the first collections of primary sources on America's frontier experience. It was an exciting time for Wilson who longed to be known among his peers for his keen analysis of politics. Still it was a challenging one as well since he was away from his wife who was pregnant again and the two little girls he loved so much. He wrote letters to Ellen that were not quite so long as the ones he penned during their courtship but still filled with his deep and abiding love for his family. In a note written to Ellen on St. Valentine's Day, he told her how much he loved being married to her:

> "I wish I could write the marriage song that my heart sings … To enjoy my sweet one proved to be to enjoy my own full powers: living with her and for her, I have lived life at its best."

Two weeks later, he was again lonesome for Ellen as he watched the snow falling in Baltimore. "I wonder if it is snowing in Middletown as it is here," he wrote. "I wonder how the day is going with my precious little wife, whether she is thinking of me and of the love for her that governs all my life?"[208]

Just as she had done in her courtship, so now in her marriage Ellen tried to be a calming influence in Wilson's life. She wrote back from snowy Middleton that

---

[207] "Wilson's Copy for the Wesleyan Catalogue for 1889-1890," *PWW*, VI, 431-432; Woodrow Wilson, "A Constitution for the Wesleyan University House of Commons, January 5, 1889," *PWW*, VI, 39-44; "A Newspaper Report of a Chapel Talk: Prof. Wilson at Brown, November 13, 1889," *PWW*, VI, 423-424.

[208] Woodrow Wilson, "Letters to Ellen Axson, February 14 and 27, 1889," *PWW*, VI, 92-93, 116-117.

her brother Eddie was in bed with the mumps. She was so tired that at times she only had the strength to sit down and sigh with exhaustion. It would not be long before first Maggie and then Jessie ran up to her and kissed her to make her feel better. While she missed Wilson, she admitted they were getting along without him. But so as not to hurt his feelings, she quickly added "the simple fact is, sweetheart, that I am not without you. I feel your presence here, close, close beside me all the time." By the fall of 1889, Ellen had another daughter, Eleanor, born in October, to keep her busy.[209]

In the following spring, the Board of Trustees of Princeton University offered Woodrow Wilson a chair in jurisprudence and political economy. He accepted the job in May and headed to Princeton to find a house big enough for his wife, three daughters, Eddie and now Stockton Axson, too. He was excited at the prospect of at last making a mark on his nation by becoming a voice about modern politics and not merely a teacher about the past. He had begun to realize, on his long journey from Johns Hopkins to Bryn Mawr and finally to Wesleyan, that his own nation fascinated him far more than any other country in history. He was ready to explore and promote the nation that he now described as stronger after its Civil War than before it.

> "We are more – much more than a preserved nation; we are a strengthened, elevated, matured nation. We have triumphed over difficulties, not by steadfastness merely but by progress also. We have had that best evidence of health, namely growth. Vastly better, greater, more worthy, whether for strength, for unity, or for achievement are the Re-United States than were the merely *United* States. We have done more than kept faith with the deeds of our Fathers; we have kept faith with their spirit also."[210]

Perhaps at Princeton he could finally write a great book that would show the world how the United States was the leader of the modern world in politics. Never before had democracy taken hold like it had in this nation of sixty million that filled up not "ridiculously small" city-states as in Greece or "snug" cantons as in Switzerland but an entire continent. Maybe he could become an inspiring voice encouraging Americans to remember the ideals upon which their nation was

---

[209] Ellen Wilson, "Letter to Woodrow Wilson, March 3, 1889," *PWW*, VI, 126-127.

[210] Woodrow Wilson, "Make Haste Slowly (title supplied by the editors): The One Hundredth Anniversary of the Inauguration of George Washington, Address Delivered April 30, 1889, at (Place Not Given). From Original Manuscript in Mr. Wilson's Handwriting, in Mrs. (Edith) Wilson's Possession, *PPWW,* I, 79 (Wilson gave the address in the North or First Congregational Church in Middleton, Connecticut; see notes on address in *PWW*, V, 176-182).

founded and so help them take their place on the world stage in the coming century. If he could write with the insights that he expressed in his speech on the centennial of the inauguration of President George Washington, then maybe there was still a chance that he could become as great a commentator on the American scene as Alexis de Tocqueville had once been:

> "It behooves us once again to stand face to face with our ideals, to renew our enthusiasms, to reckon again our duties, to take fresh view of our aims and fresh courage for their pursuit … The tasks of the future are not to be less but greater than the tasks of the past: it is our part to improve even the giant breed of which we came – to return to the high statured ages: to weld our people together in a patriotism as pure, a wisdom as elevated, a virtue as sound as those of the greater generation whom to-day we hold in special and grateful rememberance."[211]

[211] Ibid., 186.

Chapter 5

"WHEN A MAN COMES TO HIMSELF"

It is a very wholesome and regenerating change which a man undergoes when he "comes to himself"... The scales have fallen away. He sees himself soberly, and knows under what conditions his powers must act, as well as what his powers are.

Woodrow Wilson[212]

Woodrow Wilson came back to Princeton just 15 years after he had first entered the college as a freshman. Then he had been a shy and awkward boy who dreamt of one day doing brave deeds on the world stage, but who knew not a soul in town and so wandered about looking for a place to stay. But now he returned to his alma mater as a grown man with a beautiful wife and three little daughters, all who loved him dearly. Ellen's brothers Eddie and Stockton along with her little sister Margaret would also be coming to live with them. While he was certainly a success in his private life, Wilson was still haunted by the fact that he had not achieved the greatness he longed for in the realm of politics. Perhaps at Princeton he could at least write his most ambitious work that he planned to call *The Philosophy of Politics* and so become renowned in the world of scholarly men. If he did not achieve some kind of greatness among his peers, then he would be a failure, not in the eyes of his family, but in his own. Having given up all hope of achieving a political career, and now bent on attaining success in the academy, he would have been stunned to learn that within a dozen years he would be tapped to lead Princeton as its first lay president and from there head back down the path toward government which he now believed was closed to him.

---

[212] Woodrow Wilson, "When a Man Comes to Himself," *PWW*, XI, 263.

Wilson's friends, most especially Robert Bridges whom he still called "Bobby," had worked hard to win him the professorship at Princeton. Bridges was a well-known editor in New York City and had urged both the college's new president Francis Patton and members of the board of trustees to hire Wilson away from Wesleyan. While some faculty members worried that Professor Wilson was too much of a Southerner for their decidedly northern campus, Patton had read *Congressional Government* and was very impressed with its author. While Patton was a Presbyterian minister himself, he recognized the change underway in higher education. Everywhere ministers as teachers and administrators were giving way to laymen trained in new methods who proudly displayed their doctorates on their office walls. Curriculum was being modernized to move away from classical studies that emphasized Greek and Latin toward more relevant fields like economics, law, and modern history. Patton, who remained quite cautious as he transformed Princeton, thought Wilson would be the perfect man to help take the college into the future while remaining true to its best traditions.[213]

Wilson carefully laid out the new program in jurisprudence and political economy at Princeton. His courses in Public Law, General Jurisprudence, American Constitutional Law, International Law, Public Administration, English Common Law, and Advanced Economics were open to juniors and seniors. His course in Elementary Economics was a required course for all students at Princeton. Although Patton saw him as a moderate, leaning even somewhat more toward the conservative rather than to the liberal, the outlines for his courses clearly showed him to be quite modern, even "cutting edge" in his understanding of the law. For Wilson, the law was not something that had been carved in stone during some past golden age. Instead it was a dynamic and living reality which developed in the interchange of ideas and practices among men across time. The law was primarily a function of politics, not philosophy. "Law is a growth, and the result of growth," he explained in his class in Public Law, "It is the growth of society recorded in institutions and practices." Still he was not a radical and cautioned the reformers of his day never to forget the powerful influence that past laws would continue to have on the better future they hoped to create. "In so far as social reformers endeavour to establish institutions," he cautioned, "they are bound by the conditions of the life of the law."[214]

Wilson's two sides came into play in controversies that quickly developed in his own department and within the wider faculty. Soon after arriving at Princeton,

---

[213] Baker, *Life and Letters*, II, 1-9.

[214] Editorial Note, "Wilson's Teaching at Princeton, 1890-1891," *PWW*, VII, 5-7; Woodrow Wilson, "Revised Notes for a Course in Public Law," *PWW*, VII, 7-9.

Wilson wanted his assistant Winthrop M. Daniels to teach a course in sociology. However, President Patton would not allow such a class to be offered. Patton wanted no part of teaching students about human society without reference to God or his almighty providence. "He was taking no chances with an evolutionary philosophy," Daniels later remembered, "which he distrusted as essentially materialistic and anti-Christian."[215] Wilson was quite frustrated and considered the situation "extraordinary and ridiculous." He himself remained a devout Christian who was not afraid to embrace the concept that societies developed over time. He was also not frightened by Darwin's theory of evolution and could not understand why so many Protestants resisted it. Still Wilson worked out a compromise with President Patton whereby Daniels would be allowed to lecture on Public Finance. As Daniels explained, "Error in this field was but venial; in the other, apparently mortal."[216]

While Wilson was at the forefront of leading Princeton toward new fields of study that accepted the growth of human society over time, his attitudes toward student behavior remained quite conservative. Cheating among Princeton students had become legendary and the faculty struggled to overcome one scandal after another in their courses. Their main tactic was to patrol their classrooms as students took their examinations. Many southern students came to the Wilson's home and told Ellen about the shocking behavior of their fellow students, most of them northerners, who had no sense of personal honor. After listening to his wife's description of the deplorable situation, Wilson proposed an honor system where the Princeton students would be treated as men, not children. He was ridiculed by some of the older professors at the faculty meeting where he first introduced it. They sneered at his talk of the "honour of a gentleman" as a quaint idea from a bygone age. One professor said it came from the hypocritical world of aristocrats who would not cheat at cards with their fellow gentlemen but who would also not think twice about seducing innocent women. Wilson ignored these taunts and led the fight for the honor system which was instituted at Princeton in the 1893 to 1894 academic year. He also served on the Discipline Committee that oversaw the resolution of violations of the honor code.[217]

Despite his tough stance on honorable behavior, the students of Princeton came to respect and admire their new professor. Wilson's classes were often large, running anywhere from 160 to 400 students. He usually began his lectures by

---

[215] Baker, *Life and Letters*, II, 17.

[216] Ibid., 18.

[217] Ibid., 16-17; Axson, *Brother Woodrow*, 67-69; the minutes of several meetings of the Discipline Committee can be found in Volumes VI through XII of the *Papers of Woodrow Wilson*.

reading a few key points aloud that he had typed out the night before. He would then speak for the rest of the class period on these points in much more detail and with many colorful stories. Years later, his students could still recall the vivid images that their teacher had impressed upon their minds. Raymond Fosdick remembered how Wilson's powerful lectures touched the lives of all who heard them. He was especially impressed with Wilson's description of how on a dark and stormy Sunday morning in 1538 Presbyterian ministers had gathered in the Greyfriars churchyard to sign a covenant against the Stuart monarchs right in the very shadow of Edinburgh Castle. Fosdick explained:

> "Mr. Wilson was always at his best in his description of events like this. His enthusiasm was contagious, and we who had the privilege of listening to his lectures came away feeling that we had been in the presence of some Elisha upon whom the mantel of the old prophets of liberty had fallen."

Wilson's lectures were often so powerful that students cheered his remarks and burst into spontaneous applause. Year after year, he was voted the most popular professor at Princeton by his students.[218]

Most of the members of the Princeton faculty were equally impressed with Professor Wilson. They respected his profound intellect and his skill at debate, but were happy to note that strains of humor and even playfulness wove their way through his dignified personality. He was fond of telling stories that poked fun at just about everyone including himself and his own intense teaching style. One of his favorites dealt with a fellow professor who sat in on Wilson's lecture about reform politics. Anxious to see if he had impressed his colleague, Wilson asked him after the lecture, "What part did you particularly like?" "Well," his fellow professor wryly responded, "when you spoke of the 'heyday of reform,' I liked that. I've worked on a farm myself and I know what haying is like."[219] Instead of taking offense at the comment, Wilson repeated it often with much laughter at his own expense. He was also fond of telling jokes and doing playful imitations of people, even adding songs and dances when he needed to make his point. Some of his best stories were about Scotsmen or Irishmen, and were recited in the best dialects with even the dancing of reels and jigs.

Ellen Wilson helped build her husband's reputation among the faculty at Princeton through her gracious hospitality. Her brother Stockton Axson remembered how she was always entertaining professors, students, and the many

---

[218] Baker, *Life and Letters*, II, 10-13.
[219] Ibid., 20.

friends and relatives of both herself and her husband throughout their twenty years together at Princeton. "I fancy it would be safe to say that, during his entire professorship at Princeton," Axson recalled, "he and Mrs. Wilson did not sit down to a third of their meals alone, that at least two thirds of the time there were guests at the table." Talk around the table was always friendly and often touched on books and ideas. The Wilsons liked to joke that there ought to be a "revolving bookcase" in the dining room. Many a time they dispatched one of their daughters to the library or study to retrieve the *Century Dictionary* or the *Century Biography of Names* to settle an always friendly debate.[220]

The Wilson daughters were a treasure for both their father and their mother. The little girls were soon well known on the campus. Thinking them too small to attend church, Ellen let her husband go alone to worship on Sunday mornings during their first years at Princeton, but always made sure that she arrived with the children in time to greet her husband when the services were over. She was an accomplished seamstress who dressed Maggie and Jessie, both blonde and blue eyed, in "Kate Greenway" dresses with bonnets that tied under their chins with wide satin ribbons. The baby with the brunette curls, whom everyone called Nell, was always dressed in white and came along in a carriage.[221] Ellen taught her daughters at home where she schooled them not just in books but in the same devotion to their father that she herself felt. In return, Wilson took an active part in his daughters' lives, listening to their every thought and trouble with respect. Still sometimes he would twist his face into "fantastic shapes" to make them laugh when they were trying so hard to tell him something serious. He could also fascinate his little girls for hours with his storytelling and his singing of old hymns like "Watchman Tell Us of the Night" and folk tunes like "The Kerry Dancers." He could make the sound of a galloping horse by slapping his hands on his knees until it seemed as if the magical creature had come down a path toward his daughters and then passed them by. He wanted his children to dream like he once did, and so built soaring towers with their blocks and taught them geography by having them divide up the world between them. When his daughters quarreled over who should claim the United States, Wilson ended the fighting be declaring no one could own America.[222]

Young Professor Wilson lived not just at the center of his own loving family, but more and more stood at the heart of an extended group of relatives. As his own father grew older and seemed to drift, having lost all purpose in his life after

---

[220] Axson, *Brother Woodrow*, 79-80.
[221] McAdoo, *The Priceless Gift*, 172-173.
[222] Ibid., 182.

the death of his beloved wife Jeanie, many of the Wilsons turned to "Brother Woodrow" for advice. His sister Marion and her husband died within months of each other in 1890, and their children needed to be sent off to relatives throughout the south who could raise them. Annie Howe became a widow in 1895 when Dr. George Howe died of peritonitis. Wilson hoped his sister would come live with his family in Princeton, but she decided to move to Philadelphia to be near one of her sons. Still she often turned to her younger brother for help in guiding the education and careers of her four children. Jessie Bones Brower also turned to Woodrow for advice on her stepson John Le Foy as he approached college age. She pulled on Wilson's heart strings when she wrote:

> "My dear cousin, when I look back on the days when we played wild Indians … & recall your favorite amusement of shaking me out of the tree, after throwing stones at me, you being the hunter & I a squirrel, I can scarcely believe we are the same couple. Those were dear old days, and you were my only brother."

Wilson's own little brother Josie, now proudly calling himself "Joseph R. Wilson, Jr.," frequently asked his older brother for help finding work in his chosen profession of journalism. He fell in love often and finally asked for his older brother's blessing on his marriage to a beautiful girl named Katie. Both Woodrow and Ellen were later a great comfort to Josie and his wife when their twin daughters died shortly after birth.[223]

Wilson also grew especially close to many of Ellen's relatives, most especially her brother Stockton Axson, whom he considered one of his best friends. Axson had come to live with the Wilsons in 1889 so he could attend Wesleyan University and study literature under Caleb Thomas Winchester, a renowned English professor. Axson then followed in his brother-in-law's footsteps and headed to Johns Hopkins for his graduate studies. When he found the new scholarly approach to literature imported from Germany not to his liking, he came back to Wesleyan to work on his M.A. in Literature with Professor Winchester. He then taught at the University of Vermont and lectured at an extension college outside of Philadelphia. In 1906, he secured a position at Princeton teaching literature. Ellen Wilson was particularly proud of the fact that

---

[223] There are numerous letters in the *Papers of Woodrow Wilson* from 1890 to 1910 that illustrate Wilson's growing role as the leader of an extended family made up his relatives and those of his wife Ellen. The following two letters from Wilson's father are good examples: Joseph Ruggles Wilson, "Letters to Woodrow Wilson," September 15 and October 13, 1890," *PWW*, VII, 10-11, 311-312; also see Jessie Bones Brower, "Letter to Woodrow Wilson, February 14, 1897," *PWW*, X, 166-167.

the students adored her brother and frequently voted him most popular professor just like her husband. After seven years at Princeton, Axson headed to the Rice Institute, later Rice University, in Houston, Texas, where he remained as a Professor of English until his death in 1935. Although many women loved him, Axson never married and remained near the heart of Wilson's family circle throughout his entire life. He often suffered from bouts of depression and was even committed to a mental hospital in Philadelphia for a time. Still he always came back to his sister Ellen and his best friend Woodrow whose loving home was a refuge for a soul so sensitive to beauty and suffering like his own. Stockton was ever grateful that the Wilsons' love for each other never turned inward upon themselves, but always went back out into the world where it could encompass people like him. "The love of Mr. and Mrs. Wilson for each other was complete but unselfish," he explained later in his memoir about his brother-in-law, "It seemed to stimulate in them loving-kindness for others and to evoke loving-kindness from others."[224]

Outside of his family, Wilson kept up old friendships with college classmates like Bobby Bridges and made new ones with younger scholars like Frederick Jackson Turner. He was also especially close to Cleveland Dodge and Cyrus McCormick, two members of the board of trustees, who were committed to keeping a man of Wilson's caliber at Princeton. Still many of his adult friendships were with women. He often confessed to his wife that he could not resist the charms of a beautiful and intelligent girl. When away from home, he frequently commented in his letters about whether there were any pretty women to admire in the town he was visiting. His daughter Jessie later remembered that her father "liked brilliant women, enjoyed knowing them, and more talking with them." For her part, Ellen Wilson tried to accept these friendships as necessary because of her own character and that of her husband. She once confessed to her cousin Florence Hoyt that she sometimes felt she was not clever enough to keep up with her brilliant husband. "I am too grave or too sober," she explained, "I am not gamesome."[225] She encouraged Wilson to correspond with several women he had met while traveling alone or vacationing with her and the children. Although she hoped that her "dear Woodrow" would always remain faithful to her, she knew her husband had a deep craving to be surrounded by people, especially women, who adored him.

One of Wilson's most serious friendships during his Princeton years was with Edith Gittings Reid, the wife of Johns Hopkins Professor Harry Fielding Reid.

---

[224] Axson, *Brother Woodrow*, ix-xiv, 223.

[225] Baker, *Life and Letters*, II, 57; McAdoo, *The Priceless Gift*, 189.

They corresponded with each other about their day-to-day experiences, but mainly spent time discussing Wilson's many writing projects. While Wilson could be quite formal in public when dealing with men, he was always charming and gallant in his letters to women, making them feel as if they were fair maidens and he was a dashing hero who had just stepped out of the pages of a romantic novel. Few ladies could resist a salutation like the one he sent to his "dear friend" Edith Gittings Read in January 1901:

> "Yesterday was a lucky, happy day for me. The postman, instead of bringing me business letters, brought me nothing but letters from friends, and I saw your handwriting with real delight … I wish my conscience could forget how selfish and essentially unreasonable it would be for me to propose a scheme of regular correspondence,--so that my pleasure might seem less hap-hazard and I might always have the zest of expectation to go before them!"[226]

Still it was his "Eileen" whom he loved above all others. Stockton Axson later recalled that he never heard a cross word between Woodrow and Ellen Wilson. This did not mean that they agreed on everything. On the contrary, both had strong wills and definite opinions, and often engaged in lengthy discussions to reach agreement on serious matters. In fact, the couple seemed to enjoy debating with one another in calm yet firm tones that always mixed determination with gentleness. "You are wrong, my dear, you are wrong," was a frequent comment of Mr. Wilson, while Mrs. Wilson would usually answer, "Woodrow, I don't see how you can think that." Their family and friends who heard them playfully argue and finally compromise could never have imagined that their letters to one another remained as passionate in the first decade of their marriage as they had been during their courtship.[227]

Wilson's correspondence with his wife took on an especially ardent tone when Ellen visited her family in Georgia during the spring of 1892. She had gone home to show off her beautiful little daughters, now five, four, and two, to her family. She sent letter after letter to her husband filled with gentle gossip about her family and amusing stories about the children. When she first arrived in Savannah early in March, she thought she might be pregnant again, hopefully with the boy she wanted so desperately, and so lingered in case she needed to head to Aunt Lou's in Gainesville. When this proved not to be the case, she still extended her stay well into May so she could travel to Rome and visit the cemetery where

---

[226] Baker, *Life and Letters*, II, 57-62; Woodrow Wilson, "Letter to Edith Gittings Reid, January 27, 1901," *PWW*, XII, 82-83.

her parents were buried. She took much care in choosing the perfect headstone for her father's grave that had gone unmarked for eight years. In contrast to the sweet but leisurely tone in Ellen's correspondence, Wilson's letters became more and more desperate as his wife's vacation dragged on. He confessed his love for her as if he was still a suitor hoping to win her heart. He filled his notes with short quotes from Ellen's favorite poet William Wordsworth and longer ones from the Elizabethan writer Robert Herrick. "How love came in I do not know," Wilson recited, "but I as well as any other this can tell: That when from hence she does depart, the outlet then is from the heart." He begged his "own darling" to go back to those "never-to-be-forgotten times and places" in Rome where they had first met and fallen in love. There she must reach out for his love across time and space just as he was now longing for her in lonely Princeton. Sadly he added:

> "I believe that if I could hold you in my arms for just five minutes every day, look into the depths of those eyes – cover their lids, your sweet, sweet lips, your cheeks, your chin, your neck, your brow with kisses, and make just one attempt to put my love into words – I could endure the rest of the twenty-four hours, as I cannot now!"[228]

Wilson especially missed his wife every winter when he traveled to Johns Hopkins University to deliver his lectures on Public Administration. He continued to do this in part for the prestige it brought to him as a leader in this new field, but he mainly did it for the money. He lectured for six weeks in Baltimore for the income it brought him. His girls were growing and dreaming already of going to college one day. He also needed to provide for the livelihood and education of Stockton, Eddie, and Margaret Axson. Reverend Wilson came to visit often at Library Place, and Wilson knew that eventually his father would need to live permanently with his family in Princeton, especially as he was beginning to show signs of the deafness that would plague his old age. However, knowing how much his work at Johns Hopkins meant to his own career and the comfort of his family did not make it any easier for Wilson to be gone from his beloved wife each winter. He was haunted by loneliness, and found his only joy in writing to Ellen about everything that happened in Baltimore and telling her how much he missed

---

[227] Axson, *Brother Woodrow*, 224.

[228] Eleanor ("Nellie") Wilson, the third daughter in the Wilson family, tells the story of learning that her mother was disappointed that she was a girl in her adult memoir on her parents' relationship (see McAdoo, *The Priceless Gift*, 171); the many letters between the Wilsons during Ellen's trip to Georgia in 1892, including ones related to Ellen's possible pregnancy, can be found in Volume XII of the *Papers of Woodrow Wilson*. The direct quotes come from Woodrow Wilson, "Letter to Ellen Wilson, March 31, 1892," *PWW*, XII, 532-533.

her. Things that once made him happy, like the theater, no longer moved him in the same way if Ellen was not at his side to share them. Once after he had seen a performance of Lillian Russell in Baltimore, he left the theater reflecting on the contrast between the illusion of the fading beauty on the stage and the reality of the lovely woman he had left at home in Princeton. "Perhaps it is, when I see an image of life on the stage," he explained to Ellen, "... the meaning of my own relations in life, whether by contrast or suggestion, is brought vividly home to me, – the meaning of one woman's life comes back to me." To be away from this one woman was an "exile" and he counted down the days until he could return to her like a boy waiting for the school year to end.[229]

Ellen Wilson loved her husband just as dearly, but also knew that he was a man who was still searching for his true purpose in life. In contrast to Wilson's letters, her correspondence was much calmer. They were also shorter than the ones she had written during her courtship. She was now a busy mother with a large household to care for and a professor's wife with many duties related to furthering her husband's career. She entertained in their home, mothered his students, especially boys from the South, and attended lectures and other events on campus. While Ellen always told Woodrow how much she and the girls missed him, she never begged him to come home or discouraged him from seeking other opportunities to lecture throughout the country. In fact, she was proud of him as requests arrived from all over the United States for Wilson to come and speak. Soon he was traveling not just to Baltimore, but to nearly every part of the country – New York, Pennsylvania, Virginia, Illinois, and even Colorado – to address alumni groups, professional societies, and colleges, most especially at their founder's day and commencement celebrations. As all this began to happen in Wilson's life in the early 1890s, no one was happier than his "dear Eileen" who did not fear losing her husband, but who instead wanted to share his brilliance with the world.[230]

Wilson gained national attention as a public speaker in the summer of 1893 when he was invited to give a talk at the Columbian Exhibition in Chicago on whether lawyers, doctors, and ministers should first receive an education in the liberal arts. While he supported better professional training in the fields of law,

---

[229] Woodrow Wilson, "Letter to Ellen Wilson, February 4, 1894," *PWW*, VIII, 452-455; Ellen Wilson makes the following interesting comment in a letter to her husband on January 27, 1895, *PWW*, IX, 135: "It is Sunday evening. The children are at last safely asleep after a long and funny discussion as to the various things they mean to do 'in life.' (You will be grieved to hear, by the way, that they all propose to go to college!)."

[230] Stockton Axson is the best source on describing how devoted Ellen Wilson was to supporting her husband's academic and public speaking career; see Axson, *Brother Woodrow*, 102-111.

medicine, and the ministry, he could not accept the argument that the liberal arts should be abandoned as outdated in the modern world. In Wilson's mind, the practical could never be separated from the theoretical. How could an attorney ever come to know the law as a living thing if he did not understand the time out of which it came? How could a doctor determine what research he should do if he had not evaluated the benefits of its outcome? How could a minister preach if he could not think and reason with the depth of knowledge that only liberal arts could bring him? No matter how proudly "modern" the world might consider itself to be, Wilson concluded that colleges and universities, both at the graduate and undergraduate levels, must continue to train students in the ancient ways of liberal learning that shaped the whole person.[231]

On the morning after his talk at the World's Fair, the *Chicago Herald* ran a cartoon of "Dr. Woodrow Wilson" as an earnest school boy reciting a graduation essay. This was the first time that Woodrow Wilson was caricatured in a newspaper. The drawing made him seem bird-like since his head was drawn large and his legs and arms were penciled in much smaller. Wilson looked like a child whose mother had gotten him ready for school. His hair was slicked back, spectacles pinched his nose, and he wore a suit with a wide collar and short pants.[232] While the cartoon captured Wilson's youthfulness, it failed to show his impact on the crowd. The 36-year old professor might have looked like a boy, but his voice was deep and manly. Although he sang as a lively tenor, he spoke with a rich baritone. Listening to Wilson give a speech was closer to hearing an actor on a stage than watching a student recite a lecture. He carefully modulated his tones to make his points most effectively and paused when necessary to add drama to his argument. His sophisticated speaking style amazed his listeners who were more accustomed to the popular orators of the day who tried to shake the rafters with their words.[233]

Still there was something telling in the cartoonist's image of Wilson as a young boy reciting an essay on the importance of learning. While reading novels or poems, he could still lose himself in his imagination just like he had done in his childhood, and he now worried that modern literary criticism would destroy this beautiful experience forever. Scholars should modernize their methods, he thought, especially in fields like history and politics, but only to deepen

---

[231] Woodrow Wilson, "Should an Antecedent Liberal Education Be Required of Students in Law, Medicine, and Theology, July 26, 1893?" *PWW*, VIII, 285-292.

[232] A replica of the cartoon from the *Chicago Herald* (July 27, 1893) can be found in the *Papers of Woodrow Wilson* (VIII, 286).

[233] Woodrow Wilson's voice can be heard by accessing several of his speeches that are posted online at the website of the Vincent Voice Library at Michigan State University (www.msu.edu).

understanding of the human heart and not to cover it over with a kind of pseudo-science. He agreed wholeheartedly with his brother-in-law Stockton Axson who resisted teaching literature by means of modern critical techniques, and he expressed this conviction in an essay entitled "Mere Literature" which was published in the *Atlantic Monthly* in December 1893. While he recognized that the modern age was swept up in the theory of evolution, and so scientists were searching for the forms that lay beneath everything in the material world, Wilson argued that the experience of literature was different. Reading a beautiful novel or poem opened a person up to the world of spirit, and not to matter. "Literature in its essence is mere spirit," he explained, "and you must experience it rather than analyze it too formally."[234]

Wilson's romantic spirit was only heightened as he traveled the country giving lectures throughout the 1890s. The cynicism toward his country that he had felt as a child growing up in the South during the Reconstruction finally disappeared. The time when he ignored the nation's centennial celebration and laughed at the massacre of Custer and his 7th Cavalry summer of 1876 was now only a distant memory. Even his obsession with England and its parliamentary system of government lessened as he came to appreciate the wonder of democracy in his own country. When he gave an important lecture on Edmund Burke, he refrained from making his usual comments on how the American system of government was inferior to the British one. Many of his other long held opinions about the United States were discarded as he crisscrossed the country by train. He was most impressed by the sheer size of his nation. Feeling the power of America's westward pull as he headed across the Mississippi River, through the Great Plains, and into the Rocky Mountains, he became one of the earliest champions of Frederick Jackson Turner's frontier thesis. He wholeheartedly rejected the theory that "Germanic *germs*" lay at the root of American democracy. While he still believed that England played an important role in helping self-government get started on the continent, he concluded that it was the practical spirit of the British people, rather than any one political form they brought with them to the New World, that spouted in the American soil and blossomed full blown into a vibrant democracy as the nation moved westward.[235]

---

[234] Woodrow Wilson, "Mere Literature," *PWW*, VIII, 438-452. The essay was probably written early in 1893, but was not published until later in the year (see Wilson's essay in the *Atlantic Monthly*, LXXII, December 1893, 820-828). When Wilson published this essay along with several others in an edition called *Mere Literature*, he dedicated the book to Stockton Axson.

[235] Wilson's support for Turner's frontier thesis can be seen in a speech he gave at the American Historical Association convention where Turner unveiled his thesis. See also Frederick Jackson Turner, "Letter to Woodrow Wilson, December 20, 1893," *PWW*, VIII, 417.

His favorite topics for speeches and political essays became the nature of democracy, the meaning of liberty, and the true American spirit. Instead of seeing the United States as a pale reflection of England, he now praised the American character and saw it as the moving force behind the nation's democracy. "The true American spirit," he proclaimed, "is a spirit that chooses and does not obsequiously submit." This defiant spirit did not come ready made, but developed over time as an integral part of American history. Even before his friend Turner had unveiled his thesis on the impact of the frontier on the United States, Wilson was explaining his nation through the eyes of its pioneers:

> "A high-spirited and adventurous people chose a pioneer life on a new continent in preference to submitting to opinions and institutions of which they did not approve, and having subdued that new continent to the uses of civilization they established upon it a government which was meant to have as its fundamental doctrine the right of every man to choose his principles and his life."

The democracy that these American pioneers established was a truly unique one. Whereas other nations thought of democracy only in terms of majority rule, the Americans developed a system wherein parties were organized and then the majority of voters decided between them. This simple innovation made the United States a place where "officers and the law govern," and not a mob. The true American spirit was thus one of cooperation as well as independence. The nation progressed through "disciplined hosts" which directed the people, chose their leaders, and fought for laws that ensured a better future for all. By organizing "nation-strong," the issues of the day were met by a proud people who moved ever forward.[236]

Wilson also returned to the topic of political greatness that had fascinated him in childhood. Now he narrowed the question down to identifying who the greatest Americans truly were. As much as he admired Alexander Hamilton and James Madison, he believed that they were too English in their habits and sentiments to be called "American." Similarly, Thomas Jefferson was something less than a true American because of his devotion to the French Enlightenment which "permeated and weakened all his thought." Benjamin Franklin showed the first signs of being more American than European, and George Washington would be firmly in this category if his biographers had not made him so lifeless. The first truly great Americans who can be clearly identified were undoubtedly John Marshall and Daniel Webster. "In these men," Wilson explained, "a new set of ideas find

[236] Woodrow Wilson, "The True American Spirit (October 27, 1892)," *PWW*, VIII, 37-40.

expression, ideas which all the world has received as American." The greatness of these two men, who could think and speak for their nation as a whole, became clearer when they were set side by side with two more provincial types, John Adams of Massachusetts and John C. Calhoun of South Carolina. Other great Americans surely included Henry Clay, Andrew Jackson, and even Robert E. Lee whom Wilson placed in a class with other men with a fighting spirit like Patrick Henry and Sam Houston. While he still admired Lee like every schoolboy who had grown up in the South during the Civil War, he now saw Abraham Lincoln as "the supreme American of our history." Wilson had come to believe that the whole country was summed up in Lincoln. He was strong and humane like the West, conservative and respectful of the law like the East, and aware of the terrible heritage of slavery like the South. His coming to power at the exact moment he was so desperately needed in the nation's history must be considered providential. If Americans would carefully study these men, they could see the kind of leaders they would need in the future.

> "The great men of our future must be sound-hearted, hopeful, confident of the validity of liberty, tenacious of the deeper principles of American institutions, but with the old rashness schooled and sobered, and instinct tempered by instruction. They must be wise with an adult, not an adolescent wisdom. Some day we shall be of one mind, our ideals fixed, our purposes harmonized, our nationality complete ... then will come our great literature and our greatest men."[237]

At the very moment that Woodrow Wilson was beginning to understand his own country, and coming to appreciate what it meant to be an American, he was asked by the noted editor Albert Bushnell Hart to write a book on the Civil War and Reconstruction as part of a multi-volume series on the "epochs" of the history of the United States. Wilson called his most important work to date *Division and Reunion*. It was the first serious study done of the traumatic period in American history from 1829 to 1889. The book sold well for many years and was used throughout the country as a textbook on the era. In his work, Wilson became the first historian to theorize that the American nation was not truly formed until the Civil War. Through this bloody conflict, the relationship of the states to the nation was finally decided. He also tried his best to understand every side in the long struggle and concluded that both those who fought for the Confederacy and the Union were right. "The South was right in law and constitution, but wrong in

---

[237] Woodrow Wilson, "A Calendar of Great Americans, September 15, 1893," *PWW*, VIII, 368-380.

history," he explained, "The East, on the other hand, was wrong in law and constitution, but right in history."[238]

By the late 1890s, it was clear that Woodrow Wilson was coming into his own as a thinker, speaker, and writer. Yet this growth in his life and career was taking a terrible toll on his health which went largely unnoticed. During the critical year of 1896, Wilson worked at a fever pitch on a variety of projects and ignored how exhausted he was. In the early winter, he taught at an extension college in Lancaster County just outside of Philadelphia and then traveled to Baltimore where he lectured at Johns Hopkins University. While in Maryland, he oversaw the construction of a new home for his family back in New Jersey. Ellen Wilson had carefully designed the Tudor house on Library Place, but was now having a difficult time dealing with the contractors. A crisis developed when the original builder died and left no instructions on how the work was to be completed. When a new contractor showed up at the house, he asked for Mr. Wilson, and refused to deal with his wife. "He says he must see you and 'the boys,' meaning the carpenters, together – why I can't imagine!" Ellen complained to her husband. Wilson came back for a visit to Princeton to get work on the house started again. He then returned to Baltimore where he took on another writing project suggested to him by Henry M. Alden, the editor of *Harper's Magazine*. It was a biography of George Washington which he wrote both to further his own career and pay for his family's new home. He must also pay back $1500 to his father who had loaned him the price of the lot on which the house stood.

With so much of his energy now "bent to money-making," Wilson wrote the book on Washington as quickly as he could. While he kept his eye on future royalties, he greatly enjoyed working on the project. He went to Washington, D.C. to visit his old law partner Edward Rennick who was now working in the State Department. Rennick showed him many of Washington's letters and other original documents from the time of the American Revolution. Back in his boarding house in Baltimore, Wilson wrote late into the night. He was swept up in his imagination as he completed chapter after chapter, writing back to Ellen that today he was in "the thick of 1776" while tomorrow he "passed the winter of Valley Forge." It was an emotional experience for Wilson to write about Washington and helped him gain a better understanding of the cost paid by the founding generation to establish the United States of America.[239]

---

[238] Baker, *Life and Letters*, II, 123-124.

[239] See Ellen Wilson, "Letter to Woodrow Wilson, February 5, 1896, *PWW*, IX, 409, for the complaints on Mr. Titus, the new contractor; see Woodrow Wilson, "Letter to Ellen Wilson,

As he worked on the biography of Washington, Wilson also became actively involved in politics for the first time in his life. The people of Baltimore held a rally in the town's Music Hall protesting the actions of the city council. They were angry that the members of the council had decided to appoint persons to municipal offices rather than allow the voters to choose them. Wilson spoke to the crowd on the nature of good government, taking his ideas straight from the lectures he was giving at Johns Hopkins. He challenged the people to dedicate themselves to reform over the long haul, and not to give up the dream of reform when the rally was done and their enthusiasm died down. "I am a believer in the long processes of reform," he said, "Everything will come as you mean it if you only continue to mean it." He was joined on the podium by New York's reforming Police Commissioner, Theodore Roosevelt. The two men were caricatured in the *Baltimore News* with Roosevelt jutting out his strong chin and the slender Wilson, without his glasses on, pointing to the crowd as he challenged them. While the two men never become close friends, they corresponded with one another from time to time in polite letters. At Wilson's request, Teddy Roosevelt even tried to help Edward Rennick hold onto his job in the State Department after McKinley was elected later in the year.[240]

As he buried himself in his work throughout the winter and early spring of 1896, Wilson tried to deny the growing problems with his health. He thought his listless condition was due to a combination of his old stomach troubles and his current overwork. If he could just get a little rest, he was certain he would soon be better. But those who knew him were growing increasingly worried. His brother-in-law Stockton Axson noticed that Wilson's eye twitched constantly. He mentioned his concern to Reverend Wilson who said, "I am afraid Wilson is going to die." While her husband wrote from Baltimore that he had been sick, but was feeling much better, she worried when people who had seen Wilson at Johns Hopkins told her that he looked terrible. Back home in Princeton in the late spring, Wilson sometimes felt so bad that he took to his bed. Finally, on May 27, he suffered a small stroke that left his right hand useless and his right arm partially paralyzed. Doctors diagnosed his condition as "neuritis" and prescribed immediate and extended rest so he could regain the use of his right side.[241]

January 28, 1895," *PWW*, IX, 137, for the remark on "money-making;" see the comments on the Washington book in Woodrow Wilson, "Letters to Ellen Wilson, February 17 and 23, 1896," *PWW*, IX, 430-431, 443-444.

[240] "A Newspaper Report of a Reform Rally in Baltimore, March 4, 1896," *PWW*, IX, 483-486.

[241] Axson, *Brother Woodrow*, 39-41, 255; Ellen Wilson, "Letter to Woodrow Wilson, February 23, 1896," IX, 444-445.

Ellen Wilson took matters into her own hands to cure her husband. Her new next door neighbor, a wealthy older woman named Mrs. Brown, had taken quite a liking to Ellen and Woodrow. She offered to pay for a trip to England for both of them. A depressed Wilson refused the gift, but his wife accepted the offer on the condition that her husband would be allowed to travel alone. She wanted him to stop thinking for a time about his classes, his lectures, and his writings. He must go to Europe where he could relax and then come back home to his family and his work completely refreshed. Complaining until the very moment he boarded the *S.S. Ethiopia* in New York in June, he was soon grateful to Ellen for forcing him to take the trip. He relaxed on the summer cruise across the Atlantic, making fast friends with the Woods, a married couple from North Carolina. Mr. Charles A. Woods was a lawyer who enjoyed talking politics with the young professor from Princeton. He even predicted that Wilson would someday be the President of the United States.[242]

Wilson arrived first in Glasgow and then traveled by train and bicycle from Edinburgh all the way to London and then back to York. It was a pilgrimage for him as he journeyed to the many places he had heard about from his mother in childhood. He also visited the graves of his heroes Edmund Burke and Adam Smith and the birthplaces of Robert Burns and William Wordsworth. He plucked a flower from the wall near Wordsworth's cottage, and mailed it to Ellen telling her that she deserved to see these sights more than he. "I declare I hardly have the heart to tell you of being in these places," he explained to Ellen as he placed the flower from Rydal Mount in the envelope, "knowing how you will yearn when you read them, and knowing how much better *right* you have to see them than I have" At first, Wilson struggled to hold a pen, but soon he could write clearly with his left hand. His letters to his wife were travelogues in which he included his itinerary, a detailed sketch of all he saw, and finally the deepest impressions of everything he experienced. As he traveled through his favorite place, the beautiful Lake Country made famous by the Romantic poets, he came to miss Ellen and his children terribly. By the time he reached the home of Shakespeare along the Avon River, he admitted that he was even homesick for his own country. It was only in Oxford that he thought for a moment about leaving everything behind and settling permanently in England. He could barely express the beauty of the buildings and the quads as he penned his letter home to Ellen from the town's Wilberforce Hotel.

---

[242] McAdoo, *The Priceless Gift*, 201. When Wilson became president in 1913, he appointed Woods to a judgeship.

> "I have seen as much as made me feel alien as that made me feel at home since I came to England, and have been made on the whole to love America more than less … but Oxford! Well, I am afraid that, if there were a place for me here, America would see me again only to sell the house and fetch you and the children …"[243]

Wilson came back down to earth when he visited the National Gallery in London, wishing that his dear Eileen could be at his side as he wandered through the galleries lined with the masterpieces of Reynolds and Gainsborough. He ended his trip by riding first up to Lincoln, then on to York and Durham, where he visited their mighty cathedrals, and finally all the way through the Yarrow before he sailed home in August. The thought of returning to his wife and children after seeing so much beauty overwhelmed him. In his last letter home before sailing in August, he wrote:

> "This is the little note that is to go to-morrow to my sweet, sweet love, as the harbinger of my home-coming … I rode the whole length of the Yarrow yesterday morning with the poets in my heart and spent the afternoon and night beside St. Mary's lake … This is only to tell you that my heart has traveled not a step from your side all summer, – has drawn closer, rather … I know now, too, how much I love our precious children, God bless them …"[244]

Wilson came back to America a changed man in many respects. When people asked him what he thought of England, he usually answered, "I am a better American for having been there."[245] While his travels across America had already begun to lessen his adoration of England and increase his admiration of the United States, his nostalgic trip through the British Isles only confirmed this drift in his thought. Ellen Wilson recognized even deeper changes in her husband. He came home restored in mind and body, but he also had a new self-confidence that she had never seen in him before. The change was most apparent in the letters he wrote to her after his summer trip. When he now traveled about the country giving more and more speeches, he continued to correspond with her almost daily, but the desperate passion of his earlier letters had all but disappeared. Although he did not yet recognize it in himself, Wilson appeared to be on the brink of finding himself and his place in the world at last.

---

[243] Woodrow Wilson, "Letters to Ellen Wilson, June 13 and 14, July 3, 5 and 9, 1896," *PWW*, IX, 514-515, 532-534, 537-538.

[244] Woodrow Wilson, "Letter to Ellen Wilson, August 24, 1896," *PWW*, IX, 575.

[245] Baker, *Life and Letters*, II, 85.

The new Wilson – calmer, self assured, and even more profound in his insights about life in general and politics in particular – first emerged in public during the sesquicentennial celebration at Princeton in October 1896. The College of New Jersey had been founded 150 years before and was now officially rechristened as Princeton University in weeklong festivities. The celebration began on the night of October 20 as the faculty, students, and alumni marched in a procession down Nassau Street. Nellie Wilson long remembered how her father walked behind the college's marching band with a torch in hand like "a happy boy." On the next day, everyone packed into Alexander Hall to hear Wilson give a speech on "Princeton in the Nation's Service." Members of the Class of '79 stood and cheered when Wilson stepped to the podium. Ellen sat awestruck and bursting with pride just below the stage.[246] Reading from a script that he had typed himself with his left hand, Wilson captured the crowd's attention with his opening remarks:

> "We pause to look back upon our past today, not as an old man grown reminiscent, but as a prudent man still in his youth and lusty prime and at the threshold of new tasks, who would remind himself of his origin and his lineage, recall the pledges of his youth, assess as at a turning point in his life the duties of his station."

His rich voice pulled the already emotional crowd first back toward the past and then ahead toward the future. He reminded his audience how the college was founded just as the ideals of the American Revolution were beginning to stir in men's souls. Right from the beginning, the college was tied to the revolutionary spirit through the Reverend John Witherspoon, its first president and one of the signers of the Declaration of Independence. Although founded by Presbyterian ministers, Princeton had never been a narrow sectarian school. Instead it had seen its purpose right from the start as building a sense of duty in its students. In fact, said Wilson, Princeton was a "school of duty." Students came to the College of New Jersey – before, during, and after the Revolution, to serve their nation. Princeton University would continue to serve the American people. It would stand like a beacon to "illuminate the duty" through every lesson drawn from the past that was taught at the college in the present. Wilson ended by challenging his listeners – faculty, students, and alumni alike – to become a perfect place of learning. "What was that perfect place?" he asked the excited crowd. He answered:

---

[246] McAdoo, *The Priceless Gift*, 206-297.

> "A place where ideals are kept in heart in an air they can breathe. A place where to hear the truth about the past and to hold debate about the affairs of the present, with knowledge and without passion … slow to take excitement, its air pure and wholesome with a breath of faith: every eye within it bright in the clear day and quick to look toward heaven for the confirmation of its hope. Who shall show us the way to this place?"[247]

The applause was thunderous and the reaction to the speech was overwhelming. Ellen Wilson later told her cousin Mary Hoyt how the Princeton men "fell on his neck and wept for joy." The ones who could not reach Wilson shook hands with each other in a "perfect frenzy of delight." Wilson's name was spread in newspapers across the country. Many magazines printed the speech in its entirety. Requests for Wilson to speak poured in from all over the United States, and important people from around the nation and the world who came to lecture at Princeton now made their way to Library Place to discuss the affairs of the day with Professor Wilson.[248]

Having returned from Great Britain with a greater understanding of his country, and now being recognized as one of the nation's most original thinkers, Wilson felt a new sense of urgency to speak out on behalf of the American people. He continued his work on *A Short History of the United States* which he had begun after publication of the Washington biography. He also wrote about contemporary politics for major publications like the *Atlantic Monthly*. He generally admired President Grover Cleveland, defending him as his own man and as the most important political figure to come on the scene since Abraham Lincoln. He supported most of the positions that Cleveland took in his second administration including tariff reform and the gold standard. He could not understand the furor over free silver and thought William Jennings Bryan was insane for supporting it. He considered Bryan's Cross of Gold Speech nothing short of madness. While he remained a Democrat, he watched from the sidelines as his party seemed to spin out of control. Wilson was equally concerned that the drive for reform among working men was becoming more violent. He saw the growing unrest in the country as a revolt against the concentration of wealth in the East that had developed since the Civil War. However, he disliked the Populists as too emotional and unrealistic in their demands. He also could not tolerate laboring men who disrupted the flow of commerce in an effort to win their demands. When the papers were filled with stories of how Cleveland sent federal troops to break

---

[247] Woodrow Wilson, "Princeton in the Nation's Service, October 21, 1893," *PWW*, X, 11-31.
[248] Ellen Wilson, "Letter to Marie Eloise Hoyt, October 27, 1896," *PWW*, X, 37-38.

up the Pullman strike, Wilson shouted gleefully to his family, "Here is great news! Mr. Cleveland has issued a pronunciamento, declaring the railways between the East and Chicago military and post roads, and has ordered out the army to enforce the decree."[249]

Wilson also began to worry about America's growing role in international affairs. His concern became especially urgent at the conclusion of the Spanish American War. The question that haunted him, and he believed the nation as well, was a simple one – "What ought we to do?" Specifically what should the nation do now that it had acquired an overseas empire – Cuba, Puerto Rico, and the Philippines? While America had not entered the war as a conqueror, she had become one at war's end. Wilson looked back with some regret that the nation had not negotiated more carefully with Spain rather than simply plunging into a war to free Cuba at all costs. Still he could not brood about this for too long since the modern world moved at a swift pace and could not be "stayed by regrets." He and his fellow Americans must simply face the fact that there was no going back to a world where their country sought its destiny only on this continent. They must also recognize the "terrible efficiency" of their navy whose victories in Havana and Manila had "quickened our blood." As America moved farther out into this "very modern world," Wilson feared that war would be inevitable – not the romantic battles he had dreamt of in his childhood, but more terrible conflicts that would kill countless young men and send many a beautiful ship to the bottom of the sea.

Moving away at last from the romantic images of his youth, Wilson now realized how dangerous it was for a nation to have a navy. Did we build these ships, he asked himself, thinking them no more frightening than boats docked at a yacht club? America had launched her young fleet at a more "aggressive" time than the world had ever known. The "vital nations of Europe" – England, Russia, Germany, and France – were lining up with and against each other in shifting alliances to divide the world between them. On the dark and dangerous sea of modern history, Americans would have to make choices as important as the ones they made to settle a continent. They had an obligation to answer the question – "What *ought* we do?" For Wilson, the question was not a speculative one, but was instead a deadly moral challenge. If the world's greatest democracy was to do battle beyond its borders, then it must fight a different kind of war. "The work of war," Wilson concluded, must be done "with a manifest and earnest passion for

---

[249] Axson, *Brother Woodrow*, 71-73.

service, but with no love of slaughter, – with a great pity, rather, for those whom they destroy, – like the christian gentlemen we would have them be."[250]

As he worried about his country, and tried to formulate policy for it if only in memorandums to himself, Wilson continued to work at the same pace he had done before his physical breakdown in 1896. While he preferred writing with a pen, he now typed all of his lecture notes, speeches, and other works on the Hammond in his study. Ellen had made sure there was study in the new house that was lined with bookshelves. Here her husband could work at his roll top desk and look up at the crayon drawings she made for him of the men he most admired – William Gladstone, Edmund Burke, Walter Bagehot, Daniel Webster, and Reverend Joseph Wilson. His daughters remembered how they had to stay quiet in the house until they heard the desk roll shut and their father started to whistle. Then they could run to him, tell him their troubles, and listen to his funny stories. Their favorite one included Wilson's imitation of an Irishman who had a little too much to drink. While his wife feigned shock at this performance, Wilson was fond of saying that he could be a success in vaudeville if he ever gave up teaching.[251]

Throughout the late 1890s, the Wilson house on Library Place was always a lively place. The home had seven bedrooms, three for the Wilsons and four more for visitors. Wilson's sister Annie and his father were frequent guests. Ellen's family also came and went. Margaret attended Bryn Mawr, while Eddie became an engineer and moved to Georgia with his new wife. Ellen remained concerned about her brother Stockton. He had the same melancholy moods as her father once had and he complained of frequent stomach aches. Both she and her husband looked for ways to improve Stockton's mental and physical health. Wilson even wrote to one of Axson's colleagues at the University of Vermont, asking him to take Stockton along on a planned trip to Europe. Finally, in June of 1899, Ellen decided to send Stockton to Great Britain and asked her husband to accompany him. This time Wilson did not resist, knowing that the trip would be good for both of them.[252]

It was a happy crossing for Wilson and an equally memorable one for his brother-in-law. Stockton later recalled how his friend Woodrow was the leader of all the travelers on the cruise. Every night he would head to the crowded smoking room on the *Furnessia* and lead the evening's discussion. After arriving in Glasgow, they headed to Edinburgh, Wilson's favorite city in Europe. He had

---

[250] Woodrow Wilson, "A Memorandum: 'What Ought We To Do?,' August 1, 1898," *PWW*, X, 574-576.

[251] McAdoo, *The Priceless Gift*, 201, 209-210.

[252] Ibid., 201; Axson, *Brother Woodrow*, 83-84.

hoped to tour Great Britain by bike and even brought two new ones with him. But when Axson, who was not feeling well, asked if they could go mainly by train, Wilson happily agreed. He guided his troubled brother-in-law through Scotland and England by retracing the steps he had taken during his visit there three years before. They traveled first through landscapes made famous by Robert Burns, then made their way down to Wilson's mother's home in Carlisle, and finally headed to the Lake Country made famous by Wordsworth and the other Romantic poets. In Durham, Wilson visited the cathedral once again, but also sat in on a criminal court where he noticed how much swifter justice was in England than in the United States. He wrote all his observations down in long letters to Ellen and told her again that she deserved to see all these sights, not himself and her brother. He found Oxford as magnificent on this trip as when he had first seen it. However, when describing London to his wife, he made few comments on seeing Parliament, the place he had visited so many times in his imagination, and instead commented on the differences he noticed between English and American girls. He explained his observations to his understanding wife:

> "English girls, when they are interesting, are unmistakably very interesting creatures. American girls (as surely all the world must see, – for *this* part of the world, at any rate, is full of them) have a great and obvious superiority in beauty, figure, style, grace, and a sort of *effectiveness*; but English girls are, I should judge, as a rule sweeter and easier to love in an intimate, domestic fashion. When they get beauty, too, they are very dangerous."[253]

From London, Wilson headed alone to Ireland for three weeks on a biking tour where he was most impressed with the pattern of quads within quads at Trinity College. In late August, he joined Stockton in Glasgow and headed home on the *City of Rome*. One night during supper, the ship went up onto an iceberg in the fog. Wilson calmly finished his dinner before heading up on deck. Axson stayed in the dining room with the other passengers and only made his way through the broken dishes that were ankle deep once the ship had freed itself from the iceberg. He was amazed to see his brother-in-law still on deck speaking to a Presbyterian minister as if noting remarkable had happened. Later that same evening, as they headed for their cabin, Woodrow told Stockton that they should probably not get undressed tonight and instead just take their coats off just in case something happened. But beyond this, Wilson showed no outward signs of worry, not even when the ship continued to list to one side on the following morning.

---

[253] Baker, *Life and Letters*, II, 93-94.

When the ship scraped along another iceberg later that afternoon, Axson found Wilson relaxing in a deck chair. He told his brother-in-law not to worry, but Stockton could not help wondering what thoughts were running through Woodrow's mind. Was he thinking of his wife and three girls? Surely he knew he was on the brink of a great future as a scholar and even an administrator. Was he thinking of his "unfinished career?" Wilson later claimed he was simply happy he had remained so calm and thus proved to himself that "he would not be a coward in a crisis."[254]

Still something had changed deep within Woodrow Wilson and he finally recognized it in himself when he returned home from his second trip to Europe. Whether a gradual change had occurred since his attack of paralysis, or a sudden one had happened during his brush with death in the North Atlantic, Wilson understood that he had come "unto himself." The change his wife had first seen in him three years previously he now saw in himself. As he approached his 43rd birthday, he felt the dreams of his childhood disappear at last as a full awareness of his adult powers and his place in the world descended upon him. He described this new self-understanding in the most personal essay he had ever written. Calling it "When a Man Comes to Himself," Wilson began with the startling statement that a man's self-awareness comes only with disappointment:

> "It is a process of disillusionment. The scales have fallen away. He sees himself soberly, and knows under what conditions his powers must act, as well as what his powers are … He has learned his own paces, or, at any rate, is in a fair way to learn them; has found the true nature of the 'going' he must look for in the world; over what sorts of roads he must expect to make his running, and at what expenditure of effort; whither his goal lies, and what cheer he may expect by the way. It is a process of disillusionment, but it disheartens no soundly made man."[255]

Wilson believed the disappointment that woke a man up from illusions about himself could come at any time in his life. But the ones Wilson picked to illustrate the most probable times that a man would "come to himself" marked the turning points in his own life. The scales should fall off a man's eyes when he graduated from college, went off to the big city to make his way, or married the love of his life. These events showed a man the difference between dreaming about achievement and accepting the reality of his situation. Whether he understood his

---

[254] Axson, *Brother Woodrow*, 88-89.

[255] Woodrow Wilson, "When a Man Comes to Himself, November 1, 1899," *PWW*, X1, 263-264.

place in life all at once, or slowly came to see the path he must take, the result was always the same. A day would arrive when a man knew who he was and what his duty in the world must be. While the details of the duty might be different from man to man, the essence of it was identical. Men were called to love and serve one another in the same way that Jesus Christ had loved and served the world. As Wilson concluded the deepest reflection he had ever written on life, he wrote openly about religion in a way he had not done since the summer before he entered Princeton. His faith in Christ was now greater than the commitment he had made in his boyhood and much grander than the beautiful sermons he heard on Sunday mornings. It was a call to service that made all the actions of a man's life meaningful if they were done for the good of others.[256]

As Wilson reflected on disillusionment in his own life, he felt greater sympathy for others in the world who had also known disappointment. During the 1900 race for the White House, he listened more carefully to William Jennings Bryan, the Democratic nominee for president. Bryan came to a rally on the Princeton campus knowing full well that most of the students were against him. Wilson was impressed at the calm and dignified way the candidate spoke to the crowd. Bryan knew that most of the students and their fathers did not support him. Still he challenged them to open their eyes and look at the simple truth that "the government of the United States had slipped away from the masses of the people and come into the hands of a privileged few, and that this was bad for the country." Although Wilson still disagreed with many of the specifics of Bryan's reform program, he left the rally respecting him as "a sincere man with a fundamental conviction." Wilson may have been humbled by the fact that Bryan's sentiments were the same ones that had driven him from the dreams of a political career. As a young lawyer living in Atlanta, he had also come to the conclusion that politics in modern America was only for the wealthy.[257]

As Wilson at last came to himself in his forties, he decided that his main duty in life was to write his long delayed *The Principles of Politics*. He made what he thought was his last foray into politics in the summer of 1901 when he met with Vice President Teddy Roosevelt at his home at Oyster Bay on Long Island. Roosevelt asked for Wilson's help in organizing young men on college campuses throughout the country to work for reform. However, these plans were abandoned in September when McKinley was assassinated and Roosevelt became president. Back at Princeton, Wilson concluded that he would never be able to complete his comparative study of the politics of the world if he continued teaching. In the

---

[256] Ibid., *PWW*, 264-273.
[257] Axson, *Brother Woodrow*, 73-75.

spring of 1902, he waited to learn if his request for a leave of absence, which he had made a year and a half ago, would finally be granted. He planned to travel west with Ellen so she could see the Rockies and then head with her to Europe where he would complete the research on the book he believed would be his masterpiece.[258]

Certain he at last understood and accepted his place in life, Wilson was stunned when the Board of Trustees ignored his request for a leave of absence and asked him instead to become president of the university. The trustees had become increasingly disappointed with President Patton since he was not moving fast enough to modernize the institution. Wilson's closest friends on the board, Cleveland Dodge and Cyrus McCormick, were convinced that the professor who was winning national attention for his ideas and writings would be the perfect man to turn Princeton around and make it the country's leading institution of higher learning in the new 20th century. While Wilson had turned down several offers to lead other top colleges, including the University of Virginia, he accepted the offer from his alma mater on June 9, 1902, a day he and his family would always remember. Before Wilson left Library Place with his wife to make a speech on the steps of Nassau Hall to a crowd of cheering students, he went up to the bedroom where his ailing father now lived to tell him the news. After he and Ellen had left for the festivities on campus, an excited Joseph Wilson rose from his bed, paced back and forth, and shouted for his three granddaughters to come

---

[258] Wilson had made frequent notes to himself during his trip to Europe with Stockton Axson outlining *The Philosophy of Politics.* A good example of this process is his "Memoranda, P[hilosophy]. o[f]. P[olitics]., September 10, 1899," *PWW*, XI, 239; he and his family nicknamed the proposed work "P.o.P.;" Woodrow Wilson, "Letter to Theodore Roosevelt, July 28, 1901, *PWW*, XII, 172; Woodrow Wilson, "To the President and Board of Trustees of Princeton University, October 19, 1900," *PWW*, XII, 27-28.

see him immediately. "Never forget what I tell you," he said as they rushed into the room, "Your father is the greatest man I have ever known." Fifteen-year old Margaret answered, "Oh, we know that, Grandfather." The old man frowned and said, "You're too young to know. *I* know what I'm talking about. This is only the beginning of a great career."[259]

[259] McAdoo, *The Priceless Gift*, 225.

Chapter 6

The Voice of Democracy

We are not put into this world to sit still and know; we are put into it to act.
Woodrow Wilson[260]

As Woodrow Wilson headed with the rest of his nation into the 20th century, great changes were underway in his own character. He was now in his middle forties and was certain that he had at last "come to himself." He felt himself reborn as he said goodbye at last to his childhood dreams of leading men into a better future. As Wilson grew in understanding of himself, he also came to know his country in a way he had never understood it before. Instead of comparing his nation to Great Britain and finding it wanting, he now saw the United States as a vibrant democracy. The eyes of the world were on this young country as the place where people were governed most fairly. Still as the scales seemed to fall from his eyes, he was not totally uncritical of his nation. He now worried that this precious democracy could crumble in the face of growing wealth if it was concentrated in the hands of just a few. He hoped he could write a great work of political theory that showed the wonder of America as it was and as it must be preserved. But at the very moment that he dedicated his life to this purpose, the world came looking for him not as a scholar, but as a leader – first of a university, then of a state, and finally of the nation he had come to admire so much.

After Wilson had been named the president of Princeton University, hundreds of letters of congratulation poured into the family home at Library Place.

---

[260] Woodrow Wilson, "Inaugural Address as President of Princeton October 25, 1902, *PPWW*, II, 443-461.

Relatives, former students, old friends, members of the Class of 79, and even acquaintances were overjoyed that Wilson had been recognized with this high honor. President Theodore Roosevelt himself penned a short note to Wilson saying that he was delighted at Princeton's choice. "As an American interested in that kind of productive scholarship which leads to statesmanship," he wrote, "I hail your election as President of Princeton."[261] But of all the letters that flooded the Wilson home in the early summer of 1902, the most touching came from Hattie Woodrow. She was now living with her husband Edward Welles in Denver, Colorado. She told her cousin how her husband read the story of President Patton's resignation aloud to her from the local newspaper. Before he could finish the story, Hattie said, "Cousin Woodrow will fill that place some day, but he's too young for it yet." Like everyone else, she was thrilled when her husband read further that Wilson "had actually been *made* President." She was also happy that her uncle Joseph Wilson was still alive to see his son's "ability recognized and rewarded." She knew that Woodrow and Ellen were thinking of coming to Denver, and she told them to consider her house their headquarters.[262]

Wilson thanked his cousin for the generous offer of her home, but said that now he and his wife would not be able to come to Colorado. As much as he wanted Ellen to see the magnificence of the western country, it would simply not be possible. He told Hattie that he was truly surprised that this great honor had come to him. Wilson confessed that while he was excited about the appointment, both he and his wife were saddened at the thought of leaving the beautiful home they had built together. Now they would have to live in a mansion called the Prospect set aside for Princeton's president. Here their much cherished privacy would be gone and they would become "public personages." Still he hoped that he would feel the same delight so many others now felt for him once he took up his duties as the president of the college. "Dear father is quite feeble," he added, "but in good spirits and it is a great blessing to have him with us." He then closed his letter to the first love of his life by signing "Your affectionate cousin, Woodrow."[263]

Ellen Wilson experienced many of the same mixed emotions that her husband felt about his appointment as president of Princeton. In part, she was ecstatic that Wilson's talents had at last been recognized by his peers. She was well aware of campus politics and knew that the university's board of trustees rarely agreed on anything. So she was impressed that the board had voted for her husband

---

[261] Theodore Roosevelt, "Letter to Woodrow Wilson, June 23, 1902," *PWW*, XII, 454.

[262] Harriet Woodrow Welles, "Letter to Woodrow Wilson, June 12, 1902," *PWW*, XII, 417-418.

[263] Woodrow Wilson, "Letter to Harriet Woodrow Welles, June 27, 1902," *PWW*, XII, 462.

unanimously on the first ballot. As congratulations poured in from faculty, students, and townspeople alike, she wrote to her cousin Florence Hoyt that the "scenes were indescribable." She thought it especially wonderful that Wilson had received the presidency as a gift and not through any effort on his part. Surely this proved that the appointment was an "act of Providence." Still it frightened her to see how much everyone seemed to love and respect her husband. She knew this meant they would expect much from him in return. Ellen was also concerned that Wilson's life as a man of letters had probably come to an end. But there was no turning back for it was as if her beloved Woodrow was being swept along in a great wave that was meant to take Princeton into the future. She must ride the tide with him, leave the beautiful home they once shared, and move into the Prospect where she would entertain the many important people who were coming into his life. Heartbroken as Ellen Wilson might be about this, she was resolved to fulfill all of her new duties to the best of her ability.[264]

As president-elect Woodrow Wilson spent the summer of 1902 vacationing throughout New England and writing his inaugural address, his wife went to work turning the rambling mansion with more than twenty rooms into a home for her family. She found the place especially gloomy and was determined to fill it with light and color. Her letters to her husband kept him posted on the many aspects of remodeling the Prospect. By the end of August, she could write excitedly that all the repairs were underway:

> "Plumbing, heating, lighting, painting, papering, carpets, shades, bedding, hangings, upholstering, refinishing are all settled in *detail* and contracted for and everything begun and I can rather rest on my oars ... If you could see me you would certainly not be anxious for me, for I have never felt better in my life."[265]

The home was ready for the Wilsons to move into it in September. Ellen had made sure that her husband's study was one of the most beautiful rooms in the Prospect. It was in the front of the house and looked out onto the tree-lined lawn. The walls were covered with bookshelves and the crayon drawings of Wilson's heroes that Ellen had made for him. She also carefully placed Woodrow's roll top desk so it received the best light in the room. Ellen decorated the entrance hall with a bust of George Washington that Wilson's Princeton classmates had presented to him along with copies of Apollo Belvedere, the Marble Faun, and Winged Victory. Color was everywhere from the rose carpet that warmed the

[264] Ellen Wilson, "Letter to Florence Stevens Hoyt, June 28, 1902," *PWW*, XII, 463-464.
[265] Ellen Wilson, "Letter to Woodrow Wilson, August 25, 1902," *PWW*, XIV, 106-108.

marble floor of the foyer to the bright new Tiffany stained glass in the window at the top of the main staircase. Ellen Wilson also carved out one room in a quiet corner of the house just for her own family. Filling it with chairs and tables from Library Place, she lined it with her own paintings.[266]

In his new study, Woodrow Wilson worked hard on the speech he would give at his inauguration in late October. His emotions ran deep as he tried to find the words that would capture all that he felt about this momentous event in his life. In part, he was overwhelmed with gratitude for the many blessings he had already received. He had thought deeply about them as he traveled in the previous summer. Looking back on his life, he was overwhelmed at how much he was loved, especially by his wife Ellen.

> "I often marvel at the circumstances of my life, there has been so much sweetness and unmarred good fortune in it, so much love and deep content, so much quiet delight. I thank God from the bottom of my heart! I have been so trusted and loved and honoured. It is marvellous. What deep ingratitude it would be should I repine or fret at anything. And you, my darling, are the centre of it all, – all the greatest delights, all the deepest content, centre in you … "[267]

Wilson was also excited that he was now seen as one of the nation's leading educators and that his ideas on the value of a college education would be taken seriously both at Princeton and well beyond its campus. "I feel like a Prime Minister getting ready to address his constituents," he had confessed to Ellen just weeks after he had been appointed president of Princeton. Wilson was equally amazed that for the first time in his professional career he was in charge of planning for the future. From Massachusetts in August, he had written home to his wife, "I think a good deal about college affairs these quiet hours … The right to plan is so novel … it is a pleasure to think out the work that is to be done."[268]

Even as he struggled to write at least 650 words a day on his inaugural address, Wilson also contended with the growing frustration he felt over college education in the modern world, especially the one that young men were receiving at Princeton in the first decade of the 20th century. When Wilson had come to Princeton a generation before, he did so with the intent of mastering classical studies as best he could so that he could go back out into the world to serve others in some capacity. While he had come to support modernizing the college

---

[266] McAdoo, *The Priceless Gift*, 228-230.

[267] Woodrow Wilson, "Letter to Ellen Wilson, July 20, 1902," *PWW*, XIV, 29.

[268] Woodrow Wilson, "Letters to Ellen Wilson, July 19 and August 6, 1902," *PWW*, XIV, 26-27, 56-57.

curriculum, he still believed that a college education must prepare young people to serve others, especially their fellow citizens. In fact, America's colleges were vital in ensuring that the nation's democracy continued and grew even stronger. Colleges must act as a kind of leveler where young men from many different backgrounds came together as equals. Once every student, rich or poor, received the best training possible, each graduate must head back into the nation's stream of life dedicated to the principle of using their talents in service to others. In this way, colleges and universities would remain engines of democracy rather than servants of privilege.

Upon accepting his new position, Wilson had told Princeton's board of trustees that he had no intention of being the president of a country club. Nevertheless, this was exactly what he feared Princeton was becoming. In his twelve years as a professor at the college, he had watched as more and more sons of wealthy men had arrived on campus to pursue their degrees as a mere lark before they worked in business or inherited their family fortunes. If a student had enough money and his family had the right influence, he could barely attend class, fail most of his exams, and still graduate at the end of his senior year with a diploma from Princeton. Wilson was committed to putting an end to the growing influence that money and power had on the campus. He was determined to do this even though he knew one of his main duties as president would be raising money for the college through donations from the most successful alumni and the wealthiest Americans.[269]

The transformation of Princeton from a college open to the best young minds in the nation to a place of privilege for the sons of the wealthiest Americans was something that Wilson's brother-in-law Stockton Axson also saw clearly. He was a frequent visitor to his sister's family at both Library Place and Prospect, and would join the faculty just four years after Wilson became Princeton's president. Axson remembered that Princeton seemed "as simple as a village schoolhouse in the Middle West" when he first visited it in the early 1890s. The students were all considered equals with one another, and the wealthiest students did their best to blend in with the other boys. Nothing in their dress or manners could distinguish them from the poorer students. "I am satisfied that in 1890," Axson remembered, "it would have been impossible from any outward show to have known whether the Princeton student was the son of a millionaire or the son of a blacksmith."[270]

---

[269] Daniels, *Woodrow Wilson*, 76-83; Woodrow Wilson, "Letter to Ellen Wilson, July 19, 1902," *PWW*, XIV, 26-27; Hale, *Woodrow Wilson*, 109-111; Woodrow Wilson, "Letter to Ellen Wilson, August 6, 1902," *PWW*, XIV, 56-57.

[270] Axson, *Brother Woodrow*, 114.

But things had changed dramatically in the next two decades. Wealthy alumni moved to Princeton and built their mansions near the campus. They brought smart carriages and the best horses, and later their automobiles, with them, and even dressed in formal clothes for dinner. Axson mused wryly that Princeton had become a fashionable superb of New York City by the first decade of the 20th century. The change affected the students, too, with the wealthiest ones following the habits of their parents. He often recalled an incident that happened early in his teaching career at Princeton that showed the subtle changes occurring on the campus. Students often asked him to come to their rooms at night to give informal lectures. This had long been a common practice among the boys at Princeton. Professor Axson did this for about a year, always wearing the same clothes he had worn throughout the day. But one rainy night when he arrived in the same rumpled clothes that he had been in since the morning, he was surprised to see some of the boys dressed in evening wear. From then on, everyone had to dress up in tuxedoes when attending these lectures. As small a matter as this might seem in itself, Axson saw it as the subtle undermining of the democratic spirit at Princeton.[271]

Wilson agreed with his brother-in-law that Princeton was changing, but he went even further in his analysis and worried that education at the college level was being undermined at the very moment that America most needed leaders who understood its destiny. He was certain that the United States was at a great crossroads in history. As the world's largest and truest democracy, it was about to play a leading role in the future of mankind. Wilson had only come to understand and appreciate America's place on the world stage in the dozen years that he had worked as a professor of politics and law at Princeton. In fact, it had taken him more than 30 years to achieve this greater appreciation of his nation. Though born and raised in the South, he could now look back at the Civil War and the Reconstruction as a time when a national identity had at last been forged. This new identity took shape just as the frontier finally closed and the American people stepped off the western edge of their country and headed out onto the oceans of the world.

For Wilson, it was imperative that the American people understood how history had shaped them up to this momentous time and how from this point forward their ideals could shape the world. While the most powerful countries in Europe still lived in the illusion of the old order where nations were set against nations, the United States must boldly sail forward and make democracy the order of the day. The American nation could become the leader of a new and better

[271] Ibid., 112-115.

world where nations lived together as neighbors rather than as enemies. In an essay he was writing at the same time that he was preparing for his inauguration as Princeton's president, Wilson clearly stated his vision for the country:

> "Every man knows that the world is to be changed ... nations and peoples which have stood still for centuries through are to be quickened, and make part of the universal world of commerce and ideas ... it is our duty ... to moderate the process in the interests of liberty."[272]

Americans must never fear, he wrote later that same year in an article for the *Atlantic Monthly*, that they were not up to the task. He believed that the United States had become the leader of the world at a time when people everywhere craved democracy. While he again stated that the nation owed much to England, he now argued that America had surpassed the mother country in the practice of democracy and that its greatest ideals were more universally applicable than those of Great Britain. It was the duty of America's leaders to take these principles – a love of liberty joined to a keen sense of self-discipline, a rule of law that brought justice to the lowly and the great alike, and a tradition of revolution that built up rather than tore down society – to all mankind in order to "serve, not to subdue, the world."[273]

As Wilson's understanding of the destiny of his own nation deepened, he came to see a close tie between democratic practices and the education provided by colleges and universities. He meditated on the relationship between these two realities in the months before his inauguration, and was soon convinced that higher education in America existed primarily to prepare leaders who would serve the nation's ideals and so the future of the world. Once he took the helm of Princeton, Wilson was determined to be the captain of one of America's greatest democratic principles – protecting opportunity for all the students who entered his university against the creeping power of privilege. He would immediately toughen academic standards so that every young person, rich or poor, was treated in exactly the same way, and thus he would end the practice of allowing wealthy students to graduate because they had the right "pull." But since he was not the kind of leader who believed in radical, immediate, and possibly destructive

---

[272] Woodrow Wilson, "The Reconstruction of the Southern States, January 1901," *PPWW*, I, 368-395.

[273] Woodrow Wilson, "The Ideals of America, December 1902," *PPWW*, I, 416-442.

reform, he would move slowly toward the implementation of even more important changes that would ensure the vitality of democracy on the Princeton campus.[274]

October 25, 1902, the date long set aside for Woodrow Wilson's inauguration, finally dawned as a "perfect autumn day" with much celebration and even frivolity on campus. The excited students and faculty were joined by alumni from all over the country. Most notable was former President Grover Cleveland who marched at the front of the inauguration day parade dressed in cap and gown alongside Governor Murphy of New Jersey. Mark Twain, J. Pierpont Morgan, and Robert Lincoln were among the distinguished guests. Mrs. Wilson and her three daughters, Margaret, Jessie, and Nellie, now ages 16, 15, and 13, were there, too. They beamed with pride, alongside Reverend Joseph Ruggles Wilson, and were excited to be wearing store-bought dresses for the first time in their lives. Representatives came from colleges all over the county to participate in the ceremonies including Booker T. Washington from the Tuskegee Institute. One of Ellen's "unreconstructed" aunts was indignant that an ex-slave would be allowed to speak at the dinner after the inauguration festivities, but Wilson would not send him away once he had been invited. He even later told his family that Washington had given the best speech during the entire week, even better than his own inaugural address.[275]

While many of the themes in Wilson's speech were identical to those in his sesquicentennial address, he wove them together with a greater emphasis on democracy than ever before. "In planning for Princeton," he proclaimed in his opening remarks, "we are planning for the country." As universities laid their plans for the future, they must always remember that they served a country made great by the common people. "American universities serve a free nation whose progress, whose power, whose prosperity, whose happiness, whose integrity," he explained, "depend upon individual initiative and the sound sense and equipment of the rank and file." College professors and the young men they taught must never see themselves as superior to the less well educated people in their own country. If they did, then their university must consider itself a failure. Instead all scholars and students must be made to realize that they served the creative power of the American people.

One need only look at Princeton's past to understand this. More than a century before, the college mainly turned out ministers like Reverend John Witherspoon who led their flocks and their communities. Later Princeton educated men like James Madison who gave their lives to establish the American

---

[274] Hale, *Woodrow Wilson*, 112-114.

[275] Baker, *Life and Letters*, II, 138-141.

government. Now Princeton must train young men not just in the ministry or politics, but in medicine, the law, and new fields like engineering and the mechanical arts. Even in this more specialized atmosphere, students must never forget that they were being trained in careers that would serve their nation. Students would grasp this broader perspective on the purpose of their education by taking courses in the liberal arts like philosophy, history, and literature. Here they would gain a vision of the world, their place in it, and how they were called to work on behalf of the American people. Their minds would become elastic and their outlooks would grow broader and deeper. Wilson explained:

> "We seek in our general education, not universal knowledge, but the opening up of the mind to a catholic appreciation of the best achievements of men and the best processes of thought since days of thought set it."

By the time a student graduated from Princeton, the inner man would have been shaped through liberal learning, while the outer man would have perfected his talents in a specific modern discipline. America in turn would be a better place as each successive generation of college graduates would leave the academy to serve the nation, and because of the position in which the country now found itself, the world. He concluded:

> "A new age is before us, in which, it would seem, we must lead the world. No doubt we shall set it an example unprecedented not only in the magnitude and telling perfection of our industries and arts but also in the splendid scale and studied details of our university establishments."[276]

While Wilson presented his vision for Princeton in broad strokes at his inauguration, he was already thinking of specific ways to implement it. He hoped to transform the university into a place where faculty and students worked side by side with one another. He planned to organize the university into colleges and could already see where he would house them. These buildings would not be ivory towers, but living places where professors and students met and exchanged ideas that would benefit their nation and the world beyond. In this exciting new atmosphere, students would no longer loaf or coast on the reputations of their parents. Instead they would be inspired to work hard. They would embrace the new curriculum that would cut the last ties to the old classical studies, strengthen core training in the liberal arts, and create new majors in the best modern fields.

Wilson believed Princeton must make these changes since the world grew more complex each day and the methods of the past would never be able to train young men to meet its challenges. He was also determined to raise the money necessary to accomplish these reforms and estimated the cost to be in the millions of dollars.[277]

Wilson's first report to the Board of Trustees clearly outlined just how much his plans for bringing Princeton into the modern world would cost. While he knew the university currently had resources totaling less than $4,000,000, he projected that nearly three times that much would have to be raised in the next few years to implement the many improvements he would soon recommend. Down the road, he would need $1,000,000 for a school of science, close to $3,000,000 for new buildings and new faculty, and over $2,000,000 for a tutorial system that he was carefully planning. Beyond this beginning sum, Wilson told the board members that there must be an immediate outlay of nearly $7,000,000 to build a graduate school, a college of jurisprudence, an electrical engineering school, and a museum of natural science. Many men on the board were stunned at Wilson's boldness, but he had key allies like his close friends Cleveland Dodge and Cyrus McCormick who went to work raising the funds to implement their new president's vision almost without question.[278]

More like an American president issuing executive orders than a college president shaping policy, Wilson next issued a series of directives to tighten discipline on the campus. While many of his new policies appeared harsh, the president claimed that he did them in a spirit of fairness. Every student would be treated the same way and no one would ever again get special privileges. For example, if a student failed the entrance exam, he could not enroll in the college, no matter how much his wealthy father might complain to Board of Trustees or even to the president of the college himself. Once a student was enrolled, he must attend class, do his required assignments, and pass his exams. If he was caught cheating or doing anything else dishonorable, then he would be brought up before the Discipline Committee. Seniors were asked to serve on a council that oversaw the hearings of the committee. Students could be suspended or even expelled for bad behavior that ran the gamut from cheating on exams to holding drunken parties on campus. Once the mother of a student who had been expelled for

---

[276] Woodrow Wilson, "Princeton for the Nation's Service: Inaugural Address as President of Princeton University, October 25, 1902," *PPWW*, I, 443-461.

[277] Woodrow Wilson, "Princeton Ideals: Delivered at Princeton Dinner at the Waldorf-Astoria, December 13, 1902," *PPWW*, I, 462-473.

[278] Woodrow Wilson, "President's Report to the Board of Trustees, October 21, 1902," *PWW*, XIV, 150-161.

cheating came to the president's office, begging for clemency and saying she was about to have an operation and feared she might die if her son was so punished. Wilson refused to overturn the expulsion and said, "You force me to say a hard thing, but, if I had to choose between your life or my life or anybody's life and the good of this college, I would choose the good of the college." Ellen Wilson remembered that her husband returned home that afternoon deathly pale and unable to eat his lunch.[279]

While many of the these directives were meant to modernize the college, there was one area where President Wilson kept an ancient tradition alive. He refused to abandon the requirement that students attend compulsory religious services in the college chapel each morning. He saw Christianity's call to service as a golden thread coming out of Princeton's past and extending into its present. The discipline of praying in the chapel would warm the heart of every student and thus strengthen him in the performance of his daily duties. If a boy learned to discipline himself by this simple service to God, then surely he would carry this same devotion with him when he graduated from Princeton and went out into the world to serve his fellow man. Wilson still believed something about faith that he had learned in his own childhood. Young people learned more about Christianity in the presence of those who practiced it than in a catechism class. The young men who came to the Princeton chapel every morning from early fall to late spring would deepen their faith through the very atmosphere of the place. They would become more deeply Christian by the same kind of osmosis that planted faith in his own heart as he grew up in the manses of his parents.[280]

While President Wilson could make many changes at Princeton related to student life on his own, he needed to rely on the support of the faculty to make more significant changes to the curriculum. He found an important friend and ally in Henry Fine, Princeton's dean and a professor of mathematics. Dean Fine served on the important Committee on Course of Study which was charged with making recommendations on improving the curriculum. Working closely with President Wilson who chaired the committee, Dean Fine and the other members of the committee took nearly a year and a half to make their recommendations. Wilson often said that the long process was like "reconstructing a state." He was excited to spend whole days discussing ways to reorganize the college into departments along with planning degree programs that were meaningful paths of study for the students. The committee also decided that while freshmen and sophomores should

---

[279] Baker, *Life and Letters*, II, 150-152.

[280] Ibid., 152-153; Woodrow Wilson, "The Young People and the Church, October 13, 1904," *PPWW*, I, 474-486.

be required to take certain courses, juniors and seniors should take electives in their primary areas of study. He found it "all most interesting, a bit exciting, and most encouraging" to create something so meaningful rather than merely rewriting constitutions for debating societies. Even though he was so busy, he tried to keep a diary of all the work he was doing on reshaping Princeton's curriculum. He kept his wife Ellen, who was traveling in Italy with Jessie, cousin Mary Hoyt, and two family friends, informed of every detail of the process. "Today our committee on the Course of Study completed its labours and next week our report, with which we are all really delighted, … will be laid before the Faculty," he wrote to Ellen in April.[281]

Ellen's trip to Europe was a gift from her husband. Wilson's latest book, *A Short History of the American People*, had been published just before he was inaugurated as the president of Princeton. Since the royalties were substantial, he was able to afford to send his family to Rome, Assisi, Florence, and Venice. Ellen could now wander through museums, churches, and galleries in Italy, and then write home to Wilson that "every day has been an epoch in my life." In Rome, she was awestruck by Michelangelo and found Fra Angelico "adorable," but she was most amazed by Raphael. Nothing could have prepared her for the wonder of "The School of Athens" in the Sistine Chapel. She could hardly tear herself away from "all those glorious, majestic, god-like figures who are holding high converse together." Later in Florence, she visited the Uffizi, the Pitti, and the Bella Arti Galleries, and told Wilson:

> "I am left gasping – overwhelmed – almost dismayed at the feast spread before me. Everywhere I turn there is some masterpiece that I have longed to see all my life, and I run from one to another and am so overcome with rapture and excitement that I end by holding both hands in a sort of despair … "[282]

For all the joy in their correspondence, there was an underlying current of dread on the part of both Ellen and Woodrow Wilson in the letters they sent across the sea to each other in the spring of 1904. It was almost as if they sensed that the happiness they had known for so long could not last forever. Sadness had already come into their lives just the year before in January 1903 when Joseph Wilson died in Princeton. Reverend Wilson had arteriosclerosis and suffered an attack of angina the day after Wilson's inauguration. He took to his bed in the

---

[281] Baker, *Life and Letters*, II, 157-159; Woodrow Wilson, "Letter to Ellen Wilson, April 14, 1904," *PWW*, XV, 246-247.

room Ellen had prepared for him in the Prospect and never rose from it again. As he lay dying, with all of his family at his side, his last words were, "My dear, dear son."[283] Wilson buried his "life-long friend and companion" next to his mother in Columbia, South Carolina, the town where his parents had known their happiest days. Now both Ellen and Woodrow were alone in the world with no parents to comfort or support them. They seemed to know in some quiet place in their hearts that now death would stalk them and their family. "No generation ahead of me now!" he wrote to his friend Edith Gittings Reid, "I am in the firing line." Each new illness of the Wilson's daughters became especially frightening. Jessie came down with diphtheria when visiting Assisi, while Margaret and Nellie both contracted the measles. Their parents wrote anxious letters back and forth to each other promising that they would never be separated from one another by an ocean again. As he worried about his family, both at home in Princeton and across the sea in Italy, Wilson tried to find the words to tell his wife how much she meant to him.

> "I want … to make you realize – every moment of your journey – how my thoughts hover over you, night and day, with a tenderness, a pride, a joy, and yet a longing, which I have spent twenty years in the vain attempt to put into words and which, God willing, I shall spend all my life trying to put into acts of love and devotion ..."[284]

Just as Woodrow and Ellen Wilson had feared, the next few years of their lives were bittersweet. In his career as president of Princeton, Wilson still experienced the sweetness of continued success. He moved from enthusiastic approval for the new curriculum to even greater support for a project that he called the preceptorial system. He had recently become concerned that students at Princeton spent more time outside of the classroom than in it. While in class, their learning seemed to have been reduced to little more than passively listening to lectures and mindlessly giving back the information on tests. Wilson remembered the excitement of his own college days when he would talk with his friends for long hours into the night at Mrs. Wright's boarding house or at the Alligator Club. For Wilson, more learning went on in these informal sessions than in the classroom. In order to recapture what he had known, and make learning an

---

[282] Ellen Wilson, "Letters to Woodrow Wilson, April 15 and May 25, 1904," *PWW*, XV, 250-251, 348-350.

[283] Axson, *Brother Woodrow*, 24-26.

[284] Woodrow Wilson, "Letter to Edith Gittings Reid, February 3, 1903," *PWW*, XIV, 347-348; Woodrow Wilson, "Letter to Ellen Wilson, May 27, 1904," *PWW*, XV, 350-351.

exciting experience for every student who came to Princeton, Wilson planned to hire 50 "preceptors" or tutors who would live among and work with the students. They would guide them in discussions and debates held outside of the classroom, and they would also help them improve their writing.[285]

Wilson proposed the preceptorial system to the faculty early in the fall semester of 1904. He also went on the road talking to alumni throughout the country to help them understand the new system. He needed both their moral support and donations from them totaling at least $2,250,000. His explanation to the Princeton alumni, along with his pitch to the faculty and Board of Trustees, emphasized the fact that this was not a new idea. Professors had complained for some time that they were losing touch with their students. Classes held in lecture halls had been broken up into smaller sections. Wilson explained that this effort to place students in smaller classes was not working since the young men were assigned alphabetically or on the basis of their grades. "Now it so happens," Wilson was fond of saying, "that God has not classified men's abilities either alphabetically or according to grades." If a young person was engaged in true inquiry with a talented and caring preceptor, then he would strengthen his own talents and also develop a lifelong love of learning. In the spring of 1905, the Board of Trustees unanimously approved the preceptorial system, and President Wilson, Dean West, and several other professors went to work scouring the country for just the right young scholars to get the new program off the ground. While there was some grumbling among parents who feared their boys would have to work too hard, the preceptorial system was set to go into effect in the fall of 1905.[286]

Yet even as he prepared for his greatest success at Princeton to date, Wilson's life was soon touched by a serious illness and then a tragic death. Just as he was laying the final plans for the tutorial system, his own health broke down. He entered New York's Presbyterian Hospital in the winter of 1905 where he was operated on for hemorrhoids and a hernia. While recuperating, he developed phlebitis in his right leg. When he was finally back on his feet, Wilson and his family suffered the greatest shock they had ever known. In April, Ellen's brother Eddie, his wife, and one-year old son were drowned while they were trying to cross a river in Georgia. Axson and his family were in a carriage on a ferry when the boat hit a bridge. Runway horses swept Eddie, his wife, and his child into the current. He pulled his family out of the waves and had almost made it to shore when he lost all strength and went under with his wife and baby.

---

[285] Hale, *Woodrow Wilson*, 112-138.

[286] Baker, *Life and Letters*, II, 143-169.

Wilson had raised Eddie as his own son and was devastated at his lost. Axson had lived with the Wilsons from the time he was a little boy until he graduated from Princeton in 1897. Then he had gone off to Boston where he studied engineering at the Massachusetts Institute of Technology and met his wife, a violinist. They had just moved to Georgia where Eddie had a job with a mining company. Wilson's three daughters were especially heartbroken at the news of his death for they had known Eddie more as a brother than as an uncle. Wilson tried to comfort them by saying he would always keep the memory of the beautiful boy he had helped to raise ever before him when he thought of Edward Axson. However, Wilson could not help Ellen who withdrew into her own silent and private grief. For a time, she even ignored her children and their many troubles. They knew they could not come to her with any of their joys or concerns. She spent her days compulsively cleaning the house over and over again. Finally, remembering how much she had suffered from her father's collapse after her mother's death, she came out of her grief on her own, much to the relief of her family. She also followed her husband's advice and took up painting again, now of landscapes rather than portraits, with the help of local artists who lived in a colony near the family's summer retreat in Old Lyme, Connecticut.[287]

But even with Ellen's recovery, the effects of the tragic loss of Eddie Axson rippled across Wilson's family, ruining their health and spirits. Margaret Wilson, who so resembled her father in temperament and appearance, went to Italy in the fall of 1905 where she contracted malaria and later suffered a nervous collapse. Stockton Axson fell into a deep depression that led to a complete nervous breakdown. He spent much of 1905 in a mental hospital in Philadelphia. A year after the death of his brother-in-law, Wilson still cried at the mention of Eddie's name, and on the morning of May 28, 1906, he awoke to find that he could not see out of his left eye. While he had probably suffered a serious stroke, his doctor diagnosed the problem as a ruptured blood vessel in his eye. He ordered immediate bed rest and even recommended that Wilson give up some of his many responsibilities. Mrs. Wilson intervened and insisted her husband would recover completely if he rested over the summer. She packed him off for a three-month stay in Scotland and England. He returned healthy and refreshed, although he never fully recovered the sight in his left eye. Once he was home, Ellen Wilson encouraged her husband to walk more and even to play golf. She also made him

[287] Axson, *Brother Woodrow*, ix-x, 103; McAdoo, *The Priceless Gift*, 240-242.

promise that he would vacation on his own every winter in a warm place like Florida or Bermuda.[288]

Wilson came back from his trip to the British Isles, where he had spent much of his time visiting Andrew Carnegie at his castle in Scotland, ready to move on to the greatest reform that he had yet planned for Princeton. This reform came out of his deep concern that the older students at his university were bent on forming themselves into an elite class. The junior and seniors lived in "eating clubs" which had become ever more elaborate. Wilson had himself been a member of the Alligators, but it was truly an "eating club" where the boys gathered for meals and friendly discussions as if they were in their own boarding house. As sons of wealthy Americans arrived at Princeton throughout the 1890s with their cars and evening clothes in tow, the clubs had become quite luxurious. For Wilson, these places with their "dining rooms and kitchens and servant quarters – common rooms, libraries, billiard rooms, smoking rooms, private dining rooms for parties, and sleeping rooms for visitors" were a disgrace. Freshmen and sophomores, who were not allowed into the clubs, spent much of their time laying plans to get into the most prestigious clubs. The process had become so competitive that students who failed to get into the "right" clubs felt themselves failures. Some even left the college before finishing their degrees.[289]

With the beauty of Oxford and Cambridge in mind from his many travels to England, President Wilson drafted a plan for students to live in "quads." In an attempt to end the growing spirit of elitism and integrate students "pupil to pupil," Wilson proposed building residential colleges for each of the four classes. Instead of the upperclassmen housed in private clubs with the freshmen and sophomores fending for themselves in boarding houses, every class would live in its own college where the students eat and study with one another. The colleges would be built on perpendicular lines – north, south, east, and west – with all classes and all students facing each other. Every college would have a master and three resident preceptors who would watch over the students and encourage them to mingle with one another. Students would also take an active part in governing their colleges by writing the rules for life in them.

Wilson formally presented the plan to the Board of Trustees in June of 1907. In his report, he stated the reasons for the quad system with the clarity of a legal brief. He emphasized the luxury of the clubs which had become a scandal and the

---

[288] Mulder, *Woodrow Wilson: The Years of Preparation*, 184; Ellen Wilson, "Letter to Mary Hoyt, June 12, 1906," *PWW*, XVI, 423; Ellen Wilson, "Letter to Florence Hoyt, September 27, 1906," Ibid., 430.

terrible effect that not getting into the right club had on many boys at Princeton. When he personally addressed the board on the matter, he sounded like a defense attorney speaking on behalf of his client, the average boy who came to Princeton with much talent but little money or influence. The deadening spirit of privilege must decrease while democratic camaraderie must increase. He closed his argument with one final piece of evidence, a memorandum he had sent to every club on campus, assuring them that he would not close the clubs immediately. Instead, he pledged to work with club officers to make the transition to the quads a smooth one and even speculated that some clubs could be fully integrated into the new system. "No one can now predict," he explained to them, "just how the new developments would come or just what shape they would take."[290]

Although Wilson won the full approval of the Board of Trustees for construction of the quads, he soon faced the wrath of many alumni, especially the wealthiest graduates who lived in the eastern United States. For his first time ever at Princeton, either as its president or its favorite professor, Wilson was condemned for his actions and his personality. Many students and even some faculty joined in calling him a dictator who ruled the campus with an iron will and a leveler who hoped to overturn the social order. Many condemned him as a "confiscator" and even a "socialist." The outcry was so great that in October 1907 the Board of Trustees asked Wilson to withdraw his request for implementing the quad system. Wilson was stunned that the board lacked the political will and the vision to see how the quad system would improve life for the majority of students at Princeton, but he relented, knowing that many alumni had threatened to withdraw their financial support from the college. He also knew that several faculty members, including his best friend Professor John Hibben, had turned against him. The shock was so great that he later said he had come to doubt the value of friendship, and swore that he would never forgive colleagues like Jack Hibben who had failed to support him in his first crisis at Princeton.[291]

Although he had lost one major battle in the war against privilege, President Wilson refused to give up the fight. In fact, he seemed to accept the defeat as a kind of self-awakening. He now understood more clearly that he may have a destiny as a leader who championed democracy against the forces of irresponsible wealth. As a former professor of political economy, he understood the purpose of

---

[289] McAdoo, *The Priceless Gift*, 241-242; Woodrow Wilson, "Letter to Ellen Wilson, September 2, 1906," *PWW*, XVI, 445-446., Hale, *Woodrow Wilson*, 126-130.

[290] Woodrow Wilson, "Report on the Social Coordination of the University, June 10, 1907," *PPWW*, I, 499-511; Woodrow Wilson, "Address to the Board of Trustees, June 10, 1907," Ibid., 511-518; Woodrow Wilson, "Memorandum Concerning Residential Quads," Ibid., 518-521.

[291] Hale, *Woodrow Wilson*, 122-137; Axson, *Brother Woodrow*, 133-134, 204-207, 206.

money in a free enterprise system as a means of exchange. But now at the helm of one of the nation's greatest universities where he must make decisions for the good of all, he came to see that Americans had developed "too strong a tendency to glorify money merely." As the United States became wealthier, the nation was in grave danger of drifting rapidly into a plutocracy. His battle to house the Princeton students in quads and so give the boys "an education along purely democratic lines" was just one small attempt to make a course correction in the dangerous drift of his nation. Although his dream of making democracy real in the beautiful colleges and walkways of his "quads" had failed, he would never back away from trying to convince even the wealthiest students that their lives and fortunes must serve the greater whole. A Princeton graduate named E. B. Seymour came to visit Wilson in the same month that his plan for the quads was defeated. He long remembered how Wilson was "still meditating on the necessity of making Princeton democratic." Seymour never forgot the talk he had with President Wilson in that long ago October and years later could still remember how Wilson described his vision for the future:

> "At Princeton, whither come many sons of millionaires, he felt we should so impress these boys with ideas of democracy and personal worth that when they became, in the ordinary course of nature, masters of their fathers' fortunes, they should so use their undoubted power as to help, not hurt, the commonwealth."[292]

This attitude gave Wilson a new sense of purpose that served him well in the next great battle at Princeton over the graduate school. Wilson had made the building of a graduate college one of his top priorities as soon as he had become Princeton's president. Four years into his presidency, a woman named Mrs. J. A. Thompson Swann left $250,000 in her will to Princeton in order to construct the graduate school. She stipulated that the building must be on the Princeton campus, and the Board of Trustees decided that it should be built near the President's house at Prospect.

Having failed to win approval for the quad system, Wilson turned his efforts to developing the graduate school. He saw the new addition as a place where his dreams for a more democratic Princeton and a less plutocratic nation could be worked out. If he worried that wealthy students were cutting themselves off from the best aspects of college life, he was even more concerned that scholars were becoming more and more disengaged from the mass of men. As their studies became more specialized, educated men were in danger of talking only to each

---

[292] The conversation between Seymour and Wilson is quoted in Hale, *Woodrow Wilson*, 137-138.

other. Scholars might truly one day live in an ivory tower where their rarified debates bore no relation to the life that the common people lived. This dangerous trend flew in the face of everything he was trying to accomplish at Princeton. For Wilson:

> "The whole Princeton idea is an organic idea, an idea of contact of mind with mind – no chasms, no divisions in life and organization – a grand brotherhood of intellectual endeavor, stimulating the younger, instructing and balancing the older man, giving the one an aspiration and the other a comprehension of what the whole undertaking is – of lifting, lifting, lifting the mind of successive generations from age to age!"[293]

With this philosophy in mind, Wilson went to work hiring the best faculty and securing up-to-date libraries and equipment for them along with the most qualified students. As he made his plans, Wilson had little idea that Professor Andrew West, the Dean of the Graduate School, disagreed with both the overarching vision and specific plans of his president. Nor did Wilson suspect that Dean West was a determined foe who was committed to taking whatever measure necessary to defeat his plans for the graduate college. As a professor of the classics, West had little sympathy with the drive to modernize the curriculum, but had not resisted Wilson on any of his reforms so far. In fact, he had been one of the professors who worked with the president and Dean Fine to hire the first preceptors. Still he did not understand the incessant cry for greater discipline in the classroom and made little demands on his own students. He was a huge man, tall and portly, who gave the impression that nothing bothered him. In reality, something did bother him and that was President Wilson and his plans for a democratic graduate school that served the needs of each successive generation. West dreamed of a graduate college set far away on the edge of the campus where scholars lived and worked like the academic aristocrats he truly believed them to be. He even wrote a pamphlet where he described every detail of the building where these noble minds would be housed, down to the kind of wood paneling that would line the libraries and the height of the bell tower that would chime for lesser mortals to hear way off in the distance.[294]

While he seemed to live in a dream world while planning his own private paradise of a graduate school, West was practical enough to understand that his version of Princeton's newest college would only win out if he could raise enough

---

[293] Wilson's comments on his vision for the graduate school are quoted in Hale, *Woodrow Wilson*, 147.

money for it. In the spring of 1909, he convinced William Procter of Cincinnati, a manufacturer whose grandfather had made a fortune in soap with his partner James Gamble, to donate $500,000 to Princeton for the graduate school. Procter demanded that Princeton must in turn raise another $500,000 and follow West's plans to place the school on the edge of the campus. After debating the issue for nearly a year, the Board of Trustees decided to put Procter's bequest on hold. They made their decision primarily because of the passionate pleas of President Wilson to turn down the offer. He disagreed wholeheartedly with West's vision of a graduate school as an ivory tower, saying the plan failed to take disciplines like the sciences into consideration. Classical scholars might enjoy long discussions in paneled drawing rooms, but scientists needed laboratories. Wilson also railed against the creation of a scholarly aristocracy that was disengaged not just from the life of Princeton, but from the life of the nation as well. Finally, he was deeply concerned that Procter's gift came with too many strings attached. It was just another sign of the creeping plutocracy that was on the brink of ruining the American democratic spirit. Wilson knew that private colleges and universities could only survive if they raised money from wealthy donors, but if these gifts came with demands to determine policies on campus, then those institutions would have lost their very souls.[295]

After his defeat with the Board of Trustees, West went to work behind the scenes to undermine Wilson's character and his authority. He first enlisted the support of Grover Cleveland who now lived in Princeton. The former president contacted Cleveland Dodge and told him the graduate school must be set up in the way that his close friend Dean West envisioned it. West then solicited as many other alumni as possible, trying to convince them that Wilson's actions were arbitrary and truly dangerous to the very survival of Princeton. After all, the President had turned down a substantial sum of money to the college from one of the nation's most successful industrialists. West also went to work on the faculty, deepening the rift in ranks that had developed over the quad struggle. To counter West, Wilson threw himself into the fight convinced that the battle at Princeton showed the invisible fault line that ran through the academy and the nation. On one side were the reactionary forces of past academic traditions who had found new allies in the wealthy benefactors that funded them. On the other side were modern scholars like Wilson who allied themselves with the best democratic traditions of the American nation. In this fight, the old romance of his childhood seemed to return. Though still battling bad health and deep sorrow in his family,

[294] Ibid., 139-146.
[295] Ibid., 140, 144-152; Baker, *Life and Letters*, II, 221-223.

there were flashes in him of the little boy who had penned the story of life as a battle between the forces of light and darkness in the *North Carolina Presbyterian* so long ago.[296]

Wilson took his case to the people, crisscrossing the country to speak with alumni groups and defend his plans for the graduate school. Usually he was buoyantly optimistic in his talks, but in Pittsburgh on April 10, 1910, he broke down and delivered a speech only a few paragraphs long. The gloves were off and he blasted every institution that served "the classes and not the masses of people." Private universities like Princeton were bowing more and more to the wealthy and neglecting their duty to the people. That was precisely why state universities, he argued, were becoming so popular and schools like Princeton were losing all esteem in the eyes of the nation. The Protestant churches were no better. "They have more regard for pew rents than for men's souls," ranted an angry Wilson. "They are depressing the level of Christian endeavor." He mentioned a speech he had recently given at a centennial celebration for Lincoln's birth. Then he had boldly stated that if Lincoln had been a modern college man, he would never have bothered serving his country. Few college men today care anymore about helping the people. "It is for this reason that I have dedicated every power in me," shouted an angry Wilson, "into a democratic regeneration." American colleges must realign themselves with the American people. To do this, they must be "reconstructed from the top down." If the crowd who was listening to him disagreed, they should take a look at the great progressive movement sweeping through politics. The American people were demanding nothing short of a moral regeneration in their parties and among their leaders. "Only those leaders who seem able to promise something of a moral advance are able to secure a following. The people are tired of pretense and I ask you, as Princeton men, to heed what is going on." He left his stunned crowd with a warning:

> "If she loses her self-possession, America will stagger like France through fields of blood before she again finds peace and prosperity under leadership of men who know her needs."[297]

In his growing frustration as president of Princeton, first over the quad struggle and then the graduate school battle, Woodrow Wilson had turned for comfort, not to his wife, but to a friend he had met in a winter trip to Bermuda. She was Mary Peck, a beautiful American woman who was separated from her

---

[296] Ibid., 224-225.

[297] Woodrow Wilson, "Speech to Pittsburgh Alumni, April 16, 1910," *PPWW*, I, 202-203.

second husband. Wilson had gotten to know Mary Peck and a whole group of friends in Bermuda when he first ventured there in 1907. Most people in this crowd were men like Mark Twain who enjoyed trading barbs with Princeton's president and playing chess with him. But there were a few interesting women who formed a set at the hotel on the island where Wilson stayed. Some were wealthy Englishwomen who spent part of every year in Bermuda. But others were wealthy women like Mary Peck, mainly American, who had left their husbands, but who were unwilling or unable to get a divorce.

Mrs. Peck was a tall woman in her mid-forties with beautiful blue eyes. She was trim and wore her hair swept up in the style of the day. She had been happily married for a short time when young to a man named Thomas Hulbert and had a son Allen Schoolcraft Hulbert by him. After her first husband died in an accident, she married Thomas Peck, a wealthy wool manufacturer from Massachusetts, but was soon desperately unhappy. Every winter she escaped from her troubled marriage to Bermuda where her beautiful face and figure along with her vibrant personality made her the leader of the fashionable crowd. She was considered quite daring in her time not only for leaving her husband, but also for lighting up one cigarette from another. Wilson met her on his first trip to the Caribbean to improve his health on the orders of his wife. But it was not until the following year, after he had lost his battle for the quads and had turned away from his closest colleague Jack Hibben forever, that he truly became enamored of the lovely and witty Mrs. Peck. He soon called her his "dearest friend" and opened up the deepest places in his heart that he had shown no one else but his wife. When he returned to Princeton, he regularly corresponded with Mary Peck, telling her the most intimate details of his life, his woes with the Princeton faculty, and his dreams for the future. He even mocked the trustees who came to dinners arranged at Prospect by his wife. The description of one such dinner in October 1908 was particularly bitter. He explained:

> "Mrs. Wilson is the only woman at the long table, and is taken into lunch by the senior trustee present, generally some old gentleman who is *very* dull to talk to and who makes the whole thing a burden to the poor lady. The slow, elderly members gather at her end of the table, held together by a certain natural affinity, while the younger and livelier ones sit at my end, - lively talk and jest and badinage as they were thirty years ago."[298]

---

[298] Mulder, *Woodrow Wilson, The Years of Preparation*, 246; Woodrow Wilson, "Letters to Ellen Wilson, January 4, 1907 and August 27, 1908," *PWW*, XVI and XVIII, 546 and 414 respectively; Eleanor McAdoo provides the description of the elegant Mary Hulbert Peck as a chain smoker in *The Woodrow Wilsons* (New York: The Macmillan Company, 1937), 131. She also makes the

Wilson went so far as to tell Mary Peck that his battles at Princeton had plunged him into near despair. He told her often how deep and passionate his personality was and how crushed he was by every defeat. "I am a person," he explained, "...who observes no sort of moderation in anything, and when I *do* have the blues I go in for having them with great thoroughness and fairly touching bottom." In contrast, Mary seemed to be a person who was natural and spontaneous. He idealized her as "a veritable child of nature," loved by nature as her own child and adored by her own dear friends for the deep radiance that lit up her very being.[299]

More than anything else, Wilson wanted Mary Peck to be his confidante, while he would be her protector and defender in all things, especially as she tried to decide whether she should divorce her husband. He confessed his growing disgust with the wealthy people who flaunted their wealth in Old Lyme where he now summered with his family. He told her of the vocation awakening deep within him to fight for the common people. He even admitted that he still ached to go into politics, the dream he had kept hidden within himself since childhood. "This is what I was meant for," he wrote to Mary in the fall of 1909, "this rough and tumble of the political arena. My instinct all turns that way, and I sometimes feel rather impatiently the restraints of my academic position." As he opened the most hidden places of his soul to his "beloved" Mary, he begged her to unburden herself in the same way. He was certain that providence itself had brought them together at the very time they both needed each other's help. He pressed her to trust him with all the troubles she was having with her estranged husband. In one of the most emotional letters he ever penned to anyone, he wrote:

> "I will understand and I will sympathize as keenly and entirely as your heart could wish. Will you not use me and make me *feel* my use? That is what I am for. I am happy that I was sent to you at such a time."[300]

For her part, Ellen Wilson had always tried to understand her husband's deep need to be loved, not just by his family, but by a circle of true friends who included many beautiful and brilliant women. He hid none of these relationships

interesting comment that her mother's first interview included the statement that she disapproved of women smoking, another hint of Ellen's veiled dislike for Mrs. Peck; Woodrow Wilson, "Letters to Mary Peck, October 12 and 19, and November 2, 1908," *PWW*, XVIII, 448-450, 478-481.

[299] Woodrow Wilson, "Letter to Mary Peck, September 19, 1909," *PWW*, XIX, 385.

[300] Woodrow Wilson, "Letters to Mary Peck, July 18, August 1, and September 5, 1909," *PWW*, XIX, 311-314, 321-324, and 357-359 respectively.

from his "dear Eileen," not even the one with his "precious" Mary. He even filled his letters to Ellen when he was away from her with news about Mrs. Peck. On his second trip to Bermuda in January 1908, he wrote home to Ellen, "I have seen Mrs. Peck twice, and really she is fine … I know that you would like her, despite her free western manner." However, Mrs. Wilson did not like her husband's relationship with Mrs. Peck. Although Wilson continued to confess his undying love for Ellen, calling her "the one indisputable reality" in his life, she believed he had crossed the line in his friendship with Mary Peck.

While she was certain that her husband never had an actual affair with Mrs. Peck, Ellen Wilson did believe that he had been unfaithful to her emotionally. She was hurt that he had opened the deepest places in his mind and heart to this fascinating woman. Those parts of Woodrow Wilson should have belonged only to herself and she did not want to share them with anyone. The romantic friendship between Woodrow and Mary began at a particularly lonely time in Ellen's life when each one of her daughters had gone off to college. Years later she confessed to a family friend that Wilson's love for Mary Peck was the "only unhappiness" that her husband had caused her "during their whole married life." Nellie Wilson also remembered once she heard her mother weeping at Prospect while her father swore he should never have brought her there. Nellie never knew that her mother may have been crying over Mrs. Peck.[301]

Nellie Wilson also heard an even more important conversation between her father and mother on a morning in May 1910. Coming down late for breakfast, she heard her father laughing and was certain it must be good news. Her father's mood, so darkened by the struggle over the graduate school, had brightened recently. His many speeches to Princeton alumni across the country seemed to have turned the tide in his favor. There were even rumors that the Board of Trustees would soon ask Dean West for his resignation. But when Nellie walked into the dining room, her father mentioned nothing along these lines. Instead he looked grim and said, "We've beaten the living, but we can't fight the dead. The game's up." Nellie could not understand what he meant and looked at her mother who had a forced smile on her face but who said nothing. Her father was laughing bitterly because he had just learned that his archenemy Dean West had outwitted him. He had convinced Isaac C. Wyman, a wealthy Princeton alumnus, to leave $3,000,000 in his will to build a graduate college at Princeton. Wyman came from

[301] Woodrow Wilson, "Letter to Ellen Wilson, January 26, 1908," *PWW*, XVII, 607; Ellen Wilson confessed her disappointment over her husband's relationship with Mary Peck to Dr. Cary Grayson, the White House physician; see Mulder, *Woodrow Wilson, The Years of Preparation*, 263; McAdoo, *The Priceless Gift*, 240-242.

a highly respected family in New Jersey. His grandfather had loaned George Washington the enormous sum of £40,000 during the American Revolution. His father had fought with the Continental Army at the Battle of Princeton, and he himself had graduated from the College of New Jersey in 1848. Nearly 90 years old when he died on May 18, Wyman had named two trustees to oversee his bequest to the Princeton graduate school, John M. Raymond of Salem and Andrew F. West of Princeton.[302]

Woodrow Wilson had fought many a battle in his life from the time he first set foot on a phantom ship to battle imaginary pirates. Some of the most important contests he later undertook were against himself as he struggled to become a serious college student and then to work his way out of the law and back into the academy. He had won some good fights at Princeton, especially for greater discipline and a tougher curriculum, and in the process he had found a new voice for himself. He had begun to speak out for a new vision of America where the common people and the best democratic traditions of the past were cherished. He had found many enemies of this vision including America's nouveau riche and their conspicuous consumption, the lazy students of Princeton and their pampering parents, and the treacherous Dean West. While he had fought the good fight against these foes, he could not defeat a bequest as large as $3,000,000. He recommended that the Board of Trustees accept this gift and the one previously offered by Procter, the wealthy soap magnate.[303]

While in his own eyes, Wilson considered himself a failure, this is not how everyone saw him. While many of the trustees and some of the faculty had turned against him, the students still loved him. Throughout the graduation ceremonies in June of 1910, he was met with thunderous applause from the boys of Princeton. President Wilson was frequently seen fighting back tears that flowed down his cheeks as they gave him one ovation after another. He was especially touched by the song the seniors chanted about him:

> "Here's to Woodrow, King divine,
> Who rules this place along with Fine,
> We have no fear he'll leave this town
> To try for anybody's crown!"[304]

---

[302] Ibid., 262.
[303] Baker, *Life and Letters*, II, 346-349.
[304] Ibid., 351.

They were not far from the truth for many of the people who had heard Wilson speak in recent years were convinced he should run for political office. His angry speech in Pittsburgh had impressed many people far from the Princeton campus. In fact, some even said he should not be the president of a university, but instead the President of the United States. They were impressed that Wilson had not simply spent his time talking to alumni groups, but had also spoken to bankers about the responsibilities they owed to the common good even as they sought their fortunes in the marketplace. He had extolled Lee to southern audiences, and Lincoln to northern ones, while reminding both of the struggles that were underway in their nation at the present time to preserve the best ideas of the past against ever greater concentrations of wealth and power. He challenged his fellow Democrats to find a way to rein in the great corporations and trusts while still preserving the principles of personal liberty upon which the nation was built.[305]

During the years when he had battled Dean West and the Board of Trustees over the graduate school, Wilson had dreamt again of becoming a dynamic political leader, like Edmund Burke or William Pitt, the heroes of his youth. Just as he had once confessed his dreams to his cousin Jessie Bones, so he had whispered them again in passionate letters to his friend Mary Peck. But when in the summer of 1910, Jim Smith, the "Big Boss" of New Jersey's Democratic Party, asked him to accept the nomination for governor in a desperate bid to find someone who could beat the Republicans, it was Ellen Wilson who convinced her husband to accept the offer. Wilson finally agreed in September 1910 to run for the top office in the state, and in October, he submitted his resignation to Princeton's Board of Trustees. In one of the simplest letters he had ever penned, Wilson tried to explain the principles that he still held dear and to capture the sentiments that overwhelmed him as he left Princeton. To the "Gentlemen of the Board of Trustees," he wrote:

> "On the fifteenth of September last the Democratic party of New Jersey nominated me for the office of Governor of the State, and I seemed it my duty to accept the nomination. In view of Princeton's immemorial observance of the obligation of public service, I could not have done otherwise.

---

[305] Woodrow Wilson, "The Bank and the Nation, September 30, 1908," *PPWW*, II, 54-63; "Robert E. Lee: An Interpretation, January 19, 1906," Ibid., 64-82; "Abraham Lincoln: A Man of the People, February 12, 1909," Ibid., 83-101; the growing sentiments developing within Wilson with regard to the Democratic Party during the years immediately before he became the President of the United States in 1912 are best summarized in his speech entitled, "Democracy's Opportunity, June 15, 1911," Ibid., 303-309.

> Having accepted the nomination, it becomes my duty to resign the presidency of the University I have so long loved and sought to serve. I, therefore, hereby offer my resignation of this great office with which you have honoured me, and venture to express the hope that the Board will see its way to act upon the resignation at once. It is my earnest prayer that the University may go forward without halt or hindrance in the path of true scholarship and thoughtful service of the nation."[306]

As Wilson set off on a campaign trip throughout the state of New Jersey, his brother-in-law Stockton Axson noticed that a great change seemed to have come over his personality. The relentless fighter, who once divided the world between those who were with him and those who were against him, had disappeared. While he might never forgive friends like Professor Hibben or enemies like Dean West for ruining his plans for Princeton, he would in the future treat those who opposed him with greater respect. Axson was certain that the sometimes fiery and impatient man who had seemed to hold himself aloof from others was gone for good. Surely he had learned lessons that would make him wiser, more patient, and a better politician and leader. Axson had also begun to see flashes of mysticism in his brother-in-law. "His soul dwelt abroad and alone," Axson mused, as if he was caught up in a vision of his own destiny and the destiny of his nation. Wilson himself never mentioned this destiny, but rather spoke of the providence which governed men's lives and brought good out of all circumstances, even the most terrible ones. As the election approached, Axson began to see more and more similarities between his brother-in-law and Abraham Lincoln, another leader who had a strain of mysticism in his soul and a keen sense of his own destiny. Only time would tell if Woodrow Wilson might also be called to lead his nation through fiery trials toward a better future, and perhaps in the process pay the same price for greatness that Lincoln once did.[307]

---

[306] Woodrow Wilson, "Letter of Resignation from Princeton University, October 29, 1910," *PPWW*, II, 269.

[307] Axson, *Brother Woodrow*, 148-149.

Chapter 7

THE ROAD TO THE NEW FREEDOM

The New Freedom is only the old revived and clothed in the unconquerable strength of modern America.

Woodrow Wilson[308]

When people in New Jersey learned that Woodrow Wilson was running for the top office in the state, reactions to his candidacy were mixed. Some thought that since he had no experience in politics, then he most probably had no real interest in becoming governor. Many of his greatest supporters considered him a scholarly but essentially naive fellow whom they could manipulate to their own advantage, while his worst detractors dismissed him as an upstart who had merely found himself in the right place at the right time. But whether they were for him or against him, none suspected that he had prepared for this day from the moment he first heard the news of Lincoln's election when he was just a boy. In times of quiet play and imaginative reflection from his childhood through his adolescence, he had dreamt of leading men, first on the high seas against pirates and later as the Prime Minister of an idealized England. But he had pushed these dreams deep into the recesses of his own heart as he faced the many responsibilities and disappointments of his adult life. Still somewhere these ideas had remained alive – so much so that when the bosses of New Jersey's Democratic Party came looking for him, he was ready and willing to serve. In a strange twist of fate, better suited to the romantic novels he loved to read in his youth than to the life he had come to know as the President of Princeton, the world around him had somehow caught up with the world within him. By a miracle that he did not quite

---

[308] Day, editor, *Woodrow Wilson's Own Story*, 120.

understand, he suddenly found himself on the brink of becoming the leader that he had long hoped he would be.

As he headed out into the world of politics, Wilson remembered the many sea-faring tales of his youth and often described his current life in terms from long ago. "The idea of a man of fifty-four (no less!) leaving a definite career and a settled way of life of a sudden and launching out in a vast sea of Ifs and Buts. It sounds like an account of a fool," he told Mary Peck in one of the many letters he continued to write to his "dearest friend."[309] He had already sensed the tide of events that was about to sweep him forward even before he had won the nomination for governor. As he prepared his last baccalaureate address in June 1910, he was haunted by a line in a letter of Saint Paul where the apostle said that "we look not at the things which are seen, but at the things which we see not." Like all the students he was about to address, Wilson was soon to sail out onto an invisible sea where all he had once imagined for himself might now come true. Surely he could bring the words of Saint Paul to life for the young men of Princeton for he was himself living the very truth of them.

As he faced the last group of boys he would ever address in this way, with tears flowing down his cheeks, Wilson told the students not to look back too much since all the good things they had learned would stay with them. He urged them instead to look ahead to the greatness that they could achieve as they worked for the good of others. While some 20th century critics might argue that such romantic accomplishments were no longer possible in the more mechanical and scientific modern age, Wilson assured them that great individuals could still break through from the crowd as leaders who would shape the future in ways that past ages could never have imagined. As he spoke these words to the Class of 1910, he told these things even more truly to himself:

> "Perhaps not so many individuals are of significance as formerly, but the individuals who do tell more tremendously, wield a greater individual choice, command a power such as kings and conquerors never dreamed of in simpler days gone by. Their sway is the sway of destiny over millions upon millions of their fellow country-men, over the policy and fortunes of nations. There never was a time when the spirit and character of individual men was of more imperial import and consequences than now."[310]

---

[309] Woodrow Wilson, "Letter to Mary Hulbert, January 13, 1911," *PWW*, XXII, 329-330; Mary Peck had finally decided to divorce her second husband and now went by the name of her first husband.

[310] Woodrow Wilson, "Baccalaureate Address, June 12, 1910," *PPWW*, II, Part 2, 234-242.

In the summer of 1910, Woodrow Wilson embarked on the greatest adventure of his life to date, confident that all would be well as long as he remembered that he served the people whom he now so admired and the democracy that he had come to cherish. It was chilling and even frightening for him to think of what a leader could do with such power in the modern world. He was convinced that Christ still remained the model of the best kind of leader to be even in the rapid pace of a new century where facts changed right before a man's eyes as he tried to digest them. In such turbulent times, a leader's every thought must be directed toward finding the best ways to improve the lives of the common people and so raise them to a happier existence from generation to generation. The self doubt he had often felt in his childhood and in his youth now gave way to real humility as he pondered why Providence had opened this path before him which had been closed to him for so long. As he emerged more and more before the public, he was determined to begin nearly every speech with a comment that he had no illusion about his own greatness. In many respects, this was quite a change for a man who had always been thoughtful but in a rather self-centered way throughout much of his youth. He was still profoundly introspective, yet no longer just to understand himself but rather to find the best way to serve the people whom he now represented.[311]

While a somewhat shaken and much more humble Wilson felt himself moving from the shadows of obscurity into the bright light of fame, he had not been completely invisible to the Democratic leaders of his state. As the President of Princeton, he had come before the public on many occasions, most recently in his struggles to make certain that democracy remained alive and well at his university. The battle over the quads and the graduate school had played out in the state's newspapers with President Wilson being largely portrayed as the champion of the average boy and the common man. His angry speech to the alumni in Pittsburgh in April 1910 may have shocked many a professor back in Princeton but had electrified the imagination of professional politicians who needed a dynamic candidate for their party to rally around. One such man, former Senator and "Big Boss" of the New Jersey Democrats, Jim Smith, led the way in enlisting Wilson as a candidate for governor. While in private he called Princeton's president a "Presbyterian priest," Smith praised Wilson in public as the "man of the hour" who would be the "medium by which the Democratic party is to have its hunger for the plums of victory appeased after so long a wait."[312]

---

[311] Ibid., 242-243.

[312] Baker, *Life and Letters*, III, 20; Daniels, *Woodrow Wilson*, 87.

Still amidst all the certainty that his candidate could win, the "Big Boss" worried that Wilson was an unknown commodity. While Wilson's reputation as a fighter for the good of the people would probably get him and a whole slate of Democratic candidates elected in these progressive times, Smith did not want the new governor acting like a real reformer once he was in office. He had even quizzed Wilson point blank whether, once elected, he would "shut the doors in the face of the organization leaders?" Wilson assured him that he would give the party leaders a fair hearing since he himself was a firm believer in the two party system. If the top Democrats in the state came to him and recommended that certain people be appointed to his administration, he would probably do so, but only if they were the best possible men for the job. Accepting Wilson's equivocal answer as a sign that he would be able to control the inexperienced academic, Smith had no idea that Wilson intended to be a new kind of executive. Once the political appointments that Smith and the other bosses thought so important were made, Wilson planned to get down to the real business of directing his party to support his legislative program for much needed reform in the state. He was determined to see that New Jersey's chief executive acted more like a Prime Minister who crafted laws with the support of his party rather than as a mere figurehead who rubber stamped what the bosses – and in the case of New Jersey – what the trusts wanted him to do. Right from the start, Wilson was determined to be a new, more dynamic leader who pushed major reform legislation through the state house that had been stalled for years.[313]

As he launched out into his new career in politics, Wilson was certain that he would be seen as a reformer. He often quipped half in jest, but half sincerely, that in modern American politics, reform was the only option, and that an elected official who resisted reform was in danger of running aground in three deadly places. Such a politician might end up a "radical" who went too far, a "conservative" who did not go far enough, or a "reactionary" who did not go anywhere at all. In contrast, Wilson argued that the only sure course to follow was that of a "progressive." He defined a progressive quite simply as "one who (a) recognizes new facts and adjusts new laws to them, and who (b) attempts to think ahead, constructively."[314] He had come to believe that the great drive for political reform that had started in the western prairies and then swept into the nation's bustling cities came directly from the people themselves. The essentially

[313] Ibid., 98.

[314] Woodrow Wilson, "Wilson's Definitions of Different Groups," in Day, editor, *Woodrow Wilson's Own Story*, 109 (quote in this book is taken from Wilson's address before the Kansas Society in New York City on January 28, 1911).

conservative Americans who now supported the progressive movement had grown tired of a world where money ruled politics. They wanted nothing new or radical, but instead they desired the rebirth or restoration of the responsible government that had been handed to them by the Founding Fathers. Wilson believed the majority of Americans had rightly come to see that most politicians were too busy pandering to wealthy individuals and corporations to remember that they served the people, most of whom had no power or influence to sway their leaders anymore.[315]

For Wilson, the race to be the next governor of New Jersey was not simply to win a contest in the way Smith and the other bosses hoped. Instead it was to put the same kind of policies in place statewide that he had tried to institute on a smaller scale at Princeton. The next governor and the members of his party must dedicate themselves not just to taking office, dividing up appointments, and then doing nothing, but to crafting legislation that improved the lot of average men and women. To be progressive leaders, they must see government as actively changing people's lives for the better. To win an election was only the beginning of the greater story of American democracy which depended on better laws always being passed.

Wilson had placed his vision of what these new laws should be in the platform which he wrote for the party. The administration of the state would be streamlined. Unnecessary offices and commissions would be abolished and spending would be carefully monitored. While taxes must be levied, they would be made equitable, falling equally on the shoulders of the rich and poor alike. Funds for education would also be equally distributed, and the state's natural resources, including most especially water, would be conserved for the benefit of all. An active Public Utilities Commission would be put in place that truly regulated the rates that companies charged their customers. Employers would be made liable for the safety of their workers, and employees of the state would win the eight hour day. Trusts that had come to New Jersey expecting protection and preferential treatment would face new legislation that ensured fair competition. Corrupt election practices would be outlawed, and there would be civil service reform at the state, county, and municipal levels. Wilson made sure that one of his favorite national concerns, the excessively high tariff, was condemned in the party platform of New Jersey's Democrats. He also threw his support behind a

[315] Wilson developed his ideas on the nature of good government and the role of an active executive throughout the 1910 gubernatorial race and in the lead up to his run for the White House in 1912. One of the clearest statements of his developing vision can be seen in his work entitled "Issues of Freedom, May 5, 1911," *PPWW*, II, Part 2, 283-290.

constitutional amendment that would allow the people, not the legislature, to elect Senators to the U.S. Congress.[316]

As progressive as the new platform seemed to be to its author Woodrow Wilson, not all of New Jersey's Democrats who wanted reform necessarily wanted Wilson. One of his loudest critics was a tough, up-and-coming state representative from Hudson County named Joseph Tumulty. An Irish Catholic who had learned democracy in his father's grocery store in Jersey City's Fifth Ward, also known as the "Bloody Angle," Tumulty led the opposition to Wilson's nomination for governor at the party's convention in Trenton in September 1910. What could a professor from Princeton, he argued, possibly know about the troubles of working men and women? How could the darling of the bosses ever deliver on any of the reforms he promised? Even worse, how could a man with no experience in the hard knock school of state politics ever hope to beat even a weak candidate like the Republican Vivian Lewis?[317]

While Wilson won the nomination for governor on the first ballot, the party was still not unified behind him. He may have long dreamt of leading men to greatness, but now he faced his first challenge in the real world of politics. He must somehow become the standard bearer of a divided party. Smith and the other leaders of the Democratic machine were sure they had a winner in their man Wilson, but they were ready to turn on him as an "ingrate" if he dared to think for himself or do anything on his own. The progressive wing of the party, filled with young men like Tumulty, was ready to snicker at the bookworm professor, the tool of the bosses, even while they still held out the faint hope that he might turn out to be a reformer and so trump the bosses who had handpicked him. As he headed by car from his house on Prospect Avenue in Princeton to the Taylor Opera House in Trenton, he knew that he would have to give the speech of a lifetime, one worthy of his childhood heroes, if he was truly to become the leader of his party.

Most everyone waiting at the convention in Trenton had never seen Wilson in person before. In order to stir up the delegates to an even more fevered pitch, Colonel George Harvey, the editor of *Harper's Weekly* and one of Wilson's staunchest supporters, staged a dramatic entry for his candidate to the convention. "We have just received word," announced the convention's secretary at Harvey's request, "that Mr. Wilson, the candidate for the governorship, *and the next President of the United States*, has received word of his nomination, and is now

---

[316] "The Platform of the New Jersey Democratic Party," *PWW*, XXI, 94-96.

[317] Joseph P. Tumulty, *Woodrow Wilson as I Know Him* (Garden City, New York and Toronto: Doubleday, Page, and Company, Inc., 1921), 1, 11, 17-18.

on his way to the Convention." The crowd went wild, and even a disgruntled Joseph Tumulty, who laughed to himself that the "Princeton professor has left the University for the Elysian Fields of politics," slowly pushed his way through the delegates toward the stage so he could get a "close-up" look at the "man of mystery" once he finally arrived.

Like so many people in the hall, Tumulty was amazed when Wilson finally appeared and headed to the podium. He was not the bookish, ethereal creature that most had expected. Instead, he was tall, just a little under six feet, "clean-cut, plainly garbed," standing before the excited crowd, always "cool and smiling." He was not a good looking man, but when he began to speak, there was a flash in his dark grey eyes that was mesmerizing and even made him seem handsome. Tumulty, who was at first disappointed that Wilson spoke so calmly about the reforms that could be accomplished if the party worked together for the good of the people of New Jersey, soon found himself caught up in the power of the candidate's vision. Like everyone else in the hall, he was amazed how Wilson's deep and sincere voice spoke directly to the entire crowd, as if he was talking to everybody in the room one on one. There was nothing of the high drama or any of the tricks of the trade common to the great orators of the day in Wilson's manner. Instead there was only deep thought and real humility that fully won the crowd over to him. At one point, when Wilson was certain the delegates were growing tired of him, many shouted "Go on … You're all right!" The whole effect was thrilling. As Joe Tumulty, who would soon become Wilson's personal secretary, explained:

> "His words, spoken in tones so soft, so fine, in voice so well modulated, so heart-stirring. Only a few sentences are uttered and our souls are stirred to our very depths. It was not only what he said, but the simple heart-stirring way in which he said it."[318]

The most memorable moment came toward the end of the speech when Wilson looked up at the flag that hung over the speaker's stand. He caught the crowd up in pondering the ideals of America as they dreamt of her ships sailing around the whole world. While no one knew that these images came from a time long ago when Wilson spent his summers by the Cape Fear River in Wilmington, they felt the power of his love for his country. Tumulty was even certain that he heard a sob from the crowd as Wilson spoke these final words:

---

[318] Ibid., 19-20; "A News Report of Impromptu Remarks to the Democratic State Convention," *PWW*, XXI, 118.

> "When I think of the flag which our ships carry, the only touch of colour about them, the only thing that moves as if it had a settled spirit on it – in their solid structure, it seems to me I see alternate strips of parchment upon which are written the rights of liberty and justice and strips of blood spilled to vindicate those rights and then – in the corner – a prediction of the blue serene into which every nation may swim which stands for these great things."[319]

As he looked at the cheering mob all around him, Tumulty saw grown men, cynical and embittered just moments before, now weeping at the eloquence of Wilson's words. They had gone from being selfish manipulators out only for themselves to "Crusaders" who were "ready to dedicate themselves to the cause of liberating their state from the bondage of special interests." As he made his way out of the Opera House, he came upon John Crandall of Atlantic City, one of Wilson's fiercest opponents at the convention. Crandall stood hunched and silent for a moment as if in a dream, but then pulled himself up to his full height. Waving his hat and cane over his head, he shouted, "I am sixty-five years old, and still a damn fool!"[320]

After the convention came to a close, pundits in both the machine and reform wings of the party were amazed as Wilson launched into the most aggressive campaign for governor that the state of New Jersey had ever seen. He started by giving a less than inspiring speech in a hall in Jersey City, but quickly recovered and later that same day had the crowd in "the hollow of his hand" at a rally across town. He traveled by car to every county in the state and was met by large crowds in both Democratic and Republican strongholds. People came in record numbers to listen to Wilson's common sense ideas explained to them from the steps of town squares or the stages of public halls. Everywhere he went throughout New Jersey, Wilson was direct, engaging, and even funny. When a man in Jersey City shouted, "Go it, Woody! You are all right. But you ain't no beaut," Wilson, without missing a beat, recited one of his favorite limericks:

> " For beauty I am not a star;
> There are others handsomer by far;
> But my face, I don't mind it,
> For I am behind it;
> 'Tis the people in front that I jar."[321]

---

[319] Tumulty, *Woodrow Wilson as I Know Him*, 21.
[320] Ibid., 22.
[321] Axson, *Brother Woodrow*, 159-161; Daniels, *Woodrow Wilson*, 99.

Wilson would always remember his campaign for Governor of New Jersey in 1910 as the greatest one he ever conducted. The whole process seemed to be made up of one piece. All the speeches he gave in the six weeks from mid-September to Election Day in early November were linked together in a great chain of meaning. While he made sure that he spoke without any affectation which might have come from his long years in front of a classroom, he still seemed to be teaching the people of New Jersey about the great issues of the day and what he meant to do about them. Stockton Axson, who accompanied his brother-in-law on many of his campaign stops throughout the state, clearly heard Wilson's thesis. It was the simple proposition that "in a democratic government the people themselves must be brought in direct contact with their own affairs." Everything he was proposing to accomplish as governor was simply meant "to restore a government wrested from the people back to the people."[322]

In his earliest speeches and interviews with press throughout New Jersey, Wilson stressed the need for politicians to respect the very people they served. He clearly believed that Americans as a whole had woken up and were ready to speak with one voice about their common problems. "The time when you could play politics and fool the American people has gone by," Wilson said to the Trenton convention, "Now it is a case of put up or shut up." He was certain that the majority of people were tired of machine politics where politicians ran for office the same way they raced horses. For them, the contest was everything and the payoff came in dividing up the spoils of office among their supporters after each victory. Once firmly in office, the political leaders did nothing but wait for the next election. All of the growing problems of the day that impacted the lives of the electorate were ignored.

More like a prosecuting attorney than a professor, Wilson next laid out those problems clearly for his listeners. He explained how the high tariffs levied by Republican administrations in Washington were nothing but favors done for the wealthiest Americans and how these duties added to the cost of living for the average man and woman in the country. He warned of the growing power of corporations that had won full rights as "individuals" from the Supreme Court, but who in turn refused to obey any laws that were meant to regulate them. The liberty granted to them under the Republican court's interpretation of the Constitution had turned into license. Business leaders cared little for the health and safety of their workers or the need to preserve vital natural resources for the good of future generations. Instead they were content to reap profits for their

[322] Axson, *Brother Woodrow*, 101.

stockholders with no thought of the obligation they might owe to the country that had made them so wealthy.

While he stressed that the free enterprise system was part of the very fiber of the American experience, Wilson warned that corporations were now dominating the political process and blocking all reforms that would benefit the majority of the people. Corporations must be regulated and so learn to play by the rules that governed the average American. In Wilson's opinion, the idea of regulating corporations was not a radical one that needed to be silenced as "un-American." Instead it came out of the best traditions of self-government handed down to the people from the founding generation. The framers of the Constitution set up a representative democracy where the people elected leaders who acted on behalf of the majority, not the wealthiest. "This cry for quiet and peace is quite futile," Wilson explained to a reporter on the day after he was nominated for governor, "These things will not be settled until the people are convinced that they have been settled rightly."[323]

By the halfway point in his campaign, Wilson was keen on emphasizing the importance of law in the United States. Above all else, America was a nation of laws. The whole purpose of its democracy was to give the people power to elect representatives who would craft laws that made life better for everyone. Wilson had made it clear from the convention onward that he would be a new kind of governor who worked with his legislature to pass important new laws. He promised one crowd after another that bills for fairer taxation, conservation of natural resources, an effective Public Utilities Commission, direct primaries, and the regulation of corporations would be written, debated, and approved soon after he had taken office. By mid-October, Wilson could tell his audiences that his opponent was now swept up in the groundswell for reform in the state. Vivian Lewis had scrapped the Republican platform and crafted one of his own that looked amazingly like the one Wilson had written for the Democrats. "I find that it greatly *resembles my own*," Wilson joked with voters in Atlantic City, "*So I experience a sense of relief, therefore*, in finding that there is no issue between Mr. Lewis and myself." With so little difference between himself and the

---

[323] "A News Report of Impromptu Remarks to the Democratic State Convention, September 17, 1910," *PWW*, XXI, 118-120; "Two Interviews, September 17, 1910," Ibid., 120-125; "Wilson Views are Clear-Cut: Tariff Revision, Regulation of Corporations and Conservation are All Vital Issues, September 17, 1910," Ibid., 125-127; "An Interview: Crime of Trusts is Individual, Says Dr. Wilson, September 18, 1910," Ibid., 134-136; "A News Report of a Speech in Jersey City: Woodrow Wilson Raps Roosevelt's Court Criticism, September 21, 1910," Ibid., 147-148.

Republican candidate, Wilson told his audience that they must decide which man would truly deliver on his promises.[324]

As Election Day grew closer, Wilson's vision for the future of America became a prominent theme in his addresses to the people of New Jersey. At times it seemed as if he was Tommy Woodrow once again standing on the prow of an imaginary ship looking ahead into a future that his listeners could not yet see. From his high vantage point, he could tell the crowds that the United States was on the brink of becoming the leader of the world. It was therefore more imperative than ever for the American people to understand their nation and themselves. "What is the manifest destiny of America?" he asked voters midway through the campaign. It was not to rule the world by sheer physical force. It was not to pile up masses of vulgar but magnificent wealth. It was not to collcct vast amounts of money that the nation could "throw away and burn." Instead, Wilson believed that the destiny of America was "to do the thinking of the world." This thinking could not be done by an intellectual elite locked away in universities. Instead, it must come from "the pulse of the common man, the average man, of all men – the thought of humanity itself." The American spirit that had pondered long and hard on the meaning of democracy and the God-given rights upon which it was built would be the greatest treasure any nation had ever given to the world. In fact, the gift of American ideals to all mankind would make the whole world young again. Wilson's speeches became most lyrical when he tried to capture what America meant to him and hopefully one day to all the world:

> "For America, ladies and gentlemen, is not merely a piece of the surface of the earth. America is not merely a body of towns. America is an idea, America is an ideal, America is a vision."[325]

The eloquence of Woodrow Wilson on the campaign trail thrilled voters in New Jersey in a way they had never been excited before. Whether speaking to farmers in small towns or laborers in large cities, the candidate had the common touch that was soon the envy of most other politicians, especially Republicans. On nearly every occasion when he spoke, Wilson received a warm reception from the crowds that often waited long hours to hear him. During the few times that audiences seemed to be against him, he was able to win them over, usually by changing his prepared speech on the spot and talking directly to the concerns of the people standing in front of him. One such occasion occurred in late October in

---

[324] Woodrow Wilson, "Address in Atlantic City, New Jersey, October 13, 1910," Ibid., 311.

[325] Ibid., 316-320.

the little town of Carlstadt, an old Dutch settlement in Bergen County. Wilson had just received a rousing reception at a crowded high school in Passaic, but five minutes into his talk in Carlstadt, he knew no one understood a word he was saying. Instead of trying to make the same points that had been such a success just hours before, Wilson suddenly confessed that running for Governor was not all that it was cracked up to be. "You know," he said, "I have been going all over the State in an automobile. Well, I feel now after near six weeks of talking, that I am running out of gasolene." A roar of laughter went up from the people of Carlstadt who were now on his side. Once they had quieted down, Wilson asked them a simple question. What's the difference between the Democratic and Republican tickets in this election? When he answered that one ticket would work and the other wouldn't, the crowd roared again. He then reminded them that their ancestors had come to this country for the right to govern themselves, and that now it was their duty to vote and keep the American democracy going. Before Wilson left Carlstadt on his way to another campaign stop, he told one last joke. He said he finally understood why English politicians "stand" for office while Americans "run" for it.[326]

Meeting one success after another as he motored through New Jersey, Wilson finally ran into a bump on the road of his masterful swing through the state in late October. A leader of the progressive wing of the state's Republican Party by the name of George L. Record challenged the Democratic candidate to a debate. Record believed the debate would settle once and for all a gnawing question in the minds of most reform minded people in New Jersey. Was Wilson truly a progressive who would deliver on his promises if elected or merely the puppet of a boss like Jim Smith who got him the nomination and the tool of a party hack like Jim Nugent who was running his brilliant campaign behind the scenes? Like everyone else who heard Wilson, Record knew that the Democratic challenger was a brilliant speaker who could make the most complex ideas understandable and excite the people to demand reform. However, he also realized that politics in the state of New Jersey was run by two political machines, the Democratic "Old Guard" and the Republican "Board of Guardians." Once elected, neither machine thought it their duty to pass reforms that might benefit the people. Their only concern was keeping the many trusts that had found a home in New Jersey happy. A brilliant debater himself, Record was certain that his challenge would bring

[326] "A News Report of a Campaign Speech in Carlstadt, New Jersey, November 2, 1910" *PWW*, XXI, 507-508.

Wilson down from the clouds and test his mettle in order to determine once and for all if he truly meant what he said.[327]

In a letter written on October 17, Record delivered a series of 19 questions to Wilson. He explained that if Wilson answered all the questions, then this would show where the candidate stood and whether or not a formal debate was necessary. The first questions tested Wilson on specific proposals that had long been pending in the state house. Should the Public Utilities Commission have the power to set rates? Should the state determine the value of property owned by a public utility? Should the profits of public utilities be capped by law at 6%? Record then moved on to questions related to reforming politics. Should the use of primaries be extended to races for all state offices? Who should oversee primary elections? Should ballots be mailed to people's homes? Should there be a corrupt practice act? The last set of questions went directly to the issue of who actually controlled Wilson. Would he admit that the boss system existed? If so, would he abolish it? How do the Democratic and Republic machines differ from one another? Has the Democratic Party truly reorganized itself along progressive lines? Would he have progressives in the Democratic and Republican parties alike pledge to support real reforms once he was elected?[328]

Although many in his campaign urged him not to respond, Wilson answered Record in a personal letter written on October 24 in Princeton. After apologizing for taking so long to respond, saying that the demands of the campaign had prevented this, he answered "Yes" to all the questions on reforms related to the Public Utilities Commission except the one on the 6% cap on profits. Wilson believed there should be a cap, but it should be set by the commission members who understood the marketplace and not by a statute. Similarly, Wilson answered "Yes" to all the political questions, but said that ballots must be kept only at polling places and should not be mailed to people's homes. He completely agreed with Record that the state was currently under the control of the Democratic Old Guard and the Republican Board of Guardians. But if Record doubted that a change was underway in the Democratic Party, then Wilson suggested he take a look at "the spirit of the whole remarkable *Democratic revival which we are witnessing* not only in New Jersey but in many other states." It proved that rank and file Democrats were taking back control of their party from the bosses. Once the people had elected him governor, Wilson vowed that he would put an end to machine politics in New Jersey forever.[329]

---

[327] Tumulty, *Woodrow Wilson as I Know Him*, 38-39.

[328] George Lawrence Record, "Letter to Woodrow Wilson, October 17, 1910," *PWW*, XXI, 406-411.

[329] Woodrow Wilson, "Letter to George Lawrence Record, October 24, 1910," *PWW*, XXI, 338-347.

When Wilson's answers were reported in the state's newspapers, he was seen as the clear winner in the contest with Record. In fact, Wilson's answers were so close to Record's own opinions that a debate would not now be necessary. Angry Republicans blamed Record for giving Wilson the opportunity to look like a decisive leader. "Damn Record; the campaign is over," was a common complaint among the bosses in the Republican machine. Democrats like Smith and Nugent ignored the substance of Wilson's answers and instead praised their candidate for his brilliant strategy. They were certain that the letter was mere posturing on Wilson's part and that all of his responses would be forgotten after the election. As Tumulty explained it, "They simply smiled and shrugged their shoulders and said, 'This is a great campaign play'."[330]

The Democratic machine was content to let Wilson take any flight of fancy he chose for they were certain he was heading for a landslide. During a stop in Montclair, New Jersey in the last week of his campaign, Wilson's oratory became even more emotional in a speech he delivered on the meaning of the progressive government. On one level, it meant passing all the promised legislation from fairer taxation and regulation of the corporations to direct primaries and the conservation of natural resources. But on another much deeper level, it was the very idea of free government in its widest sense. The progressive movement had brought people together from many different backgrounds. Now leaders must rise up who could organize everyone and get them working together on real reform. Wilson hinted that these men must not be like leaders of the past who approached their work as they would any other job. Instead, the men who took office in these exciting times must be those "who are in love" with progressive ideas and who can translate these same ideas into action.[331]

By the time Woodrow Wilson gave his last speech in Newark, just three days before the election, the Democrats on all sides of the political spectrum felt themselves caught up in a great Crusade. They were buoyant in the certain hope that the eloquent schoolmaster who now led them would help their ticket sweep the state on November 8. Even old enemies like Joe Tumulty and Jim Smith could sit side by side in the crowded auditorium to listen to Wilson profess his faith in the plain people of America "whose names never emerged into the headlines of newspapers." Tumulty would always remember how Wilson's beautiful voice seemed to reach every ear and touch each heart. The candidate reminded everyone that the race had begun as a fight against privilege. The quest they had undertaken

[330] Tumulty, *Woodrow Wilson as I Know Him*, 42.

[331] Woodrow Wilson, "A Campaign Address in Montclair, New Jersey, November 2, 1910," *PWW*, XXI, 509.

together was not a radical one but instead was a battle filled with the common sense of living. "…you know that men are not put into this world to go the path of ease," he explained, "They are put in this world to go the path of pain and struggle. No man would wish to sit idly by and lose the opportunity to take part in such a struggle." He told his many supporters not to look back but ahead to the days when future generations would judge them and "thank God that there were men who undertook to lead in the struggle." When the speech was over, Joe Tumulty stood up to leave and felt Boss Smith tugging on his coat. With tears in his eyes, he whispered, "That is a great man, Mr. Tumulty. He is destined for great things."[332]

Wilson himself was caught up in the drama and emotion that he was now stirring in the souls of so many men and women. The old romance in his heart that had stayed with him for so long but had been dampened by the battles at Princeton came alive once again. He was at last the hero who led the people into a bright new day by his clear vision and the heartfelt eloquence of his words. Still old doubts remained that he might never be able to reach the future he had promised for the people. As he had done at other stressful times in his life, he now found comfort in a poem that he had run across in the October 1910 issue of *American Magazine*. It was Rudyard Kipling's stirring piece entitled "If." Wilson often read the poem out loud and even carried a copy of it with him in the last weeks of the campaign. Kipling's words touched him deeply and seemed to mirror the profound experience through which he was passing:

> "If you can dream – and not make dreams your master;
> If you can think – and not make thoughts your aim,
> If you can meet with Triumph and Disaster
> And treat those imposters just the same …
>
> If you can fill the unforgiving minute
> With sixty seconds' worth of distance run,
> Yours is the Earth and everything that's in it,
> And – which is more – you'll be a Man, my Son!"[333]

Wilson left Newark and arrived back in Princeton to await the election and its outcome. On Tuesday, November 8, 1910, he remained the calmest person in the

---

[332] Tumulty, Woodrow Wilson as I Know Him, 43-45.

[333] Baker, *Life and Letters*, III, 86; Wilson loved the poem "If" so much that he had a copy of it framed and displayed it in his White House study. It was also in the room in his last house on S Street in Washington, D.C. where he died in 1924.

president's house on Prospect Avenue. Ellen Wilson was relieved to see her sensitive husband so calm. She had supported him at every step of the way in the campaign and had even helped him with his speeches. He often said the lines that got the best response from the crowds were usually written by his wife. Her only fear throughout the campaign had been what might happen to her husband's spirits if he lost. Now that he seemed resigned to accept either victory or defeat, Ellen could stop worrying about Woodrow, even as she and her daughters along with all the family and friends who crowded into Prospect grew more anxious and excited by the minute. By the early evening, the phone rang every few minutes with updates on the returns. Wilson was the only person allowed to answer the phone on this critical night. Each time a call came in, he would pick up the receiver and listen without giving away any hint of what was being said to him on the other end. "Yes" and "Thank you" were his only comments. He would go back to his wife and daughters, pretending as if the news was bad. When they despaired, he teased them for their lack of faith and then told them that the returns were good. Still he cautioned his family not to be overly optimistic. However, by 10 P.M., it was clear that he had won a smashing victory.[334] He was elected the Governor of New Jersey by the largest majority in history with one exception. He carried 15 of the state's 21 counties, some of which had always voted Republican. While the Republicans held on to the senate, the Democrats took the assembly for the first time in seventeen years. While his party won landslides in many other states, Wilson's victory in New Jersey was seen as the Democrat's greatest achievement in the election of 1910.[335]

In the midst of the excitement surrounding her husband's victory, Ellen Wilson soon found her most pressing concern was to move her family from the president's house on Prospect Avenue to new lodgings. The state provided no housing for its governor and most men who held the office took rooms in hotels near the capitol. The Wilsons decided to move into the old Princeton Inn on Nassau Street. Governor Wilson would make the 10-mile trip to and from Trenton by train every weekday morning and night. Ellen Wilson packed what the family would be able to take with them and then stored the rest. "I never realized before how dreadful possessions are," she confessed to her daughter Nellie, "I shall never save anything again as long as I live." Nellie, an art student at the Pennsylvania Academy, would be coming to live with her parents. So would her sister Margaret who spent much of her time in New York pursuing a music career and Jessie who longed to become a missionary but who was content for now to work at a

---

[334] McAdoo, The Priceless Gift, 264.

[335] Baker, *Life and Letters*, III, 105-106.

settlement house in Philadelphia. The Wilsons would be able to get away in the summertime to Sea Girt, a house provided for the governor and his family on the Atlantic Ocean. The home was right next to the training camp of the state's National Guard. While Sea Girt was big and bright, filled with many rooms and soft sea breezes, it was made dusty and noisy by the men who seemed to be always drilling with their horses or shooting off their cannons.

Mrs. Wilson was determined to make both the rooms at the Princeton Inn and the rambling house at Sea Girt into retreats for her husband and children. But it was the greatest challenge of her life as a homemaker to date. With no budget from the state for entertaining as there had been from the university at Princeton, she must find a way to pay for the many guests who descended on her family out of her husband's meager salary as governor. Nellie Wilson remembered how once her mother ruefully said, "I never know whether there will be five for luncheon, or twenty." Taking matters into her own hands, the Wilson's youngest daughter decided to find a more suitable home for her family in Princeton. The cottage she chose on Cleveland Lane had been built by an artist. It had a studio perfect for the family's painting and sketching, and there was a small garden in back that her mother would love. Since her parents could not afford the rent, she suggested that Ellen Wilson ask the family friends, Mary and Lucy Smith from New Orleans, to move in with them and share expenses. They agreed and soon Governor Wilson and his family had a proper place in which to live.[336]

If Mrs. Wilson's top priority was making a new home for her family, Governor Wilson's first charge was to show the Democratic machine that he meant to keep his promises to the voters of New Jersey. One of the first people to come calling for a favor was the Big Boss Jim Smith who believed Wilson owed him something after getting him elected. He had previously been the Senator from New Jersey, and had decided after the election that he would like the position again. Smith was stunned when Wilson told him, "The primary elected Martine and there is nothing for the legislature to do but ratify that election." The angry boss reminded Wilson that James Martine, the only candidate to run in the primary, had only gotten 54,000 votes. He said this proved that everyone considered "the primary a joke." However, Wilson claimed that allowing the people of New Jersey to decide who the next Democratic candidate for Senator would be was hardly a joke. If Smith tried to get the nomination, Wilson said he would not support him. By January, the fight was on. Wilson organized rallies in Jersey City and Newark to speak out in favor of Martine as the people's choice. He buoyed up the spirits of frightened Democratic legislators by telling them that

---

[336] Eleanor Wilson McAdoo, *The Woodrow Wilsons*, 116-117, 127-129.

this was their chance to break the stranglehold of machine politics. Smith had marched into Trenton leading a big parade with a brass band loudly playing, and had then called in the party's representatives in the state house one after the other to remind them of his power as the Big Boss. Despite the fanfare, the primary results were upheld with Smith winning only ten votes, and Martine went on to be elected the new Senator from New Jersey, with Smith now getting just three votes. The party boss who was moved to tears by his candidate's final campaign speech left Trenton with only his sons accompanying him. "He wept, they say," Wilson wrote to Mrs. Peck, "as he admitted himself utterly beaten. Such is the end of political power – particularly when selfishly obtained and heartlessly used." However, Smith had not given up completely on New Jersey politics. He would rely on Jim Nugent, Wilson's former campaign manager, to thwart any reform measures in the legislature that might break the power of the Democratic machine. He would also refer to Wilson ever after as a liar.[337]

Governor Wilson had only begun to understand both the promise and the dangers of the new found power that had suddenly come to him. In part, watching Smith's downfall, had frightened him. "It is a pitiless game," he told his dearest friend Mary, "in which it would seem, one takes one's life in one's hands, – for me it has only begun!"[338] Still he had thought long and hard about the need for a strong executive in a democracy and there was no going back now. He comforted himself by remembering that he had been direct with the party bosses and the people throughout the campaign. Wilson made it clear that he would not be a "rubber stamp" for the bills that came up from the legislature, but would instead propose laws for the members of the state house to debate and approve. He felt personally responsible for fulfilling every promise he had made in the party platform. Throughout the campaign, Woodrow Wilson had often said to the many crowds who came to listen to him, "Now, if you don't want that sort of governor, don't elect me; and you can't say I didn't give you fair notice."[339]

In his first inaugural address, Governor Woodrow Wilson was determined to show the party bosses that he truly was a reformer who meant to keep his promises. Yet at the same time, he hoped to emphasize that he was not a radical. In fact, he saw no contraction in this, and instead believed his understanding of America's best political traditions had inspired him to call for reform. Wilson had

---

[337] Daniels, *Woodrow Wilson*, 100-101; Baker, *Life and Letters*, III, 117-127; Woodrow Wilson, "Letter to Mary Hulbert, January 29, 1911," *PWW*, XXI, 391-392.

[338] Ibid., 392-393.

[339] Axson, *Brother Woodrow*, 163; the exact speech to which Axson is referring was given on October 3, 1910; see *PWW*, XXI, 424-425.

always stressed that he was not against big business and now even mocked the Populist rhetoric that called corporations "hobgoblins," "unholy inventions of rascally rich men," or "puzzling devices by which ingenious lawyers build up huge rights out of small wrongs." Calling for calm in the midst of hysteria, Wilson argued that corporations were merely organizations created by the law and that now they must be regulated by the law. These new laws must be carefully crafted under the watchful eye of the people who were now "wide awake."

As he laid out the specifics of his legislative program, Wilson was careful to point out how deliberate his approach was in contrast to muckraking journalists and politicians who sensationalized every wrong in society. A good example was workingmen's compensation. When businesses were small, employers knew all of their workers and could watch out for their needs. But now with hundreds or even thousands of employees, corporations were out of touch with the demands of their workers. In this new day for capital and labor, the government must step in and find ways to protect laboring men and women. Having honed his ability to simplify the most complex matters into the turn of an elegant phrase, first in the classroom but most recently on the campaign trail, Wilson explained how he would help the workers. "New rules must be devised," he explained, "for their protection, for their compensation when injured, for their support when disabled."

Beyond delivering legislation related to workingmen's compensation, Wilson made the creation of a vibrant Public Utilities Commission one of his top priorities. Under his administration, the commission would be an active regulatory body working for the good of the people. Conservation of natural resources would also be high on Wilson's list of priorities. Water must be made pure with an adequate supply being delivered to the state's growing cities. The land itself must be preserved with careful decisions made as to what should remain forest and what should be given over to the farmer's fields. Beyond these major issues, Wilson also promised that the use of the primary must be extended to every elected office in the state, the tax burden must be equally shared by all, including the wealthiest citizens and corporations, and all corrupt practices between politics and business must be outlawed. While his program might appear too ambitious to some, especially the party machines on both sides of the aisle, Wilson reminded his fellow politicians from throughout the state of New Jersey that "We are the servants of the people, of the whole people." If they kept this truth ever before them, then they could work with the certain knowledge that they would help first this generation and then all mankind to greater progress and achievement.[340]

---

[340] Woodrow Wilson, "Inaugural Address as Governor of New Jersey, January 17, 1911," *PPWW*, II, Part 2, 270-282.

While the tone in his inaugural address had been decidedly moderate, the actions he took in leading the legislature bordered on the revolutionary. Convinced that the separation of powers had been exaggerated to the detriment of the executive, Wilson decided to take command of the legislature. He went directly to the room in the state capital where previously business leaders had come to tell the state legislators what bills could be passed and which ones must be killed. Wilson locked the door, promising that as long as he was Governor, the key would stay in his pocket. He kept his own door open to any legislator, Democrat or Republican, who wished to speak with him. He also attended conferences and caucuses among legislators at the state house. When angry politicians condemned him for overstepping the powers of his office, he argued that, as the chief executive, he more truly represented all of the people of New Jersey than anyone else in the state house. He was as direct with the politicians in Trenton as he had been with the people on the campaign trail:

> "You can turn aside from the measure if you choose; you can decline to follow me; you can deprive me of office and turn away from me; but you cannot deprive me of power so long as I steadfastly stand for what I believe to be the interests and legitimate demands of the people themselves."[341]

Despite his determination to move reform legislation through the state house, Wilson had a hard time getting members of his own party to sponsor his bills. Within just days of taking office, the new Governor threatened to keep the representatives in a special session if they failed to act on behalf of reform. If they still refused to help him, then he would go directly to the people in mass meetings all over the state and ask them to make sure their representatives voted correctly. Under such relentless pressure, E. H. Geran, an assemblyman from Monmouth County, finally agreed to support the Direct Primaries bill. This act would extend the use of the primary to all state offices as well as all positions in the two major political parties. The elections would be overseen by citizens who had passed special civil service exams. The law also prescribed how party platforms would be written. After the candidates for the legislature had been nominated, they would meet to write their party's platform and would then pledge that they would fulfill every promise they had made in it once elected.[342]

When Jim Nugent, Wilson's former campaign manager and the chairman of the state's Democratic party, called a special meeting to plan how to defeat the

---

[341] Daniels, *Woodrow Wilson*, 102.

[342] Hale, *Woodrow Wilson*, 185-213; Baker, *Life and Letters*, III, 136..

measure, the Governor showed up at the state house. He stayed at the meeting for over four hours, defending the proposed law and arguing down any charge against it. Later in an angry confrontation over the bill, Nugent shouted at Wilson, "I know you think you've got the votes." He stormed out of the Governor's office saying as he left, "I don't know how you got them … You're no gentleman!" After a party in Avon, New Jersey six months later, where Nugent toasted Wilson as "a liar and an ingrate," he was promptly removed as the state's party chairman and replaced by a Wilson supporter.[343]

The Direct Primaries Act, also known as the Geran Bill, passed the Democratic assembly with a healthy majority and the Republican senate without a struggle. By April 22, 1911, the day the legislature was adjourned, every other piece of Wilson's reform program had also been signed into law. The governor was proudest of the Corrupt Practices Act which he believed was as tough as a comparable law in England. The bill outlawed betting on elections. All campaign finance records must be open to the public. Corporations could not donate money to politicians and spending limits were placed on all campaigns. Wilson had also delivered on his promises by passing the Employers' Liability Act and a bill on the Regulation of Public Utilities. Companies were now responsible for workers injured on the job, while the Public Utilities Commission would have authority over rates for gas, water, light, and power as well as railway and trolley companies. The reform of education was underway along with the transformation of local politics since now every city in New Jersey could adopt the commission form of government.[344]

As Governor Wilson looked back over the last six remarkable months of his life, he took much of the credit for himself, at least when he confessed his accomplishments to Mary Peck in a letter written to her the day after the legislature adjourned:

> "Everyone, the papers included, are saying that none of it could have been done, if it had not been for my influence and tact and hold upon the people. Be that as it may, the thing was done, and the result was as complete a victory as has even been won, I venture to say, in the history of the country. I wrote the platform, I had the measures formulated in my mind, I kept the pressure of opinion

---

[343] Daniels, *Woodrow Wilson*, 36-37.

[344] Ibid, 72; Woodrow Wilson, "A Statement on the Work of the New Jersey Legislative Session of 1911, April 22, 1911," *PWW*, XXII, 578-579; one of the best descriptions of Wilson's accomplishments can be found in a letter he wrote to Mary Hulbert (formerly Mary Peck); see Woodrow Wilson, "Letter to Mary Hulbert, April 23, 1911," *PWW*, XXII, 581-582.

constantly on the legislature, and the programme was carried out to the last detail."[345]

Wilson admitted he was relieved that he would be able to look voters in the eyes in the upcoming elections in the fall when all the state representatives ran for office again. But Wilson also knew that his new secretary Joe Tumulty and his wife Ellen had a great deal to do with his success. Tumulty had been worried early on that Wilson was too grim in his meetings with the state legislators. He told the Governor he was "too stiff and academic" with them and many were anxious to see if there was "a more human side to him." Tumulty enlisted Ellen Wilson in finding a solution. The two were soon fast friends and even became each other's confidante in their determination to save the new governor's political career. Tumulty often came to the family home, walking past his boss and saying, "I want to talk to Mrs. Wilson – you can't come. She's a better politician than you, Governor."[346] Acting on their advice, Wilson entertained both Democrats and Republicans alike at parties where he told jokes, did impressions, and even danced a cakewalk with one of the senators. "These evenings undoubtedly played their part in the outcome," he confessed to Mary, "They brought us all together on terms of intimacy; made them realize what sort of *person* I was."[347]

Wilson was excited but overwhelmed at the thought that his success as governor might open the way for him to run for the White House, not in the far distant future but in just one year. The Democrats were looking for a dynamic candidate to run against Republican President William Howard Taft who would be trying for his second term in 1912. Taft was considered vulnerable since he was disliked by the extreme ends of his own party. Conservatives were angry at the trust busting activities of Taft's Justice Department, while progressives, most notably former President Theodore Roosevelt, criticized his hand-picked successor for failing to pass any significant reform legislation. If Taft did get his party's nomination, many Democrats predicted Teddy would run for president himself on a third party ticket. With the Republicans splitting their votes between Taft and Roosevelt, a Democrat might win for the first time since Grover Cleveland took the top office in 1892. It was also a good sign that a Democrat would win the White House in the next election after the party took the House of Representatives in 1910. While all these possibilities were exhilarating to Wilson who had dreamt of becoming a great leader since his boyhood, the reality of

---

[345] Ibid., 583.

[346] Tumulty, *Woodrow Wilson as I Know Him*, 75; McAdoo, *The Woodrow Wilsons*, 120-121.

[347] Woodrow Wilson, "Letter to Mary Hulbert, April 23, 1911," *PWW*, XXII, 582- 583.

governing even a small state like New Jersey had been a strain on him. The pressure would be even greater if he was given the chance to lead his country. He looked into his future imagining once again that he was the captain of a ship facing his own fate and the future of all mankind. He saw a great battle brewing in the distance between the forces of greed on the one side and the forces of justice and humanity on the other. "What a vigil it has been," he thought, "there is no telling what deep waters are ahead of me … God grant I have the strength enough … to tip the balance in the unequal and tremendous struggle."[348]

Even as he worried, most of his friends were overjoyed and wrote letters and telegrams congratulating him on his every success and predicting an even brighter future for him. Charles Talcott, the boy he had made the pact with to achieve greatness when still a boy, was one of the first to congratulate him when he was elected governor. "Warmest congratulations … you have certainly a great victory," wrote Talcott. Wilson's best friend from his law school days, Richard "Heath" Dabney, was even more excited. He wrote that he would jump over the rotunda of the University of Virginia and click his heels once Wilson had become governor. But when his old friend took his "seat in the chair of George Washington," Dabney would not make another leap like this one since he would be at the inauguration. "I've never seen one yet," he wrote, "but I shall not miss *yours*!"[349]

Wilson's greatest supporter for his candidacy as President of the United States was his own wife Ellen. If he ever hesitated or doubted that he should make a run for the White House, she would calmly urge him not to be so hasty. Both she and her friend Joe Tumulty were always on the look out for ways to promote his interests. They both knew that the Democratic candidate in 1912 would have to win the support of William Jennings Bryan, the party's standard bearer who, after losing three presidential elections for the Democrats in 1896, 1900, and 1908, would probably not make another run for the White House. When Mrs. Wilson heard that Bryan was coming to lecture at the Theological Seminary at Princeton in March of 1911, she invited him to dinner. She then sent word to her husband in Trenton to get back to Princeton as quickly as he could to entertain an important guest. When both men finally met, they were delighted in each other's company. They spoke not at all about politics, but instead swapped stories and jokes over dinner. "A truly captivating man, I must admit," Wilson wrote the next night to Mary Peck, while Bryan told his friends that the Governor was not a

[348] Ibid., 583.

[349] Charles Andrew Talcott, "Telegram to Woodrow Wilson," *PWW,* XXI, 583; Richard Heath Dabney, "Letter to Woodrow Wilson, September 18, 1910," *PWW*, XXI, 138.

solemn college professor, but a lively and nimble-minded fellow. Bryan was especially captivated by the charming Mrs. Wilson. Tumulty was equally excited about the amazing Ellen Wilson who had pulled off a political coup. "You have nominated your husband, Mrs. Wilson," said the overjoyed little Irishman. "It was nothing at all," answered the gracious Ellen Wilson.[350]

With the support of his friends, and especially with the urging of his wife, Woodrow Wilson set out on a speaking tour of the country in May 1911 to test the waters for his presidential candidacy. He would travel more than 8,000 miles, speaking everywhere from Kansas City, Denver, and San Francisco in the Far West back to Minneapolis, St. Paul, and Lincoln in the Middle West. He then headed to Texas, back to Kentucky, and finally to the Carolinas. Everywhere he went he found crowds waiting to hear his ideas about reforming government on a national scale. Every night he sent long telegrams back to Ellen and his daughters describing the events of the day. Then he bundled up clippings about his speeches from the local papers, mailed them back home, and prepared another talk for the next town.

The crowds especially responded to his bold call for change that was rooted at the same time in the traditions of the past. He assured them that he understood the unrest that had come up directly from the people for more than a generation. Americans were not calling for "revolution," but for "restoration." They wanted the freedom to control their own destiny once again in the way the Founding Fathers had originally intended it. Instead of government functioning on behalf of the wealthiest citizens, it would work for the good of the common man. Wilson predicted that the Democratic Party would lead the way into this better future. Unlike the Republican Party that had held power for so long as the tool of the corporations, the Democratic Party would find new ways to free the people from this grip of money and make the government a truly representative democracy once again. In one of his most acclaimed speeches in Denver, he spoke of reform not just as a part of the political traditions of the nation but as part of its religious heritage as well. Surely the Bible shows a man's right relationship to God. Once a man knows he has an eternal destiny, "he stands up a free man" who understands the role he must play for good in God's universe. As long as the nation remains Christian, Wilson affirmed that the drive to make life better for each new generation would always rise up from the very heart of a faithful people.[351]

---

[350] McAdoo, *The Woodrow Wilsons*, 123-124; Woodrow Wilson, "Letter to Mary Hulbert, March 13, 1911," *PWW*, XXII, 500-501.

[351] Woodrow Wilson gave 25 major addresses during his 8,000 mile swing through the nation; two of the most significant speeches came in Kansas City where he spoke on freedom and in Denver

As he traveled through the country that he now loved so deeply, Wilson began to envision what he would later call the "New Freedom." It was clear to him that big business had hijacked the government of the United States through its chief weapon, the Republican Party. While there was nothing wrong with business growing "big" to match the country or corporations developing as a way of "efficiency," it was dangerous for the country's political future and even for its economic one to hand all power over to the wealthy. It would also ruin the chance of the nation to become the leader of the world if democracy in America gave way to oligarchy. For Wilson, the greatest role that he or any other politician could play was as a hero who set the people free to experience once again the government as their Founding Fathers had intended it to be. So long as the Americans were held hostage by special interests and corruption, there could be no true democracy in the United States. It would be up to the Democratic Party to transform itself and be ready to lead the rebirth of democracy in America. The Democrats had long called themselves the party of the people, but they had lost their way after the Civil War with no agreement on practical ways to use their power once elected to help the people. The challenge was for the Democrats and the nation to catch up with the people. All the old traditions of the party and America, including the equality of all men and an even playing field from which people could rise up and make their dreams come true, would be reborn in the struggle to achieve the New Freedom.

Wilson came back to New Jersey and headed out onto the campaign trail to support the Democratic assemblymen and senators who had backed his reform program in the last term of the legislature. He stumped in every district except Essex County where Boss Smith and Jim Nugent still had a powerful influence. Convinced that he had led a tide for permanent reform that had come directly from the citizens of his state, he was stunned when the assembly along with the senate went Republican. As he started his second year as the Governor of New Jersey in early 1912, many were ready to dismiss him as bright dream that had faded all too quickly. Would the national party be willing to take a chance on him as their new standard bearer if he could not even hold on to the little state of New Jersey? As Wilson doubted himself, his most dedicated supporters, old and new, went to work to salvage his presidential hopes. Cleveland Dodge donated thousands to the cause and Wilson soon had a war chest of $200,000. William McCombs, a former student of Wilson's at Princeton, who had volunteered to

where he gave a talk at a celebration for the 300th anniversary of the translation of the Bible into English; see Woodrow Wilson, "Issues of Freedom, May 5, 1911," and "The Bible and Progress, May 7, 1911," *PPWW*, II, Part 2, 283-290, 291-302.

implement the state's new Employers' Liability Act, now took on the job of running Wilson's presidential campaign committee. William McAdoo, the father of a Princeton student whom Wilson had once met on a train heading to the college, had become a good friend and agreed to help on the campaign. He was a brilliant organizer who was currently directing the construction of tunnels under the Hudson River in New York City. Both McCombs and McAdoo were Southerners with Scotch-Irish backgrounds like himself, and they convinced him not to give up without a fight.[352]

Wilson's supporters decided that the best place for him to start the fight for the Democratic nomination for the presidency was at the Jackson Day Dinner in Washington, D.C. in early 1912. Over 700 party leaders including William Jennings Bryan and other serious contenders for the top spot on the ticket, like Champ Clark of Missouri and Oscar Underwood of Alabama, would gather along with their supporters at the annual ritual in the ballroom of the Raleigh Hotel. They would look back at their leader Andrew Jackson, first congratulating themselves on carrying on his principles and then convincing themselves that they could find ways to make those same ideas relevant to the modern world. At first, Wilson thought it would be demeaning for a reformer like himself to take on a crowd of party leaders, but his top advisors, along with his wife Ellen, convinced him that a speech at the dinner would be the best platform to launch his run for the White House.[353]

Woodrow Wilson had delivered many important speeches in his life, but never was so much riding on his words as on the night of January 8, 1912. He must make a magnificent speech that convinced progressives like Bryan that he was truly the new leader of their wing of the party, while at the same time assured bosses from machines like New York's Tammany Hall that he could deliver voters in traditional Democratic wards all over the country. He also knew that William Randolph Hearst sat at the main table ready to make or break him in the headlines of his newspapers on a whim. At an even deeper level, Wilson on this most important night must face up to the dreams of his youth. He now stood in the place that Pitt and Burke had once found themselves in and he would at last see if he was made out of the same stuff as his childhood heroes.

Wilson began by celebrating the achievements of the Democratic Party which stood for principles that most Americans deeply cherished. Their main belief was in the basic equality of mankind. On this one key idea, dear to the hearts of the

---

[352] Baker, *Life and Letters*, III, 191-193, 234-235.

[353] Ibid., 259-260; Woodrow Wilson, "Jackson Day Dinner Address, January 8, 1912," *PPWW*, II, Part 2, 244-251.

party's two founders, Andrew Jackson and before him Thomas Jefferson, all of the Democrats in the crowded ballroom could agree. Their disagreements came when they must decide upon methods to preserve and enhance this equality. In the last generation, the party had splintered over such methods, but not its deepest beliefs. All eyes turned to Bryan as Wilson called him the one "fixed point" that held the party together in the last generation. Nothing proved that the spirit of Andrew Jackson was alive and well in the Democratic Party more than "the character and devotion and the preachings of William Jennings Bryan."[354]

After starting with a look back, Wilson now brought his fellow Democrats into the present and made them see why the demand for reform was sweeping up from the people that their party had always served. He put on his "war paint" to show the bosses that he meant to take the fight for the people straight into the Republican camp. The government of this nation, he explained, was dangerously close to being privately controlled. The reason for this was the fact that the country had for too long been under the control of the Republican Party which was the puppet of bankers, the trusts, and railroads. For the Democrats to win in November, and so become the majority party again, they must find ways to give the government back to the people. While he said this night was not the time to hammer out these methods, Wilson listed lowering the tariff and ensuring fair competition in the face of growing monopolies as specific examples of just what the Democrats could do to rescue the people. He ended by urging the many men in the room who had worked against each other to shake hands, forget the past, and agree to work together. He closed on a decidedly progressive and highly romantic note by telling the crowd that no Democratic candidate could ever again turn away from reform on behalf of the people:

> "What a travesty it is upon the name of Democracy to see any Democrat who wishes to destroy the very thing that his principles should make him in love with, namely, the life of the people themselves."[355]

Wilson's talk in the Raleigh Hotel in January 1912 had the same effect that his speech at Trenton's Taylor Opera House had back in the late summer of 1910. For a little while, the competing factions in the Democratic Party came together in the emotions of the moment. They were overwhelmed at the power of Wilson's

---

[354] Ibid., 351-353.

[355] The comment on "war paint" comes from Tumulty's description of his boss as someone who could be charming and friendly in person but who could also give rousing campaign speeches with the best of them; see his full description of Wilson as a campaigner for Governor of New Jersey in 1910 in Tumulty, *Wilson as I Know Him*, 27-37; Wilson, "Jackson Day Dinner Address," 251-253.

oratory, and many believed there was finally a greater speaker and maybe even a better leader in the party than the "Great Commoner." William Jennings Bryan may have been the most excited person in the crowd saying "it was the greatest speech in American history." Still Wilson knew that one speech would not win him the nomination. He was soon out on the road again, talking to large and friendly crowds in Ohio, Indiana, and Illinois. He gave one of his most memorable speeches in the Virginia State Capital in Richmond where he was greeted as a native son. Everywhere he went, he told Democrats who might be worried about the new direction he wanted to take the party in was merely a course correction that Jefferson himself would have approved. He also befriended a new advisor, Colonel Edward House, a wealthy Texan who been impressed with Wilson since he first heard him speak at the Texas State Fair in October 1911, to give him practical advice on winning the nomination and the election.[356]

When the Democratic Convention got underway in Baltimore on June 25, 1912, Governor Wilson was on his summer vacation in Sea Girt with his wife, three daughters, and Joe Tumulty. When the little group had arrived there in the second week of June, Wilson reminded them that "Two weeks from to-day we will either have our sweet Sunday calm again or all-day reception and an army of reporters camped on the lawn." The reporters had already set up tents on the lawn the day before the Convention started and they were determined to stay there until Wilson's nomination was assured. He had asked Judge John Wescott to place his name in nomination, and would rely on his team, especially his campaign manager McCombs and his friend McAdoo, to win the nomination for him. While he would not take an active part in the battle at the convention, he was able to deliver 248 delegates through victories in primaries and state caucuses. He also had two phone lines installed directly from the convention hall to his house at Sea Girt. One line went up to his room, and the other went into a tiny closet on the first floor. The phone in the closet was manned by a red-faced Joe Tumulty who grew more excited by the hour and who gave a minute by minute account of the events in Baltimore. The calmest person at Sea Girt was Woodrow Wilson. He spent his days golfing and his evenings reading a biography of Gladstone aloud to

[356] Bryan made the comment of Wilson's Jackson Day Dinner Address to his friend Judge Robert Hudspeth; see Baker, *Life and Letters*, III, 266; Woodrow Wilson, "Richmond Address, February 1, 1912," *PPWW*, II, Part 2, 367-388; Woodrow Wilson, "What Jefferson Would Do, April 13, 1912," *PPWW*, II, Part 2, 424-429; also see the description of the early relationship of Woodrow Wilson and Colonel House in Baker, *Life and Letters*, III, 294-309.

his wife. In his heart, he said a silent prayer, "May the Lord have mercy on me!"[357]

He was determined to make promises to no one, most especially to the party bosses, but instead hoped to win the nomination on his own merits. Still he did everything in his power to convince the progressive wing of the party that he was the legitimate heir to William Jennings Bryan. In early June, when Bryan had asked all the candidates to support his bid to nominate a progressive as the temporary chairman of the convention, Wilson was the only one who had the courage to respond. Many in his camp had told him to ignore Bryan, but Ellen Wilson encouraged him to answer. "You are quite right," Wilson had written to Bryan, "The Baltimore Convention is to be a convention of Progressives, of men who are progressive in principle and by conviction." His telegram to Bryan had convinced many progressive Democrats heading to the convention that Wilson was their man.[358]

On June 26, the night on which candidates were to be nominated, Bryan made a daring play to keep the progressive spirit alive at the Baltimore convention. He had become concerned that the bosses, especially those from Tammany Hall, and wealthy financiers, like Thomas Ryan of New York and August Belmont of Virginia, were about to take control of the convention and block any hope of a progressive winning the nomination. So he proposed a resolution to the convention that condemned any candidate who was beholden to the likes of "J. Pierpont Morgan, Thomas F. Ryan, or August Belmont." After a bitter debate on the resolution, and the removal of the names of Ryan and Belmont who were sitting at the convention as delegates, the measure passed by a vote of 883 to 201½. Bryan was sure he had single-handedly kept the cause of progressivism alive among the Democrats, while Wilson's supporters were certain the tide would now turn in favor of Wilson once the balloting started.[359]

The nominating process did not begin until midnight when the names of Alabama's Oscar Underwood, Senator Champ Clark of Missouri, and Governor Simeon Baldwin of Connecticut were placed before the crowd. Finally at 2:15

---

[357] Wilson's attitude to his possible nomination can best be seen in his weekly letters to Mary Hulbert; see Woodrow Wilson, "Letters to Mary Hulbert, June 9 and June 17, 1912," *PWW*, XXIV, 466-467, 481-482; Eleanor Wilson McAdoo mentions the same comment ("Two weeks from to-day") that her father made in McAdoo, *The Woodrow Wilsons*, 153; the description of her parents' activities cam be found in McAdoo, *The Priceless Gift*, 272; Wilson's request for Judge Prescott to nominate him can be found in Woodrow Wilson, "Letter to John Prescott, May 29, 1912," *PWW*, XXIV, 449-450.

[358] Woodrow Wilson, "Telegram to William Jennings Bryan, June 22, 1912," *PWW*, XXIV, 493.

[359] The complete text of Bryan's initial resolution can be found in Daniels, *Woodrow Wilson*, 107; Baker, *Life and Letters*, III, 345.

A.M. on the morning of June 27, 1912, Woodrow Wilson's name was placed in nomination. Judge Wescott was an old style orator whose booming voice reached every person in the convention hall. He described Wilson in terms so dramatic that the crowd cheered for an hour and a quarter:

> "Providence has given us, in the exalted character of New Jersey's Executive, the mental and moral equipment to accomplish this reincarnation of Democracy … He has been in political life less than two years. He had no organization of the usual sort; only a practical ideal, the reestablishment of equal opportunity. The logic of events points to him … Time and circumstance have evolved the immortal Governor of New Jersey … the seer and philosopher of Princeton, the Princeton schoolmaster, Woodrow Wilson."[360]

Joe Tumulty listened to the whole thing on the phone in the closet at Sea Girt, running out to tell the family, "It's *still* going on. It isn't over *yet*! Where's the Governor?" Wilson had gone to bed, but Ellen, her daughters Margaret, Jessie, and Nellie, and Joe Tumulty would get little sleep until the balloting was finally over.[361]

The first ballot came at 7 A.M. on June 27 after two more candidates, Governor Thomas Marshall of Indiana and Governor Judson Harmon of Ohio, were nominated. The results were disappointing with Champ Clark receiving 440½ votes and Wilson garnering just 324. Neither was close to the 724 votes needed to win the nomination. On the tenth ballot, Tammany Hall gave New York's 90 votes to Clark and it looked like a stampede would soon begin for the Senator from Missouri. But the stampede never happened and the convention was soon deadlocked again. Six days into the balloting, Wilson's campaign manager William McCombs became deeply discouraged and called Sea Girt recommending that the Governor release his delegates. Ellen, with tears in her eyes, told her husband that he must have breakfast before sending the telegram. When Wilson found an undertaker's catalog in the morning mail, he tried to cheer his daughters by joking, "This is certainly prompt service. Will you help me choose a coffin for a dead duck?" While Wilson and his family were still having breakfast, Tumulty ran into the dining room. He said McAdoo was on the line claiming "McCombs was crazy" and not to give up.

---

[360] Baker, *Life and Letters*, III, 345-347; quotes from Judge John Wescott's Nominating Speech for Woodrow Wilson (June 27, 1912) can be found in Baker, *Life and Letters*, III, 345-347, and Tumulty, *Woodrow Wilson As I Know Him*, 123-124.

[361] McAdoo, *The Priceless Gift*, 272; McAdoo, *The Woodrow Wilsons*, 163.

When the fourteenth ballot was taken later that day, Bryan announced that he was throwing his support to Wilson. The convention hall went wild, but still there was no groundswell on the floor for the Governor's candidacy. The movement toward Wilson only began when thousands of telegrams poured in from Democrats all over the country demanding that Wilson be nominated. It was not until July 3, 1912 on the forty-sixth ballot that Woodrow Wilson was finally chosen as the Democratic candidate for President of the United States. When Tumulty got the word from Baltimore, he raced out onto the porch and called a brass band over that had been waiting in a grove of trees since the day before. They marched toward the house playing "Hail to the Chief."[362]

As Wilson stood with his wife on the wide porch that overlooked the lawn at Sea Girt, a reporter noticed how calm the candidate was. He said, "Governor, you don't seem a bit excited." Making fun of himself, Wilson answered, "I can't effervesce."[363] In reality, he was deeply moved, even overwhelmed at the thought of the great responsibility that lay before him. He was excited that he had been chosen to fight for the "people's cause," and he looked forward to heading up a rousing campaign as the leader of the Democratic Party. Still he knew that he would face not only the befuddled and friendly William Howard Taft who had just been nominated by the Republicans, but most probably the very "real" and "vivid" Theodore Roosevelt who claimed he was the voice of reform and the true champion of the people. Certain that Taft would come in last in a three-way race, Wilson knew the contest would be between himself and Roosevelt.

For just a moment, after Roosevelt became the candidate of the Progressive or Bull Moose Party, the dreams that Wilson held about himself as a powerful leader seemed illusions. While he had long hoped to lead his nation as a great hero, and had even recently described the modern politician as a man "in love" with the people, he knew that Roosevelt actually was a hero. Teddy Roosevelt was the kind of leader in the flesh that Wilson had always wanted to be in his dreams. He had gone with the Rough Riders up San Juan Hill and spent much of his time since leaving the White House leading hunting expeditions around the world. Teddy Roosevelt would obviously be able to capture the imagination of the American people, while Woodrow Wilson would appear as "a vague, conjectural personality, more made up of opinions and academic prepossessions than of human traits and red corpuscles."[364]

---

[362] Baker, *Life and Letters*, III, 351-353; Axson, *Brother Woodrow*, 175-176; McAdoo, *The Priceless Gift*, 273-274.

[363] Ibid., 274.

[364] Woodrow Wilson, "Letter to Mary Hulbert, August 25, 1912," *PWW*, XXV, 55-56.

Even with this sudden wave of self doubt, Wilson was convinced that Roosevelt had "promised the millennium" one too many times. He could not imagine four more years of Roosevelt in the White House. While he admitted that the former president had done a great deal to wake up Americans about the need for reform, Wilson now saw Roosevelt as a madman lost in an "insane distemper of egotism." His daughter Nellie remembered how her father could do a perfect imitation of Roosevelt accepting the nomination of the Progressive or "Bull Moose" Party. "We stand at Armageddon and battle for the Lord," he cried hysterically, and then added, "Good old Teddy—what a help he is." In Wilson's opinion, Roosevelt had become a danger to the progressive cause because he had confused reform with himself and was convinced that only he could deliver it. Instead of finding a balance between high ideals and practical action, Roosevelt promised to lead his followers down a path toward reform that only he could see. One need simply look at the laundry list of promises he had made in the Progressive Party platform to understand he had gone too far ahead of the people.

Wilson distanced himself from Roosevelt by drawing a sharp contrast between their styles of leadership. "You have no right to promise Heaven," Wilson explained to his supporters, "unless you can bring us to it." Wilson would never let the voters see how much Teddy the Rough Rider intimidated him, but would instead characterize Roosevelt as an extremist who had launched a campaign of self love rather than love for the people. In fact, the Bull Moose candidate was so caught up in leading the advance party of reform that he had lost touch with the people. Wilson was always careful to portray himself as a captain moving in the same direction as Roosevelt but with a steadier hand on the helm. With a similar vision but a more stable approach, he would be able to accomplish what Roosevelt had failed to do as President. He would lower the tariff, reform taxation, and modernize the currency system. Truly believing he was the man who could deliver the reforms so long promised to Americans, and trusting in Providence, he resolved to throw himself into the race, saying "We shall see what will happen."[365]

---

[365] Daniels, *Woodrow Wilson*, 115-117; Wilson's attitude toward Roosevelt is taken from an extended quote in Tumulty, *Woodrow Wilson as I Know Him*, 125-126; Wilson's comments on not being able to imagine four more years of Roosevelt can be found in Woodrow Wilson, "Letter to Edith Gittings Reid, May 26, 1912," *PWW*, XXIV, 445-446; his imitation of Roosevelt for his family is described in McAdoo, *The Woodrow Wilsons*, 154; see also Axson, *Brother Woodrow*, 175-179, for an excellent comparison of Wilson and Roosevelt; Wilson's fears about Roosevelt as the more "real" and "vivid" candidate can be found in Woodrow Wilson, "Letter to Mary Hulbert, August 25, 1912," *PWW*, XXV, 56.

From the moment he accepted the nomination on the front porch of Sea Girt on the afternoon of August 7 to his final campaign rally in New York's Madison Square Garden on the night of October 31, Wilson decided that he could not win the race on personality, and so he must base his campaign on principles. He would lay out a vision for the future of their country that all Americans could understand. He reminded every crowd who came to see him that they were part of a great awakening of their nation. Old ideals and duties had been forgotten, while the average person found life hard to sustain. The young saw opportunity blocked at every turn, and older men found business difficult to maintain in the face of the many special favors granted to monopolies. Cherished liberties had been wasted, while precious resources had been squandered. Despite the problems, there was no need to fear. Americans were in a new and exhilarating age where their leaders must bravely lay out plans to free the people and their political system from the control of the trusts and the corporations. As to specifics, the Sherman Antitrust Act must be enforced. The tariff had outlived its usefulness and must be reduced. Taxation must be made equitable with the wealthiest citizens and corporations paying their fair share. In foreign affairs, the nation must face the world as a democracy, not an empire. The United States held the Philippines in trust and must serve the people there until they were ready to shoulder their own freedom. Finally, the nation must find a better way to educate its people for it could neither maintain its wealth nor lead the world with an ignorant population.[366]

At first, Wilson hoped that he could run his national campaign by giving significant addresses on these principles at strategic places throughout the country. He worried that his voice was not strong enough to reach large crowds in the open air and hoped to speak with them in smaller auditoriums. However, all of his advisors, most especially his wife Ellen, urged him to go out on the road and run the race for the presidency in the same way he had campaigned for Governor of New Jersey.[367] He must meet as many Americans as possible in as many places as he could travel to by Election Day. He would have to go well beyond the 8,000 miles he traveled on his 1911 speaking tour. By car and train, Wilson set off to meet the American people he had promised to set free from special interests and the Republicans face to face. The self-doubt he felt at the moment he received his nomination disappeared as he proved himself once again to be a lively speaker on

[366] Woodrow Wilson, "Speech of Acceptance, August 7, 1912," *PPWW*, II, Part 2, 452-474.

[367] Baker, *Life and Letters*, III, 375; Baker mentions that Wilson's supporters, both wealthy ones, like Cleveland Dodge and Cyrus McCormick, and smaller contributors who gave less than $100, were able to raise $1,110,953.25 for his campaign. In fact, nearly $319,000 of the total came from people who could each give less than $100. After Wilson was elected, he was able to turn over a cash balance of $25,000 to the Democratic National Committee (see Ibid., 399).

the stump. Reporters were amazed that he was not the stiff academic they expected him to be, but a real working politician with an open and easy manner. He usually had the crowd on his side from his opening banter with them all the way to the end of his prepared speech. They noticed, too, that he was able to keep the same ideas, first presented in his acceptance speech, fresh by changing his tone and phrasing slightly to match the mood of every crowd.[368]

However, not everyone was pleased with Wilson's performance on the campaign trail. Many of the most diehard progressives in the party found him too cautious. They said he carefully avoided taking a stand on the most controversial issues of the day. The self-appointed champion of the people refused to discuss both the "Negro question" and the rights of women. In private, he met with black leaders and assured them that he would "seek to be the President of the whole nation and would know no differences of race or creed or section." In public, he said the states must decide whether women should vote. Republican politicians and the newspapermen who supported them poured through Wilson's many writings that had been published since his youth and attacked him on a variety of points. When they said his *Short History of the American People* proved he hated immigrants, he pointed to the fact that the Democrats had been the party of immigrants since the days when Jefferson and Madison led the opposition to the Alien and Seditions Acts. While some attacked him as a "Black Presbyterian" who would discriminate against Catholics, others spread rumors that he was a secret member of the Knights of Columbus. He countered by saying he was a believing Protestant who respected all religions including the "great" Catholic faith. While he was himself not a Knight of Columbus, he mentioned that his private secretary Joe Tumulty was a devout Catholic. His supporters listed the many Catholics he had picked for state offices in New Jersey. They also pointed to an important speech Wilson had given at Carnegie Hall in December 1911 defending the rights of American Jews as proof that he honored all faiths.[369]

No one was angrier at Woodrow Wilson on the stump than Theodore Roosevelt. By running as the candidate of the Progressive or Bull Moose Party, Roosevelt had assured the defeat of his former friend William Howard Taft, the Republican candidate. But instead of certain victory in the upcoming election, he now found himself locked in a race with another man he had once championed. Roosevelt was especially frustrated at Wilson for ignoring every attack he

---

[368] David Lawrence, *The True Story of Woodrow Wilson* (New York: George H. Doran Company, 1924), 56.

directed against the Democratic candidate. The dramatic Roosevelt spent much of his time on the campaign trail jousting with a shadow. Everywhere he looked Wilson was not to be found. Still when he peered into the future, he saw only Wilson. A cartoon of the day best captured Roosevelt's frustration by showing the Bull Moose candidate hunched over a crystal ball with a smiling Wilson staring back at him from inside it.[370]

For his part, Wilson ignored the attacks on him while insulting Roosevelt in a carefully calculated manner. In public, Wilson took the high road, never responding directly to Roosevelt, but usually going out of his way to be respectful toward Taft, the certain loser. Wilson even visited President Taft at the Copley Plaza Hotel when they were both campaigning in Boston.[371] In contrast, the more that Roosevelt argued he was the only man who could save the country from ruin, the more that Wilson mocked any "gentleman" who thought the government would collapse or the nation would go to pieces if he was not elected. "There is no indispensable man," he had said from his front porch at Sea Girt when he accepted the nomination.[372] The crowd loudly cheered him, knowing that this jab was meant for Roosevelt. He also liked to portray his opponent as a rabble rouser who shouted loudly but who could accomplish little. At a campaign stop in Denver, he asked the crowd to imagine Teddy convincing business leaders to give up monopolies by leading them in the Hallelujah Chorus. In contrast to Roosevelt's campaign of self adulation, Wilson emphasized the sound principles upon which he would base his actions once he was President. At a rally in Pueblo, Colorado, he explained why his approach was so much better than those of his rivals in a series of questions that sounded humble but were actually quite pointed:

> "What difference does Mr. Taft's record make to me? What difference does Mr. Roosevelt's career so far make to me? What difference does my own character … make in the presence of these tremendous issues of life? I tell you truly I can't afford to think about Mr. Taft or Mr. Roosevelt when I am thinking about the fortunes of the people of the United States … What are men as compared with the standards of righteousness?"[373]

---

[369] Baker, *Life and Letters*, III, 380-390; Woodrow Wilson, "Letter to William McAdoo, October 22, 1912," *PWW*, XXV, 442-443; Woodrow Wilson, "The Rights of the Jews, December 6, 1911" *PPWW*, II, Part 2, 318-322.

[370] Baker, *Life and Letters*, III, 269, 376; 380, 390, 394.

[371] Ibid., 392.

[372] Woodrow Wilson, "Speech of Acceptance," 473.

[373] Woodrow Wilson, "Campaign Address in Pueblo, Colorado, October 7, 1912," is quoted in Baker, *Life and Letters*, III, 376-377; similar ideas can be found in Woodrow Wilson, "Campaign

Wilson kept up this approach throughout the campaign, and only communicated with Roosevelt directly after he was shot at a rally in Milwaukee on October 14. Wilson sent a telegram to his rival saying, "Please accept my warmest sympathy and heartiest congratulations that your wound is not serious."[374] He also vowed to stop campaigning until Roosevelt had fully recovered. Just one day after Teddy Roosevelt returned to the campaign trail, Wilson held his final campaign rally at Madison Square Garden, where more than 16,000 supporters waved American flags and shouted, "We want Wilson!" for over an hour before the candidate could finally speak. When the crowd finally fell silent, Wilson in the deep tones that so characterized his voice was serious. This was his last chance to speak of his devotion to the people and his certainty that they in turn would speak in favor of his vision at the polls in less than a week. "All over the country, from one ocean to the other, … in less than a week" he quietly told the hushed audience, "the common people of America will come into their own again."[375]

At last, the exhausting campaign was over. Wilson had often admitted on the road that he did not have the "Bull Moose's strength" like Roosevelt did. On one of the toughest days of his campaign in Bryan's home state of Nebraska, Wilson made seven speeches in Omaha before racing down dusty country roads in an open car to Lincoln were he made two more. Sometimes after speaking elsewhere to crowds as large as 35,000, he lost his voice. His old stomach problems returned and he suffered from frequent indigestion. His "sick headaches" also came back with a vengeance. He worried, too, that he was gaining weight and could not seem to lose it. Friends who visited him at Cleveland Lane were surprised at his drawn and pale appearance when he returned from his campaign trips. Still he seemed to recover quickly with his wife and daughters at his side again. Once back home and restored to health, his only concern now was that the privacy of his family would disappear for good if he did win the Presidency.[376]

Speech at Colorado Springs, October 7, 1912," and "Campaign Speech at Denver, Colorado, October 7, 1912," *PWW*, XXV, 362-368 and 369-377 respectively. The "Hallelujah Chorus" comment can be found in the Denver speech.

[374] "Two News Reports: Wilson Sends Sympathy; Wilson Won't Speak with Roosevelt Ill, October 15, 1912," *PWW*, XXV, 418-419.

[375] Eleanor Wilson McAdoo gives an excellent account of her father's last campaign rally at Madison Square Garden which she and her sisters attended; see McAdoo, *The Woodrow Wilsons*, 178-180; Woodrow Wilson, "A Campaign Address in Madison Square Garden, October 31, 1912," *PWW*, XXV, 493-501.

[376] For the comment on the "Bull Moose's strength," see Woodrow Wilson, "Letter to Frank Glass, September 6, 1912," *PWW*, XXV, 113; for Wilson's overall comments on his health, see

On Tuesday November 5, 1912, Woodrow Wilson went early to a nearby fire station to cast his vote. He returned home and took a group of friends on a walk around Princeton to see places where Washington had fought his own campaign against the British. He also showed them the diploma that James Madison had received, the only Princeton graduate to be elected President of the United States so far. Later in the evening, he went back to Cleveland Lane and retired to his wife's studio where Ellen Wilson read to him from the poems of Robert Browning while he sat by the fire. Relatives, friends, and reporters filled the house, crowding around Joe Tumulty every time the phone rang with news about the latest returns. Just as in the Governor's race, the word came at 10 P.M. that Wilson had been elected. Reporters burst through the front door shouting, "He's elected!" The bell in the tower of Princeton's Nassau Hall started tolling wildly. Ellen Wilson heard the excitement, left the sitting room to make sure the news was official, and then returned to her waiting husband. She put her hands on his shoulders, kissed him, and said, "Let me be the first to congratulate you!"[377]

When Wilson came out his wife's studio, he looked serious and was not smiling. His daughters raced up to him and kissed him, while every one else came forward to shake his hand. Soon they heard students coming from Princeton toward the Wilson house on Cleveland Lane singing "Old Nassau." Tumulty ran out to the porch with a chair for Wilson to stand on so he could address the boys who stood listening to him with torches in their hands. "I have no feeling of triumph to-night, but a feeling of solemn responsibility," he told the students who were gathered in front of him. "I know the very great task that lies ahead of me and the men associated with me. I look almost with pleading to you, the young men of America, to stand behind me, to support me in the new administration." He then spoke of his sympathy for those he had defeated. Surely they had made mistakes, but they had not done so with any intention of harming the nation. He began to think, too, of how long it would take to accomplish his vision to set things right in America. It would not be one man or a single session of Congress that would achieve it. Rather, it would be a long journey that would continue on into the next generation. In the chill of the November evening, Woodrow Wilson, now captain of the ship of state, suddenly understood that he could begin the

---

Woodrow Wilson, "Letters to Mary Hulbert, September 1 and 29, 1912," *PWW*, XXV, 66-67, 284-285; one of the best comments from a friend on Wilson's appearance after returning from campaign trip can be found in a letter written by Fred Yates to his wife dated August 8, 1912. Yates was an artist that the Wilsons had met while traveling through England. His letter is quoted in Baker, *Life and Letters*, III, 402.

[377] McAdoo, *The Woodrow Wilsons*, 180-181; "News Report: Kiss from Wife Tells President He's President-Elect, November 5, 1912," *PWW*, XXV, 517-518.

journey of America toward its new freedom, but he would not be able to take the nation there by himself or in his own lifetime.[378]

[378] McAdoo, *The Priceless Gift*, 274-275; Woodrow Wilson, "Remarks to Princeton Neighbors and Students," *PWW*, XXV, 520-521.

Chapter 8

"LET THE PEOPLE COME FORWARD"

This is the high enterprise of the new day: to lift everything as concerns our life as a nation to the light that shines from the hearthfire of every man's conscience and vision of the right.

Woodrow Wilson[379]

Woodrow Wilson had campaigned for President of the United States in the certain hope that he more truly understood the American people than either Theodore Roosevelt or William Howard Taft. But when the votes were finally tallied, he had not won an overwhelming personal victory. In fact, he had received only 42% of the popular vote. He had won 6,286,214 votes, while Roosevelt took 4,126,020 with Taft coming in last as predicted with 2,483,922. Eugene V. Debs, the Socialist candidate, had won an amazing 6% of the popular vote. Wilson could be comforted in the fact that he had won a smashing electoral victory. The final tally gave him 435 votes compared to 88 for Roosevelt and 8 for Taft. Wilson had won in every section of the country with Roosevelt taking just five states, Michigan, Minnesota, Pennsylvania, South Dakota, and Washington, and Taft winning only Vermont and Utah. Wilson and Roosevelt had split the electors in California.[380] The Democrats also kept the House of Representatives and took the Senate. Even with such a hard-fought victory behind him, Wilson remained determined to find a way to speak for all the American people, including the more than six and a half million who had voted against him. In the bright days that came upon him in the fall of 1912, he decided that he must get away to a quiet

[379] Woodrow Wilson, "First Inaugural Address, March 4, 1913," *PWW*, XXVII, 151.

[380] Baker, *Life and Letters*, IV, 410.

place where he could think deeply about the direction in which he would lead everyone in his nation. He knew from his own study of history and politics that he would have but a short time to turn all the promises he had made on the campaign trail into actual laws for the entire nation. He must work quickly and deliberately while the light of reform still burned brightly in the hearts of the people he had come to love so much.

Wilson knew that many of his fellow countrymen might think it odd that he needed time to get away and think just days after his election. "One is considered queer in America," he told his daughter Nellie, "if one requires time for concentrated thought." This quiet reflection would be necessary for the President-Elect who was committed to searching deep down in his mind and heart to understand his own times and the needs of his people. As he looked back, Wilson saw how the American people had lived through a dramatic era of lost ideals, shattered dreams, and renewed hopes. Their longing for a better future had been reawakened in the three-way race for the White House in 1912. If Wilson was to be the spokesman and interpreter of these trying times and the will of the people, then he must search himself "through and through" with a "pure heart" in order to choose the "high course of action."[381]

As the leader of America's great ship of state, Wilson headed for the sea to reflect on his new life as President. His friend Mary Peck, who had retaken her first husband's name and now called herself Mrs. Hulbert, offered the use of Green Cove Cottage, her house in Bermuda, to the President-Elect. Just ten days after the election, Wilson boarded a ship bound for the Caribbean in New York City with Ellen and his daughters Jessie and Nellie. Margaret knew that she would have many duties once the family moved to Washington and decided to stay behind in New York for some final singing lessons. Wilson told his wife and two youngest daughters who were accompanying him that a trip to the Caribbean would be "an excellent tonic for us all," especially after everything they had been through in the two short years since he had officially entered politics. Relatives, friends, office seekers, newspapermen, and even sightseers had overrun the family homes at Sea Girt and Cleveland Land. The Wilson girls had gotten used to fielding questions from reporters on their every thought and responding to the countless invitations they had received since the election in November. Nellie Wilson was amused when a silk manufacturer asked her to choose the next fashionable color to replace the blue so favored by Teddy Roosevelt's daughter Alice. Each of the girls also received marriage proposals from all over the country. Their father hoped that a cruise and a vacation in the Caribbean would

---

[381] McAdoo, *The Woodrow Wilsons*, 191; Woodrow Wilson, "First Inaugural Address," 151.

help them catch their breaths before the even greater whirlwind of life in the White House had descended upon them.[382]

The Wilson family found that Green Cove Cottage was a haven where they could spend time with one another for what would probably be the last time. The large white house had a fence with a locked gate in front of it to keep out the prying eyes of the press. The windows in the back opened out toward the sea. At night, the green shutters could be closed against the wind. Nellie and Jessie were amazed at the veranda that wrapped around the house. They could jump from it right into the clear blue waters of the Caribbean. Ellen Wilson loved the vines filled with pink flowers that seemed to be everywhere and the deep red coral of the sea. She had taken her paints with her and set up her easel to capture the magical beauty of the paradise that surrounded her. She also enjoyed long carriage rides with her husband and daughters. Wilson loved filling baskets with sandwiches and heading by bike with Jessie and Nellie to picnics all over the island.[383]

The President-Elect soon settled down to the more serious business that had led him to Green Cove Cottage. His first order of business was to catch up on his correspondence, especially to the many friends and well-wishers who had flooded him with congratulations since the election. He was soon most deeply concerned about Mary Hulbert who was passing through a divorce from her second husband and the death of her mother. She had written to her "devoted friend" Woodrow that her youth seemed to disappear with the passing of her mother and she had nothing to look forward to anymore. Wilson spoke to her in terms of the sea that he loved so much. "The waters are very deep and very black," he wrote, but this was merely a passing storm and not a reason to despair. Mary Hulbert was too vibrant a person for life not to come back in her even stronger than before. He reminded her that her son Allen still needed her and assured her that her life would bloom again.[384]

While at Green Cove, Wilson also had time to read over the many promises he had made to the American people during the campaign. He was determined to find ways to meet the expectations that he believed the citizens of his nation now had for him. He had painted himself in heroic terms, saying often that he was leading them on a great crusade from imprisonment into freedom. He had even called for a "Second Emancipation" from the slavery of the trusts that would be

---

[382] McAdoo, *The Woodrow Wilsons*, 191.
[383] Ibid., 182-192.
[384] Woodrow Wilson, "Letter to Mary Hulbert, January 1, 1913," *PWW*, XXVII, 3-9.

similar to the first emancipation that freed the slaves.[385] In October, just a month before the election, he had written an open letter to the American public explicitly stating that he would rescue the nation from the grip of the monopolies that had crushed competition. This bold action would be necessary since the trusts had taken control of not just the economy but the government as well. "Until it is freed," he explained, "it cannot serve the people as a whole." He had proposed lowering the tariff as the best way to set Americans and their government free. Once the tariff was lowered, it would be clear to business leaders that they could never again seek favors from the government at the expense of the people. Monopolies could then be broken up and opportunity for all would flourish in an atmosphere of healthy competition. Only then could the government get down to its real business of passing laws that would improve the lives of all Americans.[386]

Wilson's vision had seemed so clear on the campaign trail, but now in the quiet of Green Cove, it appeared more like a dream. What was this New Freedom that people had nicknamed his campaign and now called his administration? Wilson answered the question by putting together a collection of his campaign speeches with the help of a young editor named William Bayard Hale. The book was to be published in the upcoming year as *The New Freedom* with the subtitle of "A Call for the Emancipation of the Generous Energies of a People." Wilson wanted to make sure that Americans understood that his call for the emancipation of his nation had come from the people's own cry for reform and not from some abstract concept on his part. His latest book was therefore an attempt to express the spirit of the people and to set it forth "in large terms which may stick in the imagination." By carefully laying out the best excerpts from his many speeches, he would state again his promises to lower the tariff and so free the nation from the grip of monopolies and the politicians whom they had long controlled. This would be done not to destroy business but to make it more competitive. The book would also show that Wilson had made another important promise on the campaign trail. This promise was to reform the nation's credit system. At present, credit was privately controlled by a handful of bankers in New York City. The country itself had no way to regulate interest rates. So long as this situation existed, Wilson warned that the "old variety and freedom and individual energy of

---

[385] Woodrow Wilson, "Campaign Speech in Denver, Colorado, October 7, 1912," *PWW*, XXVI, 369-377.

[386] Woodrow Wilson, "A Public Letter to the Voters of America, October 19, 1912," *PWW*, XXVI, 432-440.

development are out of the question."[387]

With the major goals of lowering the tariff, controlling the trusts, and reforming the nation's credit clearly before him, Wilson set to work picking his cabinet. He had dreamt of such a task since he wrote his first essay on "Cabinet Government" while just an undergraduate at Princeton. Cabinet officials should be the right arm of a powerful executive who helped him shape legislation that would improve the lives of all the people. Wilson's special understanding of the way in which an executive should work had only grown stronger during his one year as Governor of New Jersey. "I must have the best men in the nation," he told his college friend Walter Hines Page whom he would appoint as the ambassador to Great Britain, in order to help him craft reform legislation and push it through the Congress.[388] Wilson hoped these "best men" would stand shoulder to shoulder with him in the great battle he saw opening before him in the halls of Congress and the board rooms of the nation's businesses to free the nation from special privilege. He did not care if they were Democrats or Republicans and even said he would appoint people who had voted for Roosevelt or Taft if they were qualified. Since it was critical to build an excellent team around him, Wilson decided to choose only the top cabinet officers, ambassadors, and judges himself. In this way, he would avoid the many unqualified office seekers who would come looking for jobs after the election.[389]

Wilson had already begun to discuss possible cabinet choices with Colonel House, his new advisor. House reminded him that William Jennings Bryan would have to be given a cabinet position. This must be done in part to please the many party regulars who would demand a post for Bryan. But more importantly, it would prevent him from forming an opposition to the new President and ruining his chances for re-election in 1916. Wilson decided to offer the position of Secretary of State to Bryan, but remained determined to choose the most qualified men for the other positions. He also said he would not remove excellent workers from their jobs in the executive branch just because they were Republicans. As House corresponded with the new president about the remaining cabinet posts, he was certain that Wilson's idealism in the present would do a great disservice to him in the future. Republicans appointed to his administration would not remember Wilson kindly once they wrote their memoirs. History, House worried

[387] Woodrow Wilson, "A Preface to The New Freedom," *PWW*, XXVII, 6-7; Woodrow Wilson, *The New Freedom: A Call for the Emancipation of the Generous Energies of a People* (New York: Doubleday, Page and Company, 1913), 184-191.

[388] Wilson's remark to Page is quoted in Baker, *Life and Letters*, IV, 23.

[389] "A Warning to Office Seekers, March 5, 1913," *PWW*, XXVII, 153.

privately, would not think well of Woodrow Wilson because of this honest mistake.[390]

Determined to find the best men for his cabinet, the President-Elect spent much of his time at Green Cove Cottage creating charts on potential candidates. He listed the qualifications of each man on a separate sheet of paper. Wilson wrote down the details of their careers, their closest friends, and even what their wives were like. He then reviewed the charts over and over again, seemingly unable to make a final decision on any of them. Nellie Wilson found the process especially maddening. She finally told her father that she did not care who he chose as long as he picked his campaign advisor William McAdoo as the Secretary of the Treasury. Wilson did not tell his daughter that he had already picked McAdoo for the post, certain he would be the perfect man to help reform the nation's credit system. Instead, he teased her by saying to his wife, "Imagine! Nell wants me to appoint a man to the Cabinet just because she likes him." Ellen Wilson joined in the decision-making process in order to ensure that Joseph Tumulty would continue as her husband's private secretary. At first, Wilson worried that Tumulty might be too inexperienced and even "provincial" for Washington, D.C. But he was furious when people warned him a Catholic like Tumulty would reveal every presidential secret directly to the Vatican. Calling such a charge "asinine," Wilson agreed with Ellen and kept her best friend on as his secretary.[391]

While Wilson hoped to choose the top posts in his administration in an orderly way, he soon realized that making choices in this manner would not always be possible. When he returned to New Jersey with his family in late December, he was besieged by members of his own party who urged him to place Democratic Congressmen and Senators in his cabinet. They told him this would be the only way he could get his reform legislation passed through the House and Senate. But even when he did offer cabinet positions to Congressmen, they did not always accept. A. Mitchell Palmer, a representative from Pennsylvania and the leader of Wilson's forces on the floor of the Baltimore Convention, turned down the post of Secretary of War since he was a Quaker. Wilson also had a difficult time convincing many of his friends to take ambassadorships around the world. He wanted to appoint Princeton's Dean Henry Fine as the ambassador to Germany, but his old friend turned him down, explaining that he could not survive on the low government salary offered to him. Even men who did take

390 Colonel House, "From the Diary of Colonel House, January 8, 1913," *PWW*, XXVII, 20-23.

391 McAdoo, *The Priceless Gift*, 275-276; Colonel House, "From the Diary of Colonel House, January 8, 1913," *PWW*, XXVII, 24; McAdoo, *The Woodrow Wilsons*, 196-197.

ambassadorships later came back to Wilson saying they must resign unless they received more money to support their families. The new President would have to turn to his wealthy friend Cleveland Dodge to keep Walter Hines Page in London. Dodge agreed to pay a salary of $25,000 to Ambassador Page each year and also to keep this secret between himself, the President, and Ellen Wilson.[392]

Considering Bryan and McAdoo as his most important picks, Wilson finally decided on the rest of his cabinet early in 1913. Attorney Lindley Garrison, the Vice Chancellor of New Jersey, was made the Secretary of War. J.C. McReynolds, a government lawyer from Tennessee who had helped to prosecute the case against the tobacco trust, became the Attorney General. Franklin K. Lane, a dynamic member of the United States Commerce Commission from California, was appointed as the Secretary of the Interior. The Postmaster Generalship went to the longtime Democratic Congressman from Texas, Albert Burleson. Wilson chose his close friend Josephus Daniels of North Caroline as the Secretary of the Navy and fellow college president David Houston of Missouri as the Secretary of Agriculture. While he had hoped to appoint the brilliant Boston jurist Louis Brandeis to Commerce Secretary, Wilson offered the post to Massachusetts Congressman W. C. Redfield, an expert on the tariff in the House of Representatives, under pressure from his fellow Democrats. William B. Wilson of Pennsylvania, an officer in the American Federation of Labor, became the Secretary of Labor. Along with these top cabinet positions, President-Elect Wilson made plans to name several judges to the federal bench including Charles A. Wood, the North Carolina lawyer he had met onboard the *S.S. Ethiopia* during his first trip to Europe in 1896. Wilson also enjoyed appointing enthusiastic young progressives to posts in the government. He thought it a “capital” idea when Josephus Daniels recommended that Franklin D. Roosevelt, an attorney who had worked hard for Wilson’s election in upstate New York, be appointed as the Assistant Secretary of the Navy.[393]

Even as Wilson worked to fill the key positions in his administration with the best men possible, he was still the Governor of New Jersey and was determined to push through as much reform legislation as possible before he left for Washington. On January 14, 1913, he gave a more ambitious message to the legislature than he had ever done before. He warned corporations that New Jersey would no longer be a state where they could hide. He laid out a series of laws to

[392] Alexander Mitchell Palmer, “Letter to Woodrow Wilson, February 24, 1913,” *PWW*, XXVII, 132; Henry Burchard Fine, “Letter to Woodrow Wilson, March 12, 1913,” *PWW*, XXVII, 173-174; Woodrow Wilson, “Letters to Cleveland Dodge, July 12, 1914,” *PWW*, XXX, 277-278.

[393] Daniels, *Woodrow Wilson*, 135-140; Josephus Daniels, “From the Diary of Josephus Daniels, March 6, 1913,” *PWW*, XXVII, 157.

regulate corporations including a bill that would give the state the power to investigate any company that sold securities in New Jersey. There must be a more equitable method of tax assessment so wealthy property owners paid their fair share. Wilson called for jury reform to ensure that grand juries were not used to further the careers of ambitious district attorneys. The Public Utilities Commission must be given the authority over railroad crossings. A Full Crew Bill must be passed so that every train that came though New Jersey had enough workers to make sure its trip through the state was a safe one. The Governor next argued that cities must be given more power to rule themselves without the constant oversight of the legislature. An agricultural extension service must be set up, while plans must be laid for the conservation and preservation of the state's remaining forests. School buildings should be opened for use by the community in the evenings after the students had gone home. Finally, Wilson said that New Jersey's constitution must be modernized and so must the business practices used by the state government. In a last look at the future of New Jersey, he urged the representatives to pass the constitutional amendments on the income tax and the popular election of Senators. Knowing that many listening to him in the state house, including members of his own party, were ready to undo the reforms that had been passed once he was gone, Wilson launched one last volley at the politicians of New Jersey:

> "Woe betide the individuals or the party groups that turn away from that path! The future is with those who serve, and who serve without secret or selfish purpose. A free people has come to know its own mind and its own friends."[394]

While his last speech as the Governor of New Jersey had a fiery tone, Wilson wanted to speak in a quieter and more poetic way in his first speech as President of the United States. He had rarely gone back to Princeton since he was elected governor, but headed to the campus to write his inaugural address. He asked his friend Harry Clemens, a librarian at the university, to find him a place where he could work on his speech undisturbed. Clemens found a small alcove in the stacks where Wilson drafted his inaugural address first in shorthand before completing the final copy on a typewriter.[395] By writing only ten paragraphs, one of the shortest inaugural addresses in American history, Woodrow Wilson hoped to

---

[394] Woodrow Wilson, "An Annual Message to the Legislature of New Jersey, January 24, 1913," *PWW*, XXVII, 46-54; Woodrow Wilson, "A Statement on Signing Seven Bills Regulating New Jersey Corporations, February 20, 1913," *PWW*, XXVII, 120-122.

[395] Baker, *Life and Letters*, IV, 4.

enter the ranks of the nation's great orators like Abraham Lincoln especially. Even more importantly, he was sure that by using the simplest words possible he could heal the many wounds left over from the last campaign and clearly point the way to a future that everyone could see.

The Wilsons had chosen March 3, the day before the inauguration, as the time when they would depart for Washington. The idea of leaving Princeton was a bittersweet one for Mr. and Mrs. Wilson. The presidency was certainly the fulfillment of Woodrow's deepest hopes for himself and Ellen's most cherished dreams for her husband. Still it was hard to leave the town that had been their home for more than 20 years and the place where their children had grown up. Their final night on Cleveland Lane was almost unbearable. "One last evening in this little house," Wilson wrote to Mary Hulbert, "and we find our hearts very heavy." His mind was flooded with memories, and for at least a few moments, he could not imagine himself in the nation's capital taking the oath of office. The weather was unusually warm in the spring of 1913, and with the curtains blowing in the room where he wrote, Wilson confessed to Mary that he almost felt "that Bermuda is just outside my window, while Washington is on the far side of the globe." Still he was not totally unprepared for the move to the White House. His cabinet was nearly complete, his inaugural address had been written, and he had taken out a $5,000 bank loan to pay for the move to Washington and new clothes for his entire family. His wife and daughters must be dressed in the best styles of the day, and for the first time in their lives, all of the Wilson women bought clothes, shoes, and jewelry without worrying about the price. Even the President-Elect found he must buy new clothes and shoes if he was to play the part that Providence had chosen for him.[396]

Just as Wilson and his family were about to leave for the train station, a crowd of more than 1,500 people arrived on the doorstep of Cleveland Lane. Many in the crowd were neighbors and townspeople, but most were students who had come to wish the former Princeton professor good luck as he set off on the greatest adventure of his life. Wilson could not break away from the people who serenaded him with "My Country 'Tis of Thee" and "Hail to the Chief." He was presented with a silver loving cup from the people of Princeton who would not let him go until he said a few last words to them. Wilson was deeply touched by the outpouring of affection from the large crowd. He felt a deep love not just for the people who stood in front of him, but for all the people of the United States. He told them how this showed that true patriotism was always local. A man loved his neighbors and through them he loved his nation. One could not love a country

---

[396] Ibid., 4-5; Woodrow Wilson, "Letter to Mary Hulbert, March 2, 1913," *PWW*, XXVII, 146.

"abstractly," he insisted, but must instead love it "concretely." Right before he left the crowd of well wishers, Wilson told them that he had been trying hard since becoming President to think on behalf of the American people. He might be able to do this if he remembered how deeply connected he was to the citizens of Princeton who stood before him.[397]

When the crowd finally departed, with the townspeople returning to their homes and most of the students heading to the station to board the train for Washington, Woodrow and Ellen Wilson went off by themselves. Hand in hand, they walked to the house where they once lived at Library Place. They remembered how hard they had worked to build the only home they have ever owned. Then they walked to the depot and boarded the train for the capital with their daughters, many more relatives and friends, and hundreds of Princeton students, all dressed in the college color of bright orange and singing "Old Nassau" at the top of their lungs. When Wilson and his wife and daughters arrived at Washington's Union Station just a few hours later, they were whisked off to a suite in the Shoreham Hotel. President Taft and his wife had invited Woodrow and Ellen to tea at the White House in the late afternoon. The President-Elect would then attend a party with Princeton's Class of '79 at the Willard Hotel later that night.[398]

The excitement of the train trip to Washington and the ride to the Shoreham Hotel through the streets of the capital had almost made Nellie Wilson forget the terrible fear that had haunted her since childhood about her parents' safety. But the dread came rushing back to her as she was helping her mother dress for the tea at the White House. Ellen Wilson was especially excited to meet President Taft since they had been writing to each other about housekeeping details in the White House since the election. But suddenly all the color went out of her cheeks and she began to cry uncontrollably. Nellie ran to get spirits of ammonia to revive her mother. Ellen Wilson finally calmed down, saying the noise and the crowds had all been too much for her. After her mother left with her father for the White House, Nellie became deeply frightened by the despair she had seen in her mother's face. It was as if Ellen Wilson had looked into a terrible future for herself and her husband. Nellie now sobbed in the empty room, shouting, "It will kill them! It will kill them both!"[399]

---

[397] Woodrow Wilson, "Remarks to Neighbors in Princeton, March 3, 1913," *PWW*, XXVII, 192-193.

[398] McAdoo, The Priceless Gift, 276.

[399] Baker, *Life and Letters*, IV, 4, 276; several letters between President Taft and Ellen Wilson can be found in *The Papers of Woodrow Wilson*; see William Howard Taft, "Letter to Ellen Wilson, January 3, 1913," *PWW*, XXVII, 12-13, and Ellen Wilson, "Letter to William Howard Taft, January 10, 1913," *PWW*, 28-29; McAdoo, *The Woodrow Wilsons*, 201-202.

By the morning of the inauguration, calm had been restored to the Wilson family. They were somewhat disappointed that the sky was overcast, but still it was a warm day with spring in the air and the buds on the trees just ready to bloom. Taft arrived shortly before noon to accompany Wilson along the parade route to the Capitol. He seemed noticeably happy as he prepared to give up the reins of power. Taft had confessed to Wilson that the White House was the loneliest place on earth and he was delighted to be leaving it. As they proceeded in an open horse-drawn carriage toward Capitol Hill, Taft waved to the cheering crowd that lined the streets to catch a glimpse of the new president. Wilson's Vice President Thomas Marshall followed right behind in another carriage, while Ellen and her three daughters came next in an automobile. Wilson looked serious as he headed to his inaugural, but Taft was always smiling. He laughed the loudest when people shouted as he passed that he was a good loser. When the parade arrived at the Capitol, Taft escorted Wilson and Marshall into the Senate chamber, while Ellen and her daughters took their places near the podium on the east side of the Capitol.[400]

When Woodrow Wilson finally came out on the platform where he would be inaugurated, he noticed that the police had roped off the lawn directly below the podium where he was to speak. He asked them to take down the barricades with the simple phrase, "Let the people come forward." This line seemed to mirror all that he wished to say to his waiting nation. The cheering crowd rushed forward, excited that they would be so close to the man who would soon be sworn in as President. Mrs. Wilson also left her seat near the podium so she could stand below the platform and look directly up at her husband. When Wilson bent down to kiss his wife's small Bible that would be used in the swearing in ceremony, a shaft of sunlight broke through the clouds and fell directly on him. Wilson noticed that the Bible had opened to Psalm 119. He was deeply moved at the words upon which he would lay his hand when he took the oath of office as President of the United States:

> "So shall I keep thy law continually forever and ever.
> And I will walk at liberty: for I seek thy precepts.
> I will speak of thy testimonies also before kings, and will not be ashamed.
> And I will delight myself in thy commandments, which I have loved."[401]

---

[400] McAdoo, *The Woodrow Wilsons*, 203-206.

[401] Baker, *Life and Letters*, IV, 8-10; Axson, *Brother Woodrow*, 189; McAdoo, *The Woodrow Wilsons*, 206.

In a speech that lasted only ten minutes, President Woodrow Wilson delivered a vision of America that he hoped would truly move the people of his nation. Speaking in his deep voice that could be heard by the many thousands of people who had gathered all around him, he did not gloat that the Democrats had finally pushed the Republicans out of office. His party's victory was merely the last expression of a long revolt that had come up from the people. "We have been refreshed by a new insight into our old life," the new President explained. He asked his fellow citizens to look back at all they had passed through together in the last generation. Through the brilliant efforts of America's men, women and even children, a powerful economy had been built up. "We reared giant machinery," he said, "we were heedless and in a hurry to be great." But now it was time for the country to "count the human cost, the cost of lives snuffed out, of energies overtaxed and broken" that had been paid for this success. Above all else, the nation must face the terrible toll that this drive for wealth had taken on its politics. "The great government we loved has too often been made use of for private and selfish purposes," he explained, "and those who used it had forgotten the people."

As their president, Woodrow Wilson pledged to maintain the economic strength of the nation, while handing control of the government back to the people. "We shall restore, not destroy," he promised the crowd who stood near him and through them the American people. The tariff would be lowered and the banking and currency system would be overhauled. The resources of the nation, including the farms, the waterways, and the forests, would be preserved, while the health and safety of America's workers would be safeguarded. All this could be accomplished, Wilson explained, if the politicians who served with him remembered that they were the "spokesmen and interpreters" of the people. He ended his simple speech with a humble plea for help from all Americans.

> "This is not a day of triumph; it is a day of dedication. Here muster, not the forces of party, but the forces of humanity. Men's hearts wait upon us; men's lives hang in the balance; men's hopes call upon us to say what we will do. Who shall live up to this great trust? Who dares fail to try? I summon all honest men, all patriotic, all forward-looking men, to my side. God helping me, I will not fail them, if they will but counsel and sustain me."[402]

---

[402] Woodrow Wilson, "An Inaugural Address, March 4, 1913," *PWW*, XXVII, 148-152; Colonel House, "Diary of Colonel House, February 13, 1913," *PWW*, XXVII, 109-111.

The large crowd had been quiet, almost reverent as Wilson spoke. Once he finished, they broke into cheers that seemed to come up toward him in great waves. Most of the reporters who covered Wilson's inauguration were impressed with the serious and thoughtful tone of the new President's speech. There was no fiery rhetoric in this address as there had been in the many speeches that Wilson made on the stump during his presidential campaign. Colonel House agreed with the newspaper accounts of the talk, and had told Wilson when he first read a draft of the address that it was more spiritual than political. For Woodrow Wilson, who believed so completely that understanding the spirit of the people would lie at the heart of his presidency, there was little difference between the two.[403]

After the ceremony was over at the Capitol, President Wilson headed with his family to the White House which was now their new home. Ellen Wilson had regained her usual composure and was already planning ways to make the great old house seem more livable for them. She would have rugs and favorite furniture brought down from the house on Cleveland Lane. She would also see what paintings and sculptures could be borrowed from museums in town to make the White House more beautiful. She would lay out a rose garden and even make a small studio for herself high in the attic. As she had done in every home that she had shared with her husband, Ellen Wilson was determined to make the White House a welcome place for her family and friends. She had already planned receptions for the Wilsons, the Woodrows, and the Axsons and the Hoyts. She even engaged a social secretary, Mrs. Belle Hagner, a society matron who knew all the right people in Washington. Together they would arrange the many afternoon tea parties and the nightly dinners and receptions that were so necessary if the Wilson administration was to be a success.[404]

On his first day in the White House, President Wilson was also determined to leave his mark. While he respected tradition, especially the expectation that the new president must review the inaugural parade as it passed down Pennsylvania Avenue in the late afternoon, he would not go along with any custom that he considered frivolous. In his opinion, there was nothing sillier than the tradition that the new president must host an inaugural ball. He was appalled when he learned that Taft's inaugural ball in 1908 had cost nearly $100,000. He refused to spend public funds on such a ridiculous expense. Neither the cries of Washington's grand dames nor the pleas of his three daughters could budge him. Years later Nellie Wilson could still describe the pale blue satin dress decorated with pearls that she had purchased for the occasion in the hope that her father

---

[403] Baker, *Life and Letters*, IV, 4.
[404] Ibid., 5-7.

would change his mind and not be so "Jeffersonian." However, he did not budge and the dress stayed in its box. With no celebration to attend, Wilson spent the evening wandering through the White House with his brother-in-law Stockton Axson. They looked for any evidence they could find of Abraham Lincoln and also read the title of every book in the presidential study.[405]

Within just a few weeks of taking office, President Wilson was determined to make even more innovations. He wanted the American people to view him simply as a man, a citizen like them, who was trying his best to serve them. He was no better than anyone else and refused to be treated as special. To prove this, he would not accept the membership in the Chevy Chase County Club in Maryland that was always offered to the incoming President. He also told his staff and his guests that there was no reason for them to remain standing until he was seated. Wilson even refused to enter a room before a lady, saying if he was a gentleman before he became President, then he would continue to be one after coming to Washington. Ike Hoover, the longtime butler at the White House, could never get used to this new rule. Wilson encouraged the same informality with reporters and so became the first President to hold regular press conferences. He even confessed to the newsmen that he hoped they could help him get his message out to the people. Wilson only became angry with reporters, at least in the beginning of his administration, when they pried too closely into the lives of his daughters. The new President drove the Secret Service to distraction when he tried a similar informality with them. He liked to pull a hat down over his eyes and slip out of the White House undetected. Once agents found him a few blocks from the White House buying candy for children in a grocery store.[406]

Wilson's drive to reinvigorate the Presidency brought a new spirit to the White House. His cabinet meetings were lively exchanges of opinions and strategies among men whom the President respected. With Bryan, his Secretary of State, always on his right side, and McAdoo, his Secretary of the Treasury, always on his left, Wilson began each meeting by throwing out some key concerns, often related to specific pieces of legislation he wished drafted and approved. He welcomed the ideas of his cabinet members and listened carefully to all dissenting opinions. The new President reflected on the advice he had been given, and later wrote down his own ideas in a steady stream of letters, memorandums, and reports. The clerical staff in the White House was soon overwhelmed with paperwork. Many remembered the easy schedule they had under President Taft

---

[405] "A News Report: Wilson Opposes Inaugural Ball, January 17, 1914," *PWW*, XXVII, 59-60; McAdoo, *The Woodrow Wilsons*, 198; Axson, *Brother Woodrow*, 192.

[406] Baker, *Life and Letters*, IV, 5; Daniels, *Woodrow Wilson*, 220-242

who wrote little during his administration. Now they were kept busy typing from the moment they walked into their White House office in the morning until they went home at night.[407] While they were tired, workers throughout the Executive Branch felt the excitement of having a new President who thought so deeply about the future of his nation. The quick steps that Woodrow Wilson took as he walked through the White House seemed to match the plans he was laying for his country.

In the first weeks of his presidency, Wilson turned his deepest thoughts to how he could deliver his campaign promises to the American people. First and foremost, the tariff must be lowered. He had been in favor of a reduction of the tariff since he was a young lawyer struggling to make a living in Atlanta. He had continued to write and speak on the necessity of lowering and possibly even eliminating duties placed on goods imported to the country. During the presidential campaign, he had attacked the tariff over and over again as a tool that the wealthy used against the common man. He had claimed that high tariff rates protected companies that were already established from competition and thus raised the cost of living for the average people. Like most Americans, he was highly critical of the Tariff of 1909, better known as the Payne-Aldrich Tariff. Taft had promised to reduce tariff rates when he first ran for President and the Republicans even made it a plank of their party platform in 1908. After the election, Congressmen Sereno Payne of New York had introduced a bill to lower the tariff in a record-setting nine and a half hour speech to the House of Representatives. However, when Payne's bill was sent to the Senate, Nelson Aldrich of Rhode Island added amendments that actually raised the tariff on many items. In the final bill, duties were lowered on 650 specific imports, raised on 222 other goods, and left unchanged on another 1,150 items. The President was also given the power to add a 25% tax on imports from any nation that was "unduly discriminating" against the United States. Taft signed the Payne-Aldrich Tariff, thinking it would satisfy the many competing interests in his nation. However, most Americans saw it as a cynical attempt by the Republicans to block tariff reform. Most pundits of the day considered it the main reason why the Democrats had won control of the House of Representatives in 1910.[408]

President Wilson understood the overall history of the tariff since he had taught this topic as a regular part of his classes in history and economics. He knew that the tariff originally served two purposes. It was both a source of revenue and

---

[407] Walworth, *Woodrow Wilson*, I, 283-285, 287-290.

[408] John David Rausch, "Payne-Aldrich Tariff (Tariff of 1909)," *Encyclopedia of Tariffs and Trade in U.S. History*, Volume I, Edited by Cynthia Clark Northrup and Elaine C. Pange Turney (Westport, Connecticut: Greenwood Press, 2003), 294-295.

a way to protect the nation's infant industries from foreign competition until they were strong enough to survive without government help. Alexander Hamilton and Henry Clay had been the best defenders of the two-pronged purpose of the nation's early tariff system. However, since the Civil War, Republican congresses had set higher and higher tariff rates to protect businesses from foreign competition that were fully capable of standing on their own. Tariffs also helped monopolies crush any competition that might rise up against them in the United States. Favored companies that benefited from tariffs could thus set the prices of their goods as high as they pleased without fear of foreign or domestic competitors. In the end, it was the average working men, women, and children of America who suffered.[409]

While Wilson understood the controversy over the tariff in broad strokes, he admitted that he did not know the intricacies of the actual tariff rates well enough to propose a tariff reduction law on his own. He would have to rely on his fellow Democrats in the House and Senate who were already drafting bills to lower the tariff. His first ally in the fight against high tariffs was Oscar Underwood of Alabama. Underwood had opposed him for the Democratic nomination in 1912, but had gone on to be one of his greatest supporters on the campaign trail. He was especially successful in winning votes for Wilson among Italian Americans who were angry at tariffs that raised prices on many of their favorite foods imported from Europe. After the election, Wilson started writing to Underwood and even met with him in Princeton to lay out a plan for reducing duties on imports. The "Underwood Tariff," as it was soon nicknamed, called for lowering the overall tariff rate from 41% to 27% and declared more than 100 items duty free.[410]

For his most important campaign promise to pass the Senate, Wilson would have to call on the support of North Carolina's Furnifold McLendel Simmons, the Chairman of the Finance Committee. The conservative Democrat had opposed Wilson's nomination at the Baltimore Convention, staunchly supporting Champ Clark to the bitter end. At first, Wilson recommended to other Democratic Senators that they topple Simmons from his chairmanship, but he backed down when two members of his own cabinet, Daniels and Burleson, told him this would be a mistake. They urged Wilson to win Simmons over with the same eloquence that had made him famous on the campaign trail and at the inauguration. Once

[409] For his developing views on the tariff, see Woodrow Wilson, "The Tariff Make Believe, October 1909," *PPWW*, II, 120-146.

[410] John David Rausch, "Underwood, Oscar Wilder," "Underwood-Simmons Tariff (Tariff of 1913), and "Simmons, Furniwald McLendel," *Encyclopedia of Tariffs and Trade in U.S. History*, Volume I, 402-403; Oscar Underwood, "Letters to Woodrow Wilson, January 13 and February 22, 1913," *PWW*, XXVII, 44-45, 123.

Simmons was convinced that tariff reform was necessary, he would lead the fight on the floor of the Senate to pass it.[411]

Wilson was determined to do his part to pass the new tariff legislation that Underwood and Simmons would introduce in the Congress. While he had not spoken much on the campaign trail about his belief that a nation's executive must take an active role in crafting laws, he was as deeply committed to this principle as President of the United States as he had been as Governor of New Jersey. As the tariff debate heated up in the spring of 1913, he decided to make use of the "President's Room" in the Capitol building. Architects had designed the room for the times when the President would come to speak with the Congress. However, no one had ever used the room. In fact, since the day when Thomas Jefferson had decided never to address Congress directly, no President had ever come to Capital Hill to deliver a message to the House and Senate. Wilson stunned politicians of both parties when he came to the President's Room for meetings with Congressmen on the tariff. He went even further and urged his fellow Democrats, especially in the Senate, to "caucus" or gather together in meetings on their own to discuss strategy.[412]

On April 8, 1913, President Woodrow Wilson took an even more dramatic step to pass the tariff legislation that was now stalled in Congress. He called a joint session of the House and Senate, and went to Capitol Hill to deliver an address on the tariff. No one had done this since President John Adams had spoken before the Congress 113 years ago. Wilson was to give his speech in the House of Representatives, and the gallery was packed with people including Mrs. Wilson and her three daughters. Others lined the corridors of Congress, highly excited and dressed up as if it was opening night at the theater. Vice President Marshall and Wilson's entire cabinet, all looking very nervous, came in first and sat near the Speaker's table. Wilson came in next and was met with just a smattering of applause from the Congressmen. Champ Clark, who had just been named the Speaker of the House, mumbled an introduction. With a half-smile on his lips, Wilson began his talk in his usual calm and steady manner. He started with the simple proposition that he had taken this step to show the President of the United States was a person and not a "mere department of the Government." He used an image from the sea that he loved to make his point even more clearly. The President, he said, is not "some isolated island of jealous power." Instead he is a human being trying to communicate with other human beings about their

---

[411] "Simmons, Furniwald McLendel," *Encyclopedia of Tariffs and Trade in U.S. History*, Volume I, 341.

[412] Daniels, *Woodrow Wilson*, 220-227.

"common service" to the people of their nation. He reminded them that Americans had voted overwhelmingly for reform in the last election and so were in favor of lowering the tariff. He said the people understood the dramatic changes that the economy had undergone while the Congressmen did not. Average Americans knew that the old tariff schedules were outdated. The House and Senate must keep pace with the wisdom of the people and lower the tariff.

Wilson knew how strong the ties were between the politicians who sat before him and the many business leaders of the companies that benefited from high tariffs. He was well aware how big corporations like the sugar trust were putting enormous pressure on the Congressmen to keep the tariff rates high. He challenged both the Republicans and the Democrats to turn their backs forever on using their power to help only a privileged few. He also urged them to allow American businesses to compete on an even playing field at home and abroad:

> "We must abolish everything that bears even the semblance of privilege or any kind of artificial advantage, and put our business men and producers under the stimulation of a constant necessity to be efficient, economical, and enterprising, masters of competitive supremacy, better workers and merchants than any in the world."

The President ended his short address by thanking the Congressmen for their courtesy and telling them he would probably be back soon to recommend changes in the nation's banking and currency laws.[413]

Reactions to Wilson's trip to Congress were generally favorable and his wife congratulated him about this. As they drove back to the White House from Capital Hill, she said, "That's the sort of thing Teddy would have loved to do, if he had thought of it." Wilson could hardly contain his joy, saying, "Yes, I think I put one over on Teddy." A cartoonist had the same thought, and on the next day his newspaper published a drawing of Teddy Roosevelt biting his fingernails while he shouted, "Why didn't I think of that!"[36] Still the fight for the tariff was far from over. It took two more months for the Underwood bill to pass the House. Once it made it to the Senate, Republicans went on the attack, claiming that lowering the tariff would drastically reduce government revenues. In order to meet this challenge, Senator Simmons took proposals on an income tax, first developed in the House by Democratic Congressman Cordell Hull of Tennessee, and placed them in the bill. The Sixteenth Amendment to the Constitution, which permitted

---

[413] McAdoo, *The Woodrow Wilsons*, 246-247; Woodrow Wilson, "An Address on Tariff Reform to a Joint Session of Congress, April 8, 1913," *PWW*, XXVII, 269-272.

Congress to lay an income tax, had just been approved in February 1913, and a graduated income tax ranging from 1 to 6% on incomes over $4,000 per year was added to the bill now called the "Underwood-Simmons Tariff."[414]

As Wilson had promised, he took up the matter of currency and banking reform as soon as the Underwood Tariff passed the House of Representatives in June 1913. Just as in the matter of tariff reform, Wilson had a broad understanding of the issues involved in reforming the nation's credit system. As a professor of American history and economics, he knew that Alexander Hamilton, the first Secretary of the Treasury, had set up the Bank of the United States to house the nation's treasury, loan money to private investors, and oversee the sale of bonds which financed the nation's debt. The notes of the Bank of the United States acted as the country's paper currency. Hamilton also set up the U.S. Mint to coin money for the nation. Jefferson, the founder of Wilson's own political party, had opposed the bank as potentially dangerous to the nation's democracy, but had accepted it once he became President. James Madison had allowed the bank's first 20-year charter to run out without renewing it, but another charter was won for it in the economic upheaval brought about by the War of 1812. Nicholas Biddle, the director of the Second Bank of the United States, used the institution in part to regulate state and private banks. Periodically, the national bank would collect paper notes from other institutions and exchange them for species at the various banks. This was done to ensure that the smaller institutions actually had some hard currency on hand to back up their paper money and their investments.

Wilson, a Democrat who had made a name for himself as a champion of the people against special privilege in the early 20th century, knew that Andrew Jackson, the other founder of his party alongside Thomas Jefferson, had won a similar reputation for himself a little more than 75 years before in his own fight against the Second Bank of the United States. Jackson distrusted banks as risky businesses that often gambled away the life savings of their smallest investors. He especially hated the Second Bank of the United States as an institution of privilege used only for the benefit of the wealthiest Americans. He intensely disliked Director Biddle and accused him of bribing Congressmen and Senators to keep the corrupt institution afloat. As the champion of the people against special privilege, Jackson vetoed the renewal of the charter of the Second Bank of the United States, removed all federal deposits from the institution, and eventually bankrupted it.

---

[414] McAdoo, *The Woodrow Wilsons*, 247; Charles F. Howlett, "Underwood-Simmons Tariff Act (1913)," *The American Economy: A Historical Encyclopedia*, Volume I, edited by Cynthia Clark Northrup (Westport, Connecticut: Greenwood Press, 2003), 285.

While Jackson may have won a great victory for the people against the forces of concentrated wealth, the United States had no national banking system and thus no way to regulate the currency and credit from 1836 onward. Abraham Lincoln had signed important bills on banking and currency into law during the Civil War. These acts prohibited any institution but the federal government from printing paper money. The new legislation also established stricter rules for starting and running banks in the United States. For example, all banks were now required to have at least $50,000 to $100,000 in stable assets. However, even with this important Civil War legislation, the nation still had no way to regulate credit. During economic downturns, major banks, mainly in the Eastern United States, called in their loans and so tightened the nation's credit and therefore the money supply. Republicans who dominated the Congress after the Civil War also limited the amount of silver currency that was minted in order to maintain the value of the nation's money and so benefit the wealthiest citizens and corporations. Populist reformers like William Jennings Bryan called for the coinage of more silver and therefore an increase in the money supply to loosen credit and thus help the majority of average Americans who were not wealthy.

Wilson believed that he could find a way to create a national credit system that would help business prosper and guarantee equal opportunity for all Americans. He knew the task would not be easy. Like Hamilton, he believed a national system of banking and currency was necessary for the very survival of the United States in the modern world. But like Jackson, he was convinced that the credit system must be for all the people, not just the bankers and the privileged few. Wilson also knew that both Roosevelt and Taft had struggled with the reform of the currency and had failed mightily at the task. In 1908, Congress passed the Aldrich-Vreeland Emergency Currency Act which set up the National Monetary Commission first to study and then to recommend changes to the nation's banking system. Three years later, Senator Aldrich, the chairman of the commission, issued a 49-volume report that called for the establishment of a National Reserve Association to regulate that nation's banking and currency. The association would be made up of private bankers who would make decisions about the nation's credit with almost no government control. The proposal set off a firestorm of protests from progressives in both parties who saw Aldrich's proposal as another example of how the wealthy had taken complete control of politics in their nation.[415]

---

[415] Steven E. Siry, "Federal Reserve Act (Owen-Glass Act) of 1913," *The American Economy: A Historical Encyclopedia*, Volume I, edited by Cynthia Clark Northrup (Westport, Connecticut: Greenwood Press, 2003), 111-112.

If Wilson was to have more success than his predecessors in the matter of credit reform, he would have to create a system acceptable to wealthy and average citizens alike. It would need to appeal both to the spirit of Hamilton and Jackson, and on top of that, it must be workable. Wilson had turned to Carter Glass of Virginia, a Democrat on the House Banking and Finance Committee, shortly after the election to begin crafting such a masterful piece of legislation. They knew that most Republicans would balk at any system that took the power to regulate credit away from private bankers and placed it squarely in the hands of the government. They were also aware that most Democrats would block any attempt to set up some kind of central bank that had little government oversight. Wilson would rely on William McAdoo, his Secretary of the Treasury, to win the support of the nation's bankers for whatever system was finally developed. As the leader of the Democrats, the President would need to convince progressives in his party and cabinet, most especially Williams Jennings Bryan, that the new system would be the best thing possible for the people.

Wilson set about crafting and passing legislation creating a new banking and currency system in the same way he was fighting for tariff reform. Starting in May, he worked closely with Carter Glass on the first draft of the bill that would finally be known as the Federal Reserve Act. While he was not an expert in banking, the President was deeply aware of the political and historical currents that made the bill necessary. Congressman Glass later said that Woodrow Wilson was the "one man more responsible for the Federal Reserve System than any other living man." Wilson held many press conferences on the need to pass Glass's bill by answering questions from reporters in an open and friendly manner. When a newsman asked, "Can you tell us anything about the currency legislation, Mr. President?" Wilson answered, "That's a large order. I would have to hire a hall." To the question, "Do you hope for final action at this session, Mr. President?" Wilson answered most emphatically, "Yes, I do." The President also headed to Capitol Hill to meet with Democratic Congressmen and Senators in several conferences on the matter. He soon found out that this would be a tougher battle than the one underway on the tariff since his own party was split on the best method of reforming the nation's credit.[416]

---

[416] There are many letters between Glass and Wilson in *The Papers of Woodrow Wilson* from the winter of 1912 to 1913; however, Wilson received the first draft of the Federal Reserve Act from Glass in May 1913; see Woodrow Wilson, "Letter to Carter Glass, May 8, 1913," *PWW*, XXVII, 409; Glass' comment on Wilson as the moving force behind the Federal Reserve Act can be found in Daniels, *Woodrow Wilson*, 168; Woodrow Wilson, "Remarks to a Press Conference, May 8, 1913," *PWW*, XXVII, 408.

On June 23, 1913, one of the hottest days in early summer that anybody could remember in Washington, D.C., President Wilson called another joint session of Congress and headed up to Capitol Hill to argue in favor of banking and currency reform. Although he sympathized with how tired everyone was, he gently reminded the Congressmen that they had a duty to work for the people. They could not avoid the sacrifices to which their offices called them. But beyond this opening reference to the people, Wilson turned his attention primarily to the nation's business leaders. He told the exhausted Congressmen how business leaders everywhere were waiting for the government to make a decision on how the nation's new banking and currency system would be structured. "It is absolutely imperative that we should give the business men of this country a banking and currency system," he explained, "by means of which they can make use of the freedom of enterprise and of individual initiative which we are about to bestow on them." While Wilson knew it would be an almost superhuman task to create this new system, he encouraged them by describing the work that lay before them in heroic terms. Once they had passed the act that several Congressional committees had labored on for so long, they would strike off the shackles that the credit monopoly had placed on the nation's businesses and so unleash the imprisoned spirit of American enterprise. He ended by saying he stood ready to help them in any way possible to get the bill approved. "I am at your service without reserve," he promised, "to play my part in any way you may call upon me to play it in this great enterprise."[417]

The Owen-Glass Act, named after Robert Owen who sponsored the bill in the Senate and Carter Glass who sponsored it in the House, proposed a federal reserve system. A Federal Reserve Board would coordinate the activities of 12 Federal Reserve District Banks. Secretary McAdoo had traveled throughout the country, speaking with bankers, and recommended the cities where the institutions would be located. They were Boston, New York, Philadelphia, Cleveland, Richmond, Atlanta, Chicago, St. Louis, Minneapolis, Kansas City, Dallas, and San Francisco. All national banks would be required to join the system, while other banks could join if they met certain requirements. All member banks were required to deposit a percentage of their holdings in the Federal Reserve Bank in their respective region. The Federal Reserve Banks could in turn loan money to member banks at the prime rate of interest set by the Federal Reserve Board. The board could also raise or lower the exact percentage of deposits that banks must keep on reserve. By setting the prime rate that it charged member banks for borrowing money, the

---

[417] Woodrow Wilson, "An Address on Banking and Currency Reform, June 23, 1913," *PWW*, XXVII, 570-573.

Federal Reserve Board would be able to control the nation's credit. Higher interest rates would restrict credit and slow down the economy, while lower interest rates would increase credit and stimulate the economy. Raising and lowering the percentage of deposits that must be kept on reserve would help regulate the money supply. The seven members of the Board of Governors of the Federal Reserve, who would make these decisions, would be appointed to 14 year terms by the President of the United States with the consent of the Senate.[418]

As the two major bills of his administration fought their way through Congress in the hot summer of 1913, Woodrow Wilson often reflected on what an exhilarating experience it was to be the President of the United States. He had become the hero he had dreamt of being since his childhood. He was moving on the public stage just as Burke and Pitt had once done. In many respects, he was making the office of the Presidency over in his image. It was an image that he first envisioned as a boy in Columbia when he placed Gladstone's picture above his desk and which he dreamt of again as he sat in the stairwell of Princeton's Chancellor Green Library reading books about the great figures of English history. Cartoonists, especially William Henry Walker who worked for *Life* Magazine, seemed to grasp Wilson's view of himself and the office of the Presidency. Walker drew Wilson as an Indian chief charging on horseback against the tariffs and the trusts. He showed him as the captain of the U.S. Ship of State sailing through a storm while a businessman, who had dropped a penny overboard, demanded that they go back and get it. The cartoon that seemed to capture Wilson's best understanding of himself was called "The Professor." Dressed like a Roman soldier with sword in his hand, and a mortar board on his head, Wilson stood on top of the fallen armies of special privilege that he had defeated. In this drawing, Walker perfectly grasped how Wilson saw himself in the depths of his imagination and how Americans viewed the bold actions of their new President.[419]

Wilson often described his experience as President in humbler terms. Above all else, he was overwhelmed by the deepening ties he felt to the people. He loved to get out among average Americans and see them enjoying themselves, especially at the local vaudeville theater. His favorite performer was the comedian Will Rogers. Whenever Rogers saw the President in the crowd, he would start telling jokes about him, and the more Wilson laughed, the more the comic kept it

---

[418] "Federal Reserve Act (Owen-Glass Act), October 3, 1913," *The American Economy,* Volume II, 579-592.

[419] The originals of many of Walker's cartoons for *Life* are in the Princeton Library; see Walker's "Big Paleface Chief," "Stop the ship! I've dropped a penny over board!" and "The Professor" in *PWW*, XXIX, between pages 330 and 331.

up. The President also loved to drive in his automobile around Washington, seeing children in the street, women at the doors of their small homes, and men coming and going in the hot city. These scenes brought tears to his eyes and helped him understand the responsibility that had fallen on his shoulders. "I seem to know what they are thinking and longing for," he confessed to his family. He once told his close friend Secretary of the Navy Daniels that he was happy so many windows in the White House looked down to the Potomac and across it to the Virginia. Whenever the days grew hot and he feared that he would never be able to accomplish everything he had promised to the American people, he would look out past the river toward the hills and remember that the people were counting on him. At these moments, it was impossible to be lonely or afraid.[420]

Still Wilson had to admit that this tie to the people was draining. Since he believed that he must think of behalf of all Americans, he could never escape from the duties of his office. "One has constantly to be on the job," he wrote to his friend Mary Hulbert, "It is not safe to withdraw one's attention even for an hour." Even when he was supposed to be relaxing, his commitment to the people was always in the back of his mind. He played 10 or 11 holes of golf nearly every day and headed off to the theater a few times each week, "clad in white and looking, I would fain believe, as cool and care free as I often am on these occasions," but his responsibilities to the nation were never far from him. At these times, he understood full well the loneliness that President Taft had described on his last day in office. When overcome with this feeling, Wilson imagined that he had a magic carpet that could go out to his many friends and bring them back to the White House to be with him.[421]

While Wilson noticed the emotional changes that the job had on him, his wife was more concerned about the effects the Presidency had inflicted on his health. On a Sunday morning early in his first term, Ellen Wilson called Dr. Cary Grayson to the White House. She and her husband had met the young navy doctor when they came to tea with the Tafts before the inauguration. On the day of the inauguration, Dr. Grayson had been called back to the White House to care for Wilson's sister Annie Howe who had slipped on a staircase. Now Mrs. Wilson asked him to help her husband with his chronic stomach trouble, or the "turmoil in Central America" as the President described it. "When you get to know me better," he told Grayson, "you will find that I am subject to disturbances in the equatorial regions." After the doctor ordered him to stay in bed, Wilson joked that

---

[420] Daniels, *Woodrow Wilson*, 224-225; see Woodrow Wilson, "Letter to Ellen Wilson, August 17, 1913," quoted in McAdoo, *The Priceless Gift*, 297.

[421] Woodrow Wilson, "Letter to Mary Hulbert, August 3, 1913," *PWW*, XXVIII, 107.

it was very bad advice to tell a new President "not to go to Church." Grayson's next order was for the president to give up the many medicines he was taking and replace them with simple habits in his daily life. Wilson at first balked at the proposed regimen, calling Grayson a "therapeutic nihilist." But the doctor rightly saw that Wilson's deep emotions could be overcome by an appeal to reason. He "reminded the President that he had four hard years ahead of him and that he owed it to himself and the American people to get into as fit a condition as possible and to stay there." Grayson had touched Wilson's own deep understanding of his role as President of the United States and so had quickly won over his unwilling patient. Wilson followed Grayson's instructions to the letter from that point onward. He got plenty of rest and went on a simple diet that included two raw eggs in juice, porridge, and coffee for breakfast. He kept up his golf game, went riding in his car, and took cruises up and down the Potomac on the *Mayflower*, the presidential yacht. Grayson also treated Wilson for his chronic neuritis with heat and massages.[422]

Grayson observed how the President's health was greatly cheered by his correspondence with his many friends. Wilson kept up his letter writing even in the midst of his many new responsibilities. Dr. Grayson was especially amazed at the friends Wilson still knew from when he was a child and a young man, and how many more he was making every day. He remained close to boys from Augusta like Pleasant Stovall, the young man who had given the rose to Robert E. Lee on that day so long ago. Wilson appointed Stovall as the Ambassador to Switzerland. He corresponded with his Princeton friends like Robert Bridges, Hiram Woods, and Charles Talcott, and remained especially close with classmates Cleveland Dodge and Cyrus McCormick who had gone on to be Wilson's staunchest allies on the university's Board of Trustees. He grew close to the politicians he worked with on major bills like Carter Glass and Cordell Hill, and grew still closer to old friends like Josephus Daniels and Walter Hines Page when they worked for his administration. Wilson made new friends among some of the most brilliant minds of the day like Bernard Baruch and Louis Brandeis, and even took the time to answer the notes of rising stars in the Democratic Party like Franklin D. Roosevelt. Other leaders who at first opposed him like Samuel Gompers, the President of the American Federation of Labor, became allies through regular correspondence with the new President.[423]

---

[422] Rear Admiral Cary T. Grayson, *Woodrow Wilson: An Intimate Memoir* (New York: Rinehart and Winston, 1960), 2-3

[423] Ibid., 6-7.

Wilson opened his heart most completely to the handful of women he continued to correspond with including Edith Gittings Reid and most especially Mary Hulbert who remained his dearest friend. It was harder to write to Mary now that he was President but he still managed a letter to her at least every other week. He was always overjoyed when a member of his staff brought in the mail and he saw a note addressed to him in Mary's Hulbert's handwriting. He wrote back to her about everything he was experiencing from his struggles with Congress over the tariff and currency legislation to his ever-changing emotional reactions to being President. Sometimes he wove the most dramatic lines of his speeches into his letters to her. Right after he gave his first speech to a joint session of Congress in April 1913, he wrote to Mary that the town was "agog" over his daring address. As he had just explained in his speech, Wilson told Mary that he was not an isolated figure living on some island but was instead a man trying to work with other men on laws that would improve the lives of his fellow Americans. On days when he felt especially exhausted, he said he felt like all the "grey matter" was being drained right out of his brain as he worked to solve the nation's problems. He also confessed that at one moment he was passionately involved in the day's events, and at the next he stood back and watched everything from a distance. This old "kink" in his character troubled him. There were still other times when Wilson thought of the days in Bermuda when he first met Mary. He would give almost anything to be transported back there again. Knowing how much her husband missed seeing Mary Hulbert, Ellen Wilson invited her to the White House for a visit. But she made sure that Woodrow's cousin Helen Bones, who had come to help the First Lady with her own correspondence, always went along with Woodrow and Mary on their jaunts around town. Helen Bones thought her cousin "something of a goose to be so titillated" by his charming "playmate."[424]

Even with his continuing fascination for Mary Hulbert, Wilson still confessed that the greatest love of his life was his wife. As he struggled with the highs and lows of being President, he realized that Ellen Wilson was the main reason that he was sitting in the White House in the first place. Despite her many new duties, she still continued to read over his speeches, making recommendations on adding more dramatic lines, and also served as his key researcher in foreign affairs. He turned to her to find background information on trouble spots around the world, most especially Mexico. The greatest foreign policy problem he faced in his first year in office dealt with Mexico. During Taft's presidency, President Francisco

[424] See excerpts from several letters from Woodrow Wilson to Mary Hulbert in the first year and a half of his presidency in Day, editor, *Woodrow Wilson's Own Story*, 141-142, 144-152; Helen Bones is quoted in Walworth, *Woodrow Wilson*, I, 395.

Madero, a staunch advocate of democracy, had been toppled from power and then murdered on the orders of his successor General Victoriano Huerta. Taft had refused to recognized Huerta as the new President of Mexico and so did Wilson. Ellen read countless books on the history of Mexico and explained its complex class structure to her husband. Her insights were invaluable in helping Wilson determine his actions toward Mexico and craft a foreign policy worthy of the New Freedom.[425]

By the summer of 1913, Ellen Wilson was so exhausted from her official duties as First Lady and her special work as a key advisor in the administration that the President decided she must take an extended vacation with her daughters. Wilson could not get away, but he sent his family to a house he had rented for them in Cornish, New Hampshire. Ellen wept in the White House when the President told her she must go and continued to cry on the train to Cornish, locking herself in her compartment where she refused to speak to anyone, even her children. Wilson later scolded Ellen, saying, "Be a Spartan wife, and it will make it easy for me to be a Spartan statesman." She was happier once she arrived in New Hampshire because the cottage that Wilson had rented for his family was in the middle of an artist's colony. She soon made friends with the popular painter Maxfield Parrish and his wife as well as with the sculptor Augustus St. Gaudens. She took to the hills around Cornish with her paints and easel and worked on one landscape after another. She loved the impressionistic style that painters had taught her in Old Lyme, Connecticut where she vacationed with her husband when he was Princeton's President. Much like the French artist Claude Monet, she enjoyed painting the same scene at varying times of the day. She wrote short notes to her busy husband telling him about the family's vacation. The White House staff knew to take these letters and place them directly in front of the President as soon as they arrived. In them, Mrs. Wilson described her paintings, the many parties she was attending, and even the visit she made to the graves of her great grandparents in a beautiful cemetery near a lake high in the mountains. The Wilson daughters also loved their time away from the glare of publicity in Washington. Nellie missed her father, but was happy to see her mother feeling so much better. She was especially overjoyed when actors in Cornish cast her in a small part in a play about nature.[426]

---

[425] Baker, *Life and Letters*, IV, 244.

[426] Eleanor Wilson McAdoo chose excellent quotes from the letters exchanged between her mother and father during the summer and early fall of 1913 in her book *The Priceless Gift*; see McAdoo, *The Priceless Gift*, 277-313, for the complete selection from her parents' letters; for a general overview of the family vacation in Cornish, New Hampshire, see McAdoo, *The Woodrow Wilsons*, 249-255.

While his wife was away, Wilson poured his heart out to her in weekly letters that he wrote to her every Sunday afternoon after church. He spoke in passing about the troubles with the Congress in Washington and Huerta in Mexico. But he spent more time telling her that he could have no better wife at his side than she. He confessed that he could not bear to go near her dressing room when she was gone because then he missed her too terribly. He comforted himself by reflecting on the Providence that had sent him a woman like Ellen Axson to him. In his first letter to Ellen in August, he wrote:

> "There is no reason in the world why on Sundays I should not take time to make love to my sweetheart. What an adorable family I have, and how incomparable is the dear little lady who is its crown and glory! I shall never understand how such fortune fell to me: such a wife … I am more happy and more fortunate than any man whose life I have ever known. It seems to me that I have been lifted to such things as I have accomplished merely by the inspiration of love and faith and sweet example."[49]

Ellen Wilson was overwhelmed by the love letters she received from her husband throughout the summer of 1913. She believed these letters were the most beautiful ones she had ever received in her 28-year marriage. She said they proved that Woodrow Wilson was the best writer in the world. No one could capture heart-felt emotions in words the way her husband could. His every phrase was the source of her youth and truly renewed her spirits. She missed him so terribly that once she even came back to Washington with Nellie for a surprise visit. He was happy to see them, and later was able to come up to Cornish for a week to see Nellie perform in the play about nature. When he returned to Washington, he wrote to Ellen that the eight days he had spent with her had been another "honeymoon." He laughed remembering how spoiled they were when they lived the academic life in Princeton. They thought themselves busy then, but now they understood that they had barely known the meaning of work. Still there was one thing of which he was certain. "It seems to me that I never loved you as I do now," he told Ellen in late July.[427]

Ellen's vacation lingered on past the end of summer into the early fall. She spent some of the time in New York helping her daughter Jessie choose her wedding trousseau. Jessie was engaged to Frank Sayre, an Assistant District Attorney in New York City, who would soon become a professor at Williams College. The wedding was scheduled for late November. Both of the Wilsons were doing their best to hide the sadness they felt at the thought of losing their daughter. Jessie was the beauty of the family with a loving heart and serious nature. She had wanted to become a missionary overseas but had been turned down by the Board of Missionaries as not being physically strong enough. Stockton Axson remembered teasing the family after Jessie was turned away from missionary work by saying he had never seen such "unholy glee." Jessie had to content herself with working at a settlement house before preparing for her life as the wife of a young professor. When the House of Representatives presented her with a diamond pendant and the Senate gave her a huge silver tea service, the deeply spiritual Jessie Wilson asked her mother and sister Nellie, "What can a poor professor's wife do with such things?"[428]

One of the happiest nights of Ellen's long vacation came in September when she was upstairs in the cottage at Cornish just getting ready to go to bed. She heard a commotion downstairs and soon her daughters were racing up the stairs with a telegram. It brought the news that the tariff bill had finally passed. Ellen was so excited that on the next morning she wrote to her husband saying, "What a wonderful six months it has been! It is so splendid that everyone knows how great you are! Even when they are opposed to you they feel your power."[429] Wilson was equally overjoyed and looked forward to the official signing of the bill which was scheduled for October 3, 1913. When the day finally arrived, President Wilson signed the bill into law with two golden pens, giving one to Congressman Underwood and the other to Senator Simmons. He told the many politicians who crowded into the White House on this memorable day that he did not want to go off in some "campaign eloquence" to describe this great event, but instead he simply wanted to thank everyone present for their hard work on behalf of the American people. He also gave just a flash of insight into his own boyhood long ago when he had first began planning for such a day. "I have had the accomplishment of something like this day at heart ever since I was a boy," he admitted to the men who gathered around him, and then said he imagined that most of them in the room could say the same thing. Now they must all move on to the passage of the bill to reform banking and the currency. Speaking again out of the deep romance of his heart from which his own political life had grown, he quoted the lines from Shakespeare's *Henry V* that he had just recited at a

[427] Woodrow Wilson, "Letters to Ellen Axson, August 3 and 17, 1913,"*PWW*, XXVIII, 104-106, 179-181.

[428] Ellen Wilson, "Letter to Woodrow Wilson, July 28, 1913," *PWW*, XXVIII, 91-93; Woodrow Wilson, "Letters to Ellen Wilson, July 20 and 27, 1913," *PWW*, XXVIII, 44-45, 84-86.

[429] Ellen Wilson, "Letter to Woodrow Wilson, October 3, 1913," *PWW*, XXVIII, 255-256; McAdoo, *Woodrow Wilsons*, 114, 261.

conference with the Senate Democrats. "If it be sin to covet honor," he said in aiming to pass the Owen-Glass bill, "then I am the most offending soul alive."[430]

When Wilson's family returned from New Hampshire in the middle of October, they were happy to see how well the President looked. Never had he seemed so happy, self confident, and optimistic. There was only one "thorn in his side" and that was the continuing crisis in Mexico. Wilson still refused to recognize the government of General Huerta that had come to power through the overthrow and murder of the duly elected President Francisco Madero. Since taking office in March, Wilson had made several public statements condemning any government that came to power ignoring the rule of law and acting purely out of personal ambition. He refused to change his policy toward Huerta even after Mexico plunged into greater chaos when Venustiano Carranza, Governor of the State of Coahuila, led a revolt against the general. Wilson soon found himself under increasing pressure from American banks, railroads, mining and oil companies, and even his own Ambassador to Mexico, Henry Lane Wilson, to recognize Huerta. Business leaders grew especially anxious when Huerta said he did not have to pay back the millions of dollars his nation owed to American companies if the President did not recognize that he even existed. The pressure on Wilson to recognize Huerta intensified when many nations, which had at first agreed with Wilson's position, decided one by one to recognize Huerta. Spain, China, Italy, Germany, Belgium, Norway, Russia, most of the rest of Latin America, and finally even Great Britain made peace with the dictator.

As the situation dragged on throughout the summer and fall of 1913, Wilson refused to budge. He had learned from his wife's reports that 85% of the people in Mexico lived in dire poverty and had no voice in their government while the wealthy 15% at the top held all the power and were not interested in creating a real democracy in their nation. Wilson came to feel almost as deeply for the downtrodden people of Mexico as he did for the people of his own nation. As a writer of American history, he had always been sympathetic toward the Mexican people and even described the Mexican-American War as an unjust one. He brooded over how to shape a foreign policy that served not just the best interests of the American people, but also the best interests of the majority of the people of Mexico. He did not want to abandon the Mexicans to a tyrant, but also he did not want to invade Mexico, topple Huerta, and force a democratic government onto

---

[430] Ellen Wilson, "Letter to Woodrow Wilson, September 10, 1913," *PWW*, XXVIII, 273; Woodrow Wilson, "Remarks on the Tariff Bill, October 3, 1913," *PWW*, XXVIII, 351-352; for the final version of the bill, see "Tariff of 1913 (Underwood-Simmons Tariff," *Encyclopedia of Tariffs and Trade*, Volume III, 442-505.

the nation. He preferred to follow a policy of "watchful waiting" that would allow the Mexican people to work out their destiny without interference from the United States.

In order to learn more about the situation in Mexico first hand, President Wilson first sent William Bayard Hale, the young journalist who had worked with him on *The New Freedom*, as a special envoy to Mexico, and later sent John Lind, the former Governor of Minnesota and a close friend of Secretary of State William Jennings Bryan. This infuriated Ambassador Wilson who favored recognizing Huerta and who was eventually removed from his position when he openly criticized the President's policy on Mexico. After collecting as much information as he could from a variety of sources, Wilson finally decided to issue a challenge to Huerta. He called for an immediate end to all the fighting in Mexico, free elections as soon as possible with an assurance from Huerta that he would not run for President, and the promise that all parties would abide by the results of the election. Huerta not only ignored Wilson's challenge, but openly said he would raise an army, collect ammunition, and march as far as St. Louis, Missouri, taking back all of the southwestern United States that had been stolen from Mexico by the Treaty of Guadalupe Hidalgo which ended the Mexican-American War in 1848.[431]

As Wilson struggled with Huerta, he also struggled to create a viable foreign policy, first toward Latin America but ultimately toward the entire world, that matched his own democratic ideals. It was a far more formidable task than either the struggle to lower the tariff or the battle to reform the nation's banking and currency system. Through his own study of history and especially through his wife's research, he knew that when the countries of Latin America had broken free from Spain in the early 19th century, they had done so in the hope that they could create stable democracies throughout the hemisphere. The new nations of Spanish-speaking America had all based their constitutions on the Constitution of the United States. But none of the nations that had been created were able to achieve a stable democracy. In every country, dictators or strong men called "caudillos" had seized control of their governments and ruled on behalf of the wealthiest people in their nations. With the exception of Benito Juarez, the Indian lawyer who served as the Mexican president in the mid-19th century, most of Mexico's rulers had been dictators from Augustin Iterbide who took power in the

[431] For an example of the communications between Wilson and his special envoy Hale, see Woodrow Wilson, "Telegram to William Bayard Hale, November 11, 1913," *PWW*, XXVIII, 525; see also Wilson's first set of instructions to special envoy Lind in Woodrow Wilson, "Instructions to John Lind, August 4, 1913," *PWW*, XXVIII, 110-111.

1820s to Porforio Diaz who left office in 1910 when the idealistic lawyer Francisco Madero launched a revolt against him. After making a thorough study of Mexican history, Wilson raised a question that no other American President had ever asked. Did the United States have a responsibility to foster democracy in Mexico and elsewhere in Latin America? Like his predecessors, Wilson was committed to maintaining the Monroe Doctrine which had told the world that the United States would not tolerate the building up of empires in the western hemisphere once the Spanish Empire had been toppled. But did this doctrine also imply that the United States had a duty to build up democracy in these "green young nations" as Simon Bolivar, the Liberator of Latin America, once described the newly independent countries of Latin America?

In late October 1913, with Huerta rattling his sword at the United States and business leaders growing angrier at Wilson by the minute, the President headed to a conference in Mobile, Alabama that had been called between the southern states and the nations of Costa Rica, Bolivia, and Panama. The representatives at the meeting had gathered in Mobile to discuss the business opportunities that would surely develop between them once the Panama Canal finally opened. Wilson planned to give a speech at the conference that would allow him to share his growing vision of a democratic world led by the United States on behalf of all the people of the Americas. He explained in his talk that his opposition to Huerta did not mean that he looked down on Latin America. Instead he hoped that the Panama Canal, which would split the continents apart physically, would actually join the continents together spiritually. He hoped that South America, which had been so long cut off from the trade of the Northern Hemisphere, would now become a valuable trading partner of the United States. But he warned his brother nations to the south that they must be careful when they let foreign investors within their borders. He observed that Latin American nations too often felt beholden to foreign investors and bowed to their every demand. He urged governments throughout the region to remember that they should take an active part in controlling the companies that set up shop in their nations. They must let the world know that investing in their countries was a privilege and not a right. He also challenged his brother nations to set up real democracies and so join with the United States in showing the world what "America" actually meant. It did not mean wealth or power, but instead stood for "human rights, national integrity, and opportunity" for all. "America is a name which sounds in the ears of men everywhere as a synonym with individual liberty," he explained to the people gathered in Mobile.[432]

Even as he battled Huerta, a man whom he called a "diverting brute … so false, so sly, so full of bravado," President Wilson worked to craft a foreign policy that would break his nation free from the "Dollar Diplomacy" of his Republican predecessors. While he agreed that the growth of the American economy was important, and so foreign investment was significant and should be fostered, Wilson did not believe that it should be the most important factor in determining the nation's foreign policy. He often became frustrated in the midst of the Mexican crisis at how much time he spent worrying about American investments abroad. He once told his secretary Joe Tumulty, "I have to pause and remind myself that I am the President of the United States and not of a small group of Americans with vested interests in Mexico." Wilson had to convince himself and his nation that the United States had a duty to the world beyond making money for itself. In fact, its primary duty must be to foster liberty. The United States should be the first nation in the world to stand up and say that the old rules for shaping a nation's foreign policy were dead. America would never again conquer another piece of territory. She would be content with the territory she had won and make the best and most fruitful use of it. She would place human liberty above everything else, including her own economic self interest. In a world that seemed to grow darker each day, especially as the nations of Europe stood ready to plunge into a bloody and horrific war, the United States would hold high the lamp of liberty to light the way to a new world order. She would base her foreign policy on the highest ideal possible. "It is the relationship," Wilson explained, "of a family of mankind devoted to the development of true constitutional liberty."[433]

As he began to shape a new foreign policy based on a vision of the United States as the bold young leader of the great family of nations, his own tiny family was beginning to break apart. At 6 P.M. on the evening of November 25, 1913, he led his lovely daughter Jessie into the East Room, crowded with hundreds of family, friends, and politicians, where she married Frank Sayre, the young lawyer turned professor. During the reception that followed, Ellen Wilson was quite sad, apologizing often that she knew it was a wedding, and not a funeral, but still it seemed that happiness had somehow gone out of the Wilson home forever. The President also keenly felt the loss of his beautiful daughter Jessie and confessed to Mary Hulbert that he was grateful to have his many responsibilities as President to

---

[432] Baker, *Life and Letters*, IV, 236-264; Woodrow Wilson, "An Address on Latin American Policy in Mobile, Alabama, October 27, 1913," *PWW*, XXVIII, 448-453.

[433] Woodrow Wilson, "Letter to Mary Hulbert, August 24, 1913," *PWW*, XXVII, 217; Tumulty, *Woodrow Wilson as I Know Him*, 146; Wilson, "Address on Latin American Policy," 451.

occupy his mind during the day. In the evenings, Nelly remembered how her parents always fell to talking about one thing and one thing only, Jessie. Wilson's family would unravel even more when Nellie soon became engaged to William McAdoo, the Secretary of the Treasury, a widower more than twice her age. Nellie had been smitten with McAdoo since he first joined her father's staff during the run for White House and now planned to marry him in May 1914.[434]

In the midst of his struggle to create a new kind of foreign policy, and in his sorrow at the breakup of his family, Wilson was thrilled when the Owen-Glass Bill passed the House and Senate. The bill was ready for signing into law on December 23, 1913. At the ceremony, the President thanked everyone, especially Senator Owen and Representative Glass, for the teamwork that made the dream of the Federal Reserve a reality. Privately, he gave his greatest thanks and praise to his future son-in-law, William McAdoo, for his tireless work in winning the bankers of the nation over to the new system. Wilson was delighted that in the end so many Republicans had voted for the measure, and was equally excited that the Democrats had proven at last that they were a party that could do good things for all the people, even businessmen. He looked back to the past just as he had done when the tariff bill was signed. He reminded the men standing around him that it had taken two and a half generations from the time when Abraham Lincoln passed banking legislation during the Civil War for America's politicians to come together to create a new national credit system. Now they could clearly see that their wise actions in the present had come from the upheaval of the past fifty years when the people themselves had demanded reform.[435]

The Wilson family spent Christmas, for the first time ever without Jessie, at a plantation in Pass Christian on the Gulf Coast of Texas. They made the trip at the suggestion of Dr. Cary Grayson who continued to worry about the health of both Mr. and Mrs. Wilson, and Senator Sharp Williams who highly recommended the nearby golf course to the President. Mrs. Wilson was excited to have Mary and Lucy Smith come from New Orleans to spend the holidays with the family. They celebrated Wilson's 57th birthday on December 28, and on New Year's Eve they followed the Scottish custom of standing on chairs around a table with arms entwined while singing "Auld Lang Syne." Wilson also continued to monitor the situation in Mexico and even went out to a boat on the gulf to confer with his special envoy John Lind. He also spent time alone working his way to the

---

[434] McAdoo, *The Woodrow Wilsons*, 257-264; Woodrow Wilson, "Letter to Mary Hulbert, November 30, 1913," *PWW*, XXVIII, 597-599.

remarkable conclusion that America must find a way to lead the world by serving it.

Few Americans understood the profound shift that Wilson was making in their nation's foreign policy. Many thought he was simply waiting for the right moment to invade Mexico and topple Huerta once and for all. Wilson knew that his popularity would go higher if he led the nation into a war against the arrogant Huerta. "In a republic like ours," he told his cabinet, "the man on horseback is always an idol."[436] But he had decided to intervene only if American lives or the United States itself was truly threatened. That time finally came on April 4, 1914 when General Huerta's forces arrested crewmembers of the U.S.S. *Dolphin* as they were buying supplies in Tampico, Mexico. While the Americans were later released, President Wilson still asked Congress on April 20, 1914 for the power "to use the armed forces of the United States in such ways and to such extent as may be necessary" to enforce his demands on President Huerta and protect American citizens in Mexico. Shortly after midnight on the following day, Wilson received news that General Huerta was expecting a large shipment of guns from Cuba to use against his many enemies in Mexico. Wilson worried that these guns might eventually be turned on Americans throughout Mexico and maybe even on the United States itself. He was also concerned that the weapons had probably come from Europe, most probably Germany. This proved to be correct for the guns had been shipped from Hamburg and then transferred onto the *Ypiringa* in Havana. The President ordered U.S. Marines ashore in Vera Cruz to intercept the shipment. In the ensuing battle between the Marines and Huerta's army, 19 Americans were killed. Wilson discovered that leading men in such military engagements was an agony and not the glorious experience he had so long imagined. War could only be tolerable, he concluded, if it served the cause of mankind. At a ceremony for the slain Americans at the Brooklyn Navy Yard on May 11, 1914, he said:

> "We have gone down to Mexico to serve mankind if we can find the way. We do not want to fight the Mexicans. We want to serve the Mexicans if we can, because we know how we would like to be free, and how we would like to be served if there were friends standing by in such case ready to serve us. A war of

---

[435] Woodrow Wilson, "Remarks on Signing the Federal Reserve Bill, December 23, 1913," *PWW*, XXIX, 63-66; Woodrow Wilson, "Letter to William McAdoo, December 23, 1913, *PWW*, XXIX, 62; William McAdoo, "Letter to Woodrow Wilson, December 23, 1913," *PWW*, XXIX, 66.

[436] Tumulty, *Woodrow Wilson As I Know Him*, 158.

aggression is not a war in which it is a proud thing to die, but a war of service is a thing in which it is a proud thing to die."[437]

Wilson got a chance to practice his idealistic foreign policy in the New Year when a controversy arose over whether or not the United States should pay the same tolls for use of the Panama Canal as other nations would. In 1901, the country had signed the Hay-Pauncefote Treaty wherein the United States agreed that the ships of all nations would be treated equally as they passed though the canal. But later the Senate had revoked this part of the treaty, arguing that the United States had built the canal and therefore did not have to pay the tolls. Wilson heartily disagreed. If the United States was to lead the world toward democracy, then she must learn to play by the rule of law set for everyone else. He fought a bitter battle in both the House and the Senate on this principle with much opposition coming from his own party, especially Champ Clark who gave a fiery speech against the man who had defeated him at the Baltimore Convention. Wilson finally prevailed by a vote of 247 to 162 in the House and just 50 to 35 in the Senate. Still the vote seemed but a small victory to Wilson. Would he be able to win a victory in the future on a foreign policy issue of greater importance than the payment of canal tolls?[438]

As Wilson headed into his second year as President, he hoped the great tide of reform that had swept him into office would still carry him on to new victories for the people. The tide had helped him pass laws on the tariff and the nation's credit, and was slowly helping him shape a new kind of foreign policy. In the light of the many successes that had come his way, Wilson had a difficult time recognizing two tragedies that waited on his path in the year 1914. He was troubled by the growing hostility that existed among the nations of Europe, but he refused to believe that it would lead to all out war even as he watched the world situation grow darker each day. For nearly sixteen years, ever since the conclusion of the Spanish-American War, he had worried that the United States, whose foreign policy he was struggling to shape in a new way, was heading toward world leadership at the most dangerous time in human history. He scoured the letters and messages that came back to him from his European ambassadors but found few insights into the causes of the growing conflict. Most diplomats filled their

---

[437] Daniels, *Woodrow Wilson*, 176-185; Woodrow Wilson, "Annual Message to Congress, December 2, 1913," *PWW*, XXIX, 3-11; "A News Report: Wilson Tells Long Series of Affronts that Caused Action to Curb Huerta, April 15, 1914," *PWW*, XXIX, 440-443; Woodrow Wilson, "An Address to Congress on the Mexican Crisis, April 20, 1914," *PWW*, XXIX, 471-474; Woodrow Wilson, "A Memorial Address, May 11, 1914," *PWW*, XXX, 13-15.

[438] Baker, *Life and Letters*, IV, 394-415

correspondence with details of the problems faced by American tourists abroad. Only Walter Hines Page, his old friend and ambassador in London, seemed to see clearly through the rumors of war that swirled about him. He had become so concerned by German aggression that he had begged Wilson to come to London as soon as possible. He believed that if the Kaiser saw the President and the British Prime Minister standing side by side, then he would back down from any thought of war. Wilson hesitated saying he could not give the appearance of being anything but neutral in the coming crisis. Still he remained concerned when Colonel House wrote back with much the same sentiments. After helping Wilson pick his cabinet choices, he had played little part in domestic politics, and had instead headed to Europe to be the eyes and ears of the President. He reported that the situation was grim. Wilson still could not understand what was happening. He could only sit at the dinner table each night, repeating one word – "Madness!" – about the drift toward war in Europe.[439]

In the summer of 1914, Woodrow Wilson sensed a great darkness coming not just over the world but also into his own home. His beloved Ellen had been very tired and seemed unable, even after an Easter vacation in White Sulphur Springs in the mountains of West Virginia, to get her strength back. Wilson was certain that his wife was simply exhausted. The constant round of entertaining that she was required to do as the First Lady was too much for her. On top of that, she had been the President's special consultant on Mexican history and the death of the young Americans at Vera Cruz had troubled her deeply. She had also been hounded by social workers who came to the White House nearly every day demanding her help in ending the many growing ills in Washington. Ellen Wilson was most saddened by the terrible living conditions that blacks endured in the nation's capital. She had even taken Congressman on tours of Washington's tenements and then asked them to pass a slum clearance bill. Her heart also went out to the many government workers who must toil all day with little comforts and demanded that Congress give them lavatories. Finally, and perhaps most terribly, the marriage of Jessie in November 1913 and Nellie in May 1914 had been quite heartbreaking for her.

---

[439] There are several letters on the European situation coming from Walter Hines Page, the American ambassador to Great Britain, to President Wilson in Volume XXX of *The Papers of Woodrow Wilson*. For a representative example, see Walter Hines Page, "Letter to Woodrow Wilson, August 2, 1914," *PWW*, XXX, 329-331, where Page reports from London that there is almost "a satisfaction, that war between England and Germany is certain;" many important letters from Colonel House to the President can be found in the same volume; for a good example, see Colonel House, "Letter to Woodrow Wilson, August 3, 1914," *PWW*, XXX, 341, where House describes the coming war as "this worldwide horror."

The President thought that Ellen Wilson was simply suffering from a nervous breakdown and would soon be well. After she had a bad fall in the White House, she had taken to resting most of the day on a couch in her bedroom. Wilson would have his tea with her every afternoon. He would stand by the fireplace, never taking his eyes from her and always giving her a hug around her shoulders before he left and went back to his work. He kept hoping that her main problem was missing Nellie just as terribly as he did. The White House staff noticed how lonesome the President was once Nellie married Mr. McAdoo. Wilson and his youngest daughter shared the same devilish sense of humor and often joked that they should run away and join a traveling vaudeville troupe together. It had been terrible for him to give away the little girl he remembered working so hard for to finish his *Short History of the United States* so he could buy her a pony. Surely once he and Ellen got used to Nellie being gone, everything would be back to normal, including his wife's health.

Throughout the summer of 1914, President Wilson was simply not listening to Dr. Grayson's warnings that his wife was seriously ill. She had Bright's disease, a common form of nephritis that caused inflammation of the kidneys, as well as tuberculosis in these organs, and would not recover. The family must be sent for immediately. Wilson reluctantly did as Grayson requested and told Jessie and her husband, who were living in Massachusetts, and Stockton Axson, who was traveling in Oregon, to get back to the White House as quickly as possible, But when Theodore Roosevelt wrote a note to the President filled with his deep concern for the First Lady, Wilson answered that his wife seemed to be getting better. Finally, in the first week of August, a desperate Cary Grayson sent for Dr. E. P. Davis, an old friend of the President who had gone to college with him at Princeton. It would be Davis' job to tell Wilson's family that Ellen was dying. With Margaret, Jessie, and Nellie at the President's side, Dr. Davis let the girls know that their mother had only a few hours to live. Wilson wept bitterly and his daughters remembered that they had never seen their father cry before.

In the past few weeks, the President had spent much of his time sitting at Ellen's bedside. He had told her only good news – that Huerta had resigned, that Argentina, Brazil and Chile had offered to mediate between the United States and Mexico, and that Congress had passed her slum clearance bill. But he did not tell her that the Archduke Francis Ferdinand, heir to the throne of the Austro-Hungarian Empire, and his pregnant wife Sophie had been assassinated in Sarajevo on June 28, or that most of the nations of Europe were about to declare war on each other because of this dreadful act. Instead he usually sat quietly holding her two hands in his own, while at other times, he held just one of her hands so he could write to the leaders of Europe begging them not to go to war and offering to act as a mediator. Ellen Wilson was unaware of the troubles that were descending upon the world. She slipped in and out of consciousness, whispering her last words to Dr. Grayson, “Promise me that you will take care of my husband,” before falling into a coma. At 5 P.M. on August 6, just one day after the Great War in Europe had officially begun, Ellen Wilson died, with her husband and three daughters at her side. Woodrow finally let go of her hand and crossed her arms across her chest. Then he went over to the window and broke down, weeping like a little child and asking, “Oh, my God, what am I to do?”

On the day of his wife’s funeral, President Wilson could not face going into the East Room until the final moment before the services started. It was so painful for him that he could not bear to hear any music. So the guests sat among the flowers and palms listening to the wind blow through the curtains. The prayers over Ellen’s coffin where brief and simple. Later that afternoon, the casket was taken to Union Station where a little over a year before Ellen had arrived with her family on the way to her husband’s inauguration. On the journey to Rome, Georgia, where Ellen was to be buried, Wilson sat in the last car near the coffin. He never left her side, not even when Cary Grayson asked him to rest. “Let me alone, please, until after the services,” he said to his worried doctor, “I cannot rest until then.” The President also refused to come to the window and see the countless people who lined the railroad tracks all the way from the nation’s capital to Georgia in order to pay their last respects to nation’s gracious First Lady. In Rome, Ellen’s body was taken to the First Presbyterian Church where Wilson had first seen her on that spring morning some thirty years before. On the following day in a driving rainstorm, she was buried on a hillside right next to her mother and father. Wilson watched as they lowered her casket into the ground. He made sure that there was room beside her for his own burial one day. He chose Italian marble for the tombstone that would have a woman’s profile and a quote from William Wordsworth carved on it:

> “A traveler between life and death;
> The reason firm, the temperate will,
> Endurance, foresight, strength, and skill,
> A perfect woman, nobly planned,
> To warn, to comfort, and command
> And yet a sprit still, and bright
> With something of angelic light.”

Back home in Washington, President Wilson was inconsolable. The brave young hero who had accomplished so much, so quickly seemed to have grown old overnight. He did his duties as best he could, finding some refuge in work, but the pain was excruciating. On one terrible night, Nellie McAdoo came to visit him at the White House but the staff could not find him. Finally, Nellie opened the door into the East Room where her mother's funeral had taken place just days before. The room was pitch black, and as she stumbled for the light, she touched her father's arm. He had been sitting alone in the dark for some time. To have lost his wife, just when he had come to appreciate her so much, and at the very moment when he needed her so desperately, was simply unbearable. "I can't bear it. I can't think. I can't work without her," he said, and then began to pace the room and weep. When Nellie started crying just as badly, the President caught himself and told her, "Don't cry. She was always so brave." After he remembered this about his wife, he seemed to come out of the worst of his grief. At least, they could console themselves with the fact that she had died before the whole world came undone. "She was so radiant, so happy!" he said, "We must be grateful for her sake that she did not see the world crash into ruin. It would have broken her heart." [440]

---

[440] The best source for Ellen Axson's final illness and death can be found in the memoirs of her daughter Eleanor Wilson McAdoo. See McAdoo, The Priceless Gift, 313-316, and The Woodrow Wilsons, 296-301; there are several letters written by President Wilson in the spring and summer of 1914 in ThePapers of Woodrow Wilson that show his belief that his wife would recover; see Woodrow Wilson, "Letter to Theodore Roosevelt, August 6, 1914," PWW, XXX, 351-352 (written on the same day his wife woulddie, Wilson told Roosevelt that "we have by no means given up hope and the indications today are a little encouraging;" for Dr. Grayson's recollection of Mrs. Wilson's final illness and death, see Grayson, Intimate Memoir, 32-35; also see Baker, Life and Letters, IV, 460-481, and Walworth, Woodrow Wilson, I, 398-407; for Wilson's message to European leaders (which Ellen McAdoo saw her father write at her mother's bedside), see Woodrow Wilson, "A Press Release, August 4, 1914," PWW, XXX, 342.

Chapter 9

THE SHADOWS OF WAR AND DEATH

America asks nothing for herself except what she has a right to ask for humanity itself.

Woodrow Wilson[441]

As President Woodrow Wilson rode the train back to Washington from his wife's funeral in Georgia, he was haunted by the belief that his political ambitions had killed his dear "Eileen." He told family and friends that if he had stayed at Princeton, Ellen would still be alive.[442] The sheer weight of the office of the Presidency had fallen on her shoulders as well as on his own. His only comfort during the lonely trip back to the White House was the certainty that his wife could not have born the grief of watching Europe tear itself to pieces. As he struggled with his own grief, Wilson knew that he must also tackle the terrible problem of trying to understand why the most civilized nations in the world had launched themselves into such awful bloodletting. He would not have his wife at his side to help him unravel this mystery as she had once helped him understand the troubles in Mexico. He would have to find out on his own not just what caused the war in Europe, but even more importantly what the current conflict and its eventual peace would mean to his country and the world. He had promised the American people that he would do their thinking for them and speak on their behalf. Now he would have to reach down past his grief to the deepest levels of

---

[441] Day, editor, *Woodrow Wilson's Own Story*, 194.

[442] Wilson made the comment about his political career bringing about the death of his wife to several people including his daughters. Some of Ellen's closest relatives tried to convince him otherwise. See Mary Hoyt, "Letter to Woodrow Wilson, August 8, 1914", *PWW*, XXX, 375-376.

himself in order to interpret the meaning of this awful war and America's place in it.

Once back in the White House, Wilson read though the many condolences that had come from supporters everywhere in the country. William Jennings Bryan, the Secretary of State who had such a way with words, knew he could not find any now that would ease the President's overwhelming grief. Vice President Thomas Marshall had experienced first hand the "sacred circle" of Wilson's family and tried to comfort him by saying that the sympathy of every man who loved his wife reached out to him in a "mystic touch." Wilson's close friend Josephus Daniels, the Secretary of the Navy, wrote both for himself and his wife who had been one of the First Lady's closest friends. Knowing how sad and lonely Wilson must be, Daniels offered to come and stay with him at the White House and help him through his grief. Cleveland Dodge and his wife, who were also dear friends to the entire Wilson family, were truly heartbroken, while a "stunned" Colonel House, who had believed from the President's letters that Ellen was getting better, wrote that this sad event showed "how near to us the angel of death hovers."[443]

The letters from Wilson's family members and oldest friends were especially poignant. Ellen's cousins Florence and Mary Hoyt could hardly bear to think of Woodrow trying to go on without his beloved wife. Florence Hoyt could only send the prayer, "God help you!" Mary Hoyt had been troubled by Wilson's sad confession at the funeral that his political career had killed Ellen. She penned a note of sympathy to the President as soon as he was back in Washington, reminding him that many of the Hoyts and Axsons were "short-lived." She asked him to recall how Cousin Ellen was generous by nature and might have overtaxed herself even if she had remained a professor's wife. She told him to think back and remember how Ellen had worked in a settlement house even when she was enrolled at the Art Student's League. Robert Bridges, Wilson's longtime friend from their college days together, tried to cheer "Tommy" by reminding him what he surely knew deep in his heart. "All that she ever wished for you," he wrote, "you have achieved."[444]

---

[443] William Jennings Bryan, "Letter to Woodrow Wilson, August 6, 1914," *PWW*, XXX, 355; Josephus Daniels, "Letter to Woodrow Wilson, August 6, 1914," *PWW*, XXX, 356; Cleveland Dodge, "Letter to Woodrow Wilson, August 7, 1914," *PWW*, XXX, 359; Colonel House, "Letter to Woodrow Wilson, August 7, 1914," *PWW*, XXX, 359.

[444] Florence Hoyt, "Letter to Woodrow Wilson, August 7, 1914," *PWW*, XXX, 358; Mary Hoyt, "Letter to Woodrow Wilson, August 11, 1914," *PWW*, XXX, 375-376; Robert Bridges, "Letter to Tommy Wilson, August 9, 1914," *PWW*, XXX, 366.

One of the most beautiful sympathy letters came from Mary Hulbert, the woman who had caused Ellen Wilson the only pain in her otherwise happy marriage to the President. Wilson told Mary just a week after Ellen's death that "God has stricken me almost beyond what I can bear." Mrs. Hulbert answered, saying more clearly than anyone else who had written to Wilson, that she understood what this loss meant to him, especially as Europe descended into war. How terrible, she said, that Ellen would be taken from him "*now*, now when you need that sweet soul to help you in this terrible time." She tried to comfort him by reminding him that God was always good even when we cannot see or understand his Providence.[445]

As the President took the time to answer the many condolences piled on his desk, the press of world events could not be held back. Amid the flood of sympathy letters, there came desperate pleas from his ambassadors throughout Europe to help them understand the "awful tragedy" that had befallen the world. Just three days after Ellen's death, Walter Hines Page, writing from the Court of St. James in London, said, "God save us! What a week it has been!" Ambassador Page's letters to the President were filled with vivid images of the panic that had engulfed Europe. He told Wilson that he had seen both the British Foreign Secretary and the German Ambassador to England break down in tears over a war neither man wanted. Americans of every description were crowding into Page's office waving money in his face and demanding that he get them on the next boat out of Britain. Over 100,000 Americans were stranded in Europe and anxious to get home before the actual fighting broke out.[446]

Wilson also heard from Henry Van Dyke, the Ambassador to the Netherlands. Van Dyke had been one of the professors who opposed many of Wilson's reforms at Princeton, but the President had put these past hurts behind him and appointed him as the "best man" for the job at the Hague. Van Dyke was deeply moved that Wilson had chosen him for the job, and was soon an excellent analyst of the current situation in Europe. He provided Wilson with a clear picture of the panic on the continent as Americans rushed to their country's closest embassy and begged for a way to get home. Van Dyke had already worked out an arrangement with the government of Holland to help finance the passage across the Atlantic for Americans stranded in the Netherlands. "Pray God," the ambassador told the President, "that the neutrality of Holland and America may be preserved." While the cause of peace now looked dim, Van Dyke urged Wilson to continue to

---

[445] Woodrow Wilson, "Letter to Mary Hulbert, August 7, 1914," *PWW*, XXX, 357; Mary Hulbert, "Letter to Woodrow Wilson," August 7, 1914," *PWW*, 357-358.

[446] Walter Hines Page, "Letter to Woodrow Wilson, August 9, 1914," *PWW*, XXX, 366-371.

uphold his vision of a democratic future for all mankind. Once this "horrible war" was over, he knew that Wilson's dream would "shine brighter and be nearer than ever before."[447]

Wilson's advisor Colonel House saw the situation in Europe in much the same way as Hines and Van Dyke understood it. He had returned from the continent just before Mrs. Wilson's death and hoped to meet with the President as soon as possible to give him his impressions of top European leaders, especially Germany's Kaiser Wilhelm II. House finally got his chance at the end of August when the President invited him to his summer retreat in Cornish. The lonely Wilson gave House the room that his wife had occupied the summer before when he sent her off to New Hampshire. House was often impatient with the President for preferring to talk about his dead wife instead of discussing the war in Europe. Wilson spent hours showing him pictures of Ellen and reading her favorite poems aloud to him. He liked to sit outside at night telling stories about his wife, his father, and his mother. His mind drifted off into tales from his college days about old President James McCosh and he spun even more tales about the Scottish clans in his family tree. At last House found a way to describe the German leader to the grieving President. The Kaiser, he explained, saw himself as a man of peace who had been forced into the war once Russia had mobilized. Yet at the same time, the Kaiser was proud of Germany's powerful army that used up more than half of his nation's annual budget. He even laughed at how strong his military was in comparison to the American army. But even while major powers like Germany held American might in such contempt, House still believed that the United States would be recognized as the leader of the world once the war was over. He tried to convince Wilson, who seemed so lost in the past, that America could play a key role in mankind's future, especially in the peace that would finally settle this great and terrible war.[448]

Wilson was not so convinced. In fact, he often told House in their long talks in the evenings at Cornish that his dreams for a better future had come to nothing. If he had more time to craft his vision of America as the leader of worldwide democracy, then perhaps he could have prevented the war. At least he might have been a more acceptable mediator to the warring parties. The President looked ahead into the dark future of the world and could only see unending power struggles between nations. If Germany won the war, then America would be forced to become a militarized nation herself just to survive. But no matter who won the war, it looked like his dream of a more honorable way to run international

[447] Henry Van Dyke, "Letter to Woodrow Wilson, August 9, 1914," *PWW*, XXX, 364-365.
[448] Colonel Edward House, "Diary of Colonel House, August 30, 1914," *PWW*, XXX, 461-467.

affairs had come to nothing. Maybe one day when the war finally ended, he mused, the United States might become a leading power in half of the world with Russia controlling the rest of it. Caught up momentarily in Wilson's despair, House reminded him that China would probably be the third power to rule along side America and Russia in such a dark future.[449]

As much as Wilson suffered, he did not remain always in despair. He knew he must come to grips with the situation in Europe and try to understand its causes. With little more than the dispatches of his ambassadors to rely on, he tried to piece together the chronicle of events that had led to open war. He ordered every report that came out of the State Department to be sent to him. The accounts could not be digested in any way but must be word for word. Night after night, Wilson sat at his desk reading the reports along with dispatches from his ambassadors to understand the reasons behind the conflict. He also read an article on its causes written by Albert Bushnell Hart, one of his former editors. Hart traced the roots of the war to troubles in the Balkans and pointed to Austria's repression of peoples throughout Central and Eastern Europe as the primary cause of the war.[450] The conflict that started with the assassination of Archduke Francis Ferdinand and his wife spread beyond the borders of Austria once the many interlocking alliances made between the nations of Europe went into effect. After Austria had declared war on Serbia for playing a part in the assassination, Russia came to the aid of its ally Serbia. Germany, the friend of Austria, then declared war on Russia, and this nation in turn called on her allies, Great Britain and France, to enter the war on her behalf. Even now the conflict was widening as the Kaiser worked to bring the Ottoman Empire into the war on the side of Germany and Austria.

Wilson carefully studied the tragic events that led to the many declarations of war in the summer of 1914, but wanted to go past the immediate causes to the deeper meaning of the conflict. He was most haunted by the question of what the consequences of this awful war would mean for the future of the world once the conflict was over. Was humanity doomed to suffer a deadly fight to the finish for global domination between Germany and Great Britain? If so, what would the world be like once the battle was done? All of mankind seemed to be caught between German militarism on the one hand and the ever-growing British Empire on the other. Wilson soon found himself under great pressure to pick a side in a struggle he considered useless. Some scholars like President Charles Eliot of

---

[449] Ibid., 462-463.

[450] Charles Richard Crane, the man that Wilson wanted for ambassador to Russia (but who turned down the post), sent Hart's essay on the Austrian-Serbian connection to Wilson on April 3, 1914. See the President's response thanking Crane for the article in Woodrow Wilson, "Letter to Richard Crane, August 4, 1914," *PWW*, XXX, 343.

Harvard sent letters urging the President to form an immediate alliance between the United States, Great Britain, France, and Russia, along with Italy and Japan, to halt German aggression. Elliot advocated an immediate blockade around Europe to hamper the war efforts of Germany and her allies, warning that if this was not done, then Germany would soon attack neutral ships on the high seas. Ambassador Page and Colonel House took a similar stand, but were even more openly pro-British in their recommendations, reminding Wilson of every atrocity committed by the Germans on the people of neutral countries like Belgium as they swept westward toward France. At the opposite end, William Jennings Bryan often defended Germany, telling the President that the nation was fighting to protect herself against Britain's overwhelming sea power. He favored strict neutrality and recommended that no contraband of any kind including loans be sent to the warring parties.[451]

Wilson listened patiently to every point of view that came his way about the war in Europe, but was unwilling to take a side. He was horrified at the brutality of the German offensive and the arrogance of the Kaiser. But he was no longer enamored of Great Britain. He had lost much of his admiration for England while teaching American history, law, and economics at Princeton. Although there was a flicker of democracy in Britain, the tradition and practice of self-government burned most brightly in the United States. Even more importantly, Wilson took no immediate side in the conflict because he remembered from his own childhood how terrible war truly was. The horror of war had been ever before his mind when he refused to send an army into Mexico against Huerta. In fact, as the war raged in Europe, the situation in Mexico grew worse each day. Huerta had fled the country but now President Carranza faced a revolt from his former allies, including Pancho Villa, the daring bandit turned revolutionary who fought him in the north. Joe Tumulty recalled a chilling comment that the President made in a cabinet meeting about why he refused to fight in Mexico which also applied to his reluctance to take sides in the European conflict:

> "I came from the South and I know what war is, for I have seen its wreckage and terrible ruin. It is easy for me as President to declare war. I do not have to fight, and neither do the gentlemen on the Hill who now clamour for it. It is some poor farmer's boy, or the son of some poor widow away off in some modest

---

[451] Charles William Eliot, "Letter to Woodrow Wilson, August 6, 1914," *PWW*, XXX, 353-355; William Jennings Bryan, "Letter to Woodrow Wilson, August 10, 1914," *PWW*, XXX, 372-374.

community, or perhaps the scion of a great family, who will have to do the fighting and the dying."[452]

Even as Wilson struggled to shape a coherent foreign policy in the present, he began to look ahead to what the world might be like once the war ended. Perhaps after so many countries in the world had nearly destroyed themselves in useless combat, his belief that international relations must be built on ethical principles might seem more sensible and less idealistic. Wilson believed he had best implemented these principles in the Far East. He was a staunch supporter of independence and democracy for the Philippines. He had opposed unscrupulous bank loans to China. He had even sent Secretary Bryan to California to prevent the state from discriminating against Japanese immigrants. Now in the sorrowful days after his wife's death, as he brooded about how his own family had been broken apart, he dreamt again of a world where nations behaved toward one another like members of the same household.

He shared his vision most completely with Stockton Axson. He grew especially close to his brother-in-law after the loss of the First Lady. Axson often visited the President in the White House. The two men spent many evenings reminiscing about Ellen Wilson, but their conversations frequently turned to politics. Just a few days after the family returned to Washington following Mrs. Wilson's funeral in Georgia, the President sat in his study in the White House with this brother-in-law. He mentioned in passing that his greatest fear in the coming war was that something terrible would happen on the oceans of the world to draw America into the conflict. At the same time, he could not help but think of Napoleon whose conquest of Europe had set France and England at each other's throats a century before in the same way Germany and Britain faced one another today. Other Presidents, like John Adams, Thomas Jefferson, and James Madison, had been in the same place as Wilson now found himself. Like them, he must play a terrible waiting game of threats and maneuvers in an attempt to keep his nation out of war.

Still what troubled him most in all in this, Wilson confessed to Axson, was a statement that Napoleon had made in the midst of his own military campaigns. Even with his many victories, Bonaparte quipped that "nothing is ever finally settled by force." It was in the agreements that came after the wars were over that the future of the world was decided. Wilson added that once this awful war was done, there would be four things that would be "absolutely necessary for the ordering of the world in the future." Years later Axson could still remember the vivid words Wilson chose to make his points. First, there must never again be any

---

[452] Tumulty, *Woodrow Wilson As I Know Him*, 158.

"foot of ground" taken by conquest. Second, "small nations" must be seen as having equal rights with "great nations." Only governments, not private individuals, must manufacture weapons. Finally, there must be "some sort of association" where the territorial integrity of all member nations was guaranteed.[453]

While he brooded over the meaning of war and peace in the modern world, Wilson knew as President that he must set a course for his nation. He officially declared the neutrality of the United States in August 1914. Later in an appeal addressed directly to the people, the President reminded all Americans that they held the power in their own hands to decide how the war would affect them. Their nation would remain neutral only if they as individuals remained neutral in both word and deed. He knew this would not be easy since the ancestors of Americans had come from many different nations, some of which were involved in the war. As they headed into days that would "try men's souls," a quote that Wilson took from Thomas Paine, Americans must work together to maintain the spirit of neutrality. Then happiness would descend on the land and the nation could look forward to influencing the world for peace in the future.[454]

Wilson knew that other measures must be taken to protect his nation in this dangerous time. The most significant one dealt with shipping. The vast majority of exports from the United States were currently sent around the world on foreign ships. Wilson asked Congress to pass the Ship Purchase Bill that would allow the government to buy a merchant fleet to carry American goods abroad during the war. The government would also form a corporation to oversee the ships. Opposition to Wilson's bill in Congress was bitter. Many politicians could not understand why this expense was necessary, while others believed that buying ships from nations that were at war broke America's pledge of neutrality, especially if the rumors in Washington were true that most of the ships would be bought from Germany. Wilson gave a practical answer to the first complaint. He argued that America should buy ships now when prices were low. As soon as the war became more deadly, the cost of ships would go even higher and the expense to the taxpayers would thus be greater. To the second concern, he simply said that the nation was not buying German ships or English ships, but "ships, pure and simple." He also told Congress that by buying a merchant fleet for the nation in the midst of war, they would make America into the greatest carrier of goods in the modern world. In fact, nations involved in the conflict would have to rely on the United States to carry goods since most of their own ships would be tied up in

---

[453] Axson, *Brother Woodrow*, 193-194.

[454] Woodrow Wilson, "An Appeal to the American People, August 18, 1914," *PWW*, XXX, 393-394.

the fighting. Despite his strong defense of the act, the Congress, especially the Republicans in the Senate, were in no hurry to approve the Ship Purchase Bill.[455]

As summer became fall in 1914, Wilson knew that there were many other bills he must push through Congress. His party was facing a tough midterm election in November and he could help his many fellow Democrats if he continued to deliver progressive legislation. In September, Wilson signed a bill into law that created the Federal Trade Commission. He had worked with his friend Louis Brandeis to shape this significant piece of reform legislation. Its purpose was to break up monopolies at their very source. The President would now have the power to appoint five people to the Federal Trade Commission with the approval of the Senate. Each commissioner would serve for a seven-year term. Their job would be to investigate corporate activities and issue "cease-and-desist" orders to prevent unfair business practices. Only banks and railroads would be exempt from the control of the Federal Trade Commission, but they would instead be under the oversight of the Federal Reserve Board and the Interstate Commerce Commission respectively.

One month after the Federal Trade Commission was established, Wilson signed the Clayton Antitrust Act into law. Drafted by Democratic Congressman Henry Le Mar Clayton of Alabama, the bill came about after an investigation in the House of Representatives revealed how banker J. P. Morgan and industrialist John D. Rockefeller had built a financial empire that controlled one-tenth of the nation's wealth. They had accomplished this through the use of interlocking directorates that allowed one man to direct many companies at the same time. The new law banned interlocking directorates in companies worth $1,000,000 or more and banks with $5,000,000 or more of capital. The Democratic Congress made sure that labor unions were exempt from the provisions of the Clayton Antitrust Act. If working people organized to boycott, picket, and even strike, they would not be prosecuted under the provisions of the new law.[456]

While more progressive reforms would come forward from his administration, Wilson grew increasingly worried that everything he had accomplished on behalf of the American people in the fight against special privilege would be swept away in wartime. "Every reform we have won will be lost if we go to war," he told Secretary of the Navy Josephus Daniels. He was proud of the many Democrats who had helped him deliver on his promises to the American people. The party could face the voters, knowing they had lowered the tariff, created a new national credit system, and taken a tough stand against

[455] Baker, *Life and Letters*, V, 109-133.
[456] Baker, *Life and Letters*, IV, 373; Ibid., V, 118.

monopolies. But these reforms were all still so new that no one could be certain that they would survive as the whole world plunged into war. "We don't know yet how they will work," he complained to Daniels, "They are not thoroughly set."[457]

When the campaign finally got underway, Wilson decided not to work for any specific candidates. He thought it would look better, and thus be a greater help to the Democratic cause, if he remained in the White House, monitoring the crisis in Europe. He wrote letters on behalf of the party to Oscar Underwood, the champion of tariff reform, and Frank Doremus, the Chairman of the Democratic Party. These testimonials were in turn published for Americans all across the nation to read. In them, the President proudly told the story of how the Democrats had taken up the cause of the people in 1912, and now just two years later, they could report back on the many reforms they had passed. In private, Wilson confessed his hope that his own personal popularity would help the Democrats hold onto the House and Senate. Still he was under no illusion that Americans would always feel kindly toward him. In the midst of the campaign, he confessed to his closest friend Mary Hulbert that he well understood the fleeting nature of a President's popularity:

> "For the moment I am approved of and trusted by the party and the country and am popular. But I am not deceived. I know by what tenure a man holds popularity. It is only a tenancy at will, and may be terminated without notice. Any day I might find it my duty to do something that will make me intensely unpopular, it may be, the object of fierce and passionate criticism."[458]

When the votes were finally tallied after the election on November 7, 1914, the Democrats had held on to both the House and Senate. However, they had sustained heavy losses in the House. Sixty-three Democrats along with eleven Progressives would not be returning. Still Wilson's party would have 222 seats to 200 for the Republicans. The Senate remained unchanged with the Democrats holding a majority of ten. Wilson was surprised that the greatest losses for his party had come in the East, while the West stayed strong for the Democrats. He took it as a personal affront that the East had rejected him as the "spokesman" of their nation in the coming world crisis. Yet he was overjoyed that the West, the "real heart of America," had embraced his leadership and was now solidly in the Democratic camp.[459]

---

[457] Daniels, *Life of Woodrow Wilson*, 77.

[458] Woodrow Wilson, "Letter to Mary Hulbert, September 20, 1914," *PWW*, XXXI, 59-60.

[459] Baker, *Life and Letters*, V, 95.

Wilson's most immediate concern with the new Congress was trying to pass the Ship Purchase Bill. The Republicans in the Senate did everything to defeat it including talking on any topic possible rather than the bill itself and enlisting the support of key Democrats from the South, West, and most importantly New York. At one point, Republican Senator Reed Smoot of Utah spoke for 11½ hours straight to avoid bringing the measure to a vote. When Senator Theodore Burton of Ohio spoke for 13 hours, cots were brought in for the Senators to sleep on in the cloakroom.[460] Wilson was stunned that the Republicans would hold up a measure that he believed was good for business. His argument against their tactics was a simple one. How could American goods, he asked, get out to the world market if the ships that once carried them were now be tied up in the war? When progress on the shipping bill stalled completely after the first of the year, Wilson headed out on the stump to talk directly to the American people. If he could win them over to his cause, then maybe they in turn could put pressure on the Congress to pass the bill.

President Wilson chose the Jackson Day Dinner scheduled for January 8, 1915 in Indianapolis as the place to make his case for the Ship Purchase Bill. Placing himself squarely in the mode of Andrew Jackson who believed that "everyone who disagreed with him was an enemy of the country," Wilson launched his attack on the Senators who were blocking his bill. Characterizing Republicans as members of a party that had "not had a new idea in thirty years," he scolded them for harming the very business interests which they so cherished. In contrast to these "self-styled friends of business," the Democrats were trying to help American producers by finding a way to get the nation's goods out to the world market during wartime. "I challenge them to show their right to stand in the way of the release of American products to the rest of the world," he told the cheering crowd. He also attacked the many newspapers that mocked his "watchful waiting" policy first toward Mexico and now toward Europe. He assured them that he merely chuckled as he read the editorials written against him, knowing that he would have the last laugh because his policies were in touch with "the temper and principles of the American people." In a final blast at his opponents in Congress and the press alike, he said, "If I did not think I knew, I would emigrate, because I would not be satisfied to stay where I am!"[461]

When Wilson got back to Washington, he found that his address had infuriated the Republicans who were now more determined than ever to sink his

---

[460] Ibid., 128-129.

[461] Woodrow Wilson, "A Jackson Day Address in Indianapolis, January 8, 1915," *PWW*, XXXII, 29-41.

shipping bill. They had many reasons to oppose the President's plan for a state-funded merchant marine. First and foremost, they believed that private businesses must determine how to ship goods out of the United States even during war time. Many business leaders were not worried about having fewer ships to transport goods since this would actually cause prices to rise since demand would far outweigh supply. Secondly, great pressure was coming from England and France not to approve the bill. These nations feared that the United States would soon have the world's greatest merchant marine and so compete with their own fleets. Finally, many Senators, including the seven Democrats who had joined the Republican cause on the matter of the merchant marine, feared the growing power of the Presidency. If America did enter the war, this would increase Wilson's power even further. Therefore it was necessary to reduce his ability to control the Congress in advance of America's entry into the world conflict.

While Wilson seemed his old self again in the battle with the Senate over the Ship Purchase Bill, those close to the President were increasingly worried about him. Since his wife's death, they saw him go from a young man with a bounce in his step to an old one who walked hunched over through the corridors of the White House. His brown hair had turned pure white and his face was now deeply lined. He still worked as diligently as before but his heart was no longer in it. He had his breakfast at 8:00 A.M. and then dictated letters and reviewed reports that needed his immediate attention. By a quarter to 10, he was in his office receiving visitors until 1:00 P.M. when he had his lunch. In the early afternoon, he had more formal visits with ambassadors and foreign dignitaries. When the official business of the day was done in the late afternoon, he changed to his "play clothes," which included his favorite old grey sweater, and headed to the golf course. He played until the sun went down. Then it was back to the White House for a bath, fresh clothes, and dinner. He spent the rest of the evening attending to pressing matters in domestic and foreign affairs that he would have to deal with on the next day. Then he fell into bed totally exhausted. On the following morning, the same routine began all over again. The pattern was only broken on Sunday when he slept until church and then spent the afternoon driving through the countryside.[462]

The strict daily routine that Wilson followed since his wife's death helped him keep his mind off of his sorrow but it did not relieve the unbearable burden that the Presidency had become for him. He now described the White House as the place that had brought him "no personal blessing, but only irreparable loss and desperate suffering." When a close friend, Mrs. Nancy Toy, the wife of a professor he had known at Johns Hopkins, remarked that the old fight seemed to

[462] Woodrow Wilson, "Letter to Mary Hulbert, October 11, 1914," *PWW*, XXXI, 141-142.

have returned to him, and that he reminded her of Wordsworth's "Happy Warrior," he could only laugh. The dream of the brave hero he once longed to be was now buried with his wife on a hillside in Rome, Georgia. He could only go on in the hope that he might still do some good for the people. As he explained in a letter to Mrs. Toy:

> "I seem myself so unheroic a figure … and with none but the common tools to work with. If there is anything that can infuse the heroic into me it is the trust and confidence of those whom I honour and who know right from wrong. Any heroism I may be vouchsafed will come from the outside, not from within."[463]

Cary Grayson, the White House doctor, was the person most worried about the President. Like everyone else, he had seen how Wilson had changed physically, but he was more concerned about his mental state. He only seemed happy when his family visited. Nellie McAdoo came to the White House almost everyday, while Jessie Sayre returned in January 1915 to give birth to Francis Wilson Sayre, the President's first grandchild. But most of the time, the President was alone. Grayson soon became his constant companion, often playing golf with him in the afternoon and eating dinner with him in the evening. He also sat up with the President late at night in the White House study. While the President spent much of the time working on important business, with Grayson usually reading a book, there were times when Wilson began to talk about the past. He told stories about his father, his mother, and especially his wife. Even months after Ellen's death, he still believed his political ambitions had killed her. "I sometimes feel that the Presidency has had to be paid for with Ellen's life," he once said to Dr. Grayson, "that she would be here today if we had continued in the old simple life at Princeton."

Wilson also said that Ellen's death had made him much humbler. Grayson noticed this as he took car rides with him around Washington. The President best loved talking to people when they had no idea who he was. Once a Virginia farmer said to him, "You favor the picture of President Wilson," and he simply answered, "Yes, I have been told that." On another trip that Grayson took with Wilson on the *Mayflower* to Yorktown, the pair wandered about the historic site for some time before anyone recognized him. Finally a 12-year old girl approached and asked, "You are President Wilson, are you not, sir?" He smiled and answered, "Yes, I am guilty." The little girl then took the President, his

---

[463] Woodrow Wilson, "Letter to Nancy Toy, March 7, 1915," *PWW*, XXXII, 334-335.

doctor, and a crowd of townspeople on a tour of the Nelson House, the Yorktown Monument, and Washington's Headquarters at Temple Farm.[464]

Grayson was also worried about Helen Bones, the President's cousin who had stayed on after Ellen's death to cheer him, and Margaret Wilson who had cut back on her singing career in New York to act as the White House hostess. Grayson decided to find a friend for them. He was engaged to a woman named Alice Gordon who knew many people in Washington society. She suggested that her fiancé introduce Helen and Margaret to Edith Bolling Galt, a widow in her early forties. She was from an old Virginia family that could trace itself all the way back to Pocahontas and her husband John Rolfe. Edith Bolling had married Norman Galt, a prominent Washington jeweler, in 1896 when she was 24 years old. Two years later, she gave birth to a child who died, and after that she was unable to have children. When her husband died in 1908, her brothers took over the day-to-day business of running the jewelry store for her. She was then free to take care of her ailing mother and her sisters. Edith was a friendly and uncomplicated woman with a winning smile, and she was soon close to both Helen and Margaret. They could often be seen driving around Washington together or walking through Rock Creek Park.[465]

Helen Bones always asked her new friend to come back to the White House with her, but Edith Galt turned her down, saying she would not fit in there. She did mention that she had seen the President a few times before. Once in 1909 she happened to be in the same hotel in Philadelphia where Wilson was speaking to the Princeton alumni. She peaked into the ballroom to have a look at him. She saw him for a second time on the day after his inauguration when they both came to see the actress Billie Burke at the National Theater. Edith's seat was directly below the President's box. She saw him a third time when he made his dramatic address to the joint session of Congress in April 1914. She had taken her mother to see the President but had no ticket. She bribed a doorkeeper with a piece of candy to let her into the visitor's gallery.

In March 1915, when she finally agreed to visit the White House with Helen after a walk in the park together, Edith Bolling met President Wilson as he got out of the elevator with Dr. Grayson. The two men had been playing golf and asked Edith to stay to tea. He even told his cousin Helen to have the tea brought into the Oval Office. The President was a jolly host, telling jokes and stories to Edith, Helen, and Dr. Grayson. When she left, Grayson mentioned that Wilson had actually met Edith a few weeks before. They were driving in the President's

---

[464] Grayson, *Intimate Memoir*, 35-37, 40-45.
[465] Ibid., 50.

Pierce Arrow near Dupont Circle when Grayson bowed to a tall woman with dark hair and deep blue eyes who was standing on the curb. The President saw her, too, and asked, "Who is that beautiful woman?" Grayson was happy to see that the President could be attracted to another woman so soon after his wife's death. Although he never told the President, Mrs. Wilson had asked him on her death bed to make sure that her husband married again. She knew how emotional he was and how desperately he needed the support of a woman in his life who loved him. In fact, he had been that way since he first fell in love with his cousin Harriet Woodrow.

On March 23, 1915, just a few days after meeting the President near the White House elevator and having tea in the Oval Office, Mrs. Galt came back to have dinner with President Wilson, Helen Bones, and Cary Grayson. It was a pleasant experience for everyone, especially the President who seemed to be his old self again. After the meal, Wilson read his favorite poems to the little group. Just a few weeks later, Edith went back to the White House for one of her usual afternoon rides with Helen Bones. When they headed out to the Pierce Arrow for their trip around Washington, they were surprised to see the President already in the car, waiting to go with them. It was soon clear to everyone that Woodrow Wilson was smitten with Edith Bolling Galt.[466]

The President found in Mrs. Galt a person who in some ways was very much like himself. She had grown up in the South in the aftermath of the Civil War and knew firsthand the poverty that had come with the Reconstruction. Both her grandfather, who was a physician, and her father, who studied law at the University of Virginia and later became a judge, had served in the Confederate Army. Edith was the seventh of nine children born into a family run by her eccentric Grandmother Bolling. She was an invalid who lived in the downstairs bedroom of the ramshackle family mansion where she raised canaries and ruled the Bolling clan with an iron fist. She was also Edith's first teacher, much as the Reverend Wilson had been the first teacher of his son Woodrow. Grandmother Bolling taught Edith as best she could the fundamentals of Latin, history, and French. She loved to read classic literature aloud to her grandchildren in the evening after dinner. While the family finally raised enough money to send Edith to a boarding school in Richmond, she always believed she learned the most from Grandmother Bolling. After she married Norman Galt, an older man in his thirties who had pressed her for years to be his wife, she missed her family terribly. She found little happiness in a loveless marriage. She took some comfort in the fact that she could help to take care of her mother and many brothers and sisters. She

[466] Ibid., 51.

could also dress and travel in style. She made three trips to Europe and fell in love with the city of Paris which she considered her second home.

Like Ellen Wilson, Edith Galt could recite poetry and weave it into her conversations and her letters. Wilson noticed this love of literature in his new friend almost immediately and soon began to write to her, suggesting important things for her to read. He recommended that she study the writings of George Washington, William James, and Matthew Arnold. She read everything he recommended, and in turn, quoted whole pieces of poetry that she had learned as a child at her grandmother's side. Soon the couple was corresponding with each other every day, and sometimes Wilson even took the time to send her two or three notes. At first, he filled his letters with insights into the literature he loved. But soon he was confessing the details of his troubles with Imperial Germany over its refusal to back down from sinking ships at will on the high seas and his struggle with Congress over passage of the shipping bill. He installed a phone directly from the White House to Edith's home at 1308 Twentieth Street N.W. so he could speak to her anytime he felt like it. Soon all of Washington was gossiping about how the President's Pierce Arrow motor car could be seen parked in from of Mrs. Galt's house at all hours of the day and night.[467]

On May 3, 1915, after knowing Edith for only two months, Wilson asked her to marry him. The President's surprise proposal came after a dinner with the family at the White House. Mrs. Galt was so troubled by the offer of marriage that she went home without giving Wilson an answer. Three days later, he wrote an especially impassioned letter to Edith explaining why he had asked her to become his wife when they barely knew each other. He said that he had moved so quickly because everything in his life seemed to be going at top speed.

> "These are the supreme years of my life. Minutes count with me now more than days will sometime, – and my need is supreme. I know you can fill it because you do fill it every moment I am with you. Every power in me is happily free when you are by, with the light in your eyes I love so."

Wilson went on to explain that up until the moment he asked her to marry him, Edith Galt had only known him as the President of the United States. But now he was begging her to love the private man that the world never saw. Who was the private Woodrow Wilson? He was "a longing man, in the midst of a

---

[467] Edith Bolling Wilson, *My Memoir* (Indianapolis and New York: The Bobbs-Merrill Company, 1939), 1-58.

world's affairs – a world that knows nothing of the heart he has shown you." He ended his plea to Edith with one simple question – "can you love him?"[468]

There was a desperate tone in Wilson's letter that came from more than just his loneliness. It was also the cry of a man who was facing the greatest crisis of his Presidency to date. He had bravely declared his nation's neutrality in the terrible war that was tearing Europe apart, knowing full well that neither side would respect it. Wilson found himself in exactly the same position that Jefferson had been in more than a century before when Napoleon's conquests had set France and England against each other. Jefferson knew that trading with either nation would bring down the wrath of the opposing side on his country. To remain neutral and avoid war, he had declared an embargo on all exports from the United States. He kept the peace by simply taking America's ships off the high seas. Wilson faced the same dilemma since he knew that trading with England would harm Germany and in turn trading with Germany would harm England. With no other peaceful alternative in sight, Wilson pressed forward with his demand that the warring nations respect the right of neutral countries like the United States to trade with whomever they pleased.

By the spring of 1915, it was clear that neither side would respect the rights of a neutral nation. Great Britain had placed a blockade around Europe to break the power of Germany, Austria, and the Ottoman Empire. The British navy boarded any ship bound for Europe at will, removed all goods meant for Germany or her allies, and then let the ship go safely home. Britain later paid the country for the goods that were confiscated. Germany used its submarine fleet to sink ships bound for England, certain that most of them were carrying goods needed in the war effort. While President Wilson was angry at both nations, he was more troubled by the actions of Germany than those of Great Britain. He told his cabinet that Germany's disregard for human life was a more terrible crime than Great Britain's confiscation of property. He sent word through James Gerard, the American ambassador to Germany, that he would hold the government of Imperial Germany directly responsible for any American ships destroyed or any American lives lost on the high seas. He was sadly convinced that a day would come when Germany would commit such a heinous crime on the waters off the coast of Europe that he would be forced to take America into the war.[469]

---

[468] Ibid., 60-67.

[469] Woodrow Wilson, "Letter to Edith Galt, May 5, 1915," quoted in Edwin Tribble, editor, *A President in Love: The Courtship Letters of Woodrow Wilson and Edith Bolling Galt* (Boston: Houghton Mifflin Company, 1981), 11-12.

On the afternoon of May 7, 1915, President Wilson left a cabinet meeting and met his executive secretary Rudolf Forster who was waiting for him with a telegram. Wilson was on his way to his regular golf game but canceled it when he read the cable. It told him that a British passenger liner called the *Lusitania* had been sunk in the North Atlantic. The ship was the star of the Cunard line and was scheduled to make the trip from the United States to England in less than five days. Just fifteen miles off the coast of Ireland, a torpedo sent the *Lusitania* along with 1198 passengers, including 128 Americans, to the bottom of the sea. Wilson was so distraught when he received the news that he retired to his study and refused to listen to any more details of the tragedy until he could collect his thoughts. Thousands of telegrams soon poured into the White House demanding that Wilson ask the Congress to declare war on Germany. Ambassador Page and Colonel House were among the loudest voices in the administration urging the President to abandon neutrality once and for all. Only Secretary of State William Jennings Bryan remained a strong advocate of neutrality and reminded the President that the hold of the *Lusitania* had been loaded with the weapons and ammunition bound for Great Britain. He had negotiated dozens of treaties between the United States and other nations guaranteeing peaceful relations between them and was more determined than ever to keep the nation out of war.[470]

While Wilson did not fully agree with Bryan's position, he was not ready to give up neutrality and lead the nation into the conflict. He knew that the American people were furious over the sinking of the *Lusitania*, but as their President, he must think calmly and carefully about the right course of action to take. On May 10, he headed to Philadelphia where he spoke to 4,000 people who had just become American citizens. Wilson was so swept up in the emotion of his address to the crowd that he could later barely remember what he had said. He seemed to have been elevated to some higher plane as he spoke. He told the crowd that while the sinking of the *Lusitania* was a terrible tragedy, he still favored peace over war. If there was a reason for the United States to enter the fight, he still could not see it. Until he could clearly understand and describe what America's entrance into the war would mean, he would not waver from the path of peace. He promised to keep his nation on a steady course above the fray with words that would soon come back to haunt him:

> "The example of America must be an example not merely of peace because it will not fight, but of peace because peace is the elevating and healing influence

---

[470] Baker, *Life and Letters*, V, 322-360.

> in the works and strife is not. There is such a thing as a man being too proud to fight. There is such a thing as a nation being so right that it does not have to convince others by force that it is right."[471]

In the midst of this international crisis, a letter finally came from Edith Bolling in response to Wilson's declaration of love just days before. She confessed that she was hesitant to love again since her first marriage had not been a happy one. She even felt dead inside and feared that she might always prefer to live in the shadows of the past rather than in the bright light of a new love. Still Wilson's confession of his deep feelings had overwhelmed her and given her courage. "We will help and hearten each other," she wrote, "I pledge you all that is best in me – to help, to sustain, to comfort." Yet even while she made this promise, Edith Bolling Galt was still frightened and asked the President to treat her kindly. "Into the space that separates us," she wrote, "I send my spirit to seek yours. Make it a welcome guest." She could have written nothing better to a man whose boyhood dreams seemed dead and buried. He could now be the hero once again by protecting Edith's delicate spirit. "I will be its knight," he answered, "and feel myself grow a better, purer man in the service."[472]

Wilson felt a similar heroism coming back in his relationship with the American people. By defending neutrality, he would become the guardian of his nation just as he was the protector of the spirit of Edith Galt. However, many Americans did not see Wilson as a brave leader rescuing his nation from war. They instead considered him a coward who would not join the fight against an immoral power like Germany. Several major newspapers ridiculed his decision not to go to war as too self-involved. They especially attacked the line in Wilson's Jackson Day speech where he described himself as a "man too proud to fight." No one was a louder critic of Wilson as a senseless coward than Teddy Roosevelt. He had returned to the Republican fold and was prepared to do anything in his power to help his party defeat the spineless Wilson in the upcoming election. British officials also joined in the attack on the President of the United States. Just days after Wilson made his "too proud to fight" speech in Philadelphia, Lord Bryce, the former British ambassador to the United States, issued a report detailing the atrocities that the German army had committed in neutral Belgium. The implication was clear. If Wilson continued to back neutrality, even after the

---

[471] Woodrow Wilson, "An Address in Philadelphia to Newly Naturalized Citizens, May 10, 1915, *PWW*, XXXIII, 147-150.

[472] See the letters between Woodrow Wilson and Edith Galt from May 9 through 20, 1915 in Tribble, ed., *A President in Love*, 15-29.

sinking of the *Lusitania* and the ravaging of the Low Countries, then he was little better than the "Huns" who were tearing Europe apart.[473]

Despite the bitter attacks on his leadership, Wilson refused to steer away from the neutral course he had set for his nation. Yet he was also determined to take as strong a stand against Germany as possible short of war. He drafted a letter to the German government protesting the sinking of the *Lusitania* and held a stormy cabinet meeting on May 13 to make final changes to the document. Over the protests of Secretary of State William Jennings Bryan, the final letter condemned unrestricted submarine warfare and declared the right of every American citizen to travel anywhere in the world on land or sea during wartime. Even though the entire cabinet approved the document, Bryan questioned why the President ignored every violation of American neutrality by the British while at the same time he condemned Germany's actions on the high seas. Wilson answered that Britain's actions merely violated the rights of property, but Germany's actions violated the rights of humanity. Less than one month later, on June 8, when Wilson issued a second letter of protest that condemned Germany in even stronger terms, Bryan resigned his position as Secretary of State.[474]

After Wilson issued a third letter of protest over the sinking of the *Lusitania*, Germany promised never again to attack a ship without warning. It was not the response that the President had hoped for, but it would prevent America's entrance into the war for at least a time. With the crisis of the *Lusitania* behind him, Wilson headed to Cornish for a summer vacation in August 1916. He took his daughter Margaret, Stockton Axson, and his cousin Helen Bones with him to New Hampshire along with Mrs. Galt. He spent his days playing golf and his evenings reading to Edith and his family.[475] When he returned to the White House in September, the President was ready to announce to the world that he was engaged to be married. He soon found himself embroiled in a crisis that rivaled the furor over the sinking of the *Lusitania*.

Members of his own party were shocked that the President had decided to remarry so soon after his first wife had died and were certain that the romance would ruin their chances for re-election in 1916. They had heard the many rumors circulating in the capital about the President's romance with the Washington widow. Many were especially shocked when Mrs. Galt accompanied him on official trips including a tour of the American navy along the Hudson River in New York City. At a time when Democrats needed a leader who appeared as

---

[473] Baker, *Life and Letters*, V, 287, 328.
[474] Ibid., 349-357.
[475] Edith Bolling Wilson, *My Memoir*, 68-74.

dedicated to his nation in wartime as Lincoln had once been, they found that their President was instead behaving like a lovesick schoolboy. Democratic leaders were convinced that the announcement of the President's engagement or even worse his actual marriage before the next election would lead to a crushing defeat for the party. Everyone in the cabinet agreed that the President should not think about remarrying until after his re-election bid, except his close friend Secretary of the Navy Daniels who told his fellow Democrats to face the fact that there would be a new Mrs. Wilson before the year was out.[476]

By mid-September of 1915, the situation grew even more troublesome when rumors circulated that letters between Woodrow Wilson and Mary Hulbert were about to be made public. These documents revealed that the President had been deeply involved with Mary Hulbert, better known as Mrs. Peck, perhaps even having an affair with her while he was married to Ellen Wilson. There was also talk that the President had recently given Mary Hulbert a large sum of money. Wilson's closest supporters, namely Joe Tumulty, William McAdoo, and Colonel Edward House, went into action to avert a crisis that might destroy the President's career. They decided that House must be the person to bring these rumors to the President's attention. After House confronted him about the letters, Wilson said his relationship with Mary Hulbert was strictly platonic, but he did admit that his correspondence with her was inappropriate for someone in his position. He also confessed that he had sent $7500 to his friend Mary, but it was for her son Allen and not to keep her quiet. In order to avoid any further scandal, House recommended that Wilson keep his engagement to Mrs. Galt a secret until after the election in 1916.[477]

Embarrassed by the revelation of his emotional affair with Mary Hulbert, Wilson felt compelled to explain his behavior to Edith Galt in person. He drove to her house in Washington on the night of September 18 and confessed that he once had a relationship with Mrs. Peck. He called it "a folly long ago loathed and repented of." "Stand by me," he begged Edith, "Don't desert me!" She was stunned and refused to promise anything. After Wilson had gone back to the White House, she stayed up all night in a chair in her parlor looking out the front window. It was a place where she had sat many an evening before when she was worried or had to make a decision. After a long night of wrestling with her sudden doubts about Wilson's character, she wrote him a note saying she would stand by him as she originally promised. "This is my pledge, dearest one, I will stand by

---

[476] Baker, *Life and Letters*, VI, 49-50.

[477] Ibid., 50-51; Lawrence, *The True Story of Woodrow Wilson*, 134; Edith Bolling Wilson, *My Memoir*, 75-76.

you," she wrote, "not for duty, not for pity, not for honor – but for love – trusting, protecting, comprehending love."[478]

Edith was surprised as the next day wore on and she did not hear from Wilson. Then late on the afternoon of September 19, Dr. Grayson arrived at her front door. He told Edith to come quickly to the White House because the President had been taken ill quite suddenly. When she entered Wilson's darkened bedroom, she found the President lying down with his worried valet sitting at his side. She grabbed his ice cold hand and was soon left alone with him. He told her that he had collapsed when her note came since he was certain that she had turned on him. Assuring him that she would keep her promise to stand by him and become his wife, the President quickly recovered. The same men who had opposed the President's engagement, most notably Colonel House, now supported the marriage since they would rather see Wilson alive and happy than in such despair. On October 7, 1915, the President officially announced his engagement to Mrs. Galt, and a little more than two months later, on December 18, 1915, he married his fiancée in a small ceremony at her home on Twentieth Street. When Wilson took his new bride to Hot Springs, Virginia for their honeymoon, he confessed that he had carried the note she had written to him on September 19 in his pocket but had never opened it. Now he asked Edith to read it to him. "And no matter whether the wine is bitter or sweet," it said, "we will share it together and find happiness in the comradeship."[479]

Wilson was overjoyed that he had found a companion who could help him carry the burdens of the Presidency. His daughters Margaret, Jessie, and Nellie and his closest relatives like Stockton Axson were relieved that his marriage to Edith Galt had brought him out of the despair he had known since the death of Ellen Wilson. Wilson was convinced that his "dear Eileen" would have approved of the marriage and truly believed that Edith had been sent as a "special gift from Heaven." She would help him "forget the intolerable loneliness and isolation of the weary months since the terrible war began." Still the President knew that the speed of his courtship and marriage to Edith Galt had shocked many people, especially his closest women friends. He told Edith Gittings Reid that it seemed the whole world was moving faster since Ellen's death and the start of the war in Europe. "The last fourteen months have seemed for me, in a world upset, like fourteen years," he had explained just days before his engagement was

---

[478] See the letters between Woodrow Wilson and Edith Galt from September 9 through 30, 1915 in Tribble, ed., *A President in Love*, 171-191; the letter from Edith to the President on September 19, 1915 (where she describes the "don't desert me!" comment of Wilson) is fully quoted in Edith Bolling Wilson, *My Memoir*, 76-77.

announced. "It is not the same world in which my dear Ellen lived." He hoped Edith Reid would sympathize with him and so approve of the marriage.[480]

Three days before his engagement was announced, he had confessed to Mary Hulbert that he would soon be married. The letter was a short note telling her that she was one of the first people to learn of the "good fortune" that had befallen him. He was engaged to Mrs. Norman Galt of Washington, D.C. He said he was certain that Mary would love and admire the woman who would soon be his wife. Everyone who met Edith came to appreciate what a fine person she truly was. He added that he considered his engagement to Mrs. Galt a blessing from on high. After writing so many long and impassioned letters to Mary Hulbert during the last eight years, he closed this one quickly and with little emotion. "I am writing in great haste, amidst a pressure of clamorous engagements that cannot be gainsaid," he explained, "but you will know in what spirit." He added that Helen Bones sent her love. After she received the letter announcing Wilson's engagement, Mary Hulbert never wrote to the President again. He sent a few more notes urging her to write, but she did not answer. Her silence showed that the relationship, which he now dismissed as a "folly," had meant much more to her. She could not bear to read Wilson's description of his newfound happiness in letter after letter. Instead she preferred silence and the immediate end of her friendship with Woodrow Wilson.[481]

Many of Wilson's opponents on Capitol Hill noticed that his engagement and marriage to Mrs. Galt had seemed to make him more reasonable. He had finally recognized that his stubborn stand on the merchant marine had accomplished nothing. He decided that a new approach would be necessary if he was to secure ships for the country. In his annual message to Congress, delivered just a week and a half before his marriage to Edith Galt, the President said that it was still necessary for the United States to build a "great merchant marine." However, he was no longer tied to the specific provisions of the original shipping bill and promised that a new version of it would soon be introduced to the Congress. "I am not so much interested in the particulars of the programme," he explained, "as I am in taking immediate advantage of the great opportunity which awaits us if we will but act in this emergency."[482]

---

[479] Ibid., 84-88.

[480] Woodrow Wilson, "Letter to Edith Gittings Reid, October 5, 1915," as quoted in Baker, *Life and Letters*, VI, 48.

[481] Woodrow Wilson, "Letter to Mary Hulbert, October 4, 1915," as quoted in ibid, 47-48; see also Mulder, *Woodrow Wilson: Years of Preparation*, 261-263.

[482] Baker, *Life and Letters*, VI, 303-310.

Shortly after Wilson returned to Washington in January 1916, Congressman Joshua Alexander of Missouri introduced a shipping bill with the purpose of "encouraging, developing, and creating a naval auxiliary and naval reserves and merchant marine." Even this milder bill did not pass the House until May and the Senate until August. On September 7, 1916, more than two years after the original act was first introduced to the Congress, Wilson finally signed the shipping bill into law. The scars left behind on both the President and the Republican Senate from the battle over the merchant marine ran deep and would not be soon forgotten. Wilson was more determined than ever to prove that he was the true voice of the American people and the spokesmen for their future. The Republicans were equally determined to defeat and even humiliate Wilson in order to win back the power that they believed the President had taken from them.

As Congress finally took action on a new version of the shipping bill, Wilson continued to monitor the tense situation on the high seas. While the German government had promised that its commanders would give a warning to any passenger liner before attacking it, submarines continued to torpedo ships on the Atlantic and in the Mediterranean. Since the *Lusitania* had gone down in May, more passenger liners had been sunk, and each time the Central Powers made excuses for the attacks. After the *Arabic* was sunk in August 1915, the German Ambassador to the United States had assured the President that every commander in his nation's submarine fleet had been instructed to attack passenger ships only after giving a warning. Three months later, the *Ancona* was sunk in the Mediterranean by a submarine of the Austro-Hungarian Empire. Officials of the Central Powers again assured Wilson that warnings were always given before an attack on a passenger liner. While Wilson was away in Virginia on his honeymoon in late December 1915, the *Persia* was torpedoed and sunk, taking many American lives with it including Dr. Robert McNeely, the American Ambassador stationed in Aden. The governments of each of the Central Powers denied that their fleets had anything to do with the loss of the *Persia*.[483]

Wilson was soon under pressure to take some kind of action to prevent further loss of life on the high seas. Congressmen Jeff McLemore of Texas and Senator Thomas Gore of Oklahoma crafted a resolution that banned Americans from traveling on the passenger liners of belligerent nations and authorized the government to deny passports to anyone who ignored this warning. By keeping Americans off the high seas, they hoped to avoid any confrontation that might lead to war. The resolution had strong support from millions of Americans of

---

[483] Daniels, *Life of Woodrow Wilson*, 243-265.

German descent.[484] In contrast, political leaders like Theodore Roosevelt, who sympathized with Great Britain, called for immediate preparations for war against Germany including the institution of a draft. Roosevelt believed that Wilson was secretly supporting Germany and doing everything in his power to help the Central Powers win the war. He mocked Wilson as a coward who was afraid of offending the populist wing of his own party and an opportunist who had his eye on the German American vote in the upcoming presidential election. In private, Roosevelt launched a bitter personal attack on Wilson as a "physically timid man" who was "entirely cold-blooded" and "self-seeking." He was convinced that if a powerful man like Jackson or Grant, or even more certainly Washington or Lincoln, was leading the nation, then such a person could rouse the American people to fight on the side of mankind against Germany and her allies. "If the President told them," Roosevelt wrote to an English friend, "in trumpet tones, that their honor was at stake, that not only the welfare and good name of the United States but considerations of broad humanity demanded action on their part, and if he led them in such action, they would respond."[485]

Wilson was determined to steer a middle course between these two extreme positions. He agreed with Americans who did not want to enter the war, but mainly because he believed that the nation was simply not ready for it. In fact, he had no sympathy for anyone who opposed America's entrance into the war by making excuses for Germany's aggression on the high seas. He believed he was doing his best to interpret the meaning of the war for the American people, and he concluded that Germany's unrestricted submarine warfare ignored international law. While Wilson still could not see how America's involvement in the conflict would lead the world into a better future, he was certain that Germany was taking humanity a step backward by sending so many passenger liners to the bottom of the sea. For this reason he opposed the McLemore resolution as a cowardly submission to the immoral actions of the Central Powers. When the leaders of his own party told him the resolution would pass overwhelmingly in the House and Senate, he went to Capitol Hill and lobbied successfully for its defeat.[486]

As much as he disliked the many critics who condemned him for not taking America into the war, especially after the sinking of the *Lusitania*, Wilson was more in sympathy with their ideas than he was willing to admit publicly. He had approved loans early in the war to Great Britain, mainly on the advice of his

---

[484] Baker, *Life and Letters*, VI, 164-165.

[485] Theodore Roosevelt, "Letter to Arthur Hamilton Lee, September 2, 1915," *The Letters of Theodore Roosevelt*, Volume VIII, edited by Elting E. Morison (Cambridge, Massachusetts: Harvard University Press, 1954), 967-969.

[486] Baker, *Life and Letters*, VI, 166-174.

Secretary of the Treasury William McAdoo who argued that England and her allies could not survive without them. He would continue to approve loans to England, but would insist that all repayments must be in gold. Wilson was certain that his battle to strengthen the nation's merchant fleet clearly proved his commitment to the growing preparedness movement. His caution came not from any cowardice on his part, but from the belief that the majority of Americans had simply not made up their minds to fight. He was fond of telling his cabinet that if he could not lead his nation into the war with a "whoop," meaning the full support of the people, then the United States would remain neutral. He also could not accept a peacetime draft since he was convinced that most Americans would resent the creation of a standing army. In fact, he had identified the nation's long hatred of militarism as one of the main reasons for neutrality as early as his annual address delivered to Congress in December 1914.[487]

When advocates of preparedness, like Theodore Roosevelt and his closest ally General Leonard Wood, organized parades and marches all over the country in support of their cause, Wilson took to the stump on his own self-styled preparedness tour. He headed first to New York and then to Pittsburgh before traveling to Cleveland, Milwaukee, Chicago, Des Moines, Kansas City, and St. Louis. Everywhere he went people lined the train tracks cheering him on and hoping he would stop and talk to them. Party leaders met with him in every town where he spoke and told him what the chances were for the Democrats in the upcoming election. In his formal addresses to crowds that often reached nearly 20,000, he did his best to explain his own understanding of the complex nature of the modern world and America's place in it. His first speeches were measured and calm, but once he came to Ohio, they took on a more fiery quality as if he himself finally understood his own vision. He was most intent on making his Midwestern audiences think about the role that their nation would one day play as the leader of the world. The United States, he explained, had long been blessed with a "provincial" existence. Protected on either side by two great oceans, the nation had grown up from its earliest days with little interference from the outside world. The nation's first presidents had wisely guided the United States away from "entangling alliances" with Europe and had instead turned the country westward on its march across the continent. While such a policy of neutrality was necessary in the nation's first one hundred years, isolation from the world would no longer be possible in the 20th century. Wilson believed that Washington himself, who first crafted the policy of strict neutrality, would today agree that it had outlived its usefulness. The rest of humanity would not allow the United States to stand

[487] Woodrow Wilson, "Annual Message to Congress, December 8, 1914," *PWW*, XXXI, 414-424.

alone on the other side of the oceans of the world. "It would be a hopeless price of provincialism to suppose that because we think differently from the rest of the world," he said, "that the rest of world will permit us to enjoy that thought without disturbance."

If it was inevitable that the America would be drawn into world affairs, the President warned, then the nation must face the fact that the Great War raging in Europe was probably the event that would bring this about. Wilson believed that the terrible conflict was unlike any other war in history since it was shaking the very foundations of the world. The old political, economic, and social order was passing away in a manner that no one yet clearly understood. "The world will never be the same after the war," he told the thousands who had gathered to listen to him in auditoriums, convention halls, and armories all over the Midwest, "The change may be for weal or it may be for woe, but it will be fundamental and tremendous." Wilson had come to believe that the new world that would arise from the rubble of a shattered Europe must be built on the principles that now only the United States held dear. The very ideals that the American people had once cherished in such splendid isolation, most especially the rule of the people and the respect for the laws which they created, must be laid down as the foundation of a better world. Peace was good, but an unwavering commitment to one's principles was better. "One can not pay the price of duties abdicated," he warned all Americans who would listen to him, "of glorious opportunities neglected, of character, national character left without vindication and exemplification in action." While no one could say in the winter of 1916 "whether the United States will be drawn into the struggle or not," there was no doubt that America had a job to do in creating a new and better world in the future. As the supposedly civilized peoples of the world behaved like barbarians on the battlefields of Europe, the United States must "keep law alive while the rest of the world burns." Once the awful bloodletting was over, America must somehow help to create an "international tribunal" and "joint guarantee of peace on the part of the great nations of the world."[488]

Even after he returned to the White House in February 1916, Wilson continued to think deeply about what his nation's role in the world would be after the terrible war across the Atlantic ran its course. Like many of his fellow Americans who looked toward Europe in the winter and spring of 1916, he could not see a future but instead saw only a meaningless bloodbath. In battles that

---

[488] See Baker, *Life and Letters*, VI, 24-40, for an excellent summation of the main themes in Wilson's "preparedness" addresses; for specific addresses (most notably, the addresses in New York City, Pittsburgh, Chicago, Saint Louis, and Des Moines), see *PPWW*, IV, 3-114.

dragged on for months, the nations of Europe were losing more men in a single campaign than the United States had lost in the entire Civil War. German troops under the command of Crown Prince Frederick Wilhelm launched an attack on the well-fortified city of Verdun in late February 1916. They met stiff resistance from the French Second Army under General Henri Pétain, and after six months of fighting, had only moved four miles. Nearly a million men were killed or wounded in the battle for Verdun which in the end remained in French hands.

In late March, the eyes of the whole world, including those of the President, turned away from Verdun and toward the English Channel where a French steamer named the *Sussex* was sunk by a German torpedo. Hundreds of men died, although none of them were Americans. Many people, especially members of Wilson's own cabinet, hoped that the President would take a bolder stance against Germany than sending carefully worded diplomatic notes that expressed his displeasure. Robert Lansing, who had been appointed Secretary of State after Bryan's resignation, wrote to Wilson demanding swift action. The time for "writing notes discussing the subject has passed," he argued, adding that "the present method of submarine warfare is intolerable." He told the President that an ultimatum must be delivered to the German government. If Germany did not immediately abandon unrestricted submarine warfare, then the United States must sever all diplomatic ties with Berlin.

A frustrated Robert Lansing was coming to see the President in much the same light as people like Theodore Roosevelt saw him. Lansing grew increasingly frustrated with a President who made decisions so slowly and who was unwilling to commit his nation to a specific course if he could not see its outcome. Wilson seemed to be a leader who could not make a decision unless he could intuitively grasp the proper course of action. More like a woman than a man, the President seemed to use his feelings, not his reason, to work his way to a decision. He was neither stubborn nor egotistical, but instead was afflicted with the "mentality of a woman." Lansing was not surprised when Wilson finally answered that he would not make any decision until he knew for certain that a German submarine had actually sunk the *Sussex*. The President also worried that breaking diplomatic ties with Germany might end any chance that the United States could influence the outcome of the war which might in turn drag on indefinitely.[489]

---

[489] Robert Lansing, "Letter to Woodrow Wilson, March 27, 1916," *PWW*, XXXVI, 371-373; Lansing's observations on Wilson's womanly consciousness can by found in a diary entry entitled "The Mentality of Woodrow Wilson, October 20, 1921," which is excerpted in *Wilson*, edited by John Braeman (Englewood Cliffs, New Jersey: Prentice-Hall, Inc., 1972), 86-87; Woodrow Wilson, "Letter to Robert Lansing, March 30, 1916," *PWW*, XXXVI, 382-382.

The President's advisor Colonel House saw both the situation in Europe and the character of Woodrow Wilson in much the same way as Secretary Lansing did. While Wilson trusted House implicitly, believing that they thought as one and did not have to explain their ideas to each other, the Colonel did not hold the President in such high regard. Like Lansing, House saw Wilson primarily as an emotional man who could not see the obvious course of action to take. He had fretted over the President's breakdown at the loss of his first wife and had then been equally alarmed as Wilson's swift engagement to Edith Galt. Now he stood by and watched his "friend" agonize over every ship that went to the bottom of the sea while at the same time being unable to make a rational decision on how to respond to Germany's aggression. House had no sympathy for Wilson's vision of himself as a leader who was thinking his way through to the best future for America and the world. Instead he saw the President as a vain man who must be approached first through flattery and only then by reason. He was so determined that the President must act swiftly against Germany that he went to Washington to speak with him in person. Wilson made House wait for three days before they could speak together about the loss of the *Sussex*. When they finally met, it was clear to House that Wilson was not ready to take the nation into the war and would try again to word an ultimatum that would cause Germany to back away from unrestricted submarine warfare.

Neither Lansing nor House appreciated how deeply the President was meditating on the meaning of the war in the history of their nation and in the greater story of mankind. In Wilson's opinion, humanity was passing through "solemn days" where the moral principles of all men and women were being put to the test. The world was in this horrific contest so that all nations would learn to live together in peace. No country would ever again be allowed to conquer the territory of another nation. War itself would be seen as a useless enterprise that ruined the lives of the present and future generations. People would recognize that the technology of the modern world made each new war more terrible than the one that preceded it. The leaders of nations would find ways to talk to each other in the open and negotiate settlements before their disagreements led to war.

As he slowly worked his way to this new vision for all of mankind, not just the United States, he decided to confront Germany's attack on the *Sussex* through diplomatic notes and not through a declaration of war. He headed to Capitol Hill and explained to the Senate, and so to the American people, that Germany must abandon unrestricted submarine warfare or face the severing of all diplomatic ties with the United States. He told the Congressmen, Senators, and visitors who packed the galleries of the House that America must take these measures as the "responsible spokesman of the rights of humanity." Back in the White House, he told Colonel House to deliver the news to Prince Berntoff, the German Ambassador, and cabled James Gerard, America's diplomat in Germany, to relay the ultimatum to Kaiser Wilhelm. Gerard found the Kaiser at his headquarters in Charleville, France. They argued for three days, mainly over why Wilson considered Germany's submarine attacks on Allied shipping a violation of human rights while he remained publicly silent on the British naval blockade of the continent that had reduced Germany to starvation? Finally, on May 4, the Kaiser and his staff relented. They pledged that German submarines would give a warning to ships before attacking them and would do everything in their power to protect lives on the high seas. However, ships must not attempt to escape or resist in any way. The Imperial German government also hoped that the United States would now come forward and openly condemn the blockade that had brought so much suffering to its own people. If this problem was ignored, then "the German government would be … facing a new situation in which it must reserve itself complete liberty of decision."[490]

After some debate in his cabinet, especially between Secretary Lansing and himself, Wilson accepted the "Sussex Pledge" and responded on May 8 with a simple statement that made it seem America had won a complete victory over Germany through diplomacy alone. He looked upon the pledge as Germany's declaration that it had abandoned the policy of unrestricted submarine warfare which "seriously menaced" its relations with the United States. On behalf of his nation, the President also expected Germany to execute this new policy "scrupulously." The United States would neither entertain nor discuss any suggestion that Germany's respect for the rights of Americans on the high seas be tied to the demand that the United States demand that Great Britain lift its blockade around Europe. Wilson's response to the *Sussex* pledge ended with a simple phrase that carried an implied warning to Germany. "Responsibility in such matters is single, not joint; absolute, not relative."[491]

The exhausted President left the White House and headed down the Potomac and up the James River on the *Mayflower* for a long rest arranged by Edith Wilson who was worried about her husband's health. His old stomach troubles had returned and the daily tension of keeping the nation out of war while at the same time carving out a vision of America's place in world affairs was almost

[490] Colonel House, "Diary Entries for March 27 and 28, 1916," *Intimate Papers of Colonel House*, II, 226; Woodrow Wilson, "An Address to a Joint Session of Congress, April 19, 1916," *PWW*, XXXVI, 506-510; the many drafts of the American response to the sinking of the *Sussex* can be found in *PWW*, Volume XXXVI; see also Robert Lansing, "Letter to Woodrow Wilson, May 6, 1916 with Enclosures I and II, May 4 and 5, 1916," *PWW*, XXXVI, 620-627.

[491] "An Enclosure from Woodrow Wilson to Robert Lansing, May 7, 1916," *PWW*, XXXVI, 649-650.

unbearable. Trips on the Presidential yacht had become a favorite pastime of the First Lady who loved to go exploring with her husband who became almost like a little boy again on their journeys together. Wilson loved to read maps as they traveled and often asked the Captain to put them on shore whenever he saw an interesting spot. He was always delighted when the people who lived along the river recognized him and shook his hand saying, "We think a lot of you down here." The trip this time past Washington's home at Mount Vernon was as memorable as always. The Captain made sure to dip the colors of the *Mayflower* as they passed Washington's tomb. Then "Taps" was played followed by a jolly rendition of "The Star Spangled Banner." But even with the fun of this happy and relaxing trip, Wilson's typewriter was not far away. He brought it everywhere he went and had his staff set up an office even on the *Mayflower* so he could continue to work out his vision of the world's future.[492]

The trip along Virginia's historic waterways in May 1916 deepened Wilson's resolve to see clearly a new and better future into which the United States could lead all mankind. As he looked back toward Europe, he saw only a military and a moral deadlock. The record-setting bloodbath at Verdun had made Europe numb to the slaughter in which they were caught up. In just a matter of weeks, the British would sustain heavy losses at the Battle of Jutland fought against the German navy in the North Sea. Eleven British ships and nearly 6,100 men would be lost, while Germany would lose 12 ships and more than 2,500 men. The British navy would limp home to port bruised but still confident that it retained control of the oceans of the world. Another battle between the British and the Germans along the Somme River would break out in June. Once the battle was over, no territory would be gained for either side and the casualty list would climb close to 1,100,000. At the same time on the eastern front, the Russians were gearing up for an offensive in Galicia where more than 1,000,000 men would be killed or wounded in a campaign against the armies of the Austro-Hungarian Empire. Both the Allies and the Central Powers were also finding new ways to destroy their opponents. Tanks would be used for the first time along the Somme, while pilots armed with machine guns could now shoot enemy planes down from the sky.[493]

Wilson slowly came to realize that America's history might be the key to the role the nation would soon play in world affairs. The United States was a place where people of many different backgrounds had come together to form a nation. As "a sort of prophetic sample of mankind," America could show the old world

---

[492] Edith Bolling Wilson, *My Memoir*, 95-98.

[493] Jay Winter and Blaine Baggett, *The Great War and the Shaping of the Twentieth Century* (New York: Penguin Studio, A Division of Penguin Books, 1996), 83-106, 155-173.

what the new one must look like. Nations must somehow learn to come together in the same way the people of the United States now lived side by side. It was as if God himself in this terrible war was pressing the nations of the world down to their barest elements to reshape them into a more unified whole. Wilson knew that he was not the only person thinking along these lines. He gathered a folder together with newspaper clippings and magazine articles about efforts around the world to form some kind of formal organization to bring all nations together to discuss their mutual problems. His friend from law school Richard Heath Dabney even sent him a preliminary constitution of such an organization. This new body would be a place where the nations of the world spoke openly with one another and worked together for the good of humanity.

By late May 1916, Wilson was ready to present his new vision of the world to the American public. He chose the convention of the League to Enforce Peace, one of the many organizations attempting to prevent the outbreak of another world war, held at the Willard Hotel in Washington, D.C. His speech followed one by Republican Senator Henry Cabot Lodge of Massachusetts who spoke first in favor of creating an international forum similar to the one Wilson envisioned. The President began and ended his speech with a theme he had struck on his preparedness tour through the Midwest. While the United States had not caused the Great War, it was profoundly affected by it. The war itself had come about through secret councils. If the United States had been a part of open councils between nations, perhaps it could have prevented this terrible conflict. Even as the war continued to rage, America and the world should commit itself to a "new and more wholesome diplomacy" and the same high code of conduct between nations that "we demand of individuals." All countries must recognize that they are now neighbors. The charter for this neighborhood must include at least three basic principles. Every nation must choose its own sovereignty. Small states must be afforded the same respect as big nations. All countries have the right not to be disturbed by aggressor nations. He concluded by offering to mediate among the warring nations to bring peace at last.[494]

As Wilson carefully thought through the role America would play in the world once the bloody war was over, he was also gearing up for his re-election bid in 1916. The demand for reform that had swept his party into power in 1912 now seemed a distant memory drowned out in the steady drumbeat of war. Party leaders hoped that the election could be won if Democratic candidates from Wilson on down reminded the voters of the many reforms that had made it through Congress and that the President had kept them out of war. The Democrats

[494] Woodrow Wilson, "Speech to the League to Enforce Peace, May 27, 1916," *PPWW*, IV, 185-188.

had lowered the tariff, set up the Federal Reserve, and broken up monopolies. Under Wilson's "hands on" leadership of the Congress, the party was working to pass the Farm Loan Act that would make credit available to farmers at twelve land banks across the nation. Many more bills had passed to conserve water, end child labor, protect wildlife, and preserve natural resources. The President had established an important oil reserve for the American navy at Teapot Dome in Wyoming. He had opened up the Alaskan Territory for settlement. He would soon win the eight-hour day for railroad workers in the Adamson Act after a bitter battle with railroad owners, the unions, and the Congress. He had also fought hard against any change to immigration laws that would turn people away from this country if they could not read or write English. While his first pick to the Supreme Court, his own Attorney General James MacReynolds, had turned out to be more conservative than he would have liked, the President had just put forth the nomination of his friend Louis Brandeis, a well-known progressive, for a spot on the bench. The populist wing in his own party could head to the polls knowing Wilson had succeeded beyond their wildest dreams in achieving reforms. He had failed only in two significant areas. He still favored state action rather than federal action on the issue of women's suffrage and he had refused to speak out against the practice of segregation that had come into the many departments of the executive branch once his administration took over Washington.[495]

If the Democrats were ready to stand behind Wilson in the race for the White House in 1916, the Republicans were just as united in their crusade to topple him. Theodore Roosevelt had come back to his party with a burning hatred of Wilson and the determination to make him a one term President. He held out hope that he would win the nomination, and if this failed, he wanted his friend General Wood at the top of the ticket. Instead, the party picked Justice Charles Evans Hughes who stepped down from the Supreme Court to run against Wilson. Modeling himself after the President who had so often taken his case to the people, Hughes hit the campaign trail speaking to as many voters as possible, especially in the West where Wilson was the most popular, before the election on November 7. He had help from embittered Republican Senators like Henry Cabot Lodge who had gone down to one defeat after another at the hands of a President who spent much of his time on Capitol Hill directing legislation. Lodge called Wilson the worst President in history, at least since James Buchanan. Hughes focused on Wilson's failure in foreign policy, especially his "watchful waiting" toward Mexico and

---

[495] See Baker, *Life and Letters*, V, 101-102, 118, and VI, 111-113, 161, 261, 274; for a good example of his attitude on the race question during his Presidency, see Woodrow Wilson, "Remarks on the Race Question, December 15, 1914," *PWW*, XXXI, 464-465.

Europe. Mexico was still in chaos with Carranza fighting to hold onto the presidency and Pancho Villa raiding along the Texas border. The fact that Wilson had sent General John Pershing on an expedition into Mexico to hunt down Villa only proved how inept the President was in foreign affairs. If Wilson was allowed a second term, Hughes and the Republicans could only shiver at the thought of what ruin the United States might come to if German aggression was ignored. While Wilson had easily made the decision to send troops into Nicaragua and Haiti when democracy seemed to be in danger, Hughes mocked him for being unable to make the same decision when he looked across the seas toward Europe. The Republicans were also prepared to spread rumors about Wilson's alleged affair with Mary Peck. They would also let the nation know that the newly married President neglected his wife's grave and may even have hurried her death along the summer before in order to pursue other women.[496]

The Democrats met for their convention in St. Louis in early September. It was a foregone conclusion that Wilson would be nominated for a second term. Wilson did not attend the convention but kept in touch with the delegates through a direct phone line from the White House. He also made sure that the party's platform was largely his doing. Wilson was nominated on the first ballot and Thomas Marshall of Indiana was again chosen as his Vice President. Former New York Governor Martin Glynn gave a thrilling address on Wilson's leadership in the world crisis that left the crowd shouting first "Wilson" and then "Bryan." "It may not satisfy the fire-eater or the swashbuckler," he said with a clear reference to Teddy Roosevelt, but "it does satisfy the mothers … the fathers … and the sons of this land, who will fight for our flag, and die for our flag."

Wilson appreciated the support of the convention, but he felt little enthusiasm for the campaign ahead. Exhausted from the battles over the *Sussex* pledge and the Adamson Act, he headed to a house called Shadow Lawn in Long Branch on the New Jersey shore that he had rented for his family. He hoped to spend much of the late summer there with his wife, daughters, and closest friends. He was also deeply worried about his sister Annie Howe who was sick and probably dying at her home in New London, Connecticut. He visited her once but the strain on his own health was so great that Dr. Davis, Wilson's old college friend who had cared for Ellen Wilson in her last days and who now watched over Annie Howe, recommended that Mrs. Wilson get her husband back to the quiet of Shadow Lawn. "He is under terrific strain and there is nothing he can do," Davis explained to Edith Wilson, "I will stay and do what I can, but I do not answer for the consequences if he does not get away and have some let-up." Annie Howe died a

[496] Walworth, *Woodrow Wilson*, II, 55, 59, 61-65.

short time later and Wilson headed to Columbia, South Carolina for her funeral. The services were held at the Presbyterian Church where Reverend Wilson had once preached. She was laid to rest under a canopy of flowers in the churchyard where her mother and father were buried. After the funeral, Wilson walked to the boyhood home that his mother had built for the family so long ago. There he had spent some of the loneliest days of his youth in the ruined city dreaming of fighting pirates on the high seas and leading his nation to greatness with the power of his words. It was a terrible thing for him to realize that he was now living in the very fulfillment of those dreams from times gone by as the President of the United States in the midst of world war.[497]

Back at Shadow Lawn, Wilson finally accepted the nomination on September 23 with a speech where he again laid out his vision of America's role in leading the world to a better place in the future. The old fight seemed to be back in him when he characterized the Republicans as the party of the past that "cannot meet the new conditions of a new age." But he soon disappointed his closest advisors by telling them that he planned to do little campaigning in the race. In fact, he even thought he could run an old fashioned campaign from the veranda around Shadow Lawn. The press could tell him the latest things Hughes and the other Republicans had said about him and he could throw back witty comments that would make all the papers of the country. Secretary of the Treasury McAdoo was so upset that he was ready to resign. He was certain Wilson would lose the election if he did not get out and meet the people. The President seemed happier than he had ever been since the death of his wife, but something seemed to have changed within him permanently with her passing. The old fight that had sent him on a wild campaign throughout the state of New Jersey to win the governorship had gone out of him. He also sensed the change in himself and often said that his battles to keep America out of war and craft a place for his nation in the world's future had cleansed him of all partisanship.

But finally the President listened to McAdoo, as well as his other advisors like Colonel House and Joe Tumulty, and hit the campaign trail. Starting on October 5, he made weekly trips to the Midwest where he and party leaders knew the battle for votes would be most desperate. He gave two speeches to large crowds in Omaha, and in the next week, went back in Indianapolis where he gave three more addresses. On October 19, he was in Chicago speaking again to three audiences, and on October 26, he gave a record four addresses in Cincinnati. He ended his campaign for re-election like he ended the one for his first term with a rally in Madison Square Garden where the crowd gave him an ovation that lasted

---

[497] Baker, *Life and Letters*, V, 231-261, 276.

for more than an hour. Everywhere he went he was dismayed at the campaign slogan of his followers – "He Kept Us Out of War." He expressed his frustration to his Secretary of the Navy Josephus Daniels by saying:

> "I can't keep the country out of war. They talk as though I were a god. Any little German lieutenant can get us into war at any time by some calculated outrage."[498]

On November 7, President Wilson went to the polling station not far from his house at Shadow Lawn. Then he and his wife waited for the results of the election which most experts believed would not be good for the President. Maine and New Jersey had already held many state races with big wins for the Republicans. Many newspapers were gearing up to run front-page stories about Charles Evans Hughes and his wife. Wilson himself was sure he would win right up to Election Day, but now seemed resigned to the fact that in a few days he would no longer be the President of the United States. He even wrote to Robert Lansing to let him know that he would resign immediately after the election since President Hughes would need to take over the job right away at this critical time. His three daughters did not take his impending loss so calmly. They were furious at the American people for apparently turning on their father. Edith Wilson was not surprised that the news was so bad since she had believed all along that her husband would lose the election. While she was disappointed that her new life as the First Lady would soon end, she was glad that the burdens of office would be lifted from the man she called "her dear one." "Well, little girl, you were right in expecting we should lose the election," he said to Edith as only bad news came into Shadow Lawn, "Frankly, I did not; but we can now do some of the things we want to do." They planned to take a cycling tour of Europe once the war was over. Wilson had even tried to teach his new wife how to ride a bike, much to the amusement of the Secret Service.[499]

One person in Wilson's administration refused to give up even as state after state went for Charles Evans Hughes. Joe Tumulty, the President's personal secretary, manned an office in Asbury Park and remained convinced throughout the day that the tide would turn for Wilson once the votes were counted in the west. By the late evening, it was clear that the President had lost much of the East

---

[498] Woodrow Wilson, "A Campaign Speech at Shadow Lawn, September 23, 1916," *PWW*, XXXVIII, 212-219; Daniels made the Wilson comment to Ray Stannard Baker in 1929; see quote in Baker, *Life and Letters*, VI, 258.

[499] Edith Bolling Wilson, *My Memoir*, 113-116.

and Middle West. The New York *World*, one of Wilson's staunchest supporters, published a bulletin that Hughes had been elected. Soon the New York *Times* and the Brooklyn *Eagle* followed suit. When Wilson called from Shadow Lawn, Tumulty gave him the bad news, but assured the President that the tide would turn in his favor. He heard him chuckle on the other end before he said:

> "Tumulty, you are an optimist. It begins to look as if the defeat might be overwhelming. The only thing I am sorry for, and that cuts me to the quick, is that the people apparently misunderstood us. But I have no regrets. We have tried to do our duty."

Still Tumulty remained guardedly optimistic, especially after a call from a friend at the New York *Evening Post* who told Ohio had gone into the Wilson column while Kansas, Utah, and the Dakotas were leaning in his favor. Tumulty also took calls from a mysterious man who claimed to be phoning from Republican headquarters. He said top leaders were on their way to tell Roosevelt that "the jig is up" and Wilson was elected. Finally on the morning after the election, the New York *Times* ran an extra announcing that there were growing signs that the President had been re-elected. Margaret Wilson knocked on the bathroom door where her father was shaving to tell him the news. He was certain his daughter was playing a practical joke on him and told her "to tell that to the Marines!" But when the votes were finally counted in California, Tumulty could tell the doubting President that he had been right all along. Wilson won California by 4,000 votes which pushed him over the top in the electoral count. He had beaten Hughes by more than 600,000 popular votes and with an electoral count of 277 to 254.[500]

President Wilson could think of only one thing after his upset victory and that was peace. He knew that he could now go back on the world stage as the leader of the American people. This might give him the prestige he needed to end the terrible war raging in Europe. Identifying with Lincoln who had coined the phrase "with malice toward none" in the closing days of the Civil War, he proposed a "peace without victory" in a letter to the warring nations that he prepared himself on the typewriter in his office. After consulting with Colonel House and Robert Lansing about changes to his first draft, Wilson issued the letter to the belligerents on December 18, 1916. He told them point blank that the causes of the war were obscure and that the conflict had bogged down into a stalemate. It was time for all sides to discuss the terms of the settlement. Wilson did not offer to mediate, but

---

[500] Tumulty, *Woodrow Wilson As I Know Him*, 216-224.

urged the creation of a league that would bring all the nations of the world together and so ensure that a war like this never happened again. Reaction to the letter overseas, especially in Great Britain, was swift and severe. Many Europeans condemned Wilson as an "antique god" who had suddenly descended from his high place to direct the lives of lesser mortals. At home, Teddy Roosevelt led the charge against the idea of a league. He won key support from Republican Senators, most notably Henry Cabot Lodge who disavowed his former support for a league, saying that the United States should confine its foreign policy activities to the western hemisphere.[501]

When the leaders of the world, and many in his own government, rejected his plea for peace, he went over their heads directly to the people. It was a campaign method he had used many times before to great success. When opposed by Princeton's Board of Trustees, he turned to the alumni. In the fall of 1910, he spoke on the stump in every county in New Jersey, stunning the party bosses who thought they could control him. Five years later, he traveled across the country to trump the loudest voices for war with his own version of preparedness. On the afternoon of January 22, 1917, he headed to Capitol Hill as he had done so many times before to talk to the American people and through them the people of the world. He gave the clearest explanation of his vision for the future of the world to date. The war must end and peace must come, but it must be a new kind of peace that was guaranteed by all the nations of the world. The United States must play a part in it by showing the world how "peace between equals" would work. All nations must be allowed to govern themselves without interference from the armies of other nations. In essence, the Monroe Doctrine must be extended to the world. As the President saw it, "no nation should seek to extend its polity over any other nation or people, but … every people should be free to determine its own polity." Even more simply, he explained, "I am proposing government by the consent of the governed," not just for America, but for the world. He closed his address with an appeal to people everywhere to embrace the vision which he had struggled for so long to see. "These … American principles," he concluded, "They are the principles of mankind and must prevail."[502]

President Wilson delivered his speech unaware that Germany had already decided on January 9, 1917 to resume unrestricted submarine warfare. A zone would be placed around England, France, and Italy, and any ship going to or from

---

[501] Woodrow Wilson, "An Address on Abraham Lincoln, September 1916," PWW, XXXVIII, 142-145; see Edith Wilson's analysis of the speech on Lincoln in Edith Bolling Wilson, *My Memoir*, 105; Robert Lansing, "An Appeal for a Statement of War Aims, December 18, 1916," *PWW*, XL, 373-376.

those countries would be sunk without warning and without help to the survivors. The Kaiser along with officials in his high command had made the decision weeks before in a desperate bid to break the British blockade around Europe. They were convinced that the American President who had taken so long to craft his ultimatums and speeches in the past would take no action against them in the present or future. When Tumulty laid the press release that reported Germany's decision on the President's desk on the afternoon of January 31, Wilson turned pure white and said "This means war. The break we have tried to prevent now seems inevitable." But he quickly regained his composure, and still unwilling to commit American troops to war, he called his cabinet together and asked, "What should I do?" He wanted more time to lay out the basic principles upon which the post-war world would be built, but his cabinet was in near revolt. Robert Lansing argued that merchant ships must be armed and diplomatic relations with Germany severed. Wilson worried that severing relations would lead inevitably to war. He still could not imagine himself sending young Americans to fight overseas. Wilson even wrote to his nephew George Howe that "I pray God there be no need to call you." He brooded over how a war of this magnitude would transform his nation. He had seen its terrible effects on the South in his own childhood. He knew it would take a total commitment on behalf of all Americans to win the war, and he feared that the democracy he so cherished might not survive the nation's entrance into the conflict.[503]

On February 25, President Wilson received a telegram from Walter Hines Page, his ambassador in London, which finally convinced him to take action against Germany. The British Naval Intelligence Service had intercepted a cable from the German Foreign Secretary Arthur Zimmerman to his country's ambassador in Mexico City. The ambassador was to make a deal with the Mexican government to declare war on the United States if America declared war on Germany. Once the war was over, the German government would return New Mexico, Texas, and Arizona to the Mexican people. On the next day, Wilson addressed a joint session of Congress and asked them to approve the arming of merchant ships. He did not reveal the contents of the Zimmerman telegram fearing that the outcry from the people and the press would be so overwhelming that he would be forced to declare war immediately. The bill passed the House by a vote of 403 to 14, but twelve Senators, including Wisconsin's progressive leader Robert LaFollette, threatened to filibuster to stop any chance of passing the bill in

[502] Woodrow Wilson, "An Address to the Senate, January 22, 1917," *PWW*, XL, 533-539.

[503] Tumulty, *Woodrow Wilson As I Know Him*, 254-255; Baker, *Life and Letters*, VI, 454-460; Baker also quotes the February 13, 1917 letter from Wilson to his nephew George Howe in Ibid., 464.

the regular session. Wilson lost his temper and issued a short statement that he later regretted. It simply said that:

> "A little group of willful men, representing no opinion but their own, have rendered the Government of the United States helpless and contemptible."[504]

In the midst of the battle with the Senate, Wilson's second inauguration came almost as an afterthought. He took the oath of office in the White House on March 4, and on the next day headed to the Capitol under the strictest security any President had known since Abraham Lincoln. He had come to identify even more strongly with Lincoln whose name he had first heard on that day in Augusta so long ago when he ran to his father asking what war was. Like him, he felt the deep solitude of being President in the midst of a terrible war. He knew what it was to retreat into himself and try to understand the destiny of his nation in the history of the world. Like Lincoln, he felt a keen sense of the principles upon which the nation was founded. In his second inaugural address, he did his best to state those principles again. They were freedom for all people, government derived from the consent of those people, and the equality of all nations in a great brotherhood of mankind. These principles would be the foundation on which America would assume its place as the leader of the world.[505]

For much of the rest of the month, he secluded himself in his bedroom in the White House thinking his way toward war and the future of his nation and the world. When the Senate refused to act on the bill arming the merchant marine, he issued an executive order on March 12 stating that an armed guard would be placed on "all American merchant vessels sailing through the barred areas." Still he remained in his private quarters on the second floor of the White House, seeing only Cabinet officials as well as his family and members of his personal staff. Ike Hoover, the President's butler, noted in his diary how serious Wilson always looked. The President often said that he had done everything in his power to prevent war and still Germany refused to abandon unrestricted submarine warfare. What would the world be like, he brooded, if Germany, which had showed such little respect for life and law, won the war and dictated the peace? Wilson's dream of mankind made young again through democratic principles would come to nothing. Instead the entire world would be transformed into an armed camp and

---

[504] Baker, *Life and Letters*, VI, 473; for the direct quote on the "willful men," see *PPWW*, IV, 433-435.

[505] Walworth, *Woodrow Wilson*, II, 91-92; Wilson, "Second Inaugural Address, March 5, 1917," *PPWW*, III, Part 1, 1-5.

the wars would go on forever. As he thought his way through to the painful conclusion that he must lead his nation into war against Germany to prevent this terrible future, he was comforted by the many letters and messages that poured in from labor leaders all over the country saying they would stand by him in the fight for democracy. He received even better news when word came from Russia that Tsar Nicholas II had abdicated. If the United States declared war on Germany, then the nation would truly be fighting for a better future alongside three fellow democracies – Great Britain, France, and Russia.[506]

On the evening of April 2, 1917, President Woodrow Wilson walked into the House Chamber where just four years before he had caused a sensation when he broke precedent and personally asked the Congress to lower the tariff. He was met on this important night with the loudest applause he had ever received in the Capitol. He sat down at the Speaker's table, rested his arm on the desk and read from his speech in the deep and emotional tones that the Congress knew so well. Rarely looking up from the address that lay before him, he recounted the tale of all his nation and the world had suffered on the high seas at the hands of Germany's submarine fleet. One ship after another – passenger liners, merchant vessels, and even hospital boats filled with wounded soldiers – had been "sunk with the same reckless lack of compassion or of principle." Germany had gone past the very pale of humanity in its attacks on the world's shipping and thus her aggression was a war against mankind. "The wrongs against which we now array ourselves," he explained, "they cut to the very roots of human life." He asked Congress to declare war on Germany to end the unlawful practices of this nation and to create a better future out of the ashes.

What would this new world be like? It would be a place "made safe for democracy" and its ideals. Nations would be ruled by the same principles that now governed the United States. The rights of the people would be protected. Their voice would be heard in the governments which served them. The democratic nations of the world would live side by side with each other in peace. They would respect the rights of their own people and the rights of other nations. They would behave as honorably toward one another as citizens did within the borders of their own countries. Wilson assured all who listened that Americans would not fight for these ideals so that they might win anything for themselves. They would seek no territory nor would they take any indemnities once the war was over. They fought for no selfish purpose, but only for the rights of humanity. Quoting Abraham Lincoln, he challenged Americans to brace for the "fiery trial"

---

[506] For President Wilson's order, see Josephus Daniels, "A Memorandum Regulating the Conduct of a Merchant Vessel, March 13, 1917," *PWW*, XLI, 395-399.

that lay ahead of them. They must at last give up their isolation and their neutrality for something more "precious" than peace. That something was the honor of fighting for what was right – not just for America but for the world. In words that echoed the Declaration of Independence, which Wilson believed now belonged to mankind, Wilson concluded:

> "To such a task we can dedicate our lives and our fortunes, everything that we are and everything that we have, with the pride of those who know the day has come when America is privileged to spend her blood and her might for the principles that gave her birth and happiness and the peace which she has treasured. God helping her, she can do no other."[507]

[507] Woodrow Wilson, "For Declaration of War Against Germany, April 2, 1917," *PPWW*, III, Part 1, 6-16.

Chapter 10

A DREAM RUNS AGROUND

The world has been made safe for democracy, but democracy has not been finally vindicated.

Woodrow Wilson[508]

On the night of April 2, 1917, Woodrow Wilson found himself in the place he had dreamt of being since his childhood. Like William Pitt, the British Prime Minister he so admired, he had just given an address to his fellow countrymen calling them to war and so changing the course of their nation's history. But now as a grown man, he found that the experience was not the glorious one he had first imagined it would be when he was a schoolboy in Columbia and a student at Princeton. He had made the agonizing decision to go to war only after overcoming a great hesitation on his part to lead his country into a conflict so "grim and terrible."[509] As he made his way with his wife back to the White House in the warm spring of 1917, he could not help but brood over the tragic days that lay before the nation. While he had often been met with a cool response from Congress when he asked for peaceful measures like lowering the tariff, he was now greatly troubled that they had cheered him wildly when he called for war against Germany. The crowds who lined Pennsylvania Avenue applauded him just as loudly. Wilson's secretary Joseph Tumulty was the first person to greet the President when he arrived back at the White House. "Tumulty," Wilson said,

---

508 Quote from Wilson's "State of the Union Message" on December 2, 1919 in Day, editor, *Woodrow Wilson's Own Story*, 349.

509 Woodrow Wilson, "Letter to John D. Sprunt, April 5, 1917," quoted by Baker in *Life and Letters*, VII, 49; quotes on Wilson's comments to Tumulty are taken from Alden Hatch, *Edith Bolling Wilson: First Lady Extraordinary* (New York: Dodd, Mead & Company, 1961), 102.

"think what it meant, the applause of the people in the capitol and the people lining the avenue as we returned. My message tonight was a message of death to our young men. How strange to applaud that!" Both his secretary and his wife tried to comfort him. Surely a bright future lay ahead for the world once the war was over. Wilson would be able to lead all mankind toward democracy. Tumulty long remembered how nothing could comfort him. The President let his head fall down on his desk and "cried like a baby."[510]

Secretary of the Navy Josephus Daniels was one of the few people close to President Wilson who understood just how terrible the war would be and how much it would change the nation. He had watched from the steps of the Capitol as the cavalry followed the President's car back down Pennsylvania Avenue. "If I should live a thousand years," he would later recall, "there would abide with me the reverberations of the fateful, ominous sound of the hooves of the cavalry horses as they escorted Mr. and Mrs. Wilson back to the White House."[511] Like Wilson, Daniels knew there would be little glory in a conflict where countless American boys would be needed to break the stalemate on the western front that stretched through Belgium and France. They must be well-equipped and sent in large enough numbers to break the deadlock of trench warfare. Never before in history had such an offensive been launched. Somehow the United States must quickly organize itself and deploy millions of men across the North Atlantic where German submarines were already waiting for them.

The draft was soon the first order of business for the wartime administration of Woodrow Wilson. Thousands of young Americans had already joined the army even before the President officially signed the declaration of war against Germany on April 6. By the beginning of May, at least 75,000 volunteers had joined the 300,000 regulars already in the army. These numbers were impressive but nowhere near the half a million men that Wilson estimated would be necessary to get the American Expeditionary Force up and running. At the request of the President, Congress passed the Selective Service Act on May 18, 1917. The bill required all American men between the ages of 18 and 30 to register for the draft. Members of National Guard units would also be available for service in the army. On June 5, nearly ten million men peacefully registered with their local civilian draft boards throughout the United States. Congress later raised the age limit of the draft from 30 to 45 years. Wilson himself drew the first number from this larger draft pool in a ceremony at the White House. When he called out "322," a guard named Mr. Gilbert stepped forward to say that it was his son's number. "I

[510] Ibid., 101-102.
[511] Daniels, *Life of Woodrow Wilson*, 284-285.

give the best I have to help you," Gilbert proudly told the President. Overcome with emotion, Wilson could hardly speak. He shook Gilbert's hand and finally said, "God grant he may come back to you!" By the end of the war, approximately 2,200,000 men had been drafted while more than four million were in uniform. Mr. Gilbert's son would be one of the millions who would make it back, but more than 100,000 would never return from the battlefields of Europe.[512]

There was one recruit that the army did not want and that man was Theodore Roosevelt. He arrived at the White House promptly at noon on April 10, just four days after the official declaration of war against Germany, asking if he could raise a company of volunteers and lead them to France. He slapped Tumulty on the back and shook Wilson's hand as if they were old friends. Roosevelt left the meeting convinced that the President would grant his request. He even told the many reporters who were waiting for him in front of the White House that his commission was practically a done deal. Wilson turned the matter over to top army officials who promptly turned Colonel Roosevelt down. Not only was the 58 year old former President well beyond the age limit of the draft, but he was also an amateur with little experience in real warfare. The daring courage and high drama that had taken him up San Juan Hill in 1898 would be out of place in the kind of modern warfare raging in Europe since 1914. Wilson was relieved that he could stand behind the army when turning down Roosevelt's request. He had been worried that America might appear foolish in the eyes of her allies and enemies alike for sending the colorful Roosevelt into such a deadly serious conflict. He also confessed privately to his wife's cousin Florence Hoyt that he could not have Teddy running loose in France and managing Europe's affairs. The final decision to deny Roosevelt's request fell on the shoulders of Newton Baker, the Secretary of War. Baker thought it would be a tragic mistake to entrust the lives of young American soldiers to an amateur like Roosevelt the Rough Rider. He also thought it might be difficult for an ex-President to take orders from a commanding officer in the field. Wilson explained his decision in a telegram to Roosevelt on May 19, assuring him "that my conclusions were based entirely on imperative considerations of public policy not upon personal or private choice."[513]

---

[512] Ibid., 286; Walworth, *Woodrow Wilson*, II, 106-107; Woodrow Wilson, "Second Conscription Proclamation, August 31, 1918," *PPWW*, III, Part 1, 244-245; Edith Bolling Wilson, *My Memoir*, 139.

[513] Wilson's telegram to Roosevelt is quoted in Baker, *Life and Letters*, VII, 76; see also Woodrow Wilson, "Declining Roosevelt's Offer of Service in France, May 18, 1917," *PPWW*, III, Part 1, 40-41; his letter to Florence Hoyt dated May 19 1917 is also quoted in Baker, *Life and Letters*, VII, 76-77; see Pages 11, 48 and 49 of the same work for more details.

Wilson was sincere in his belief that the United States was involved in a new kind of war that must be fought in a professional and efficient manner from the top down if it was to be successful. He quickly overcame the deep emotion he felt after asking Congress to declare war on Germany and resolved to oversee the day-to-day operations of the conflict as efficiently as he had once run Princeton and the state of New Jersey. He would take the same "hands on" approach to directing the war as he had taken when ushering his progressive legislative program through Congress during the first years of his Presidency. Edith Wilson noticed the calm determination that seemed to descend on her husband in the opening weeks of the war. He was extremely patient and always optimistic. Even when severely criticized for not allowing Teddy Roosevelt to serve overseas, he did not lash out against his enemies. He remained open to anyone who sought his help or counsel, even though his days now began at dawn and continued well past midnight. In the midst of his many new duties as the leader of his nation in wartime, he still took time to answer the many letters that came to him from his family and friends. He responded to the many worried mothers who wrote to him about their sons in the army and to progressive leaders who were concerned that no new reforms would be passed now that the nation was at war. In the midst of his deep concern for others, Wilson tried to maintain his own health by taking up horseback riding as his main exercise and by heading to the theater every Saturday night. His sense of humor remained alive and well, and after a night out on the town, he often joked that he would give anything to exchange jobs with Primrose, the Minstrel Dancer.[514]

But he was deadly serious about the war effort, especially getting American boys overseas without major loss of life. Never before in history would so many men have to cross the oceans of the world on their way to war. Wilson loved the sea his whole life and had studied the navy since his boyhood. He had been concerned since the war broke out in 1914 that the British took few measures to protect their ships. The obvious solution to the problem of trying to cross the ocean in the face of German submarine attacks was to use the convoy system. Ships must never leave port alone. This made them an easy target for submarines that could strike without warning and then head back down into the sea to attack later on. If ships always crossed the sea in groups, submarines would be more vulnerable. Even if one ship went down, the others could spot and sink the attacking submarine. Secretary Josephus Daniels always credited Wilson's idea of the convoy as the reason why so few American soldiers were lost when crossing the Atlantic. Of the nearly 2,000,000 men who would be sent overseas to fight in

[514] Edith Bolling Wilson, *My Memoir*, 145.

the American Expeditionary Force, only 758 would be lost as result of submarine attacks on shipping. Remarkably, 630 of these men were on one British transport that was sunk near the Orkney Islands.[515]

Wilson was equally committed to organizing the government in the most efficient way to prosecute the war. He set up a "super cabinet" that met every week to give him advice. This group included Secretary of the Navy Josephus Daniels, Secretary of the Treasury William McAdoo, and the noted financier Bernard Baruch. Wilson took the most serious problems to these men for their recommendations. He also set up the Council of National Defense with leaders from government, labor, and business who would help coordinate the war effort. The council itself was subdivided into smaller boards that were assigned specific tasks. The most powerful subcommittee was the War Industries Board under the leadership of Bernard Baruch that was given near total control over the nation's industrial production and price structure. The Food Administration distributed the nation's food supply both for the soldiers overseas and the men, women and children who remained behind. Americans soon were used to "Meatless Tuesdays" and other innovations that made sure the army and navy received the best food possible. Prohibition was also the order of the day with Wilson banning the use of any agricultural product in the creation of malt liquors. Other councils like the Fuel Administration controlled the distribution of oil and coal while the Railroad Administration took control on the nation's private railway lines. The remaining councils controlled such important areas as trade, welfare, shipping, and publicity. Wilson kept in close contact with every council and took a "hands on" approach to the management of the war. In fact, he read every cable that came through the Army and Navy Departments, and kept a close watch on battlefield maneuvers once American troops finally landed in France in June 1917.[516]

As a former professor of history and economics, the President was well aware that the cost of the war would be enormous. In order to defeat Germany, the United States would have to spend more money in the first year of the war than it had spent in its entire history. To raise the billions of dollars necessary to prosecute the war, Wilson asked Congress to pass the War Revenue Act. This bill raised taxes both on incomes and wartime profits. When it was clear that the added revenue from higher taxes would still not be enough to cover the cost of the war, Secretary of Treasury William McAdoo organized a nationwide project to sell bonds known as "Liberty Loans." Close to 18.5 billion dollars worth of

---

[515] Daniels, *Life of Woodrow Wilson*, 285-286; Woodrow Wilson, "Annual Message to Congress, December 2, 1918," *PPWW*, III, Part 1, 308-309.

[516] Baker, *Life and Letters*, VII, 5-8, 33, 46, 69, 168-169; Daniels, *Life of Woodrow Wilson*, 283.

interest bearing bonds were sold at parades and rallies throughout the country. Wilson spent $10,000 of his own salary to buy bonds and appeared with his wife at Liberty Loan rallies in Boston, New York, and Baltimore. The President always tied the sale of the bonds directly to the war aims he had set for the nation. "The might of the United States is being mobilized and organized to strike a mortal blow at autocracy in defense of outraged American rights and of the cause of liberty," he proclaimed at the outset of the Second Liberty Loan Drive. While the President was always met by enthusiastic audiences when he spoke at rallies and marched in parades, movie stars like Douglas Fairbanks, Sr. and Charlie Chaplin drew even bigger crowds. At a rally on the steps of the old Federal Court House in lower Manhattan, Chaplin thrilled the tens of thousands of people who had packed Wall Street by sitting on the shoulders of Fairbanks and waving his hat wildly to the crowd.[517]

Wilson saw himself as cheerleader who must encourage all Americans to participate in the war effort. "The supreme test of the Nation has come," he said in an address written to the country just days after war was declared, "We must speak, act, and serve together." The majority of Americans might not be heading to the battlefield, but their hard work would supply everything that the nation's soldiers and sailors would need to defeat Germany. Ships by the hundreds must be built overnight. Coal must be dug out of the mines to fire the factories at home and fuel the ships that must make the perilous journey across the Atlantic. Steel must be produced for arms and tanks, while the nation's railroads must run round the clock to meet the demands of war. Farmers in the north, south, and west must raise the crops necessary to feed and cloth the millions of young men heading overseas. Cattle, mules, and horses would also be needed.[518]

In the first months of the war, President Wilson personally addressed dozens of groups across the country, calling on them to unite behind the war effort. Whether speaking or writing to organizations like the Red Cross or the American Federation of Labor, his theme was always the same. "This is a time when words seem empty," he explained, "only actions seem great!" Wilson directed many of his messages to the women of America who would have to make so many sacrifices for the war. They would have to send their husbands, sons, and brothers into combat. At home, they would head into the factories and replace the hundreds

---

[517] Baker, *Life and Letters*, VII, 46-51; Walworth, *Woodrow Wilson*, II, 115; Woodrow Wilson, "Appeal for the Second Liberty Loan, October 12, 1917," *PPWW*, III, Part 1, 105; Gerald Johnson, *Woodrow Wilson: The Unforgettable Figure Who Has Returned to Us* (New York and London: Harper & Brothers, Publishers, 1944), 150-151.

[518] Woodrow Wilson, "The Supreme Test of the Nation Has Come, April 16, 1917," *PPWW*, III, Part 1, 22-27.

of thousands of men who had left for the frontlines. They would have to find ways to feed their families especially on days when most of the best food in the nation would be overseas feeding the troops in Europe. Besides speaking with women, President Wilson was most fond of encouraging students to play a part in the war effort. He urged them not to give up sports, but to engage in them wholeheartedly to build up the patriotic spirit of the country. Whether addressing housewives, labor unions, or college football teams, Wilson reminded his fellow countrymen that all Americans were now in the army of the nation that "was born to serve all mankind." In an address to a crowd at Arlington National Cemetery on Memorial Day in 1917, he explained:

> "The industrial forces of the country, men and women alike, will be a great national, a great international, Service Army, -- a notable and honored host engaged in the service of the Nation and the world, the efficient friends and saviors of free men everywhere."[519]

In the midst of such high idealism, Wilson did not think it was a contradiction that he was also a firm supporter of censorship. Just three weeks after war was officially declared against Germany, he ordered government surveillance of all telephone and telegraph lines. He also placed every wireless station under the control of the Navy for the duration of the war. He supported the Committee on Public Information that was set up by Congress under the leadership of George Creel, a journalist formerly known for his progressive opinions. Creel and his committee banned the study of German in schools, removed the works of German authors from libraries, and renamed German words like "sauerkraut" with "American" ones like "liberty cabbage." Congress gave Wilson and the government even more power to control public opinion by passing the Espionage Act in 1917 and the Sedition Act in 1918. Wilson accepted these measures as necessary for protecting the war effort from the handful of mischievous souls who would willfully damage the nation's war effort. Under these laws, it was illegal to interfere with the draft, promote disloyalty to the United States, or disrupt the sale of Liberty bonds. Anyone convicted of speaking, writing, or publishing abusive statements about the war or the government that was prosecuting it would face

---

[519] Woodrow Wilson, "Needs of the Red Cross, May 12, 1917," *PPWW*, III, Part 1, 32-35; Woodrow Wilson, "Address the American Federation of Labor Convention, November 12, 1917," *PPWW*, III, Part 1, 116-124; Woodrow Wilson, "An Appeal to the Women of the Nation, July 28, 1917," *PPWW*, III, Part 1, 80-81; Woodrow Wilson, "College Sports: A Real Contribution to National Defense, May 21, 1917," *PPWW*, III, Part 1, 45; Woodrow Wilson, "America Was Born to Serve Mankind, May 30, 1917," *PPWW*, III, Part 1, 52-53.

stiff penalties. They could pay fines up to $10,000 and spend up to 20 years in prison. More than 1,500 Americans would be sent to jail for violating provisions of the Espionage and Sedition Acts. Eugene V. Debs, the leader of the Socialist Party, was sentenced to 10 years in a federal prison for speaking out against the war in a speech in Canton, Ohio.[520]

Throughout the war, Wilson ignored the fact that many politicians, especially several Republican Senators, went along with the war as their patriotic duty but with a growing resentment toward the President and his power. Senator Henry Cabot Lodge of Massachusetts was the leader of a group of Congressmen who despised Wilson as a politician and as a person. The President and his wife got some inkling of this hatred in an encounter with John Singer Sargent, the noted American painter. Sargent came to the White House in the summer of 1917 to paint the President's portrait. Mrs. Wilson did everything possible to put the artist at ease, but he always seemed uncomfortable while he worked on the painting. He even told the First Lady that he had never been so nervous over a portrait in his life. Once the painting was finally done, Mrs. Wilson was very disappointed in it. She felt it was lifeless and made the President appear much older than he actually was. Nevertheless, the portrait was donated to the National Gallery just a few blocks from the White House. Edith Wilson later learned the cause of Sargent's strange behavior. He had met with Senator Lodge the night before he was to start work on his portrait of the President. Lodge said he was happy that Sargent would be able to do a great service on behalf of the Republican Party. He knew that Sargent was famous for finding a person's counterpart in the animal world and so drawing out the darkest traits of his subject. Lodge was convinced that there was something "sinister" behind Wilson and he was certain that Sargent would find it for the whole world to see. Although under great pressure to study Wilson and "probe his very soul," Sargent later confessed to a friend that he could find nothing "hidden or unworthy."[521]

Such petty squabbles seemed strangely out of place to Wilson as he tried to steer his nation through a terrible war and then toward a better future where peace would be the normal state of affairs, and not a distant dream. While Lodge continued to ridicule him as a man who could only see the world "according to Wilson," the President sincerely believed that he was thinking his way through the bloodshed and toward the peace on behalf of the American people who had elected him. Delegations from America's new allies came to the White House

---

[520] Walworth, *Woodrow Wilson*, II, 112-114; Woodrow Wilson, "Letter to Honorable Edwin Y. Webb, May 22, 1917," *PPWW*, III, Part 1, 46.

[521] Edith Bolling Wilson, *My Memoir*, 148-150.

asking the President for immediate help in winning the war that was on the brink of being lost, but also for his vision about why the war had started and what the peace would mean. British Foreign Secretary Alfred Balfour along with Marshall Joffré and René Viviani from France confessed that the war was going far worse than the Allies had previously admitted. There was some hope of victory against the Ottoman Empire in the Middle East. Baghdad would fall to the British in June 1917, while troops under General Edmund Allenby would take Jerusalem just six months later. But on Europe's Western Front, there had been little movement. Germany and her allies still controlled much of Belgium and northern France along with Poland, Serbia, Romania, and Montenegro. Luckily for the Allies, so many Germans had died fighting to take and hold this territory that they had retreated eastward behind the fortified Siegfried Line. The Allies had attacked the fortifications they called the Hindenburg Line, but fell back with heavy loss of life and no territory gained. The bloody trenches with the hopeless "No Man's Land" in between stretched for what seemed endless miles on the western front. The fighting seemed so useless to the men in the trenches that 16 French army corps mutinied in the spring of 1917. Both the British and the French begged President Wilson to send American troops quickly and, even more importantly, to spell out the meaning of the war and the reasons why the fighting should continue.[522]

American troops under the command of "Black Jack" Pershing landed in France on June 26, 1917. The first words of Charles Stanton, a colonel on Pershing's staff, best expressed the enthusiasm of the new recruits. "Lafayette, we are here," he said to Marshall Ferdinand Foch. The Americans would not enter the trenches until October and would not face their first major test until September 1918 at Saint Mihiel. As the Americans prepared to do battle, Wilson insisted that his nation's troops must not be used as replacements in the French and British lines. He demanded that his soldiers fight as units. There must be a clearly identified American army engaged in combat on the Western Front. However, he also recommended that Marshall Foch assume the direction of the combined Allied forces. This finally happened in March 1918. "Such unity of command is a most hopeful augury of ultimate success," Wilson cabled Foch, "We are following with profound interest the bold and brilliant action of your forces."[523]

Wilson took the charge to come up with the reasons why this war must be prosecuted to the finish quite seriously. He sat at his typewriter in his office working on a list of goals that the Allies were fighting for, but which up until

[522] Hatch, *Edith Bolling Wilson*, 105-108.

[523] Woodrow Wilson, "Message of Congratulations to General Foch, March 29, 1918," *PPWW*, III, Part 1, 197.

now, no nation had clearly expressed. David Lloyd George, the British Prime Minister, was also working on crafting a vision of the purpose of the war. When Lloyd George delivered a speech on this topic to Parliament in the New Year of 1918, Wilson put aside his ideas, believing that England's leader had captured everything he wanted to see. Still his closest advisors, especially Colonel House and Joe Tumulty, urged him to express his own vision of why the world was at war and what must come about once an armistice was settled. On January 8, 1918, Wilson addressed a joint session of Congress to lay out his vision of where the world must head once the war was concluded. He opened his address by expressing his deep concern for Russia. In November, the Bolsheviks led by Vladimir Lenin had overthrown the more moderate government of Kerensky and his Mensheviks. The new government, proclaiming its commitment to the principles of Karl Marx, condemned the war as a meaningless fight between the ruling classes of Europe. Lenin's government was currently negotiating with Germany to end the war on the Eastern Front. It was now more imperative than ever that the leader of the world's greatest democracy speak with a clear voice about his vision of a better world for all mankind.

For Wilson, the war that raged throughout the world may have started as a useless battle between the royal houses of Europe, but it could not end that way. When America finally entered the war, the character of the conflict changed. The United States joined the Allies, England, France and Russia, then all democracies, to once and for all turn the world away from autocratic governments that did not speak for the people. The world of kings and emperors was coming to an end at last in the bloody trenches of Europe. America would make certain that the new world that arose from the rubble would let men and women everywhere choose their own governments and dwell in peace together forever. He said again that his nation led this noble cause for no personal gain.

> "What we demand in this war … it is nothing peculiar to ourselves. It is that the world be made fit and safe to live in, and particularly that it be made safe for every peace-loving nation which, like our own, wishes to live its own life, determine its own institutions, be assured of justice and fair dealing by the other peoples of the world as against force and selfish aggression. All the peoples of the world are in effect partners in this interest, and for our own part we see very clearly that unless justice be done to others it will not be done to us."[524]

---

[524] Woodrow Wilson, "The Fourteen Points Speech, January 8, 1918," *PPWW*, III, Part 1, 155-159.

The President then explained that the goal of America in the war was peace and only peace. "The program of the world's peace, therefore, is our program," he asserted. Wilson then laid out the basic principles that must be accomplished after the war ended in order to achieve this peace. There must be open, not secret agreements between nations. Wilson knew that the secret interlocking agreements between the world's nations had led them down the road to war after the assassination of Archduke Francis Ferdinand and his wife. He was adamant about this first point, and directed Secretary of State Robert Lansing to enforce this principle in no uncertain terms. Wilson went on to say that there must be absolute freedom of the seas and an end to all trade barriers between nations. Weapons and ammunition must be reduced to the lowest point possible in every country in the world. Colonial claims must be settled between nations, and Russia must be respected. All territory taken from Belgium, France, and Italy must be restored. All the peoples of the Austro-Hungarian Empire must be set free to establish nations and rule themselves. Romania, Serbia, and Montenegro must be independent. The many peoples in the Ottoman Empire must be set free and a separate nation must be created for the Turkish people. Poland must be free and independent once and for all. Finally, a League of Nations should be established where all the nations of the world could bring their grievances and settle them short of war.[525]

Wilson's dramatic address was quickly nicknamed the "Fourteen Points." Copies of the speech were dropped by airplanes over many of the war torn nations in Europe. For years afterward, this address along with many of Wilson's stirring addresses on the nature of democracy and the future world of freedom and equality for all were reprinted in collections that sold on every continent. British and French officials congratulated Wilson on the clarity of his vision, believing it would boost morale in their nations, and members of his own cabinet, most especially his close friend Josephus Daniels, called it the "Magna Charta" for the modern world. Daniels believed that two addresses given by Wilson later in the year on the meaning of democracy were even more dramatic and deepened his vision of the future into which he was leading the world. The first speech was made at Mount Vernon on July 4, while the second one was delivered at the opening of the Fourth Liberty Loan campaign in New York City on September 28. It was clear to those closest to the President that he saw something wonderful coming out of the ruins of the old world and that the secret to understanding it was in the history of the United States.[526]

---

[525] Ibid., 159-161.
[526] Daniels, *Life of Woodrow Wilson*, 317, 350.

At Mount Vernon, Wilson's words turned into pure poetry as he described the drama of the war as a "supreme tragedy." The plot, he explained, was "written plain upon every scene and every act." On the one hand, there stood America, born from the ideal that all men must be free. The gallant men, like George Washington and the other Founding Fathers, who led the Revolution for this ideal fought not for one class or one nation, but for the entire world. Look who was standing at America's side, Wilson told his many listeners, and they would see all the peoples of the earth "who suffer under mastery but cannot act." On the other side, Wilson saw the "master of many armies" who were driven by their own selfish ambitions. They reign over conquered nations where the people are nothing more than "fuel" to serve their own private ends. These governments were clothed in the "strange trappings" of a primitive age that should have passed away long ago. "The Past and the Present are in deadly grapple," he explained in terms reminiscent of an essay he had written years before for the *North Carolina Presbyterian*, "and the peoples of the world are being done to death between them." He described the principles that this new army of right was fighting for by reducing his fourteen points to just four. Every arbitrary power that attempts to destroy the peace of the world must be destroyed. The settlement of every question must be based on the will of the people who will be affected by that same settlement. Nations must treat each other with the same respect that is required of citizens in civilized societies. An "organization of peace" must be established to act as the final tribunal to which all nations must submit. Wilson concluded by telling the crowd that the drama which began when the Americans rose up against the British on behalf of the rights of mankind was now working its way through to its final conclusion in this awful world war. He took one last shot at Germany by saying:

> "The blinded rulers of Prussia have roused forces they knew little of … forces which, once roused, can never be crushed to earth again; for they … are deathless and of the very stuff of triumph."[527]

Wilson was so determined to get his vision out to the people that he condensed it into a "Four Minute Address" which was read by "Four Minute Men" in nearly 5,300 meetings in towns and cities throughout the nation on the same day. Wilson reminded Americans of the wonder of the freedom born in the nation on that first Fourth of July. It was a shout of freedom not just for Americans, but for all mankind. Year after year, the nation watched as freedom

---

[527] Woodrow Wilson, "The Four-Point Speech, July 4, 1918" *PPWW*, III, Part 1, 231-235.

for others seemed to work its way slowly around the world. But now the "old insolence" of kings and noblemen had armed itself again against the aspirations of mankind. After suppressing self-government in her own nation, Germany had set off on the destruction of freedom in every nation that dared to oppose her. "No fear has deterred them," said a President who still smarted from his failure to stop unrestricted submarine warfare, "and no bribe of material well-being has held them back." But Germany must not be allowed to turn back the clock to a thousand years ago when kings and their armies ruled the world and trampled over the rights of the people. The whole world, especially the long repressed nations in Eastern Europe, would not allow that to happen. "I ask you fellow-citizens to unite with them," the President concluded, "in making our Independence Day the first that shall be consecrated to a declaration of independence for all the people in the world."[528]

By the early fall, Wilson had become concerned about the mechanism that would put this vision in place. More and more, he pinned his hope on a tribunal that he had named the League of Nations. When he spoke at the rally in New York kicking off the Fourth Liberty bond drive in September, his reasons for the league and its purpose were much clearer. He asserted that the constitution of the league must be an essential part of the actual settlement of the war. The conflict was underway to end war for all time, and the league would play a critical role in achieving an enduring peace. This new organization would ensure that nations worked together for the good of mankind in one "general and common family." The league would embody the very justice and fair dealing for which America and her allies were now fighting.[529]

As Wilson prepared for the awful trials that American soldiers would have to undergo in order to win these ideals on the battlefield, he came to believe he was listening to the very heart of the world. This "very authentic throb" came to him through the countless letters, dispatches, and official reports that arrived on his desk from all over the world. Somehow he was the champion of the people because he listened to this "great voice of the world." Wilson was convinced, in fact, that in the future "it will be very dangerous for any statesman not to pay attention to."[530] He could hear it in the war itself even when no one else could. Two million American boys would fight and 100,000 would die for the heartbeat of the world that was calling for freedom and victory. Already the Americans

---

[528] Woodrow Wilson, "Four-Minute Address," *PPWW*, III, Part 1, 236-237.

[529] Woodrow Wilson, "Address Opening the Campaign for the Fourth Liberty Loan, September 27, 1918," *PPWW*, III, Part 1, 253-261.

[530] Woodrow Wilson, "On Woman Suffrage, October 13, 1918," *PPWW*, III, Part 1, 272-273.

were helping to throw back the Germans who had broken out of the Siegfried Line. The 4th Marine Brigade stopped the German advance on the road to Paris in the Belleau Wood and lost nearly 8000 men. American soldiers pushed back the Germans at Château-Thierry and so prevented them from heading across the Marne to Paris. Five major campaigns had been underway since the summer of 1918 when Marshal Foch attacked the Germans along a line that ran from Reims to the North Sea. American troops stood their ground at Saint Mihiel. Nearly 1,200,000 Americans fought in the Argonne Forest with one out of every 10 men being killed or wounded. All along the western front, the Germans were retreating. Americans had also landed at the port of Archangel in northern Russia to protect supplies from Lenin's Bolsheviks. To the south and east, the Austrian drive into Italy had been smashed with the army cut in two and nearly destroyed.[531]

By October 1918, the Americans along with their allies were only 120 miles from the German border. Sailors in the Imperial Navy had mutinied months before, and now soldiers were rising up all along the German line demanding food and ammunition if they were to carry on the fight. General Hindenburg, Commander of the German forces, told Kaiser Wilhelm that the war was lost. The Kaiser appointed Prince Max of Baden as Germany's new Chancellor. Upon assuming his position, the Prince promptly asked President Wilson for an armistice. Wilson directed his Secretary of State Robert Lansing to inform the German government that Marshall Foch had been authorized to draw up the armistice.[532] On November 7, a German delegation headed to Foch's headquarters in the Compiègne Forest. Foch gave the Imperial Army 72 hours to accept his terms. They must give up all conquered territory, surrender all arms and warships, withdraw all forces that were west of the Rhine, return all prisoners, and allow the victors to occupy German territory. Four days later on November 11 at 5 in the morning, Germany's Secretary of State Matthias Erzberger signed the armistice in a railway car in the Compiègne Forest. Six hours later at 11 A.M. on November

[531] Winter and Baggett, *The Great War and the Shaping of the Twentieth Century*, 83-106, 155-173

[532] Woodrow Wilson, "Reply to the German Peace Proposal of October 6, October 8, 1918," *PPWW*, III, Part 1, 274-275; Robert Lansing, "Dispatch to the German Government, October 14, 1918," *PPWW*, III, Part 1, 277-279; Robert Lansing, "Message to the German Government, October 23, 1918," *PPWW*, III, Part 1, 283-285; Robert Lansing, "Message to the German Government, November 5, 1918," *PPWW*, III, Part 1, 291-292; Woodrow Wilson, "Announcement of the Signing of the Armistice, November 11, 1918," *PPWW*, III, Part 1, 293.

11, 1918, Marshall Foch ordered all soldiers and sailors to lay down their arms for the war was over.[533]

On the same day, Wilson presented the entire armistice agreement to a joint session of Congress. He saw no glory in winning the war and took no pride in having defeated Germany. Instead he saw the grim but magnificent duty that lay ahead for America as she shaped the peace and guided the world into a more humane future. The United States of America and her allies had brought an end to "armed imperialism" once and for all. Now the victorious nations were united in their commitment to a peace where justice would prevail for the weak and strong alike. Wilson described the war that had just been concluded in terms of the fall of "ancient governments" and the rise of a revolution to bring democracy to the European continent. It was as if, he concluded, that Europe was waking in a dark and bloody wilderness. "We must hold the light steady," he said, "until they find themselves."[534] In his own mind, Wilson was most committed to bringing the light of democracy to Germany and to the many peoples of the now fallen Austro-Hungarian Empire. He also believed that the nations crushed under the weight of the Ottoman Empire must be set free. He had publicly committed himself to allowing Jews, who had had been so mistreated elsewhere in the world, to return to Palestine as long as the rights of the people already living there were respected.[535]

These were the main details of the vision he held for peace in the world in the weeks following the Armistice. He looked back and saw how American soldiers had stepped in at the right moment of history to make a course correction in favor of democracy. In his annual message to Congress in December 1918, his words took off into poetry to capture his own long view of this historic moment:

> "What we all thank God for with deepest gratitude is that our men went in force into the line of battle just at the critical moment when the fate of the whole world seemed to land in the balance and threw their fresh strength into the ranks of freedom in time to turn the whole tide and sweep of the fateful struggle, – turn it once and for all, so that thenceforth it was back, back, back for their enemies, always back, never again forward!"

---

[533] Marshall Foch, translated by Colonel T. Bentley Mott, *The Memoirs of Marshall Foch* (Garden City, New York: Doubleday, Doran and Company, Incorporated, 1931), 489-496.

[534] Woodrow Wilson, "Address to a Joint Session of Congress, November 11, 1918," *PPWW*, III, Part 1, 274-302.

[535] Woodrow Wilson, "The Tasks that Lie Ahead of Us, December 28, 1918," *PPWW*, III, Part 1, 306-307; Woodrow Wilson, "Letter to Rabbi Wise, August 31, 1918," *PPWW*, III, Part 1, 243.

It was his responsibility to secure the great turn in the history of the world that the American boys had won on the battlefield by going to Paris where he would help write the treaty with Germany. "It is now my duty to play my full part," he told the Congress, "in making good what they offered their life's blood to obtain." He was certain that the Allies accepted the principles he had laid out a year before and expected him to be in Paris to secure these ideals in the final settlement with Germany. He promised to stay in touch with the Congress and had even set up a special telegraph line between Paris and Washington, D.C.

Like a young knight going off to battle himself, Wilson ended his speech with one pledge after another. In every sentence, there was the unwavering romantic hope that he need only envision the world's future, stand shoulder to shoulder with his allies and the leaders of the fallen nations, and somehow the world would be transformed. "I am the servant of the Nation," was his first pledge to the Congress. Then he promised to do his duties as President on the other side of the sea to the best of his ability. He hoped he could count on the full support of the Congress. He said he would give his all, hold no private thoughts of his own, but share everything with the House and Senate. He would make his absence brief and return as soon as he was able to translate into action the "great ideal for which America has striven."[536] Like a Crusader swearing an oath in a cathedral flooded with sunlight long ago, Wilson took up his sword to fight for a dream so right he was certain no one would question it.

The President boarded the *George Washington* with his wife Edith, his daughter Margaret, his secretary Joe Tumulty, and his doctor Cary Grayson on December 4, 1918, and set sail for France. He had appointed a four man team to help with the negotiations. Colonel House would remain his top advisor and continue the diplomatic work he had done throughout the war. He was already in Europe with Gordon Auchincloss, his son-in-law, who would act as his aide. Secretary of State Robert Lansing was also part of the team. Wilson was unaware just how deeply both men were committed to helping America's allies, especially Great Britain, rather than supporting his own ideals. Lansing was especially hostile to Wilson's reliance on the League of Nation as the world's future peacekeeper. The Secretary of State also resented the fact the President would once again rely on Colonel House for advice. Wilson had invited one Republican, Henry White, the Ambassador to Italy, to join the team since he had found his advice invaluable during the war. General Tasker H. Bliss, the U.S. Army Chief of Staff, rounded out the team of American negotiators. Hundreds of advisors in

[536] Woodrow Wilson, "Address to a Joint Session of Congress, December 2, 1918," *PPWW*, III, Part 1, 308-323.

history, law, and economics whom House had called together the year before would also make the crossing.[537]

Joe Tumulty later recalled how the first trip of a sitting President across the Atlantic was an exhilarating and troubling one for Wilson. He often saw his boss surrounded by reporters and telling jokes. He handed the President the many messages of good will that were cabled to the *George Washington*. One of the most beautiful ones came from Stockton Axson, now an official of the Red Cross, who wrote:

> "I wonder if you fully understand how entirely you carry overseas with you the hearts, and hopes and dreams, and desires of millions of Americans. Your vision of the new world that should spring from the ashes of the old, is all that made the war tolerable to many of us."

But Tumulty also saw Wilson standing alone in his heavy coat on the bow of the ship looking out toward Europe. He was certain that his boss was worried about sailing overseas without the full support of the Congress. The President had not actively campaigned in the midterm races in November, but he had issued a statement a week before the election on the need for a Democratic Congress. He told the American people that while the Republicans had been pro-war and so were good patriots, they had not given him the full support he needed to finish the war and establish the peace. "In ordinary times I would not feel at liberty to make such an appeal to you," he confessed, "But these are not ordinary times." He begged the American voters to give him the backing he needed at home and "among our associates on the other side of the sea." However, they ignored his pleas and gave the Republicans a one seat majority in the Senate and a 45 seat majority in the House. Wilson's greatest critic, Senator Henry Cabot Lodge, had won his re-election bid by defeating Boston's popular Democratic Mayor John Fitzgerald, better known as "Honeyfitz," by just 30,000 votes, and would now assume the role of the Chairman of the Foreign Relations Committee in the next Congress.

Just days before the President sailed for Europe on the *George Washington*, Teddy Roosevelt, sick and dying at his home at Sagamore Hill on Long Island, issued a bitter statement to America's allies, enemies, and Wilson himself. He said that the President had no authority to speak for the American people at this time.

---

[537] Walworth, *Woodrow Wilson*, II, 236-238.

> "His leadership has been emphatically repudiated by them. The newly elected Congress comes nearer than Mr. Wilson in having a right to speak the purposes of the American people at this moment. Mr. Wilson and his Fourteen Points and his four supplementary points and his five complementary points and all his utterance every which way have ceased to have any shadow of right to be accepted as expressive of the will of the American people."

With words like these still ringing in his ears, Wilson mused to Tumulty whether he was sailing into "the greatest success or the supremest tragedy in all history."[538]

As the *George Washington* made its way across the cold Atlantic, Wilson found himself worrying not just about opposition at home, but the troubles that lay ahead. During the final year of the war, he had been convinced that the allies were firmly behind his principles. Wilson knew about the secret Treaty of London written in 1915 where Britain, France, and Russia had agreed to carve up Germany, Austria-Hungary, and their empires in case of a future war. He was certain that the victorious nations had abandoned these plans. Wilson was therefore surprised when Colonel House cabled him about a meeting between the "Big Three," David Lloyd George of Great Britain, George Clemenceau of France, and Vittorio Orlando of Italy, each the Prime Minister of their respective nations, had agreed among themselves that they would get everything out of Germany that they possibly could. He cabled back that the peace would be determined on principle alone. There would be no looting or spoils of war for those days were over. There would be peace and justice for the victors and vanquished alike. More and more during his crossing, he came to believe that the league would be the only way to secure his vision for the world.[539]

When Wilson sailed into the harbor at Brest on December 13, 1918, he saw for the first time the adulation that would greet him throughout Europe. The harbor was filled with every kind of boat including warships that shot their cannon off in honor of him. Batteries along the Seine did the same all the way to

---

[538] See Tumulty, *Woodrow Wilson As I Know Him*, 235-249 for concerns on the growing Republican resentment in the Senate and for Roosevelt's comments; see Walworth, *Woodrow Wilson*, Volume II, 204, for the final vote count, and 320-321 for Axson's telegram and the comments on the success or tragedy of the trip to Europe; see Woodrow Wilson, "Appeal for a Democratic Congress, October 25, 1918," *PPWW*, III, Part 1, 286-288, for the President's remarks on the need to defeat the Republicans in the 1918 midterm elections. Edith Wilson later called this speech the worst mistake of her husband's life. It is interesting to note that Rose Fitzgerald, the daughter of "Honeyfitz," had given birth to John Fitzgerald Kennedy in May 1917. Edith Wilson's last public appearance would be at his inauguration as President in January 1961.

[539] See Grayson, *Intimate Memoir*, 57-59 for an excellent description of the situation and the toll it was taking on the President's health.

Paris where hundreds of thousands of people lined the streets waving and cheering him with "Vive Wilson!" He was praised in meetings, receptions, and dinners as the savior of France. In every place he went, he responded with great humility and always said Americans were proud they had won the war, but even happier they would establish the peace on the "eternal principles of right and justice." Wilson along with his wife and daughter were taken to the palace of Prince Murat, one of the most magnificent houses in the city of Paris. This would be their home throughout the treaty negotiations that were to take place at Versailles. Wilson's staff, including his top advisors House, Lansing, White, and Bliss, would be housed at the Hotel Crillon. He had a direct phone line connected between Murat's Palace and House's room at the Crillon. The President expected to get to work immediately, but the Allies had other plans. Both the French and the British hoped to delay the start of the negotiations for as long as possible since they feared Wilson would get everything he wanted in the midst of such overwhelming adulation.[540]

On the day after Christmas, President Wilson and his wife headed to London where they were greeted at Buckingham Palace by King George V and his wife Mary. As he stood on the balcony, Wilson was amazed that the crowd stretched more than a half a mile in every direction in front of the palace. "We Want Wilson" was the cry that came up from the people. The President was overwhelmed at the outpouring of love that came his way. He believed it showed how deeply the longing for a better world ran in the hearts of men and women everywhere. At a dinner with the royal family on the next evening, Wilson spoke of this great tide in the hearts of all people who "had never been so conscious of their brotherhood." He headed on to the town of Carlisle where his mother had lived as a girl. A large crowd gathered in the pouring rain to see the President enter the church where his grandfather Reverend Woodrow had once preached. Edith Wilson always remembered how her husband was nearly overcome with emotion. He told the people who had packed into the little church that memories of his grandfather, his mother, and his father were flooding back to him. He remembered how they had gone about their duties so simply, and how the whole world was now turning away from the path of savagery toward duty once again. "It is from quiet places like this all over the world," he said, "that the forces accumulate which presently will overbear any attempt to accomplish evil on a large scale."[541]

---

[540] Ibid., 62-65; Walworth, *Woodrow Wilson*, II, 236-239.

[541] Daniels, *Life of Woodrow Wilson*, 298, 302-304; Woodrow Wilson, "At His Grandfather's Church in Carlisle, December 29, 1918," *PPWW*, III, Part 1, 345-346.

From England, Wilson and his wife headed back to the continent where they made their way through France to Italy. At the border between the two countries, King Victor Emmanuel was waiting for them in his royal train. They joined the king and headed to Rome. They saw bonfires lit up in the night in honor of President Wilson all the way to Italy's ancient capital city. The crowds in Rome were larger and more enthusiastic than the ones in either Paris or London. Wilson was made a citizen of Rome and a member of the Royal Academy of Science. Pope Benedict XV invited him to a private audience and gave him a present of a beautiful mosaic. A noted archaeologist took him on a tour of ancient places in the city including the tomb of Romulus. He gave the President wreaths of laurel and myrtle, and said, "You Americans have something more sacred still, but you may carry it in your heart – love of humanity." Wilson traveled to Genoa where he visited a monument in honor of Christopher Columbus, and Turin where he laughed with the crowd about the many Italians who had emigrated to America. "I am sorry we cannot let you have New York," he said, "which I understand is the greatest Italian city in the world." In Milan, the adoration of the Italians for Wilson became so great that he was actually frightened, especially when he saw people in the square of the great cathedral kissing his picture and lighting candles around it. He knew that the crowds would love him until he made decisions at the treaty negotiations that might go against their nation. "I am at the apex of my glory in the hearts of these people," he told Cary Grayson, "I am afraid they are going to be disappointed and turn about and hiss me."[542]

The treaty negotiations to settle the war with Germany finally began on January 18, 1919 in the Room of the Clock at the palace of Versailles. Separate treaty negotiations were underway with Austria, Bulgaria, Hungary, and Turkey. Wilson faced three tough negotiators in the leaders of Great Britain, France, and Italy. Lloyd George may have wished to follow Wilson on principle into a better world, but he was the leader of a divided coalition government. He was duty bound to defend his nation and its empire around the world and on the high seas. Clemenceau was a devoted nationalist who was at first totally opposed to all of Wilson's ideas. Above all else, he was determined to protect France from any future invasion from Germany. He would not even consider joining the League of Nations unless Great Britain and the United States agreed to fight alongside his nation if France was invaded. Orlando had come to fight for the city of Fiume on the Adriatic and would be satisfied with nothing less. While Wilson came to the treaty negotiations convinced that the Allies agreed with all of the principles he

---

[542] Daniels, *Life of Woodrow Wilson*, 306; Woodrow Wilson, "Speeches at Turin, January 6, 1919," *PPWW*, III, Part 1, 380-386; Grayson, *Intimate Memoir*, 66.

had announced the year before, he soon realized that they were still deeply wounded from the war and would need a long time to heal. The losses on all sides had been staggering. Britain had lost 900,000 dead, an entire generation of the best and brightest. In France, 1,400,000 soldiers had been killed, while Italy had lost 650,000. Total casualties, killed and wounded, among the Allies topped 22,000,000 people. Germany and the Central Powers lost 15,000,000.[543]

Wilson spoke at the first session on the opening day only long enough to propose that George Clemenceau be named the permanent chairman of the peace conference. He praised France for all she has suffered, and then asked that the negotiations proceed quickly in a spirit of friendship and accommodation. People everywhere were waiting for the treaty to be written so that they might return to the calm and happiness of their daily lives. He refused to acknowledge publicly what everyone in the room knew. The victors did not share Wilson's vision of a peace settlement that would prevent future wars. While they also wished to prevent further conflicts, they thought the way to accomplish this was by punishing Germany. At the start of the second session on January 25, Wilson got his chance to counter the vengeful mood of the conference by proposing a League of Nations that would be the instrument to prevent war and bring his vision of a better future into view. This new and peaceful world would be a place where nations no longer attempted to conquer one another, but where they instead lived in harmony and mutual respect. They would trade freely with one another on the high seas that would always remain free. In every country, the people would govern themselves and so protect the rights guaranteed to them by their very nature. War would have no place in this world. It was for this vision "of justice and of liberty for men of every kind and place" that the United Stated had entered the war. He concluded with an almost boyishly optimistic view of himself that made his nation and his vision seem so young in a dark and ruined world:

> "I have only tried in what I have said to give you the fountains of the enthusiasm which is within us for this thing, for those fountain spring, it seems to me, from all the ancient wrongs and sympathies of mankind, and the very pulse of the world seems to beat to the surface in this enterprise."[544]

Sometime later at a private session of the Council of Four, nicknamed the "Big Four," Wilson was stunned when Lloyd George, Clemenceau, and Orlando

---

[543] Daniels, *Life of Woodrow Wilson*, 306-307; statistics on killed and wounded compiled by the Department of War (February 25, 1924 and June 30, 1928).

[544] Woodrow Wilson, "Address before the Second Plenary Session of the Peace Conference, January 25, 1919," *PPWW*, III, Part 1, 395-400.

dismissed his vision of post-war peace as proof that he was "pro-German." They accused him of wearing the Kaiser's helmet. Wilson was so shaken that he asked Cary Grayson to go for a drive with him through the Bois during the lunch break. He said nothing during most of the long ride, but finally told Grayson what the other leaders had said about him. "I want you to come into the room with me," he said, "Those men have gone a step too far and I don't know what may happen." Wilson went back into the private negotiating session and stood in front of Lloyd George, Clemenceau, and Orlando who were all seated. Wilson said that he was not now nor had he ever been an admirer of Germany or its culture. When Clemenceau stood to speak, Wilson whirled about and said, "You sit down. I did not interrupt you when you were speaking this morning." Clemenceau, who was nicknamed "Napoleon" by Lloyd George, sunk back in his chair. He agreed that Germany must be punished, but it must be a just and righteous sentence. If France punished Germany too severely today, he warned, then Germany would punish France tomorrow. Vengeance would build up in the souls of the German people until it became an obsession. The cycle of misery would never end but would instead be played out in wars for future generations to fight. "It is not only the innocent children of Germany that I am thinking of," he told his fellow leaders, "I am thinking of the children of France, of England, of Italy, of Belgium, of my own United States, of the whole world." For just one afternoon, the other leaders were overwhelmed by Wilson's eloquence. Clemenceau shook his hand, telling him he was not just a great, but a good man, too. Lloyd George nodded in agreement, while Orlando stood by the window wiping his eyes.[545]

Cary Grayson never forgot what he had witnessed, knowing that this was only one of the many "tilts" that Woodrow Wilson, the knight of the new order, would have against the champions of the old one. As his personal physician, he was growing increasingly worried that the President's health would soon break under the strain. Wilson worked from morning until night everyday of the week including Sunday. His life was an unending round of negotiations, official receptions, and visits to the wounded in local hospitals. The President took the time to speak with every soldier he met in the crowded wards, but was always overcome with emotion when he met a young man blinded in the war. He would always grip their hands for a long time, unable to speak while tears rolled down his cheeks. Grayson rightly observed that the adult Woodrow Wilson remained a boy with the "heart of a child, tender, susceptible to the griefs and burdens of others." His natural sympathy for humanity had only deepened after he spoke to hundreds of thousands of people in his travels through war torn Europe. In fact,

[545] Grayson, *Intimate Memoir*, 75-79.

Grayson was convinced that Wilson had spoken to more people than any other person in history. The strain of this experience was complicated by growing battles within his inner circle. Lansing's resentment that he was not the lead negotiator increased daily, while Colonel House seemed to becoming more arrogant. Wilson was disturbed when he overheard Gordon Auchincloss comment to his father-in-law, "Well, what shall we make the President say today?" Still he remained loyal to House even in the face of his wife's growing distrust of him. Edith Wilson had come to dismiss House as a colorless "yes, yes man" who played the game of flattery only to manipulate her husband. She also suspected him of leaking unfavorable stories about Wilson to the press. The President could not believe this, but he took the precaution of hiring a young newspaperman named Ray Stannard Baker to act as his official press secretary.[546]

Through all the stress and strain, Wilson was still able to put his best efforts into crafting the constitution of the League of Nations which he called a "covenant." He chose this word because the league meant more to him than just a mere part of a treaty. It was the point where history would begin again after the world had plunged into the ruin of the recent war. It was the promise of a better day ahead just like the rainbow in the sky when God promised Noah after the flood that he would never destroy the world by water again. On February 19, Wilson presented a draft of the document, and even more importantly the vision that lay behind it. He stood directly under the ornate timepiece for which the Room of the Clock was named, facing the delegates, and Mrs. Wilson and Dr. Grayson who stood hidden at the far end of the hall behind heavy drapes in an alcove. The President described the league as the "instrument" that would bring a more perfect future into being. All the nations of the world would sit together in a great council where they would listen to the troubles of their brother nations and act on the behalf of all mankind. The power behind the league would be the "moral force" of public opinion rather than the "armed force" which now prevailed. The league of all the nations would secure the world's peace by righting the wrongs of a past grown old in centuries of fighting and misery. The "underdeveloped" peoples of the world would advance under the guidance of the more advanced nations who would act not as conquerors but as elder brothers of younger ones. No nation would ever be allowed to conquer territory from another nation again. All secret diplomacy would come to an end as the nations of the world came together as one family. So many terrible things had come out of this war, Wilson noted, but many "very beautiful things" had come out of it, too:

---

[546] Ibid., 83-85; Hatch, *Edith Bolling Wilson*, 161-162; Edith Bolling Wilson, *My Memoir*, 226-227, 236, 250-252.

> "Wrong has been defeated, and the rest of the world has been more conscious than it ever was before of the majesty of right. People who were suspicious of one another can now live as friends and comrades in a single family, and desire to do so … Men are looking eye to eye and saying, "We are brothers and have a common purpose. We did not realize it before, but now we do realize it, and this is our covenant of fraternity and friendship."[547]

When the President was done speaking, there was silence for a moment, but then the delegates burst into applause. Wilson's league had already won the unanimous approval of the 14 nations that served on the committee that drafted the document. Now the entire convention voted to accept the draft for discussion and inclusion in the Treaty of Versailles. The First Lady, who stood weeping behind the curtains, finally peaked out and saw her husband "slender, calm, and powerful in argument." She felt at that moment as if she could see the upturned faces of the countless men, women, and children of the world, "crowding round and waiting for his words." She remained hidden until all the delegates left the room. Then she raced outside where she found Wilson waiting for her in the car with the Presidential flags flying from it. He was sitting in the back with his tall silk hat off and his head leaning against the seat. Wilson was tired but happy, and told his wife that this was the "first step forward." He knew there were deep wounds remaining in the souls of the men who would write the final treaty. This would lead them to make many mistakes. But as long as the league was set up, this would not matter. "For once established the League can arbitrate and correct mistakes which are inevitable in the Treaty," he told his wife as they drove through the streets of Paris on the way back to Murat's Palace. "It will act as a clearing house where every nation can come, the small as well as the great," he said. He then turned to her and smiled, knowing that tomorrow they would board the *George Washington* and head for America. "It will be sweet to go home, even for a few days," he confessed, "feeling I have kept the faith with the people, particularly with these boys. God bless them."[548]

On February 16, Wilson left for the United States where he would sign bills and give a few speeches on the peace negotiations before returning to France to finish his work on the treaty. He left Colonel House in charge in Paris, even giving him the authority to negotiate with the other members of the "Big Four." The President enjoyed the crossing back to the United States and spent a great

---

[547] Hatch, *Edith Bolling Wilson*, 163-165; Woodrow Wilson, "Presentation of the Covenant of the League of Nations," *PPWW*, III, Part 1, 413-428.

deal of time with his Assistant Secretary of the Navy Franklin D. Roosevelt and his wife Eleanor. Edith Wilson also found the Roosevelts to be "very delightful companions." When the *George Washington* docked in Boston on February 24, Republican Governor Calvin Coolidge was waiting to greet him and escort him to Mechanic's Hall where he gave a speech to an enthusiastic crowd. "I wonder if you are half as glad to see me as I am to see you," he said, "I have been very lonely, indeed, without your comradeship and counsel." He assured them that, in every step of his work, he tried to recall what he was sure their advice would be.

From Boston, the President headed by train back to Washington, D.C. At the advice of Secretary of State Lansing, Wilson broke another precedent and invited the Foreign Relations Committees of both the House and Senate to meet with him at the White House. Lansing was deeply worried that the treaty including the league would have difficulty passing a Republican Senate. Wilson had sent a draft of the League of Nations to the Congress, and now asked if the treaty was presented to the Senate, would it pass? Senator Lodge answered in a manner that could be taken in two ways. "If the Foreign Relations Committee approves it," he said, "I feel there is no doubt of ratification." Wilson looked directly at him and asked if he could go back to Paris knowing Lodge and his associates were behind him? Lodge nodded his head in the President's direction and Wilson took it as a "Yes." After the meeting, he and the First Lady headed up to New York City for another speech at the Metropolitan Opera on March 4. He confessed to the crowd that he was baffled as to why people would even think of opposing his efforts to achieve a lasting peace in the world. William Howard Taft joined him on stage and praised Wilson's dream of heading to a better world through the League of Nations. Before sailing back to France, Wilson launched one more volley at those who opposed him. He issued a statement accusing a "group of men in the Senate," who had refused to turn control of the railroads back to private hands, as obstructionists who were simply bent on embarrassing the administration.[549]

As Wilson headed back across the Atlantic, he found it hard to believe that the treaty would not pass the Senate. He knew that he would probably not win everything he hoped for in it, but if he could at least win the league, then somehow everything would work out right in the end. Edith Wilson later recalled that her husband was as "happy as a boy" as he sailed back across the Atlantic to France. When the *George Washington* arrived back into the harbor at Brest, gunboats came out again to escort him. All seemed as it had been before when he

---

[548] Hatch, Edith Bolling Wilson, 165-166.

[549] Edith Bolling Wilson, *My Memoir*, 243-245; Woodrow Wilson, "Statement Issued on the Adjournment of Congress, March 4, 1919," *PPWW*, III, Part 1, 456.

left France just weeks ago, but he began to sense that there might be trouble when he saw Colonel House coming out on a small boat toward him. The President asked his wife to take over the official duties of greeting the many French dignitaries who had come onboard, while he spoke with Colonel House. When Edith Wilson later returned to the Presidential cabin, she was stunned at the appearance of her husband. He seemed to have aged ten years in the short time since she had left him. She asked, "What happened?" and he answered that House had given away everything he had won in the treaty including the League of Nations. House confessed to the President that reporters had convinced him the treaty would not pass the Senate if the league was in it. With growing opposition to the league in the United States, and since America's allies were not really interested in it either, he had agreed to remove the League of Nations from the treaty. Edith Wilson remembered to the end of her life that on this terrible day Wilson's life started to unravel. She saw him set his chin the way he always did whenever he was making a "superhuman" effort to control himself. "Well, thank God, I can still fight, and I'll win back or I'll never look those boys I sent over here in the face again," he vowed to his wife, "They lost battles – but won the War, bless them. So don't be too dismayed." But she was dismayed, even certain that Woodrow Wilson had lost his youth forever and started down the road to long years of illness and the wreckage of his plans for a new and better world.[550]

Wilson headed back to Versailles determined to win back all he had lost including most especially the league but also a lessening of the punishments heaped on Germany. The Allied leaders were still just as determined to make Germany pay for the war, both morally and financially. Clemenceau had been wounded in an assassination attempt during Wilson's absence and was even more of a roaring lion than he had been earlier in the year. He urged Wilson to take a tour of France and Belgium to see just what the Germans had done. Wilson finally set off with his wife to see the devastation in places like Rheims, Chemin des Dames, and Soissons. But when he returned to Paris, he said again that while he believed Germany must be punished for starting the war, the sentence must not be so severe that it laid the seeds for a future war. He also would not abandon the League of Nations as the instrument to prevent war for all time. Showing he would not back down from this point, he issued statements on March 15 and March 27, 1919, demanding that the League of Nations be considered an integral part of the treaty. After much debate, Lloyd George and Clemenceau reduced the heavy reparations on Germany, while Wilson agreed to several modifications in the covenant of the league. The strain was now so great on Wilson that his health

[550] Edith Bolling Wilson, *My Memoir*, 243-245.

broke at last. He came down first with influenza and then asthma. Dr. Grayson was often called to the President's room late at night to help him breathe. Wilson, who had always been able to sleep whenever he pleased, was now awakened throughout the night with coughing fits.[551]

On June 28, 1918, the Treaty of Versailles was finally ready for signing. It was only fitting that Wilson had been given the official responsibility of inviting the Germans to Versailles in April so that they could learn the final details of the settlement. Neither Wilson on the one hand nor Lloyd George, Clemenceau, and Orlando on the other had gotten everything they wanted. In fact, Wilson had won many of his original "Fourteen Points." Land taken from France by Germany had been restored. Belgium was also returned to its former borders. Poland was now an independent nation. The old empire of the Hapsburgs was broken apart with the new democracies of Czechoslovakia and Yugoslavia formed out of the wreckage of the old order. The League of Nations was established and so the better world that Wilson envisioned all along would hopefully come into being one day. While Germany was forced to accept full responsibility for the war, the reparations placed on her were much lower than the 100 to 115 billion dollars originally demanded by England and France.

Crowds packed the roads leading out from Paris to Versailles and made it almost impossible for the delegates to get into the Hall of Mirrors where the treaty would be signed. Wilson had suggested that Germany sign first so the delegates could not change their minds. The remaining nations were then asked to sign in alphabetical order. This made the Étas Unis – the United States – the next in line. Wilson signed first and walked back to his place, flashing a big smile at his wife Edith who was seated in the crowd. People again pushed in on the delegates as they left Versailles. Wilson's guards had to gather quickly about him to protect him from the crush of well-wishers who shouted over and over, "Vive Wilson!" Later that night, French President Raymond Poincaré held a grand party for all the foreign dignitaries at the Elysée Palace. Edith Wilson was impressed with the brilliantly decorated rooms of the palace that were filled with all the peoples of the world in their best party dress. On the next day, President Wilson and his wife boarded the *George Washington* in Brest and sailed for home. French destroyers followed them out to sea while a band played "The Star Spangled Banner." Wilson was relieved to have the treaty signed, but found himself suddenly plagued with an ancient dread that he might have tempted the fates by hoping for

---

[551] Ibid., 234-235; Woodrow Wilson, "League an Integral Part of the Treaty of Peace, March 15, 1919," *PPWW*, III, Part 2, 457; Woodrow Wilson, "Defense of the League of Nations Commission, March 27, 1919," *PPWW*, III, Part 2, 459; Grayson, *Intimate Memoir*, 85.

too much in this lifetime. “Well, little girl, it is finished, and, as no one is satisfied,” he sighed to Edith, “it makes me hope we have made a just peace; but it is all on the lap of the gods.”[552]

On the bright summer day of July 8, 1919, Wilson arrived in the harbor of New York City to meet his destiny. Boats of every description filled the harbor and escorted the *George Washington* to the dock in Hoboken. Two days later, the President formally presented the Treaty of Versailles to a joint session of Congress. His speech was one of the longest and most complex ones he had ever given. He knew that the Congress had been apprised of every facet of the treaty negotiations, but he wished again to explain why America had entered the war, the part she played in writing the treaty, and the place the nation now had in the eyes of the world. The United States had joined the conflict to turn the course of history in a different direction. The world had forever turned its back on the rule of kings and their noble houses. Democracy would now come alive everywhere with the world’s first democracy, the United States of America, leading the way. He ended with a description of the course he had set for the world in words so simple they seemed more poetry than prose:

> “The stage is set, the destiny disclosed. It has come about by no plan of our conceiving, but by the hand of God who led us into this way. We cannot turn back. We can only go forward, with lifted eyes and freshened spirit, to follow the vision. It was of this that we dreamed at our birth. America shall in truth show the way. The light streams upon the path ahead, and nowhere else.”[553]

Wilson was so enamored of the vision he had charted for his nation and so convinced that the League of Nations was the sure instrument to lead the world there that he could not imagine people might oppose him. In Wilson’s mind, to oppose the league was to oppose his vision, and thus he would have no part of it. But people did oppose the league, especially Republican Senators called the “Irreconcilables” who were led by Lodge of Massachusetts. Senator Lodge found the President’s vision of a better world laughable and had been long determined to find the weak point in the league to sink Wilson’s dreams. He found it in Article X of the Covenant of the League of Nations which read:

> “The High Contracting Parties undertake to respect and preserve as against external aggression the territorial integrity and existing political independence of

---

[552] Woodrow Wilson, “Presenting the Treaty for Ratification, July 10, 1919,” *PPWW*, III, Part 1, 542-543, 545-555; Edith Bolling Wilson, *My Memoir*, 267-271.

[553] Woodrow Wilson, “Presenting the Treaty for Ratification,” 551-552.

> all States members in the League. In case of any such aggression or in case of any threat or danger of such aggression the executive Council shall advise upon the means by which this obligation shall be fulfilled."

If the United States joined the League of Nations, then the control over American foreign policy, which had been given to the President and the Senate in the Constitution by the nation's founders, would be handed over to an international council. Instead of Wilson's dream of a bright future, the people of the United States would be dragged into one war after another, not of their making and without their consent. Unless there were several modifications in the Covenant of the League of Nations that guaranteed the sovereignty of the United States, the Irreconcilables would sink the Treaty of Versailles. They soon won the support of several progressive Senators, Democrats and more moderate Republicans alike, who feared that Wilson had completely forgotten domestic reforms in his drive to fix the problems of the world. Even more Congressmen worried that the treaty pointed the finger only at Germany as the cause of the war. They feared it would be impossible to win elections in districts where Americans of German descent were in the majority. If the President did not compromise with the "reservations" of the many politicians who as Senators were fighting to win back their role in shaping American foreign policy, and also as Republicans to win back the White House, Wilson's dreams of a better world would run aground.[554]

On a warm night in August 1919, Wilson sat out on the back portico of the White House with his wife and brother-in-law Stockton Axson talking over the troubles that he was having passing the Treaty of Versailles in the Senate. As he listened to the conversation, Axson became deeply worried about how different the President seemed since he came back from Europe in July 1919. He knew that Wilson had been quite ill in Paris with bouts of the flu and asthma, but there seemed to be something even more seriously wrong with him. It was as if he had lost the "elasticity" that usually marked his thinking. Axson feared he had become a "worn-out man" who was strangely retreating into old ideas from his youth. Wilson mused that if he had the powers of a Prime Minister, rather than a President, then he could dissolve the Congress, go directly to the American people who largely supported the League of Nations, and hold national elections that would sweep candidates who supported him into office. Finally he came back to

---

[554] Tumulty, *Woodrow Wilson As I Know Him*, 522-523; Woodrow Wilson, "Presentation of the Covenant of the League of Nations," 416; for the list of Senator Lodge's 13 specific "reservations" (the fourteenth reservation dealing with America's honor was rejected by the Foreign Relations Committee), see Daniels, *Life of Woodrow Wilson*, 324-325.

the present and brooded how only labor leaders seemed to understand that modern problems must always be seen in international terms. Future generations, he predicted, would have to realize that problems no longer belonged to one country, but to the entire world. This change would in turn profoundly affect the office of the Presidency. "The man who is going to direct the future of America as an able president should always direct it," he explained, "has got to be a man who reflects long and deeply on these complicated relationships of our time and the time immediately pending."[555]

Although as President he could not dissolve the Congress in the way that a Prime Minister could turn out the Parliament, he could go over the heads of the Senators who opposed him and take his case directly to the American people. On September 3, 1919, he and his wife Edith set off on a speaking tour of the country that would take him from big Midwestern towns like Columbus and Indianapolis all the way westward to every major city in the Far West and the Rocky Mountains. Cary Grayson had begged the President not to make the trip, but Wilson shot back:

> "You must remember that I, as commander in chief, was responsible for sending our soldiers to Europe. In the crucial test in the trenches they did not turn back – and I cannot turn back now. I cannot put my personal safety, my health in the balance against my duty – I must go."[556]

In just 22 days, Wilson traveled close to 8,000 miles and delivered more than 30 major addresses. Everywhere he went – from Billings, Montana to Tacoma, Washington and then on to San Francisco, California and Salt Lake City, Utah – large crowds waited for him at railway stations, accompanied him to his hotels, and then cheered him on as he spoke in auditoriums and other public places. Mrs. Wilson later remembered the trip as a blur of parades in flower-strewn automobiles with young children waving to the President along the way. When she begged her husband to cut back on his speaking schedule, he simply said, "I am an attorney for those children," and refused to slow down. She could only watch and worry as Wilson complained of headaches that would not go away. She often summoned Dr. Grayson who had accompanied them on the trip to find some kind of relief for her husband's suffering. Little could be done for the President if he insisted on making so many speeches in the midst of the late summer heat wave that was plaguing the western states. The President was also exhausted from

[555] Axson, *Brother Woodrow*, 196-198, 238.

[556] Grayson, *Intimate Memoir*, 95.

meeting with Democratic leaders at dinners, lunches and receptions from morning until night in every city.[557]

In Los Angeles, Woodrow Wilson met a ghost from his past. Mary Hulbert asked if she could visit the President and his wife at their hotel. Edith Wilson wanted very much to meet her and assure her that she did not believe the gossip about her relationship with her husband. When the former Mrs. Peck finally arrived, she was no longer the beauty the President had so long remembered. She now seemed a faded, almost pitiful figure who talked incessantly about the troubles that had befallen her. Edith Wilson found the woman strangely obsessed with her son, an only child. She seemed unaware that the President of the United States had pressing commitments and could not listen to her all afternoon. When he finally had to leave for another engagement, Mary stayed behind, telling her troubles to Edith and waiting for her old friend Woodrow to return. She finally left much later in the evening when it was already dark and the President had not come back.[558]

The strain on the President's health grew more intense as he left Los Angeles and traveled throughout the Southwest. His speeches became longer and more complex as he headed through Nevada, Utah, and Colorado. Wilson usually began his talks by telling the people who had come to listen to him that he chafed at the confinement of Washington. "Things get very lonely in Washington sometimes," was a favorite saying for the President on his whistle stop tour of the west. He then said it was only right to leave Washington where the Treaty of Versailles was bogged down in the Senate and head out to the country to speak directly to the people. In Wilson's opinion, he owed a report on the treaty only to his fellow citizens and not to the Congress. He next moved on to every major complaint that had been brought against the treaty. As to the matter of reparations, Wilson argued that Germany had to pay some price for attempting to turn the clock backward on civilization. But he also reminded everyone that the punishments that were laid on Germany were temporary in nature and would soon be lifted. Wilson asked the crowds to remember that most of the provisions of the Treaty of Versailles were quite positive. Even the much questioned Article X of the Covenant of the League of Nations did not strip the sovereignty away from any country, but instead brought countries together to prevent war. Finally and most importantly, Wilson argued that the treaty placed Europe on the road to democracy and away from autocracy. The Austrian Empire would be broken up, and the many peoples who were once repressed under the rule of the Hapsburgs

[557] Ibid., 96-97; Edith Bolling Wilson, *My Memoir*, 273-280.
[558] Ibid., 281.

would now be allowed to govern themselves. Germany would also become a democracy. "That is the American principle," he explained, "and I was glad to fight for it." He reminded his audiences that revolution followed naturally from political repression and therefore the treaty would prevent the kind of horrors now occurring in Russia. He always made a plea for the League of Nations as the most democratic part of the treaty. It would force governments to reveal their true motives to the world. Even in foreign affairs, governments would have to act for the good of all mankind and in accordance with the will of humanity.[559]

Wilson was at his most poetic in the final moments of every speech. He clearly believed that Americans must face the fact that they were now the leaders of the world. They must play the part that Providence had written for them and so act on behalf of all mankind. This was a special destiny since never before had a people led the world, not just for themselves alone, but for humanity itself. Other nations had ruled much of the known world for selfish purposes only. Unlike these former great powers, the United States would not be a conqueror or usurper. Instead, Americans would be the "friends of liberty" and the "eternal champions of what is right." Wilson often left his listeners breathless with his closing vision of America's place in the history of the world. He thrilled the crowds by saying:

> "America is made up of the peoples of the world. All the best bloods of the world flows in her veins, all the old affections, all the old and sacred traditions of peoples of every sort throughout the wide world circulate in her veins, and she said to mankind at her birth: 'We have come to redeem the world by giving it liberty and justice.' Now we are called upon before the tribunal of mankind to redeem its immortal pledge."[560]

Everywhere Woodrow Wilson went on his western pilgrimage, his message was urgent, but his mood was upbeat. He was like the captain of ship whose crew expected to be in their home port soon but who now must push on to uncharted waters. He had to convince them that their time at sea would be a great adventure unparalleled in the history of the world. He tried to hold them steady as he described a vision of America leading mankind into a better future for all. Wilson reminded them that the millions of young men who had been sent to fight in France were the first to understand this new role for their nation. "They were going forth to prove the might of justice and right," he explained, "and all the

---

[559] Woodrow Wilson, "Speech at St Louis, Missouri, September 5, 1919," *PPWW*, III, Part 1, 643-644; all of Wilson's prepared addresses on his western tour from September 4 through September 25, 1919 can be found in *PPWW*, III, Part 1, 590-645, and Part 2, 1-416.

[560] Woodrow Wilson, "Speech at St Louis, Missouri," 645.

world accepted them as crusaders, and their transcendent achievement has made all the world believe in America as it believed in no other nation organized in the modern world."[561]

If only his listeners could look into the eyes of the mothers that he had met in France, they would agree with his vision of America's role in the world. He loved to tell the story of his visit to a cemetery on a hillside in Suresnes just outside of the city of Paris. Many American soldiers who had died in the Great War were buried there. French mothers who had lost sons in the war came every day to place flowers on the graves of the dead Americans. Over and over, the women had told him that "France was free and the world was free because America had come!" In the last speech he gave in Pueblo, Colorado on September 25, Wilson made a final plea to the American people not to turn their backs on the world that needed them so badly.

> "There is one thing that the American people always rise to and extend their hand to, and that is the truth of justice and of liberty and of peace. We have accepted that truth and we are going to be led by it, and it is going to lead us, and through us the world, out into pastures of quietness and peace such as the world never dreamed before."[562]

By the time Wilson left Colorado on his way to Kansas, he was so sick that he finally considered stopping the tour. He had pressed on with the growing dread that a more terrible war would descend on the world if the Treaty of Versailles was defeated. He worried that another bloody conflict was already brewing in the awful Providence of God. Instead of a few hundred thousand people dying, many millions would lose their lives in the next war to "accomplish the final freedom of the peoples of the world." But twenty miles outside of Pueblo, President Wilson ordered the train to stop. His constant headache was almost unbearable. Cary Grayson convinced him to get off the train and get some exercise by walking in the Colorado countryside. The President along with his wife and his doctor started down a dusty road near the train tracks. They met a farmer who gave the President a cabbage and some apples for dinner. Farther up the road, Wilson noticed a sick young man in a soldier's uniform sitting on the porch of an old farmhouse. He climbed a fence and ran up to shake the boy's hand much to the surprise of his parents. Back on the train, Wilson promised to rest completely until the next stop at Wichita. But when his secretary Tumulty asked him to shake hands with a

---

[561] Woodrow Wilson, "Speech at Pueblo, September 25, 1919," *PPWW*, III, Part 2, 414.

[562] Ibid., 415-416.

crowd waiting for him just down the tracks at Rocky Ford, he could not refuse. He stood at the back of train and reached out to as many people as possible. Then he waved to the large crowd as the train headed on toward Kansas.[563]

Edith Wilson was relieved as the train rolled across the darkened plains and her husband finally fell asleep. But as the dawn broke on the morning of September 26, she felt her life would never be the same again. She knew that her husband was desperately ill and that she would spend the rest of her life pretending otherwise. Still exhausted and in pain when he awoke, Wilson finally agreed to end his speaking tour and hurry back to Washington. When the train pulled into Wichita, Tumulty told the waiting crowd and the press that the President was ill and would not be speaking in town. Then the tracks ahead were cleared and a 1,700 mile race back to the capital began in earnest. People gathered at every station where the train had to stop or slow down. Mrs. Wilson closed the shades in her husband's compartment so no one could see how much he was suffering. The First Lady would long remember how the train ride home seemed like a funeral cortège.[564]

At 11 A.M. on Sunday morning September 28, 1919, the President's train pulled into Union Station. It had taken only 48 hours to make the trip back from Kansas. Wilson was able to walk from the train to a car where his daughter Margaret was waiting for him. Cary Grayson was worried that the President's left eye was twitching uncontrollably and saliva was dripping from his mouth. He refused to let Wilson go to his regular Sunday church service, but he did let him take a drive through the countryside later in the afternoon. Back at the White House, the President wandered about like a ghost in between his office and his wife's bedroom. His terrible headache seemed like a demon that had come to torture him.

Finally just three days later on October 1, Wilson seemed to improve. His headache subsided enough for him to watch a movie in the White House and later play billiards with Cary Grayson. But later that night, Wilson seemed forgetful. He came to his wife's bedroom and read a chapter of the Bible to her, something they had done together every night during the war. But when he went back to his own room, Edith Wilson noticed that he left his watch on her nightstand. She took it to him and he said this bothered him. It was not like Wilson to forget things. Edith knew her husband was afraid that the tight hold he had so long kept on himself might be loosening. She came back nearly every hour to check on him. At 8 A.M. on the morning of October 2, she found him sitting on the edge of his bed

---

[563] Grayson, *Intimate Memoir*, 97-99.

[564] Edith Bolling Wilson, *My Memoir*, 283-285.

unable to use his left hand that lay limp at his side. She helped him get to the bathroom and then left to call Dr. Grayson. While on the phone, she heard Wilson fall. She found him unconscious on the bathroom floor. Even before Dr. Grayson arrived, Edith Wilson knew that her husband had suffered a massive stroke. She and the doctor lifted the President into his bed, grateful that he had asked for a glass of water before slipping into unconsciousness.[565]

For days, the President drifted between life and death. Cary Grayson and the other doctors called in on the case told the First Lady that if the clot dissolved, then the President would live. If it did not, there was nothing they could do for him and the President would die shortly. The clot dissolved and Wilson was soon out of immediate danger. His left arm and leg were useless, but his mind and speech seemed unimpaired. But two weeks after his stroke, he developed a bladder infection. The doctors were convinced that a blockage of some kind was causing the infection. They asked Mrs. Wilson if they could operate, but she refused since she was certain that the procedure would kill him. The crisis passed when the President's fever broke and his bladder began functioning normally again.[566]

In the first weeks after his stroke, Wilson was exhausted and spent much of the day and night sleeping. His family took turns sitting at his bedside. He loved a small dwarf pine that someone had sent to the White House as a get well present. The President asked that a light be kept on over it at all times so he could see it even if he woke up in the middle of the night. He told his family that he could imagine himself in a forest if he looked at the little tree long enough. One afternoon when Nellie McAdoo was watching him, Wilson opened his eyes and smiled exactly the way he used to before his stroke. He said he had been dreaming of a trip that he, his three daughters, and his wife Ellen had taken long ago to Canada. "I was back on the island of Muskoka," he said, "Do you remember our picnics there, and your mother reading poetry under the pines?" He told Nellie that he wished he could hear Ellen's voice. "I owe everything to your mother," he confessed, "you know that, don't you?" Memories of their life together flooded back to him as he lay in his sick bed. He could see Ellen again, so brave and radiant. She had devoted her life to her husband and children with no thought of herself. Before he drifted back to sleep, he asked Nellie to tell her children about Ellen Wilson.[567]

---

565 Ibid., 286-288.

566 Ibid., 288.

567 McAdoo, *Woodrow Wilsons*, 300-301.

With the President physically weak but still mentally sound, decisions needed to be made about whether he should resign or step down temporarily until he was better. Wilson had begged his wife to tell no one, meaning she was not to announce how grave his condition truly was to the American people. He thought it would break their spirit in the fight for the treaty that lay ahead. Cary Grayson only commented to the press that the President had suffered a nervous breakdown. He knew that Edith Wilson had often helped the President review important papers during the war. She was with him every night when he received a stack of papers concerning the most pressing matters that must be taken care of on the next day. The papers were always left in a small box on the desk in his office. The President would stay up late, reviewing each one and sending them back with comments to various cabinet officers and other government officials. Now he and the other doctors suggested that a system be set up where important questions that needed to be decided should go first to Mrs. Wilson. She would review the matter and determine if a cabinet officer or someone else in the government could handle it. If it was an issue that needed to go to the President, she would write a summary of the key points involved and present it to him. In turn, she would convey her husband's wishes back to the cabinet or other important members of Congress like Gilbert Hitchcock of Nebraska who was leading the fight for the Treaty of Versailles on the floor of the Senate. Her personal secretary Edith Benham would help her with the typing. Miss Benham was soon so overworked that she suffered a complete nervous collapse in the following March and had to be replaced. Vice President Thomas Marshall and his wife would do their part by taking over the duty of entertaining important guests. Edith Wilson would maintain for the rest of her life that she had no personal wish to assume such an important role in her husband's administration, but that she went along with it to keep her husband alive. She also agreed to her new role in order to keep people away from the President she had come to distrust like Lansing and House, and others whom she considered common like Tumulty. To the end of her days, Edith Wilson would describe this time in her life in terms of her "stewardship" for the President and her nation.[568]

Within the President's inner circle of family and friends, only his brother-in-law Stockton Axson, who had known Woodrow Wilson since he was a little boy in Rome, Georgia, sensed the tragedy of the arrangement. He knew that Wilson was an extremely sensitive man whose feelings had always been deferred to by his family and his closest friends. Now his doctors were trying to protect him in the same way from the harshness of the world. They saw him as a man with

[568] Edith Bolling Wilson, *My Memoir*, 288-289.

nerves so frayed that he would die at the mere suggestion of giving up the Presidency or at any disagreement over policy. They were so bent on keeping him isolated, and therefore in their opinion alive, that they failed to see how the stroke and his illness had changed him. Axson knew that Wilson, who had been hypersensitive in his youth, had become a man who learned to work with others to achieve his dreams, especially after he had suffered the defeat over the quads and the graduate school at Princeton. He had gone on to be a successful politician because he had worked well with others and did not bully them. Even in Paris, he had been an able negotiator who had given up much to win many of his ideals. But all this disappeared from his personality as he lay flat on his back in his darkened bedroom in the White House. "A sick man is seldom sweetly reasonable," Axson later recalled, "A sick man with the will of Woodrow Wilson is most unlikely to be extremely accommodating." He could only watch as Wilson seemed to revert to an earlier time when he did not work well with others, but instead issued manifestos "like a rallying battle cry."[569] He seemed a little boy again chasing pirates about the world and readying to take his ship down rather than surrender it. He was so committed to his own vision of the future that he forgot he would never reach it if others refused to come along with him. Sadly, the very people who could have helped him negotiate a compromise on the Treaty of Versailles – most especially his wife Edith Wilson and his doctor Cary Grayson – joined in the battle against all who might question or oppose the President, believing that in so doing they were keeping him alive.

One person outside of Wilson's inner circle tried to undo the arrangement that had essentially made Edith Wilson into the President's Chief of Staff. That man was Robert Lansing, the Secretary of State. On Tuesday October 7, just five days after the President had suffered a stroke, Lansing stormed into Tumulty's office and demanded that Wilson resign if he was incapacitated. He read aloud the section from Article II of the Constitution that described how the Vice President must assume the top office if the President could not discharge his duties. Edith Wilson had not allowed Tumulty to see Wilson, but he was so loyal to the President that he shouted back at Lansing, "I have read the Constitution and am not in need of any tutoring at your hands in the provisions you have just read." Lansing demanded that either Tumulty or Grayson announce that Wilson was unable to fulfill his duties as President. "You may be sure that while Woodrow Wilson is lying flat on his back in the White House," Tumulty roared back, "I will not be a party to an attempt to oust him." At this point, Dr. Grayson came into Tumulty's office. He told Lansing that he would never declare the President

[569] Axson, *Brother Woodrow*, 238.

incapacitated and would publicly disavow the Secretary of State if he tried to remove Wilson from office.[570]

The first great test of the new system of Edith Wilson's stewardship came with the first vote on the Treaty of Versailles. It was apparent to everyone but the President that the treaty would go down to defeat as written unless some compromise was reached with Senator Lodge and the Republicans who supported him. Edith Wilson let none of the President's many allies, who came to the White House urging a compromise, in to see him. She was convinced that any discussion of the matter would so upset him that another, more deadly stroke would kill him. She turned Bernard Baruch away after he urged her to tell the President that "half a loaf is better then none." On November 19, just one day before the vote, a desperate Senator Hitchcock told the First Lady that the treaty was heading for certain defeat if Wilson did not compromise. He was very upset that the battle had now become a personal one between Wilson and Lodge with the treaty and its supporters caught in the middle. Mrs. Wilson was moved by Hitchcock's pleas and went into her husband's bedroom to suggest a compromise. "For my sake," she asked him, "won't you accept these reservations and get this awful thing settled?" He turned his head on the pillow, stretched his hand toward his wife, and said, "Little girl, don't you desert me; that I cannot stand." He then explained that if the United States changed the treaty already signed in Paris, then every nation, even Germany, would also have the right to change it. The country's honor was at stake. "Better a thousand times to go down fighting" he said quietly, "than to dip your colours to dishonorable compromise."[571]

Mrs. Wilson went back out to talk to Senator Hitchcock, telling him that she felt as if she had betrayed her husband for even asking such a question. She was now firmly on his side on the matter of the treaty and would never again ask him to compromise. She went back to the President's bedroom where he dictated a letter to Senator Hitchcock stating that any reservations added to the treaty would nullify it. He trusted that all true friends of the treaty would vote against the reservations. On the next day, two votes were taken in the Senate on the Treaty of Versailles. First, the treaty with Lodge's reservations in it went down to defeat and next the treaty without reservations in it also failed. When his wife finally told him about the two votes, he simply said it was all the more reason for him to get better and try again to make his country understand its great responsibility to the

---

[570] Hatch, *Edith Bolling Wilson*, 224.

[571] Edith Bolling Wilson, *My Memoir*, 297.

world. He could also proudly stand on the prow of his ship of state knowing that he had not dipped his nation's colors.[572]

In March 1920, the Democrats tried again to pass the Treaty of Versailles, and this time the President let it be known that he might accept some compromises. He was willing to change the wording of the treaty in a number of key places to win the support of the Republicans. But Senator Lodge intervened and made sure that all of his defeated reservations were placed back in the treaty once it came to the floor for a vote. Again the Treaty of Versailles went down to defeat. By this time, Wilson was well enough to sit up in a wheel chair and even go outside on the south portico of the White House to take in some sun. Tumulty finally got a chance to talk to him and tried to cheer him up. The President was deeply saddened that the United States of America had been "shamed in the eyes of the world." He blamed his enemies, most especially Senator Henry Cabot Lodge, for making Americans believe that the League of Nations was a "juggernaut" that would lead the country into war rather than peace. If only he had stayed well, he brooded, he could have convinced the people that the league was their last real hope, perhaps even their last chance, to save humanity from a coming war whose horror would be unimaginable. Tumulty read aloud from Wilson's *History of the American People* to buoy up his flagging spirits. He chose a dramatic portion of a chapter on Jay's Treaty where Alexander Hamilton was stoned by the people as he stood on the steps of New York's City Hall defending the document. Tumulty went on to read how Washington had been vilified for supporting the treaty that the people eventually realized was a good one. Wilson thanked his old friend, saying "You have placed me in mighty good company."[573]

After the final defeat of the Treaty of Versailles, Wilson thought about resigning. He imagined how he would wheel himself into the House, read his address to the nation, if he had the strength, and then wheel himself out again. His doctor Cary Grayson suggested that he should try and hold a cabinet meeting as a test of whether or not he could still function as the President. On April 14, 1920, Wilson called his first cabinet meeting since the previous year. Just two months before in February 1920, Robert Lansing had called the only other cabinet meeting since the President's stroke. He had received an angry letter from Wilson who told him that only the President of the United States could call the heads of the executive departments together for a meeting. Lansing promptly resigned and was replaced by Bainbridge Colby. Wilson's inner circle, most especially the First Lady and Joseph Tumulty, were happy to see a man as disloyal as Lansing finally

---

[572] Ibid., 296-297.

[573] Tumulty, *Woodrow Wilson As I Know Him*, 454-456.

go. Before the April cabinet session, Wilson had arranged a way out of the meeting if it became too taxing for him. It was to start promptly at 10 A.M. and Cary Grayson was to come in one hour later to see how the President was doing. If Wilson shook his head, this meant Grayson was to leave and come back later. Wilson was fine at 11 and 11:15, but at 11:30 Grayson returned with Mrs. Wilson and the President decided he was done for the day.[574]

The meeting seemed to cheer Wilson, and for awhile he even began to speculate on whether he might run again for a third term. He still felt that he had power as President if only to veto measures coming from the Congress that he was certain the American people did not want. In May, he vetoed a joint resolution of the House and Senate declaring that the war with Germany and the Austrian Empire was over. There would not be an official treaty with Germany until after the 1920 election. In the last months of his Presidency, he would veto the Volstead Act that implemented prohibition across the land in accordance with the recently passed 18th Amendment, changes to the Clayton Antitrust Act, and an Emergency Tariff Bill that sent rates back up on agricultural goods. He also became an outspoken supporter of the 19th Amendment and urged politicians in state houses throughout the nation to give women the right to vote. He took a deep interest in political campaigns once again. He was certain that if the Democratic Convention in San Francisco deadlocked in early July 1920, the delegates would need a compromise candidate who could take the case for the League of Nations back to the people. Although he knew a third term would probably kill him, he made up his mind to accept the nomination if it was offered to him. If nothing else, he thought that he would at least be able to save the party from another disastrous run by William Jennings Bryan.

As he predicted, the convention could not agree on a candidate in a three-way race between James Cox, the progressive Governor of Ohio, William McAdoo, the former Secretary of the Treasury who had made a name for himself as an able administrator in the recent war, and A. Mitchell Palmer, the Attorney General who had won recent fame for himself by launching raids all across the country in an effort to hunt down "reds." Wilson became so anxious over the balloting that he suffered asthma attacks which made him feel that his lungs had no air in them. The convention finally picked Governor Cox along with his running mate Franklin D. Roosevelt, who was recognized for the important work he did alongside Josephus Daniels to build up the navy during the war. If Wilson was disappointed that his political career was over at last, he never mentioned it to anyone in his inner circle. He thought Cox the weakest candidate of the three, but

---

574 Grayson, *Intimate Memoir*, 113.

was happy that both he and Roosevelt were staunch defenders of the League of Nations and promised to make the election a referendum on it. He was convinced they would win a smashing victory in November 1920.[575]

Since his stroke, Wilson had been isolated from the reality of American politics by nearly everyone in his inner circle. They were convinced that if they told him anything upsetting, he would surely die. Stockton Axson became concerned when he learned that the President was convinced that Cox and Roosevelt would win in a landslide. Axson found such an attitude "not only pitiful but dangerous." He guessed rightly that there would be a landslide, but it would be for the Republican candidate Warren G. Harding and his running mate Calvin Coolidge. The two men were campaigning on the rejection not just of the League of Nations, but the entire progressive reform movement that Wilson had so brilliantly led since 1912. Edith Wilson well understood the "will o' the wisp" call of Harding's campaign. She knew the idea of a "return to normalcy" had a powerful, if in her opinion illusory, pull on the American people. But like everyone else, she refused to tell Wilson the truth about the impending election. Finally, after pleading with Cary Grayson to "prepare him for the shock," Axson took on the job himself. He told his brother-in-law that Harding was heading for a record-breaking victory. "You pessimist! You don't know the American people," Wilson answered, "They always rise to a moral occasion. Harding will be deluged." Up until the day before the election, Axson could make no impression on Wilson. He was relieved that once Harding and Coolidge were swept into office, Wilson remained serene. He did even seem to mind that Eugene V. Debs had gotten a million votes as the Socialist Party's candidate for President while serving his sentence for speaking out against the war. "I have not lost faith in the American people," he calmly said, "They have been temporarily deceived. They will realize their error in a little while."[576]

It was soon clear to all that Woodrow Wilson was not the fragile figure that those closest to him had believed him to be since his stroke in October 1919. He accepted the loss of the Democrats with grace and continued on with the few duties that remained to him. He was awarded the Nobel Peace Prize in December 1920, and he asked Ambassador Schmedeman, America's representative in Norway, to deliver a short address on his behalf. In his last message to Congress which he delivered in the same month, there was no condemnation of the Senate for failing to do his will. He spoke a great deal about the tariff and the budget of the United States as well as about loans to other countries around the world. He

---

[575] Ibid., 114-119.

[576] Axson, *Brother Wilson*, 198-199.

tried his best to urge his fellow Americans one last time to realize that they were the leading force for democracy in a world that was crying out for it. When America was born, he reminded the Congress, a hope came into the world that "a new order would prevail throughout the affairs of mankind." This new order which broke upon the world in 1776 was democracy. It was the "manifest destiny" of the world's first democracy, the United States of America, to make certain that this new spirit of freedom prevailed. This spirit had led the nation into war and this faith in democracy had sent "our gallant men … into the fields and out upon the seas to make sure victory." He quoted the words of the President with whom he most identified, Abraham Lincoln, by saying, "Let us have faith that right makes might, and in that faith let us dare to do our duty as we understand it."[577]

Mrs. Wilson tried her best to make the transition from the Wilson administration to the Harding administration a smooth one. She made charts with her husband listing the advantages of five cities to which they might retire – Washington, Baltimore, Richmond, Boston, and New York. They finally agreed on Washington, and Edith Wilson went out nearly every day trying to find an acceptable and an affordable house. She also invited the Hardings to tea at the White House just as the Tafts had hosted Wilson and his first wife Ellen before the inauguration in 1913. She was astounded at how rude Mrs. Harding was and how the President elect sat in the Red Room with his leg dangling over the arm of a chair. While neither one of them seemed interested in talking with her husband, Edith Wilson noticed that Florence Harding, a loud woman who wore too much rouge, already felt at home ordering the servants about and shouting out to the newspaper men, "her boys" as she called them, in front of the White House.

Ike Hoover ignored the new First Lady's request to have the Wilsons moved out of the White House before the inauguration. After the President had left for the swearing in ceremony, Hoover stayed behind, packed everything up, and then headed to the house on S Street so he could set up Wilson's bedroom and study just as they had been in the White House. Mrs. Wilson thanked the butler she had relied on for so much and headed off to the Capitol in an open car with Mrs. Harding. She was furious when the Hardings got out of their cars and bounded up the steps of the Capital leaving Wilson to go up the elevator to the ceremony all alone. Wilson could now walk with a cane and slowly made his way to the platform where Harding was inaugurated. Later that day after the ceremonies were over, the Wilsons headed to their new home. Edith was still fuming, but the now

---

[577] Woodrow Wilson, "Annual Message to Congress, December 7, 1920, *PPWW*, III, Part 2, 513-521.

former President could only laugh. He felt no ill will toward Harding or to the nation that had so soundly rejected him. The burdens of the office had been lifted at last from his shoulders. His faith in God whose Providence ruled the affairs of men was stronger than ever. He was grateful that he would have time left to him to live in peace with his family and friends. Maybe, he thought, he could also finally write his great study *The Philosophy of Politics*.[578] He did not even care what place he would have in history or whether people would ever remember him. He had glimpsed a better world where one day all mankind would live in peace and freedom together. He was content to remember that he had played a part in steering his nation on a course toward it.

[578] Edith Bolling Wilson, *My Memoir*, 316-319.

EPILOGUE: "CROSSING THE BAR"

There is a Providence to which I am perfectly willing to submit.

Woodrow Wilson[579]

Woodrow Wilson retired with his wife Edith to a house they had purchased on S Street not far from the White House. He was still not a completely well man and would never fully recover from the stroke that had felled him in October 1919. His left arm remained limp at his side and he could walk only with a cane. But perhaps even more terribly the stroke had robbed him of his mastery over words. He could still speak clearly and entertain the many people who came to visit him with stories of the past and pleasant conversations about the present. But he could no longer craft long written pieces with ease. Working at his typewriter was now an agony as he struggled to find the words that would capture his thoughts. Even with the help of his new secretary, Edith's brother John Randolph Bolling, his ideas did not flow as easily as they once had. More sadly, Wilson recognized that his voice was no longer heard in a world that had moved past him. Like a captain who had gone down with his ship, but who still survived in the wreckage, he could see his nation sailing into the future without him. He could only hope that America would remain true to the course he had charted for her.

Edith Wilson made sure that her husband had a daily schedule that kept him occupied and so with little time to brood about the failures of the past. He rose at 9 A.M. in the morning and had breakfast in his bedroom that was in a sunny part of the house. Then he headed down to his office where he dictated as many as 25 to 40 letters a day to his secretary John Bolling. He took a nap at noon and had his midday meal in his bedroom. Usually his wife read to him as he ate. After another nap, he received visitors at 3 P.M. in the afternoon. Promptly at 4 P.M., he and

Edith took a drive. He plotted out his four favorite routes through Arlington, the Virginia countryside, just across the border in Maryland, and around Capitol Hill. Back home on S Street, he had dinner in the library and again listened to his wife read to him. He loved detective stories the most, but when Edith mentioned that she found herself always thinking in terms of crime, he asked her to read magazines like the *Atlantic Monthly* to him. She also read all the favorite novels of his youth including the major works of Charles Dickens and Sir Walter Scott. Wilson liked to play solitaire after the reading was done and loved having his wife keep score. He also enjoyed listening to the radio that his wife had installed in the house for him. By 10 P.M., Wilson was in bed, sleeping soundly until the next morning when the routine began all over again. The only change in the schedule came on Saturday evenings when Wilson, his wife, and his faithful butler Charles Scott headed to Keith's Theater in downtown Washington. The actors loved him and always gave him a bouquet of roses after every performance. He even came on snowy winter nights, telling the crowds who waited to see him, "You know I am not a quitter." Wilson loved to come home to his bedroom where his wife had sandwiches and ginger ale waiting for him. They stayed up late talking over all the jokes and routines they had seen at the theater.[580]

For a time, Wilson thought he would be able to take up his legal career again. He formed a partnership in Washington with Bainbridge Colby, the man who had replaced Robert Lansing as Secretary of State. They opened an office in the city and clients soon came calling with retainers as high as $500,000. Wilson turned most clients down when he learned their business "touched in some way on the Government structure." Colby often left the Wilson house on S Street frustrated that the former President turned away business that would make their law firm successful. He finally confessed his concerns to Edith Wilson. "It is a sublime position on the part of your husband," he explained, "and I am honoured to share it as long as I can afford it." Edith apprised her husband of the situation and gently urged him to dissolve the partnership. Wilson felt terrible that he had been so caught up in his own scruples that he had never given Colby's need to make a living a thought. He took some comfort in the fact that he could use the money from the one retainer he did take to buy Edith an electric automobile. She loved the car and often drove Wilson around the Virginia countryside. Once they saw a rusty horseshoe on the road. She got out of the car and retrieved it for her husband. He kept it on a lamp in his bedroom for good luck.[581]

---

[579] Daniels, *Life of Woodrow Wilson*, 356.
[580] Ibid., 345-347.
[581] Edith Bolling Wilson, *My Memoir*, 327-329.

Above all else, Edith Wilson tried to keep her husband's spirits up. It was not easy for a man who had been so active in the world to live as an invalid. He was often severe in his judgments and impatient with the very people who were trying so hard to help him. But while he could be unbearable in his darkest moods, he was often childlike in his deep concern for others, sometimes crying like a little boy over his inconsiderate words and actions. Those closest to him, especially his wife, his doctor Cary Grayson, and his brother-in-law Stockton Axson, understood that the extremes in his moods came from his illness. They were always patient with him, waiting for his true personality, filled with warmth and humor, to return. He seemed happiest when he was sitting at his desk in the old wooden chair he had brought with him from Princeton. "This chair stood by me through stormy weather," he was fond of saying, and now it stayed with him in his last long battle against failing health.[582]

Wilson was not lonely in his retirement since family and friends came in a steady procession to his new home to visit him. Edith Wilson's family, including her mother and many brothers and sisters, came often to parties. Margaret Wilson usually traveled down from New York City every Christmas for a visit. Cousin Helen Bones was also a frequent guest. Wilson saw Nellie McAdoo and her two daughters less often since she had moved to California with her husband. Jessie Wilson Sayre now had three children, a boy and two girls, and visited her father on S Street on a frequent basis until her husband Frank Sayre took a position as a legal advisor at the Court of Siam. Friends from Wilson's Princeton days like Robert Bridges, Hiram Woods, and Frank Glass came to see him along with Cyrus McCormick and other members of the college's Board of Trustees. Cleveland Dodge surprised his old friend on his 67th birthday with a present of a silver Rolls Royce. Other important American leaders like Samuel Gompers and foreign dignitaries like George Clemenceau and Lady Asquith, the wife of the former British Prime Minister, visited with much pomp and fanfare.

Wilson took no part in official Washington politics until November 11, 1921 when he was asked by the administration of President Harding to participate in the parade for the Unknown Soldier who was to be buried in Arlington Cemetery. He asked the White House staff if they could provide an open carriage for him and if he could go along in the parade as far as Arlington Cemetery. Much to Wilson's disappointment, they turned down both requests. His brother-in-law Robert Bolling hired a rig and his butler Charles Scott drove the carriage in the parade, turning back before crossing the Potomac as ordered by the Harding administration. Wilson was saddened that he could not follow the casket of the

---

[582] Axson, *Brother Woodrow*, 238; Grayson, *Intimate Memoir*, 132.

fallen young soldier to Arlington, but he was thrilled by the loud cheers that came up from the people who lined the streets. They crowded around his hired carriage to cheer him on and wish him well. Just two years later, when President Harding died suddenly, Wilson was gracious enough to attend the funeral of the man who had tried so hard to keep him away from the dedication of the Tomb of the Unknown Soldier.[583]

In his retirement, Wilson remained interested in politics but stayed out of the day to day workings of his own party. He had supported Cox in 1920, but refused to back him as he geared up for another run for the White House in 1924. He was certain Cox would not win and so refused to play along with the rest of the Democrats. Wilson was more concerned about the strange tendency in modern politics for dictators to rise up from the people. This was a dark side of popular government that he had never considered in his own study of politics. In the summer of 1923, he became particularly troubled about the Russian Revolution and was determined to write an article about it. After struggling for weeks, he sent a short essay entitled "The Road Away from Revolution" to the *Atlantic Monthly*. While he sympathized with the plight of the Russian people, he could not accept the "irrational revolution" orchestrated by Lenin and his followers. He was stunned that "ignorant and insolent" royalty had been toppled only to be replaced by a new breed of dictators who were dangerous not just to democracy but to civilization itself. He believed that civilization would survive if it renewed itself in the spirit of Christ. "Only then," he wrote, "can discontents be driven out and all the shadows lifted form the road ahead." Wilson was happy to be in print again, while his wife was relieved that the magazine paid $300 at a time when she was struggling to make ends meet.[584]

Wilson got another chance to tell his ideas to the American public in the fall of 1923. He was asked by a group of young people to give a radio address on the anniversary of the Armistice. Wilson struggled for weeks to put his ideas on paper so he could read them to his waiting public. He stood in his library on the first floor of his house on S Street holding his cane and speaking into a microphone. He described those who had opposed the League of Nations as "ignoble" and "cowardly." They would one day recognize their "fatal error" and realize that the United States must play a vital role in the world. He urged all Americans to turn away from selfishness and go back out onto the world stage to serve others. Wilson was deeply disappointed with his performance and certain that he had

[583] Edith Bolling Wilson, *My Memoir*, 329.

[584] Woodrow Wilson, "The Road Away from Revolution, August 1923," *PPWW*, III, Part 2, 536-539.

moved no one. But the street outside his home soon filled with people who had heard the speech and came to cheer him. Newspapers throughout the country noted that Wilson had touched more people in this one short radio address than he had ever reached in his many travels across the country.[585]

Despite the sad tone of his speech, Wilson was not bitter about the failure of his nation to join the League of Nations. He did not brood over the fact that the Congress had rejected the Treaty of Versailles. When top Democrats came to visit him on January 15, 1924, he said he did not regret that he had broken down in his fight for the league. He would rather have failed in his attempt to win it than never to have tried at all. Wilson was sure that God had a better plan in mind and that one day his Providence would bring peace into the world. His faith in the American people never wavered. "The American people are thinking their way through, and reaching their own decision," he explained, "and that is the better way for it to come." Still he was often fond of saying as he looked ahead, "It will all have to be done over again in twenty years and at ten times the cost."[586]

The Democrats who called on their fallen leader in January 1924 were shocked at how terrible he looked. He sat slumped in the couch with his paralyzed left arm hidden in the cushions. His face was deeply lined and marked with pain. It was clear that the former President was failing. Cary Grayson had noticed in the previous autumn that Wilson had suffered minor hemorrhages in his retina. He could no longer recognize the faces of people on the street as he rode by them in his car. Even with new glasses, he still could not see any better. On January 31, 1924, Wilson's stomach was so upset that his wife sent a telegram to Grayson to hurry back from his hunting trip in South Carolina. When he arrived in Washington on the next day, he told his old friend that the end was near. Wilson answered calmly that to die now was better than lingering on any longer as an invalid. His final words to Grayson were simple ones. "I am ready," he said. He slipped in and out of consciousness with his wife Edith, his daughter Margaret, and his brother Josie at his side. Finally at 11:15 on Sunday morning February 3, 1924, Woodrow Wilson died. Those with him were amazed at how his face changed in death. He looked like he was no more than 35 or 40 year old. His face was smooth and beautiful "as if a distant sunrise had touched the features."[587]

Edith Wilson was broken hearted at the loss of her husband and could not decide where he should be buried. He had asked only that his funeral be a private

---

[585] Woodrow Wilson, "High Significance of Armistice Day, November 10, 1923," *PPWW*, III, Part 2, 542-543.

[586] Daniels, *Life of Woodrow Wilson*, 355; Johnson, *Woodrow Wilson*, 292.

[587] Grayson, *Intimate Memoir*, 138-139; Daniels, *Life of Woodrow Wilson*, 347.

one and that he not be buried in Arlington Cemetery. His wife first thought of burying him in Staunton but he had no family there. She then considered laying him to rest near his mother, father, and sister in Columbia, South Carolina until she learned that there was no room left for him in the tiny churchyard. She never thought of taking him to Rome, Georgia to rest in the plot that was waiting for him next to his first wife Ellen. She finally decided on the new National Cathedral just being built on Mount Saint Alban, the highest point in Washington, D.C. Only the nave of the church had been built but plans were made for Wilson to be buried there in a stone sarcophagus. Edith Wilson chose this location since her husband had made his career in Washington and it seemed fitting that his final resting place should be there. She also decided that the funeral would be a public one with friends and family, former political allies, honor guards from the Army, Navy, and Marine Corps, and President Calvin Coolidge and his wife attending the services in the half-built church.

On February 6, 1924, thousands of people lined the two mile route from the Wilson home up Mount St. Alban to the nave of the National Cathedral. As the cortege passed, many felt a sense of awe that the man who had made such a powerful impact on their country for so many years was finally gone. He had permanently changed the office of the Presidency by insisting that the executive take an active role in shaping legislation. All of his successors would call joint sessions of Congress in order to give their State of the Union messages and other important addresses. Wilson had reinvigorated the nation's top post by showing how the Chief Executive must go past the mere description of his tasks in the Constitution to become a living spokesman of all the people. By so doing, he joined the ranks of Washington, Jefferson and Jackson. He was equally committed to the belief that the President must be the person who leads the nation into the future because he most clearly sees the connections between the past and the present. In this regard, he most resembled Lincoln. Americans now expect their President to craft a vision of the future and lead them into it as a matter of course. This expectation places a demand on any President who strives for greatness to be also a master of words. From Wilson's perspective, the campaign for the White House thus never truly ends. A President finds he must continually go back to the people to win their support. Wilson embarked on this course convinced that a President who served all Americans could circumvent the special interests that were determined to interfere with the will of the people. He did not foresee the day when politicians would need so much money to reach the people that they would be more beholden to special interests to fund their campaigns than ever before in American history.

As the coffin of President Wilson was brought into the nave of the cathedral, the mourners were met with the sweet aroma of countless bouquets that filled every nook of the church. Episcopal Bishop Freeman and Presbyterian minister Dr. Taylor, who conducted the funeral service together, led the crowd in psalms and prayers. The mourners included the President's widow, his daughters Margaret Wilson and Nellie McAdoo, his brother Joseph Wilson Jr., his doctor Cary Grayson, friends from the Princeton Class of 1879, former cabinet officers and the many Congressmen who had stood by him in their frequent battles on Capitol Hill along with dozens of young men from the military. Jessie Wilson had not been able to make it back from Siam, where her husband was serving as a legal advisor, to be at the funeral. When the casket was finally lowered into the stone sarcophagus, Bishop Freeman read the poem "Crossing the Bar" that Tennyson had written shortly before his own death. The tale of a brave captain who set out into the darkness of his final voyage seemed to have been written for Woodrow Wilson himself.

"Sunset and evening star,
And one clear call for me!
And may there be no moaning of the bar,
When I put out to sea,
But such a tide as moving seems asleep,
Too full for sound and foam,
When that which drew from out the boundless deep
Turns again home."

After the casket was laid to rest, a soldier played "Taps" and the sad melody could be heard all the way back down the hill toward Washington. The stone placed on top of the coffin had only one simple decoration – a Crusader's sword with a cross as its hilt. No better symbol could have been found to capture the romantic spirit of Woodrow Wilson – the little boy who once chased pirates in his lonely dreams, the professor and the politician who came at long last to love his country and its people, and the President who set his nation on the uncharted course of service to all mankind.

"Twilight and evening bell,
And after that the dark!
And may there be no sadness of farewell
When I embark;

For though from out are bourne of Time and Place
The flood may bear me far,
I hope to see my Pilot face to face
When I have crossed the bar."[588]

---

[588] Edith Bolling Wilson, *My Memoir*, 362-375; Johnson, *Woodrow Wilson,* 285-291.

BIBLIOGRAPHY

The sources on Woodrow Wilson are extensive. This bibliography provides only a short list of the major primary and secondary sources on the life of Woodrow Wilson and his Presidency. The list also includes related studies used in the research and writing of this work.

PRIMARY SOURCES

Axson, Stockton. *Brother Woodrow: A Memoir of Woodrow Wilson*. Princeton: Princeton University Press, 1993.

Baker, Ray Stannard. *Woodrow Wilson: Life and Letters, 8 Volumes*. Garden City, New York: Doubleday, Page & Co., 1927.

Day, Donald, ed., *Woodrow Wilson's Own Story*. Boston: Little, Brown and Company, 1952.

Foch, Marshall. Translated by Mott, Colonel T. Bentley. *The Memoirs of Marshall Foch*. Garden City, New York: Doubleday, Doran and Company, Incorporated, 1931.

McAdoo, Eleanor Wilson, Editor. *The Priceless Gift: The Love Letters of Woodrow Wilson and Ellen Axson*. New York: McGraw-Hill, 1962.

___. *The Woodrow Wilsons.* New York: The Macmillan Company, 1937.

Seymour, Charles, ed. *The Intimate Papers of Colonel House*. Boston: Houghton Mifflin, 1926-1928.

Tribble, Edwin, ed. *A President in Love: The Courtship Letters of Woodrow Wilson and Edith Bolling Galt*. Boston: Houghton Mifflin, 1981.

Tumulty, Joseph P. *Woodrow Wilson as I Know Him*. Garden City, New York: Doubleday, 1920.

Wilson, Edith Bolling. *My Memoir*. Indianapolis: Bobbs-Merrill, 1918.

Wilson, Woodrow. *The Papers of Woodrow Wilson* (69 Volumes). Edited by Arthur S. Link. Princeton, New Jersey: Princeton University Press, 1966.

____. *The Public Papers of Woodrow Wilson* (4 Volumes). Edited by Ray Stannard Baker and William E. Dodd. New York and London: Harper & Brothers Publishers, 1925.

SECONDARY SOURCES

Alsop, Em Bowles. *The Greatness of Woodrow Wilson 1856-1956*. New York And Toronto: Rinehart & Company, Inc., 1956.

Anderson, David D. *Woodrow Wilson*. Boston: Twayne Publishers, 1978.

Auchincloss, Louis. *Woodrow Wilson*. New York: Viking/Penguin, 2000.

Blum, John Morton. *Woodrow Wilson and the Politics of Morality*. Boston: Little, Brown and Company, 1956.

Brands, H. W. *Woodrow Wilson*. New York: Henry Holt and Company, 2003.

Bragdon, Henry W. *Woodrow Wilson: The Academic Years*. Cambridge, Massachusetts: Belknap Press, Harvard University Press, 1967.

Bullitt, William C. and Freud, Sigmund. *Thomas Woodrow Wilson (Twenty-eighth President of the United States): A Psychological Study*. Boston: Houghton Mifflin Company, 1967.

Cooper, John Milton, Jr. *The Warrior and the Priest: Woodrow Wilson and Theodore Roosevelt*. Cambridge, Massachusetts: Harvard University Press, 1983.

Daniels, Josephus. *The Life of Woodrow Wilson 1856-1924*. Chicago, Philadelphia and Toronto: The John C. Winston Company, 1924.

Ferrell, Robert. *Woodrow Wilson and World War I 1917-1921*. New York: Harper & Row, Publishers, 1985.

Ford, Henry Jones. *Woodrow Wilson: The Man and His Work; A Biographical Study*. New York and London: D. Appleton and Company, 1916.

Garraty, John. *Henry Cabot Lodge*. New York: Knopf, 1953.

______. *Woodrow Wilson*. New York: Knopf, 1956.

George, Alexander and George, Juliet. *Woodrow Wilson and Colonel House*. New York: J. Day & Co., 1956.

Grayson, Cary. *Woodrow Wilson, An Intimate Study*. New York: Holt, Rinehart & Winston, 1960.

Hale, William Bayard. *Woodrow Wilson: The Story of His Life*. Garden City, New York: Doubleday, Page & Company, 1912.

Hecksher, August. *Woodrow Wilson*. New York: Charles Scribner's Sons. 1991.

Johnson, Gerald W. *Woodrow Wilson: The Unforgettable Figure Who Has Returned to Haunt Us*. New York and London: Harper & Brothers, Publishers, 1944.

Lawrence, David. *The True Story of Woodrow Wilson*. New York: George H. Doran Company, 1924.

Link, Arthur S. *Woodrow Wilson and the Progressive Era 1910-1917*. New York: Harper & Row Publishers 1954.

____. *Woodrow Wilson: Revolution, War, and Peace*. Arlington, Heights, Illinois: Harlan Davidson, Inc., 1974.

Manela, Erez, "Imagining Woodrow Wilson: Dreams of East-West Harmony and the Revolt against Empire in 1919," *American Historical Review* (Volume XI, Issue 4), December 2006.

Mulder, John M. *Woodrow Wilson: The Years of Preparation*. Princeton, New Jersey: Princeton University Press, 1978.

Northrup, Cynthia Clark and Turney, Elaine C. Pange, eds. *Encyclopedia of Tariffs and Trade in U.S. History* (3 Volumes). Westport, Connecticut: Greenwood Press, 2003.

Northrup, Cynthia Clark, ed. *The American Economy: A Historical Encyclopedia* (2 Volumes). Westport, Connecticut: Greenwood Press, 2003.

Osborn, George. *Woodrow Wilson: The Early Years*. Baton Rouge: Louisiana State University Press, 1968.

Smith, Gene. *When the Cheering Stopped*. New York: William Morrow, 1964.

Viereck, George. *The Strangest Friendship in History*. New York: Liverwright, 1937.

Walworth, Arthur. *Woodrow Wilson* (Second Revised Edition). Boston: Houghton Mifflin Company, 1965.

Weinstein, Edwin. *Woodrow Wilson: A Medical and Psychological Biography*. Princeton: Princeton University Press, 1981.

White, William Allen. *Woodrow Wilson: The Man, His Times and His Task*. Boston and New York: Houghton Mifflin Company, 1924.

Winter, Jay and Baggett, Blaine. *The Great War and the Shaping of the Twentieth Century*. New York: Penguin Studio, A Division of Penguin Books, 1996.

INDEX

A

D

E

F

G

H

I

M

N

O

P

S

T

U

V

Y